נחמה ליבוביץ / עיונים בספר במדבר

NEHAMA LEIBOWITZ

STUDIES IN BAMIDBAR (Numbers)

Translated and adapted from the Hebrew
by

ARYEH NEWMAN

The World Zionist Organization,
Department for Torah Education and Culture
in the Diaspora

JERUSALEM 5740/1980

עיונים בספר במדבר
בעקבות פרשנינו הראשונים והאחרונים
מאת נחמה ליבוביץ
מהדורה אנגלית בעבודו ובתרגומו של אריה ניומן
בהוצאת המחלקה לחינוך ולתרבות תורניים בגולה
ההסתדרות הציונית העולמית
ירושלים, תש"ם

Printed in Israel at the Ahva Press under the supervision
of the Publishing Department of the Jewish Agency

TRANSLATOR'S FOREWORD

Studies in Bamidbar ("Numbers") is a continuous, revised edition of all of Nehama Leibowitz's *Studies in the Weekly Sidra** as they appeared in my English adaptation in leaflet form, week by week, for over a period of seven years from 1955 to 1962, and which have long since been out of print. The new book format has involved the translator in re-arrangement of the material and some pruning to avoid unnecessary duplication. As far as possible I have followed the same principles as in the first two volumes (*Bereshit* and *Shemot* I and II). For details of the author's lifework and the perspectives of her original approach to and outstanding pedagogic achievements in Jewish Bible study in Israel and abroad, as well as the principles which have guided my translation, readers are referred to my comprehensive introduction to *Studies in Bereshit* and foreword to *Studies in Shemot*. For background details of most of the commentators cited, readers are referred to my biographical notes on them at the end of the aforementioned volumes.

Sidra = "portion" or "lesson" into which the Pentateuch is traditionally divided for the purpose of the annual cycle of Sabbath readings in the synagogue, starting with the first Sabbath after Simḥat Torah ("Rejoicing of the Law") and ending with the Sabbath before the feast of Tabernacles.

Other volumes in this series
STUDIES IN BERESHIT (GENESIS)
STUDIES IN SHEMOT (EXODUS)
STUDIES IN VAYIKRA (LEVITICUS)
STUDIES IN DEVARIM (DEUTERONOMY)

PREFACE

Heartened by the ardent reception accorded to the first three volumes of Nehama Leibowitz's commentary on the Pentateuch, the WZO Torah Education Department now offers the devoted Bible student the fourth volume — *Studies in Bamidbar.*

With the vast majority of the Jewish people still in the "wilderness" of the diaspora, the perennial message of *Bamidbar* addresses itself to this generation with a poignant urgency. To the modern reader "every man by his own standard" (2,2), might almost instinctively suggest anarchic, relativist individualism. This is patently wide of the mark. What the Divine wisdom is submitting to the wandering Israelites in their incessant peregrinations through History, is the blueprint of Jewish existence. In it integration is the keyword. From the Sanctuary's Holy of Holies there flowed the life blood through to the bones, tendons and tissues of the communal organism. It gave it direction, it spelled life.

With consummate skill Nehama gently guides us through the rocks and dunes, the snares and pitfalls, fantasies and hopes of the desert, *Bamidbar.* Thus, duly braced and enlightened we reach, with Israel of old, the gateway to the Promised Land, to meet the challenges that persist to engage the Jewish body and mind.

AVNER TOMASCHOFF
Director, English Section
Torah Education Department

CONTENTS

Translator's Foreword

Preface

III

V

BAMIDBAR

Introduction — Ramban's (Naḥmanides) summary of the book — the
Tabernacle a mobile Sinai (Jacob) — camp is the body, Tabernacle the
heart (Kuzari) — Abravanel's synopsis of Bamidbar — the camp, its
structure and deployment a matter of military logistics (Rashbam,
Luzzatto) — Hirsch works out Ramban's idea — Israel the army of
the Lord (Midrash).   1

1. *The second roll-call of Israel* (Num. 1, 1—3) — the lesson of Mosaic
statistics — spotlight on Israel's survival despite persecution and
decimation (Naḥmanides) — balance between strategic and religious
lessons — the parallel between Biblical and later history (Baḥya).   10

2. *Forbidden and permitted census* — Abravanel points out a
contradiction between the census in Exodus and here — same
conditions applied to second census (Rashi, Ramban) — no
connection between half-shekel and census (Abravanel and Sefer Ha-
ḥinukh) — contradiction from King David's offence (2 Sam. 24,
2—10) — army as an end or means.   17

3. *The danger of the holy things* (Num. 4, 19) — meaning of *ke-vala'*
(Rashbam) — two rabbinic views on the penalty for looking at the
holy things — difficulty v. responsibility — danger of seeing the letter
and ignoring the spirit (Hirsch) — penalty for flying too high
(Abravanel) a warning to moderate the pride of Kohath's sons (Ḥefeẓ)
— a technical measure to ensure order and discipline (Sforno).   24

4. *Haftarah (Hosea 2,1—22)*—what's in a name?—*ishi or ba'ali?*—
Fear v. Love (Rashi) — idolatry v. monotheism (Radak) — debasing
the role of God (Buber) — God not a supplier of material wants —
God purifies those who purify themselves — Israel's purification
followed by the world's (Sa'adia).   32

NASO

1. *Robbery of the Proselyte* (5, 5—8) — connective links between the varied items covered in the sidra — word-association (Ibn Ezra, Cassuto) — contrast between Divine esteem for proselyte and disparagement of disobedient Israelite (Midrash) — oblique reference to proselyte (Rashi) — more on Divine esteem for proselyte. 38

2. *Guilt-offering for robbery (asham gezelot)* — (syntax of 5, 6—7) — comparison with Lev. 5, 21—23 — oral confession a religious precept (Maimonides) — purpose and character of oral confession (Sefer Ha-ḥinukh, Hirsch) — option of atonement privilege of one who admits guilt (Maimonides) — study of *ve-natan la-asher asham lo* (5, 7). 44

3. *Laws of the Nazirite* (6, 1—11) — asceticism and negation of life hallmark of "religious" as opposed to "halakhic" personality (Soloveitchik) — rabbinic controversy over the "sin" of the Nazirite — R. Eliezer extols the ascetic — R. Eliezer Ha-kappar condemns ascetic — Maimonides extols the golden mean — Naḥmanides condemns the "holy" ascetic who reverts to worldly life — nazirite regulations drastic remedy for drastic condition (Midreshei Torah). 51

4. *The Priestly Blessing* (6, 22—27) — role of priests and God in the blessing — priests bless Israel and God the priests (Talmud) — priests invoke God's blessing (Tanḥuma, Rashbam) — priestly blessing only a human wish — God the exclusive source of blessing (Hirsch) — Divine requires human preparation — explication of the priestly blessing, phrase by phrase (Rashi, Ha'amek Davar). 60

5. *The Lord lift up His face to you* (6, 24—26) — correspondence between increasing number of lexical items and increase in blessing — blessing of plenty followed by blessing to guard us against temptation of plenty (Abravanel) — study of the imagery — God's lifting His face — showing favour to those who show Him favour (Midrash) — third blessing the end itself — previous blessings the means to the end: nearness to God. 68

6. *Princes with a past* (7, 2) — identity of princes with Israelite taskmasters — they shielded the people — good and bad deeds not forgotten — the balance-sheet of history (Midrash) — the princes demoted for their pride — uniqueness of the individual. 74

7. *The lesson of Samson — Haftarah* (Judges 13, 2—25)—Samson— an experiment in unsuccessful combination of physical and spiritual strength (Kariv) — comparison between message received by Samson's mother and her report of it to Manoah — analysis of differences (Midrash, Abravanel, Alshikh, Malbim) — Nazirite vows

VIII

meant to curb temptations of unusual physical strength — tragedy of
Samson's failure — not in conformity with prophetic pattern
exemplified in Samuel his successor (Kariv).

80

BE-HA'ALOTKHA

1. *When the ark set forth* (Num. 10, 35—36) — passage enclosed in
   inverted *nun* — a book on its own (Talmud) — partnership of Moses
   and God in leading Israel (Sifrei) — the enemies of Israel the enemies
   of God — Israel's link with Torah source of tyrants animosity towards
   them (Hirsch) — a timeless invocation to remove tyranny and bring
   rest to Israel and the world.   88

2. *The fish we ate for free* (11, 4—7) — the Egyptians gave them no
   straw never mind fish — *ḥinam*: free from burden of Judaism (Sifrei),
   for free (Ibn Ezra, Naḥmanides, Abravanel) — Pharaoh fed them well
   to drive them harder (Midreshei Torah) — Herodotus cites diet of
   Egyptian slaves (Luzzatto) — deeper psychological truth of Talmudic
   explanation — Israelites preferred licence to responsibility — 11, 10
   "weep throughout their families" — resented restrictions on their sex
   relations.   94

3. *We want meat!* (11, 13—21) — no real grievance, only rebellion
   against God — analysis of Moses' reaction — Rabbi Akiva finds
   Moses over-reacted — casting doubt on the Almighty's capabilities —
   R. Shimon: Moses over-protective — feared the anger of God on His
   people — R. Gamliel: Moses told God it was impossible to satisfy
   them — they were only seeking a pretext.   105

4. *The murmurings: A repeat performance* — one and same incident
   referred to in Exodus, Numbers and Deuteronomy 33, 8 (Bechor Shor)
   — repeat performance in different circumstances — comparison with
   David's sparing of Saul on two occasions (1 Sam. 24 and 26) — to
   prove David's magnanimity — second Israelite murmurings the most
   reprehensible.   113

5. *Would that all the Lord's people were prophets* (11, 29) — an
   evaluation of Moses' rejection of responsibility of leadership (Arama)
   — turned into a new challenge — comparison with Israel's demand
   for a king in Samuel — humility of Eldad and Medad rewarded —
   Moses unselfishly wishes permanent prophetic status on everyone
   (Buber).   121

6. *Blackening the Beautiful* (12, 1) — Miriam's complaint against Moses
   — in defence of prophet's wives (Rashi, Avot de Rabbi Nathan) — the

IX

Cushite woman, a reference to Zipporah — a second wife Moses took (Kaspi) — temptation of the small to belittle the great (Bahya) — the generosity of Moses.

129

SHELAH

1. *Fact and opinion in the spies' report* (13, 2—32) — the sending of the spies not a divine command — *efes* "nevertheless": the word that gave the spies away — Arama's analogy of the buyer — stronger than Him or us (v. 31) — the deeper meaning of a surface ambiguity (Midrash) — solving a self-contradiction in the spies' report (Sforno). 135

2. *A reason to weep* (14, 1) — the sending of spies, purely a military decision (Nahmanides) — rejection of Eretz Israel symptomatic of rejection of God (Arama). 143

3. *Back to Egypt* (14, 4) — their murmurings from bad to worse — the demand for a new leader an expression of idolatry (Rashi) — link with 15, 22—31 — the inadvertent sin of the congregation of Israel — comparison with Leviticus 4, 13 — the definition of inadvertent idolatry — communities and individuals without benefit of Jewish education (Nahmanides) — no opting out of Judaism — return to Egypt return to heathen way of life. 147

4. *Moses' intercession after the sin of the spies* (14, 13—19) — compared with his intercession after the golden calf — in the latter, 3 arguments — in the former, only one — "that the Lord was unable..." — why should God take notice of fools? (Arama, Abravanel) — Ezekiel's (36, 17—36) answer: out of concern for humanity (Nahmanides) — every soul contributes to the wholeness of the Name — Agnon's Kaddish for martyrs of Israel. 157

5. *Had God changed His mind?* (14, 28—44) — when God opposed *aliya* — Isaiah supports the hawks (7, 4), Jeremiah the doves — God neither hawk nor dove — His message is a token not a type (Buber) — Jeremiah's call for surrender — no longer possible to build and plant — the generation of the desert had displayed their unfitness for their mission — it was handed only to a new generation. 165

6. *The precept of Zizit* (15, 38) — equal in weight to all the other precepts (Talmud) — switching from third to second person — tautological construction — the wearer has to be aware of the symbolism — seeing leads to remembering leads to doing (Talmud) — symbolism of the blue thread — reminder of the Throne of Glory — image of the sea:fear; of the heavens: love (Kli Yakar) — the uniform

of the army of the Lord — *ẓiẓit* more important than a *tallit* (Ibn Ezra).   171

7. *The roving eye* (15, 39) — two kinds of looking — duty of contemplating the world and reflecting upon the greatness of its creator (Baḥya) — the key to fear and love of God (Maimonides) — distinction between walking and roving — looking with a positive and negative purpose.   177

KORAḤ

1. *An unholy controversy* — Ethics of the Fathers ch. 5, 17 — controversy between Koraḥ and his congregation (Malbim) — united in their disunity — a group of individuals not a community.   181

2. *The grievances of Koraḥ and company* — a body of malcontents — mutiny set in motion when morale was low (Naḥmanides) — the sob story of the widow (Midrash) — the gullibility of man.   186

3. *Israelite's role in the Koraḥ mutiny* — what was Israel's sin in Koraḥ's mutiny? — Moses misunderstood the Divine message — not Israel to be consumed but Koraḥ and company (Rabbenu Ḥananel) — Israel guilty of passive sympathy with Koraḥ's aims (Naḥmanides) — Moses again the intercessor — the community was required actively to dissociate itself — no facing-both-ways — Israel's half-hearted dissociation (Alshikh).   194

4. *Dathan and Abiram* — Midrash on Koraḥ's silence — the mocking repartee of Dathan and Abiram to Moses analysed — reversal of Jewish values — exile becomes homeland.   203

5. *Sin is a killer* — The quelling of the Koraḥ mutiny did not cure Israel — comparison with impact of Elijah's victory over the Ba'al (1 Kings 18, 22—40) — the doubters are never convinced — man's victory over himself the only answer (Mishnah Rosh Ha-shanah 3, 8).   212

6. *The firepans* (17, 1—3) — why did the instruments of sin become holy? — served as holy vessels (Rashi) — served as a moral lesson (Naḥmanides) — link with Nazirite who likewise "sinned with his soul" (Ha'amek Davar) — symbolised victory over falsehood (Arama) — behaving like Koraḥ or suffering his fate — ambiguity of 17, 5 (Rashi v. Biur).   219

7. *The prompting of the holy spirit* — Moses deals with Koraḥ without specific authority from God — he received instructions when "he fell on his face" 16, 4 — an implied authority: the Lord confirms the world of His servant — God subjects nature to the needs of the faithful

(Albo) — inspired by Holy Spirit (Naḥmanides) — the promptings of conscience called spirit of the Lord (Maimonides) — miracles convince the convinced — lack of faith is lack of will.   225

ḤUKKAT

1. *Mystery of the Red Heifer* — a mystery that eluded the wisest of men (Midrash) — a humanistic explanation (Bechor Shor) — an allegorical approach (Sforno) — R. Yoḥanan suits his answers to the audience — no magical properties just a disciplinary excercise.   233

2. *Moses' sin* — referred to on four different occasions — Moses displayed a fit of anger unbecoming to a prophet (Maimonides) — Naḥmanides takes Maimonides to task offers Rabbenu Ḥananel's explanation: Moses failed to give God His due — acted as fugitives and not as leaders (Ibn Ezra) — Moses failed to impress them with a miracle (Albo) — Albo's explanation angrily dismissed by Arama — left with simplest explanation and most ancient and most modern — spoke to instead of striking rock (Midrash, Luzzatto) — "speak to the rock *before their eyes*" (17, 8) — an opportunity for making a spiritual impact missed (Ha-ketav Veha-kabbalah).   236

3. *The deputation to Edom* (20, 14) — why mention Kadesh? — to show Moses' loyalty to his task despite exclusion from Eretz Israel (Midrash) — two deputations compared — Eretz Israel gained through suffering (Tanḥuma).   248

4. *What made the king of Arad fight?* (21, 1) — an exception to the rule — heard Aaron had died and clouds of glory dispersed (Talmud) — comparison with what made Jethro come — the answer in the text: "by way of Atharim" — a reference to the spies (Ibn Ezra, Naḥmanides) — they noted the Israelites' loss of morale.   255

5. *The copper serpent* (21, 4—9) — significance of shift from singular to plural (Rashi) — equated the servant and Master — Midrashic parable of unawareness of bounty of God — difference between *va-yishlaḥ* and *va-yeshallaḥ* — between sending and letting them do their job — the power of the serpent was the power within themselves (Talmud, Zohar, Hirsch).   260

6. *Fear him not* (21, 34) — no direct mention of Moses' fears — what had the prophet of God to fear? — parable of Tiferet Yisrael — greatness of man and Moses in triumphing over the flaws in his character — difference between physical terror and awe — the good even in the enemy — only God can draw up the balance-sheet of human worth and unworthiness (Maimonides).   266

XII

7. *Jephthah's vow* (Haftarah) — Midrash dramatises the debate between Jephthah and his daughter—she fell between two stools — vow meant literally (Tanḥuma, Naḥmanides) — vow of celibacy (Rashi, Radak, Ralbag) — Jephthah the victim of his own lack of learning   272

BALAK

1. *Prophet or sorcerer* — comparison with wording of Divine call to Hebrew prophets — latter do not run after prophecy — Balaam tries to impose his will on God — prophets strive to raise themselves to God (Naḥmanides) — Balaam enlightened, instructed or forced to bless (Talmud, Midrash, Naḥmanides) — Balaam second-class prophet — unlike Hebrew prophets did not speak explicitly in name of God — change in attitude at end — blessed Israel willingly (Hirsch) — rabbis detected a false note.   282

2. *Anatomy of blessing* — first blessing reflects Balaam's sense of Jewish historic continuity — Balaam's gradual progress towards unqualified blessing — linguistic and time variations in the three blessings — water-imagery — from object of blessing to source of blessing.   290

3. *Balaam and his ass* (22, 21—28) — meaning of rabbinic dictum that the ass's mouth was created on Sabbath-eve — world programmed at Creation — "miracle" also part of nature — the ass-encounter a dream (Maimonides, Kaspi) — the ass's speech a human reconstruction — "as if" (Luzzatto) — a story to discredit magical practices — no enchantment in Jacob — spiritual blindness of Balaam contrasted with the ass's "far-sightedness".   297

4. *The impact of curse and blessing* — why was it necessary to take action against Balaam's curse? (Abravanel) — to teach Balaam a lesson — to benefit Israel — blessings and curses: no objective impact only subjective, psychological (Kaspi, Abravanel) — to scotch superstition and prevent ḥillul-ha-shem (Luzzatto, Astruc).   303

5. *Man leads himself down the garden path* — the puzzle of to-go or not-to-go — the change of orders prompted by Balaam's response — not a change in the mind of God (Naḥmanides) — the textual clue: going with them v. going *along* with them (Rashi, Ha-ketav Veha-kabbalah, Malbim) — Balaam's seeking permission to go reprehensible (Arama) — pushed himself to his own doom (Midrash).   308

6. *Balaam's parting shot* (24, 10) — places and purpose (Hirsch) — Balaam's advice: Not to worry in the here and now (Bechor Shor, Abravanel) — a plan to corrupt Israel (Rashi, Rashbam) — Balaam

XIII

reverts to form — from prophet to provocateur — an Israeli educator reconstructs Balaam's state of mind (Joseph Schechter).   316

7. *Balaam: the heathen Moses* — greater than Moses (Sifrei) — God gave equal opportunity to all nations — Midrash contrasts the use made of these opportunities — Solomon v. Nebuchadnezzar; David v. Haman; Hebrew prophets v. Balaam — bestowal and withdrawal of prophecy no arbitrary decision (Ephraim Urbach)—all can achieve sainthood of Moses or villainy of Balaam.   323

PINḤAS

1. *Coping with zeal* — Midrash scripts the seduction of Israel — commentary on Pinḥas' zeal — Sages wished to excommunicate him (Jerusalem Talmud) — Holy Spirit testified his zeal was selfless — why Samuel Ha-katan was entrusted with the fulmination against the heretics (*birkat ha-minim*) in the *amidah* (Rav Kook) — covenant of peace represented antidote to trauma of Pinḥas' act of zeal (Ha'amek Davar).   328

2. *Designs on Israel's soul* (Num. 25, 16—18) — Amalek threatened the body, Midian the soul — foundation of Israel's survival — the family (Midrash).   334

3. *A shepherd for the congregation* (27, 18) — Torah cannot be bequeathed — rabbis detect a note of grievance in Moses request for a successor — parable of the king and orphan maid (Midrash) — Moses pleads the case of his sons — meritocracy wins — ordination as ordered and implemented — generosity and magnanimity of Moses.   340

4. *The kindness of thy youth* (Haftarah, Jeremiah 1—2, 3) — analysis of last two verses (2, 2—3) — added to end on a hopeful note — original merit of Israel stressed (Rashi, Radak) — difference between the two commentators — original kindness of God stressed (Luzzatto) — a study of the use of the word *ḥesed* — Ezekiel's picture of the "original" (first) ugly Israelite (Ezek. 16, 4—8) — Hosea and Jeremiah describe Israel's "first" merit — Israel accepting the Torah at Sinai, God's great "find" (Buber).   347

5. *An almond rod I see* (Haftarah, Jeremiah 1, 11) — three prophetic readings of retribution (Abudarham, Zevin) — six verbs: 4 of destruction, 2 of construction (Jer. 1, 10) — a semantic analysis (Malbim) — destruction precondition of rebuilding (Alshikh) — the rod signifies the road of correction — the almond tree the first harbinger of spring — blossoms in twenty one days — catastrophe

XIV

limited to that period "between-the-straits" *ben ha-meẓarim* (Midrash)
— charity of God in mode of punishment — retribution expedited for
benefit of Israel (Malbim).   358

6.   *I am a child* (Haftarah, Jeremiah 1, 6) — prophets are essentially the
     vehicle for the Divine message (Heschel) — why then do they refuse
     the job? — Jeremiah: refusal prompted by his tender years
     (Abravanel, Radak) — his inexperience and lack of charisma (Rashi,
     Alshikh) — fears for his own safety (Midrash) — borne out by
     implication of text — "be not dismayed . . ." — prophet is basically a
     human being — only a man can be an emissary of God.   366

MATTOT

1.   *The lesson of Balaam's end* (31, 8 and 16) — Balaam's link with sin of
     Ba'al Peor revealed — because only then had he learnt of the Israelite
     promiscuity with Moabites (Luzzatto) — other examples of deferred
     information in the Bible — Balaam's complicity not mentioned in
     context — so as not to excuse the people from their moral
     responsibility — but at Balaam's death his complicity revealed.   375
2.   *Mammon or Eretz Israel* — career or mission? — origin of the term
     ḥaluẓ — a life that began with *mikneh* (cattle) and ended with *mikneh*
     (cattle) — analysis of the dialogue between Moses and tribes of God
     and Reuben — ducats before daughters — Moses rectifies the
     perspective: "before the Lord" — they loved their money and settled
     outside Eretz Israel (Midrash).   379

MASEI

1.   *The lesson of an itinerary* (33, 2) — geography-cum-archaeology or a
     philosophy of life — a Divine command (Ibn Ezra) — a Divine secret
     (Naḥmanides) — to publicise the lovingkindness of God (Rashi) —
     parable of the sick prince returning home after a long journey in search
     of a cure—to authenticate the Biblical account—(Maimonides)—to
     emphasise the hardships endured by Israel (Sforno).   388
2.   *The commandment to settle (in) Eretz Israel* (33, 50—53) — a
     question of syntax—the ambiguity of a *vav* again: *and* or *then*—two
     occurrences of *ve-horashtem*—securing the borders (Rashi)—a
     command to take possession, settle and live in Eretz Israel
     (Naḥmanides) — the command applies to the Biblical borders — live
     in Israel amongst heathens rather than outside amongst Jews (Talmud
     and Codes) — title to land by divine right.(Rashi) — all nations have

XV

similar title to their homelands (Amos 9, 7) — Israel's title conditional
on moral and religious integrity. 395

MATTOT-MASEI

1. *The consequences of following vanity* (Haftarah, Jeremiah 2, 4—28)—
    study of verse 5 — estrangement presupposes intimacy (Midrash) —
    divorce motivated by discovery of defect in the partner or a rival
    (Malbim) — following valueless things and becoming valueless — the
    question they did not ask — "where is the Lord?" Abravanel's
    explication of this question. 404
2. *Though you wash yourself with nitre* (Haftarah, Jeremiah 2, 4—28)—
    a final appeal to mend their ways — the laundry metaphor — why
    cannot stain of sin be "laundered" if the people repent? — sin too
    great to be expiated by repentance alone — suffering is necessary as
    well (Radak) — difference between "laundering" a sin and washing it
    out completely (Abravanel) — shame not of the crime but of being
    found out (2, 26, Malbim). 412

Index of Biblical and Rabbinic Sources   421
Index of Commentators and Authors   432
Subject Index   438

Bamidbar

INTRODUCTION

In his introduction to the fourth book of the Pentateuch, Nahmanides summarises its general character and significance, placing it in the context of the arrangement of all the five books of Moses:

In the third book, Vayikra, the Torah explained the laws of the sacrifices. Now we are instructed regarding the precepts connected with the Tent of Meeting. God hedged the Tabernacle around with restrictions just as He did with respect to Mount Sinai when His glory rested thereon. Compare: "The stranger that draws nigh shall be put to death" (Numbers 1, 51) with "And thou shalt set bounds to the people round about, saying, take heed to yourselves, that ye go not up to the mount, or touch the border of it: whoever touch the mount shall be surely put to death" (Exod. 19, 12). In Bamidbar (4, 20) the Almighty commanded: "But they shall not go in to see when the holy things are covered, lest they die", in Exodus (19, 21) it is stated: "Charge the people — lest they break through unto the Lord to gaze, and many of them perish". Regarding the Tabernacle it is stated: "And ye shall keep the charge of the sanctuary . . . that there be no wrath on the children of Israel" (Num. 18, 5). Regarding Sinai it is stated: "Let the priests also who come near to the Lord sanctify themselves lest the Lord break forth upon them (Exodus 19, 22).
Bamidbar contains detailed instructions therefore regarding the charge of the Tabernacle, the order of the encampments, the standing of the people afar, only the priests coming near the Lord . . . all to enhance the glory of the Tabernacle, as our Sages said: "The palace of the king which is surrounded by sentinels cannot be compared to that which is not so surrounded". This whole book is concerned with temporary precepts, commanded them for their stay in the wilderness and the miracles performed for them, to relate all the wondrous deeds of God . . . It relates that He began to deliver their

1

enemies to them by the sword and contains instructions how they were to divide the land.

There are few precepts of permanent validity in this book. It also finishes off the subject of the sacrificial laws begun in Leviticus.

According to Naḥmanides then, the Tabernacle which moved in the midst of the camp was a kind of mount Sinai on which the Torah was given, accompanying them on all their journeyings. Benno Jacob in his work on the Pentateuch follows up this idea of Naḥmanides:

> The Lord transferred His presence from Sinai to the Tabernacle, from the sanctuary of the Lord which *His hands* had established to the sanctuary which *Israel* had made. The Lord would henceforth speak to Moses from the Tent of Meeting and indicate to Israel by means of the cloud when to journey and when to encamp. The Tabernacle was a mobile Sinai in the midst of them, the heavens and heavens of heavens (the holy place and most holy place) transplanted and brought down to earth.

We may now understand the reason for the detailed treatment given by the Torah in the first sidra of Bamidbar to the camp, its arrangement and standards. That same camp housed — one boundary within another — the Tabernacle which accompanied them in their midst.

As R. Judah Halevi explains in his *Kuzari* (II, 26): "The camp and its divisions are to be compared to the body and its constituent limbs, the Tabernacle being to the camp what the heart is to the body". This is the reason for the detailing of the bearers of the Tabernacle and its various appurtenances. Again we shall resort to Halevi's explanation:

> All these appurtenances required bearers. The Levites were specially assigned to this task because they were nearer to God, especially after the incident of the golden calf, when they alone had shown undivided loyalty to the Almighty (Exodus 32, 26). Eleazar the priest being the most distinguished of them was chosen for the most sacred and refined task of taking charge of: "the oil for the lamp, the incense, the continual meal-offering and oil of anointing" (Num. 4, 16) — all of which are distinguished

by the pure fire, and the light of wisdom and knowledge; and what is more — the light of prophecy in the Urim and Thummim. The most distinguished Levitical clan after him — the sons of Kohath were assigned the task of bearing the inner limbs such as the ark, table, candlestick, altars and holy vessels for service. Of them it is stated: "For the service of the holy things belonged to them; they bore them upon their shoulders".

Let us compare this view of the role of the camp and its structure with that emerging from Abravanel's introduction to Bamidbar:

> The *first book* of the Torah, Bereshit, traces the ancestry and origins of the children of Israel from the creation of the world until they entered the Egyptian exile; the *second book* relates of their exile and redemption, in the physical sense from Egyptian bondage, and in the spiritual, from the idolatrous beliefs they entertained and from which they were weaned at Sinai and how they were commanded to build the Tabernacle so that the Divine Presence could rest on them. The *third book* initiates them into sanctity and purity and into the service of the Sanctuary, exhorting both the priests and people to refrain from abominable and evil rites. The *fourth book* relates of the leading of the people, their system of journeyings and encampments, their vicissitudes on the way, explaining why they were delayed forty years there, until the generation that had left Egypt had died out, and what happened to Korah and his company who rebelled against Moses and Aaron.
>
> Incidentally, for reasons which will be explained, this account introduced precepts specifically ordained for all time such as that of *zizit*, the Red Heifer, the laws of inheritance, the priestly blessing, the suspected adulteress, the Nazirite, the cereal burnt-offering and its libations, the continual offerings and appointed seasons' additional offerings, vows, cities of refuge and levitical and priestly gifts, the order of their journeyings — all dictated by Divine wisdom and leadership.
>
> This book describes in its ten sections how Moses led and provided for the people when they were in the wilderness, the acts of their power and might, order of their journeyings and their encampments and battles and what befell them with Moab and Midian, Balak and Balaam and the war of Sihon and Og the kings of the Amorite and the granting of their land to Reuben, Gad and half the tribe of Manasseh and all else that befell them till they came to their resting place and inheritance. The ten sections which comprise Bamidbar can be divided into two parts, the first comprising the first five:

3

Bamidbar, Naso, Beha'alotkha, Shelaḥ, Koraḥ; the second, the remaining sidrot: Ḥukkat, Balak, Pinḥas, Mattot, Masei.

Our sidra then comes to tell us of "the leading of the people, their system of journeyings and encampments". Describing the lay-out of the camp, the Biblical narrative notes:

אִישׁ עַל־דִּגְלוֹ בְאֹתֹת לְבֵית אֲבֹתָם יַחֲנוּ בְּנֵי יִשְׂרָאֵל מִנֶּגֶד סָבִיב לְאֹהֶל־מוֹעֵד יַחֲנוּ׃

Every man of the children of Israel shall pitch by his own standard, with the ensign of their father's house: far off the Tabernacle of the congregation shall they pitch.

2, 2

Some commentators consider that the arrangement of the camp of "every man by his own standard" and the roll-call of the people that preceded, bear the character of military preparation for conquest of the land. This indeed is the view taken by Rashbam who is a master of brevity and is always concerned to bring out the plain, literal meaning of the text or *peshat,* as it is termed in Hebrew.

Commenting on the verse (1, 2) "Take ye the sum of all the congregation of Israel", he states that the Almighty ordered them to be numbered from twenty years old and upwards, in the struggle for the Promised Land to which they had begun to proceed, directed by the pillar of cloud which arose on the twentieth of the second month (Numbers 4, 2). It was in preparation for this, that the Almighty commanded them to be numbered at the beginning of the month. Rashbam explains further, that the Levites were not numbered along with the children of Israel, because they were not eligible for army service, but were appointed to watch over the Tabernacle of Testimony (Num. 1, 50). Other commentators take up the same attitude and explain the arrangement of the ensigns as one of military order, adopted in the interests of security. In this connection, the comments of Luzzatto (Shadal) are worth quoting:

After the Tabernacle had been erected and they were proceeding towards the Promised Land, to conquer it under Divine leadership, it was desirable for them to be divided in accordance with their standards and groupings, so that *everyone would know his place and the camp be properly ordered,* that they should not appear as runaway slaves, but constitute a people ready for battle. They were therefore numbered as a part of the policy of instituting order. In this connection, our Sages rightly made the point that, "when He came to rest His Divine Presence amongst them, He numbered them".

It is surprising that Luzzatto does not sense that the whole attempt to supply strategic or military motives for the camp arrangement is not in consonance with, or, at least, does not offer an adequate explanation for the complete understanding of all that was involved in the arrangement of the tribes around the Tabernacle, their numbering and the exclusion of the Levites from the roll-call. Indeed, the suitability of this type of explanation is vitiated rather than supported by Luzzato's Rabbinic quotation to the effect that when God came to rest His Divine Presence on them he numbered them. Indeed a better understanding of the whole chapter can only be arrived at, when we remember that the focal point of the camp was the Tabernacle, and the tribe of Levi that encamped round about it. This was the Tabernacle which Naḥmanides considered to be a sort of substitute for Mount Sinai, a projection of it that moved in the midst of the camp as stated in our citation of his introduction to Bamidbar:

God hedged the Tabernacle around with restrictions just as He did with respect to Mount Sinai when His glory rested there.

Hirsch makes the following illuminating comment on the parallels between Mount Sinai and the Tabernacle, in his commentary, at the end of the book of Exodus.

"So Moses finished the work. And the cloud covered the Tent of the Congregation, and the Glory of the Lord filled the Tabernacle" (Exodus 40, 33). This signified that the whole process of erecting the Tabernacle had been accomplished in consonance with the Divine will "as God had commanded Moses", and that its original purpose, as expressed in the phrase, "They shall make Me a sanctuary and I shall dwell therein", had been achieved. The same as it is recorded regarding Mount Sinai (Exodus 24, 16) that "the Glory of the Lord above upon Mount Sinai . . .", so it was now, after the Torah had found its earthly resting place in the Tabernacle, in the place set aside for the revelation of God's Glory below. This same thought is expressed in Psalms 68, 18, "The Lord is among us, as in Sinai, in the holy place". Just the same as it is recorded regarding Mount Sinai that "the cloud covered it six days, on the seventh day he called unto Moses out of the midst of the cloud" (Exodus 24, 16), so the point is made (Exodus 40, 35) regarding the Tabernacle that, "Moses was not able to enter the Tabernacle of the congregation because the cloud abode thereon". Only after that does he state at the beginning of Leviticus (1, 1) that "And the Lord called unto Moses and spoke unto him".

It quite clearly emerges that the Tabernacle that went in the midst of the camp of the Levites was the centre of the camp of Israel just as the heart is the centre of the body, as Halevi noted in our quotation from the Kuzari. The arrangement of the camp, the ensigns and the roll-call are thus seen in another light from that viewed by the "literalists" (*pashtanim*) whom we cited earlier. To these, the strategist among them, we may tender the same answer as that given by the king of the Chazars when he heard the words of the philosopher whose reasoning appealed to his mind but not his heart. He said: "In these Divine matters there are secrets beyond those you have mentioned, O philosopher".

Now it is time to turn to the inspiring words of the Midrash and its treatment of the verse "Every man by his own standard with the ensign".

"איש על דגלו": הדא הוא דכתיב (דברים לג): "ימצאהו בארץ מדבר ובתהו יליל ישימון". מציאה גדולה מצא הקב"ה את ישראל שנאמר (הושע ט): "כענבים במדבר מצאתי ישראל" — כך "ימצאהו בארץ מדבר": מדבר היה העולם עד שלא יצאו ישראל ממצרים; "ובתהו יליל ישימון" תוהו ולילה היה העולם עד שלא יצאו ישראל ממצרים ועד שלא קבלו את התורה . . . כיון שיצאו ישראל ממצרים וקבלו את התורה — מהו אומר? (דברים לג): "יסובבנהו, יבוננהו, וצרנהו" — "יסובבנהו" —

שהקיפן בעבני כבוד; "יבוננהו" — שהבינם בדברי תורה; "יצרנהו" — אשרי
האזנים ששמעו עד היכן חבבן, עד היכן שמרן, עד היכן נצרן! כביכול עד "כאישון
עינו"! ראה היאך שמרן! היאך נצרן! שאמר אלוקים למשה: "משה אמור להם, שיעשו
משכן ביניהם. כביכול אני מניח את העליונים ויורד ושוכן ביניהם". ולא עוד אלא
שעשה אותם דגלים לשמו. אמר הקב"ה למשה: "עשה אותם דגלים לשמי"! למה?
שהם בני — שנאמר (דברים יד): "בנים אתם לה' " והם צבאותי, שנאמר (שמות ז):
"והוצאתי את צבאותי את עמי בני ישראל מארץ מצרים. וכן הוא אמר דגל מחנה
יהודה תימנה לצבאותם. ולפי שהם צבאותי אעשה אותם דגלים לשמי!"

This verse recalls Deuteronomy 32, 10 where it states "He found him in a
desert land and in the waste, a howling wilderness". The Lord recovered a
valuable lost property in Israel, as it is said (Hosea 9, 10): "As a vine in the
wilderness I found Israel" — so, "He found him in a desert land". The world
was desert until the Israelites went from Egypt. "And in the waste, a howling
wilderness" — Waste and dark (*Lailah*) was the world before Israel left
Egypt and before they had received the Torah . . . but as soon as Israel had
gone from Egypt and received the Torah — what then does it say? "He
compassed him about", implying that he compassed him or surrounded him
with clouds of glory; "He instructed him" — with words of Torah; "He
watched over him" — happy the ears that heard how much He loved them,
watched over them and guarded them, as if they were the apple of His eye,
so to speak!

See how He watched and guarded them! God said to Moses: Tell them to
make a Tabernacle in their midst as I am leaving my upper realm, as it were,
and descending to dwell amongst them. Moreover, He made them serve
under His ensign. The Holy One said to Moses: Make them ensigns in My
name. For what reason? Because they are my children, as it is written: "Ye
are the children of the Lord your God" (Deuteronomy, 14, 1) and they are
My hosts, as it is stated (Exodus 7, 4): "And bring forth My armies and My
people the children of Israel out of Egypt". For this reason it states: "The
standard of the camp of Judah southward. according to their armies".
Because they are My armies I shall make them into My standard-bearers.

(Bamidbar Rabbah 2, 5)

Questions for Further Study

1. Abravanel divides Numbers into two parts of five sidrot each.
   What reason can you for suggest distinguishing these two sets of

sidrot from each other   (*Bamidbar-Korah; Hukkat-Masei*)?
2.   Study carefully the following diagram and then answer the following questions:

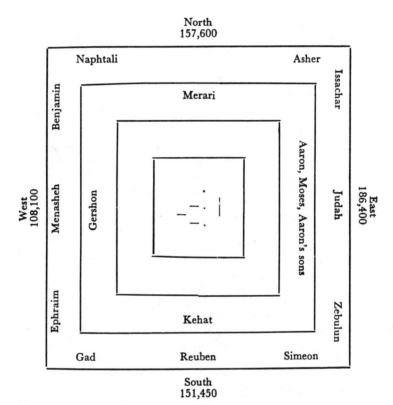

(a)   According to what plan are the tribes distributed in four groups and how are they joined together in threes? Note that the order is not in accordance with their age.
(b)   Why is the order of the tribes given in chapter 2 different from that mentioned in chapter 3?

(c) Commentators have found it difficult to explain verses 2 and 3, Psalm 80. Some of them resolve the difficulty by reference to our chapter (see diagram). What is the difficulty and its solution?

THE SECOND ROLL-CALL OF ISRAEL

וַיְדַבֵּר ה׳ אֶל־מֹשֶׁה בְּמִדְבַּר סִינַי בְּאֹהֶל מוֹעֵד בְּאֶחָד לַחֹדֶשׁ הַשֵּׁנִי בַּשָּׁנָה
הַשֵּׁנִית לְצֵאתָם מֵאֶרֶץ מִצְרַיִם לֵאמֹר׃
שְׂאוּ אֶת־רֹאשׁ כָּל־עֲדַת בְּנֵי־יִשְׂרָאֵל
לְמִשְׁפְּחֹתָם לְבֵית אֲבֹתָם
בְּמִסְפַּר שֵׁמוֹת כָּל־זָכָר לְגֻלְגְּלֹתָם׃
מִבֶּן עֶשְׂרִים שָׁנָה וָמַעְלָה כָּל־יֹצֵא צָבָא בְּיִשְׂרָאֵל
תִּפְקְדוּ אֹתָם לְצִבְאֹתָם אַתָּה וְאַהֲרֹן׃

**And the Lord spoke unto Moses in the wilderness of Sinai, in
the tabernacle of the congregation, on the first day of the
second month, in the second year after they were come out of
the land of Egypt, saying,
Take ye the sum of all the congregation of the children of
Israel,
after their families, by the house of their fathers,
with the number of their names, every male by their polls;
From twenty years old and upward, all that are able to go
forth to war in Israel:
thou and Aaron shall number them by their armies.**

(1, 1—3)

The fourth book of the Pentateuch, Bamidbar, opens with the census
conducted by Moses and Aaron of all the tribes from which it derives
its name "Numbers". The first chapter is replete with numbers of
each tribe and the total aggregate. This is also not the first census

taken of the Children of Israel. They had already been numbered prior to the erection of the Tabernacle (Exodus 30, 11—16; 38, 25—26). The sockets of the Tabernacle were made from the proceeds of the money contributed by those that were numbered. In our sidra they are numbered again; every detail is carefully given including the date — "on the first day of the second (i.e. Iyar) month in the second year" — one month after the erection of the Tabernacle.

The question that immediately arises is what need had the divine Law to include this minute statistical data? What moral purpose does it serve for future generations and why had Moses been commanded so solemnly to number them a second time, on this particular date? Our common sense interpreters, the leading representative of whom is Rashbam (Rashi's grandson) proffers a clear-cut explanation.

> "Take the number of all the congregation": This was on account of the fact that they had to enter Eretz Israel and those from twenty years and upwards were eligible to go forth in the army into battle. For on the twentieth day of the second month the matter was broached, as it is written in Numbers 10, 11, 29: "We are journeying to the place which the Lord hath promised to give to you"; for this reason the Holy One blessed be He ordered them to be numbered at the beginning of this month.

This census, according to this explanation, was therefore of a military nature in order to determine the forces at Moses' disposal and organize them for battle. This seems reasonable enough especially since the census only applied to those who had reached the age of twenty and upward, an age which was considered also by our Sages as the ideal one as far as physical endurance and capacity when they said "twenty year old to pursue" (Pirkei Avot). This explanation receives added confirmation from the fact that the Levites were not numbered along with the rest of the tribes, as it is written:

11

אַךְ אֶת־מַטֵּה לֵוִי לֹא תִפְקֹד
וְאֶת־רֹאשָׁם לֹא תִשָּׂא
בְּתוֹךְ בְּנֵי יִשְׂרָאֵל:
וְאַתָּה הַפְקֵד אֶת־הַלְוִיִּם עַל־מִשְׁכַּן הָעֵדֻת
וְעַל כָּל־כֵּלָיו וְעַל כָּל־אֲשֶׁר־לוֹ
הֵמָּה יִשְׂאוּ אֶת־הַמִּשְׁכָּן וְאֶת־כָּל־כֵּלָיו וְהֵם יְשָׁרְתֻהוּ
וְסָבִיב לַמִּשְׁכָּן יַחֲנוּ:

**Only thou shalt not number the tribe of Levi,
neither take the sum of them
among the children of Israel:
But thou shalt appoint the Levites over the tabernacle of
testimony,
and over all the vessels thereof, and over all things that belong
to it:
they shall bear the tabernacle, and all the vessels thereof; and
they shall minister unto it, and shall encamp round about the
tabernacle.**

(1, 49—50)

It is clear from here that the Levites were not numbered because of
their special role in the sacred service on account of which they were
relieved from military duties.
But there are still a number of difficulties which remain unexplained.
Why did the Torah elaborate so much on the details of the census
instead of merely informing us of the total number of Israelites at the
disposal of Moses for the purpose of battle? Naḥmanides, who seeks
to distil the maximum moral and mystical significance from the
sacred text suggests three approaches to this problem:

It was necessary for the Torah to record the total number after giving the
details because Moses and Aaron had been commanded to ascertain the
number of the people and the number of each tribe, for this was the manner
of kings to number the people. But I have not understood the reason for this
commandment, why God ordered it (i.e. to record the general total). It was

necessary to know the number of each tribe separately for the purpose of the arrangement of the camp according to standards, but why was it necessary to know the general number? Perhaps the idea was to make known His lovingkindness unto them, that when their fathers went down to Egypt they numbered only 70 souls and now they were as the sand of the sea. And after every pestilence and plague He numbered them in order to make known that Though He woundeth, His hands make whole again, in accordance with what our Sages said "out of an abundance of love for them He numbers them frequently".

Further he that comes before the father of all the prophets (Moses) and his brother the consecrated of the Lord (Aaron) and is known to them by his name gains thereby merit and life . . . For they would place upon them their eye for good and beseech mercy for them: "May the Lord God of your fathers add unto you according to this a thousand times" and not diminish your number . . .

I have further seen in Bamidbar Rabbah on the text "With the number of their names . . . by their polls" as follows: The Holy One blessed be He ordered Moses to number them in a manner that would confer honour and greatness on each one of them, individually. Not that you should say to the head of the family: "How many are there in your family? How many children have you?" But rather all of them should pass before you in awe and with the honour due to them and you should number them. That is what is meant when it states: "According to the number of names from the age of twenty years and upwards *by their polls*".

Perhaps in addition this was also the manner of kings when going to war. Now the Children of Israel were ready to enter the land and do battle with the kings of the Amorites who were on the other side of the Jordan, as it is said "we are journeying towards the place which the Lord has said"; and Moses and the Princes required to know the number of soldiers available... For the Torah does not rely on miracles that one should pursue a thousand, and this is the reason for the statement "all that are able to go forth to war in Israel".

(Naḥmanides on Numbers 1, 45)

Naḥmanides gives here three reasons, mentioning last the strategic, military consideration which Rashbam referred to. Naḥmanides in emphasising that we must not rely on miracles but must make all the necessary preparations for meeting the enemy is true to his approach in other places, particularly with regard to the spies, the dispatch of which into the Holy Land he regarded as a correct expedient adopted by all conquerors, since the Torah would not advocate relying on miracles. Nevertheless, we have no greater believer in miracles, both hidden and revealed, in Jewish history than Naḥmanides. It was he who said:

> No one of us can have a portion in the law of Moses our teacher until we believe that in all matters and circumstances affecting us we are surrounded by miracles and that they are not just natural and ordinary phenomena, whether concerning the public or the individual. All happens according to the decree on High.

On this same theme Naḥmanides makes another observation:

> The Torah orders matters to be conducted in the normal human fashion, leaving the miracles to be performed for the God-fearing in secret, since it is not the divine desire to change the nature of the world.

> (Naḥmanides on Deuteronomy 20, 8)

We may learn from these statements a valuable lesson regarding the maintaining of the judicious balance between trust in God and self-help, avoiding the twin dangers of relying overmuch on God in the sense of: "the heavens will be merciful", and human vainglory in the sense of: "my power and the might of mine hand have gotten me this wealth". On account of this Naḥmanides does not rest content with the strategic rational motivation of this census but adds a further reason and explains as well why this numbering had to be individual. Special importance is attached to this latter consideration in our days, in view of the ideologies that subject the individual to the mass and see in him a cog in the machine of state assuming that if one human being is destroyed there is always another one to take his place. In contrast to this, Naḥmanides emphasises that the census was personal and individual "according to their polls" impressing on us the value and sterling worth of each and every soul which is a unique specimen of divine creativity and a world of its own. Isaac

Arama in his Akedat Yizhak calls attention to this same feature of the census which came to demonstrate that:

> They were not just like animals or material objects, but each one had an importance of his own like a king or priest and that indeed God had shown special love towards them and this is the significance of mentioning each one of them by name and status; for they were all *equal* and *individual* in status.

The other reason mentioned by Nahmanides, alluded to first, and probably first in importance in his opinion, is the fact that this census was designed to call attention to the miracle of our existence. This idea is uppermost in the verse which we recite on the Seder night in relating the miracle of the Exodus:

בְּשִׁבְעִים נֶפֶשׁ יָרְדוּ אֲבֹתֶיךָ מִצְרָיְמָה
וְעַתָּה שָׂמְךָ ה' אֱלֹהֶיךָ כְּכוֹכְבֵי הַשָּׁמַיִם לָרֹב:

Thy fathers went down into Egypt with threescore and ten persons;
and now the Lord thy God hath made thee as the stars of heaven for multitude

(Deuteronomy 21,22)

Nahmanides further points out that this census took place after the pestilence and plague. He points to the moral of Jewish history: we have not succumbed in spite of decimation through suffering and persecution. On the contrary we have increased and multiplied.

Our sidra refers then in the dry language of statistics and numbers to the miracle of Israel's survival. This idea is phrased in philosophical terms by Bahya in his Hovot Ha-levavot:

> If someone will in these days (when the age of miracles is no more) seek a parallel to what took place in our ancient history (i.e. the miracles in the Bible), let him look frankly at our status among the nations from the time of

15

the exile and our relationships with them. In spite of the fact that we neither publicly nor privately fall in with their ways and they are aware of this, it is as He our Creator has promised us (Leviticus 26, 44): "And yet for all that, when they be in the land of their enemies, I will not cast them away, neither will I abhor them . . ." and it is said (Psalms 124, 1—2): "If it had not been the Lord who was on our side now may Israel say; If it had not been the Lord who was on our side, when men rose up against us . . ."

FORBIDDEN AND PERMITTED CENSUS

וַיְדַבֵּר ה׳ אֶל־מֹשֶׁה בְּמִדְבַּר סִינַי בְּאֹהֶל מוֹעֵד:
בְּאֶחָד לַחֹדֶשׁ הַשֵּׁנִי בַּשָּׁנָה הַשֵּׁנִית לְצֵאתָם מֵאֶרֶץ מִצְרַיִם לֵאמֹר:
שְׂאוּ אֶת־רֹאשׁ כָּל־עֲדַת בְּנֵי־יִשְׂרָאֵל
לְמִשְׁפְּחֹתָם לְבֵית אֲבֹתָם בְּמִסְפַּר שֵׁמוֹת כָּל־זָכָר לְגֻלְגְּלֹתָם:

And the Lord spoke unto Moses in the wilderness of Sinai, in the tent of meeting,

on the first day of the second month, in the second year after they were come out of the land of Egypt, saying:

Take ye the sum of all the congregation of the children of Israel,

by their families, by their fathers' houses, according to the number of names, every male, by their polls.

(1, 1—2)

Abravanel formulates the following question on the above verses:

Surely this is just the opposite of what the Torah had commanded on an earlier occasion (Exodus 30, 12): "When thou takest the sum of the children of Israel, according to their number, then shall they give every man a ransom for his soul unto the Lord, when thou numberest them". Rashi explains this to mean: when you desire to discover their total number, do not number them by their polls, but let each one give a half a shekel and by numbering the shekels you will know their number". How then could the Almighty have commanded them here to number them by their polls?

This contradiction between the first command to number the children of Israel before the erection of the Tabernacle and the one here has been noted by most of our ancient commentators. Rashi answers it simply by stating:

"By their polls" — i.e. through shekels, a half shekel per poll.

Similarly Ramban observes:

"Ye shall number them" (תפקדו) — an expression of visitation, remembrance and providence. Cf.: "And the Lord remembered (*pakad*) Sarah" (Genesis 21, 1). This is its implication in every context. It also expresses the idea of "bailment" (*pikadon*), something entrusted to someone's care for safekeeping. When the Almighty commanded Moses to number the children of Israel and said "ye shall number them", it implied that he should not actually count them but that each one rather should entrust to him a ransom of his soul of half a shekel...

But Abravanel and several other commentators maintain that this explanation runs counter to the sense of the verse, which explicitly states that they were numbered by their polls, and not through the medium of a shekel or other intermediary. Abravanel therefore maintains that the first counting in Exodus, through the medium of the shekel, bore no special significance, in respect of the method of counting to be followed by future generations. He states:

That counting was because the half-shekel was needed to provide sockets for the construction of the Tabernacle. The half-shekel was not a requirement of the counting, for he that fulfils the command of God will come to no hurt.

In other words, no one had the power except God Himself to inflict harm on man, and the giving of the shekels cannot be understood as a subterfuge to save the children of Israel from a plague that might befall them, had they been counted directly. Abravanel stoutly opposes any suggestion that they were numbered in the wilderness, through the medium of shekels, rather than by

heads, and rejects the idea that a plague would have come upon them
had they not been numbered by shekels:

> Now that the counting itself was an essential requirement, the Almighty
> commanded that it should be done without resort to a half-shekel or any
> other medium out of fear of a plague, since those discharging a religious duty
> can come to no harm. Let him not fear nor be dismayed by the pestilence
> that walketh in darkness, nor of the destruction that wasteth at noonday.

In support of this we may note that the enumerators of the
precepts of the Torah never connected the giving of the half shekel
with the operation of taking the census of the children of Israel, but
as the *Sefer Ha-ḥinukh* simply states:

> Every Jew from the age of twenty upwards, whether rich or poor is obliged
> to give annually to the priests a half-shekel . . . It was placed in one of the
> Temple chambers to be expended on the purchase of the continual and
> additional burnt offerings.

> (Ki Tissa, 105)

But there is one major objection to Abravanel's thesis. If there is
no religious objection to counting heads wherein lay the offence of
King David described in the second book of Samuel, Chapter 24?
There it is related how he took the census of the children of Israel
and how both he and the people were severely punished for this
operation.

וַיֹּאמֶר הַמֶּלֶךְ אֶל־יוֹאָב שַׂר־הַחַיִל אֲשֶׁר־אִתּוֹ שׁוּט־נָא בְּכָל־שִׁבְטֵי יִשְׂרָאֵל
מִדָּן וְעַד בְּאֵר שֶׁבַע וּפִקְדוּ אֶת־הָעָם וְיָדַעְתִּי אֵת מִסְפַּר הָעָם: וַיֹּאמֶר יוֹאָב
אֶל־הַמֶּלֶךְ וְיוֹסֵף ה' אֱלֹהֶיךָ אֶל הָעָם כָּהֵם וְכָהֵם מֵאָה פְעָמִים וְעֵינֵי אֲדֹנִי־
הַמֶּלֶךְ רֹאוֹת וַאדֹנִי הַמֶּלֶךְ לָמָּה חָפֵץ בַּדָּבָר הַזֶּה: וַיֶּחֱזַק דְּבַר־הַמֶּלֶךְ אֶל־
יוֹאָב וְעַל שָׂרֵי הֶחָיִל וַיֵּצֵא יוֹאָב וְשָׂרֵי הַחַיִל לִפְנֵי הַמֶּלֶךְ לִפְקֹד אֶת־הָעָם
אֶת־יִשְׂרָאֵל: וַיַּעַבְרוּ אֶת־הַיַּרְדֵּן וַיַּחֲנוּ בַעֲרוֹעֵר יְמִין הָעִיר אֲשֶׁר בְּתוֹךְ־
הַנַּחַל הַגָּד וְאֶל־יַעְזֵר: וַיָּבֹאוּ הַגִּלְעָדָה וְאֶל־אֶרֶץ תַּחְתִּים חָדְשִׁי וַיָּבֹאוּ דָּנָה
יַּעַן וְסָבִיב אֶל־צִידוֹן: וַיָּבֹאוּ מִבְצַר־צֹר וְכָל־עָרֵי הַחִוִּי וְהַכְּנַעֲנִי וַיֵּצְאוּ
אֶל־נֶגֶב יְהוּדָה בְּאֵר שָׁבַע: וַיָּשֻׁטוּ בְּכָל־הָאָרֶץ וַיָּבֹאוּ מִקְצֵה תִשְׁעָה

חֲדָשִׁים וְעֶשְׂרִים יוֹם יְרוּשָׁלָיִם: וַיִּתֵּן יוֹאָב אֶת מִסְפַּר מִפְקַד־הָעָם אֶל־
הַמֶּלֶךְ וַתְּהִי יִשְׂרָאֵל שְׁמֹנֶה מֵאוֹת אֶלֶף אִישׁ חַיִל שֹׁלֵף חֶרֶב וְאִישׁ יְהוּדָה
חֲמֵשׁ־מֵאוֹת אֶלֶף אִישׁ: וַיַּךְ לֵב־דָּוִד אֹתוֹ אַחֲרֵי־כֵן סָפַר אֶת־הָעָם וַיֹּאמֶר
דָּוִד אֶל־ה' חָטָאתִי מְאֹד אֲשֶׁר עָשִׂיתִי וְעַתָּה ה' הַעֲבֶר־נָא אֶת עֲוֹן עַבְדְּךָ
כִּי נִסְכַּלְתִּי מְאֹד:

And the king said to Joab the captain of the host that was with
him: Go now to and fro through all the tribes of Israel, from
Dan even to Beer-sheba, and number ye the people, that I may
know the sum of the people. And Joab said unto the king:
"Now the Lord thy God add unto the people, how many
soever they may be, a hundredfold, and may the eyes of my
lord the king see it; but why doth my lord the king delight in
this thing?" Notwithstanding the king's word prevailed against
Joab, and against the captains of the host went out from the
presence of the king, to number the people of Israel. And they
passed over the Jordan, and pitched in Aroer, on the right side
of the city that is in the middle of the valley of God, and unto
Jazer, then they came to Gilead, and to the land of Tahtim-
hodshi; and they came to Dan-jaan, and round about to
Zidon, and came to the stronghold of Tyre, and to all the cities
of the Hivites, and of the Canaanites; and they went out to the
south of Judah, at Beer-sheba. So when they had gone to and
fro through all the land, they came to Jerusalem at the end of
nine months and twenty days. And Joab gave up the sum of
the numbering of the people unto the king; and there were in
Israel eight hundred thousand valiant men that drew the
sword; and the men of Judah were five hundred thousand men.
And David's heart smote him after that he had numbered the
people. And David said unto the Lord: "I have sinned greatly
in what I have done; but now, O Lord, put away, I beseech
Thee, the iniquity of Thy servant; for I have done very
foolishly".

(Ibid. 2—10)

20

But the above story poses a difficulty even for Naḥmanides, who maintains that the command to count the children of Israel through the medium of shekels was a practice binding on all future generations.

> It sounds far-fetched to me that David should not have borne in mind Holy Writ, which states that (Exodus 30, 12): "Every man shall give a ransom for his soul . . . when thou numberest them; that there be no plague among them, when thou numberest them". If David did overlook the matter why did not Joab make the necessary shekels? Surely David's action was abhorrent to Joab, as it is said (1 Chronicles 21, 3): "But, my lord the king, are they not all my lord's servants? why doth my lord require this thing? why will he be a cause of guilt unto Israel?" Why then did not Joab number them through shekels in order to avoid sin?
>
> (Naḥmanides)

Many answers have been suggested. Here we cite one given by Gersonides, whom Abravanel also quotes with approval:

> David's offence lay in that he, the Lord's anointed and sweet singer of Israel should place his trust in the weight of numbers rather than in God alone, whose salvation does not depend on numbers, whether great or small.

To this Abravanel adds:

> I maintain that the seriousness of the offence lay rather in the high status of the offender rather than in the actual deed. David himself was by nature unassuming and humble: "Lord, my heart is not haughty, nor mine eyes lofty" (Psalms 131, 1). He always placed his trust in the Almighty: "In Thee O Lord have I taken refuge" (Psalms 71, 1). After serving God with such perfect devotion for seventy years he deserved severe punishment for becoming in the end overconfident and boastful and putting his trust in numbers by commanding Joab to count the people and pride himself in front of his enemies.

From the context, it would appear, that the census was taken for military reasons, since the duty of counting was imposed on Joab, the commander of the host and the numbered were valiant men that drew the sword. We know only too well that the Torah far from condemning human efforts to defend and protect its interests, preserve life and develop it, encouraged such action as a cardinal religious duty. The army of Israel was a necessary defence against its enemies. Why should King David then be condemned for taking measures to secure his people's safety? Even the census which the Almighty Himself had commanded Moses in our sidra was inspired too by the military purpose of the conquest of the Holy Land.[1]

It may be suggested that this puzzling story of King David's census is meant to teach us the important lesson of the difference between an army formed as a legitimate means for defence and as a body existing for its own sake. The census which David ordered was for the creation of a permanent force, after the Almighty had given his peace from all his enemies round about and he had no longer any need of military defence. But he wished, as Abravanel suggests, to boast and pride himself before his enemies. It is worth noting that Joab the born soldier who had fought all David's wars is the one who tries to prevent David doing this:

וְיוֹסֵף ה' אֱלֹהֶיךָ אֶל־הָעָם כָּהֵם וְכָהֵם מֵאָה פְעָמִים וְעֵינֵי אֲדֹנִי־הַמֶּלֶךְ
רֹאוֹת וַאדֹנִי הַמֶּלֶךְ לָמָּה חָפֵץ בַּדָּבָר הַזֶּה:

Now the Lord thy God add unto the people, how many soever they may be, a hundredfold, and may the eyes of my lord the king see it; but why doth my lord the king delight in this thing?

(2 Samuel 24, 3)

Joab puts the case even more clearly in the account in I Chronicles, emphasising that David no longer required the army for military purposes:

וַיֹּאמֶר יוֹאָב . . .
הֲלֹא אֲדֹנִי הַמֶּלֶךְ כֻּלָּם לַאדֹנִי לַעֲבָדִים לָמָּה יְבַקֵּשׁ זֹאת אֲדֹנִי...

And Joab said . . .
But, my lord the king, are they not all my lord's servants? why
doth my lord require this thing? . . .

(Ibid. 21, 3)

In short, the army and the soldier are only required in time of
need, but should not be gloried in, as having any intrinsic
importance.

ה׳ עֹז לְעַמּוֹ יִתֵּן
ה׳ יְבָרֵךְ אֶת־עַמּוֹ בַשָּׁלוֹם:

The Lord will give strength unto His people,
the Lord will bless His people with peace.

(Psalms 29, 11)

NOTE

[1] See the previous chapter, p. 11

THE DANGER OF THE HOLY THINGS

This sidra deals with the arrangement of the camp and the method of transporting and setting up the Tabernacle. We shall deal with the last three verses of the sidra:

אַל־תַּכְרִיתוּ אֶת שֵׁבֶט מִשְׁפְּחֹת הַקְּהָתִי מִתּוֹךְ הַלְוִיִּם:
וְזֹאת עֲשׂוּ לָהֶם וְחָיוּ וְלֹא יָמֻתוּ בְּגִשְׁתָּם אֶת־קֹדֶשׁ הַקֳּדָשִׁים
אַהֲרֹן וּבָנָיו יָבֹאוּ וְשָׂמוּ אוֹתָם אִישׁ אִישׁ עַל עֲבֹדָתוֹ וְאֶל־מַשָּׂאוֹ:
וְלֹא־יָבֹאוּ לִרְאוֹת כְּבַלַּע אֶת־הַקֹּדֶשׁ וָמֵתוּ:

Cut ye not off the tribe of the families of the Kohathites from among the Levites;
but thus do unto them, that they may live, and not die, when they approach unto the most holy things:
Aaron and his sons shall go in, and appoint them every one to his service and to his burden;
but they shall not go in to see the holy things, as they are being covered, lest they die.

(4,18—20)

This passage poses, first of all, a linguistic difficulty. What is the meaning of the strange phrase: "They shall not go in to see *kevala' et ha-kodesh?*" Rashbam regards the word *ke-vala'* as indicative of destruction and demolition:

Kevala' et ha-kodesh — i.e. when they dismantled the tabernacle the Lord was revealed, and if they saw, they would die. cf.: Lamentations 2, 2: "The

24

Lord hath swallowed up (*bila*) and unsparingly" and "Have swallowed up thy paths (*bileu*) (Isaiah 3. 12)... In this view we have the observation that the sons of Kohath stood afar off when they began to dismantle the tabernacle, as it is written: "When the camp setteth forward, Aaron shall go in, and his sons and they shall take down the veil of the screen . . . *after that,* the sons of Kohath shall come to bear them" (Num. 4, 5, 15).

But in spite of Rashbam's citations from the use of the word *bala',* in other contexts, his view that it means dismantling or demolition in our context has met with little acceptance, since one cannot compare the careful dismantling, piece by piece, of the tabernacle to the action of destruction and "swallowing up", implied in all the verses quoted by Rashbam. For this reason, Rashi's explanation is to be preferred, that it refers to the *covering* of the vessels, placing each one carefully in its container. But the real difficulty in the verse is not one of language but of content. Our commentators have been puzzled by this warning against gazing on the vessels.

The ominous ending of this passage is puzzling. What was the sin which the Levites had to fear when engaged in transporting the holy appurtenances that warranted such a dire penalty? Here are two different views propounded in the Midrash.

R. Eleazar Ben Pedat said, in the name of R. Yose Ben Zimra: The sanctity of the ark caused the people to be struck down by it, and all would run away preferring, at all costs, to take some other vessel, the table, the candlestick and the altars. The ark would thereby be slighted and the Holy One blessed be He would be angry with them. It was for this reason that the Holy One blessed be He, said to Moses and Aaron: Institute a precautionary measure for the sons of Kohath that they should not be cut off, to ensure that they would not leave the ark and run away. "Cut not off the tribe of the families of the Kohathites", but let Aaron and his sons come along and give each man his task and burden so that they will not be able to transfer from one service to another and from one burden to another.

R. Samuel bar R. Naḥman said: Heaven forfend, that the sons of Kohath should leave the ark and run to the table and the candlestick. On the contrary, they were ready to give their lives for the ark. What was the meaning, then of the admonition: "Cut not off the tribe of the families of the

Kohathites?" — They knew that whoever carried the ark merited greater reward. All would then leave the table and the candlestick and come running to the ark, in order to reap a greater reward (in the hereafter). As a result of this, quarrels would arise and each one would claim the right to carry the ark, thereby slighting the other appurtenances. For this reason God said to Moses: Institute a precautionary measure that they should not be destroyed from the world. Arrange them according to the tasks and the burdens, that they should not quarrel with one another, and all claim the right to carry the ark. The Holy One, blessed be He said: let Aaron and his sons come along and give each one his burden, as it is written, "Aaron and his sons shall go in, and appoint them every one to his burden and to his service".

(Bamidbar Rabbah)

Two different approaches are here outlined. R. Eleazar found that the danger which the Almighty wished to guard against, was that the Levites would shirk the more difficult task, and prefer one which demanded less responsibility. They would run to carry the table and the candlestick but would avoid ministering to the ark. R. Samuel took the opposing view. He maintained that the danger here would be that they would all prefer the responsible task, which carried with it more prestige and honour, and neglect the less responsible and more humdrum ones. Who would then be found to carry out these smaller but still necessary chores? For this reason, it was said: "every one to his service and to his burden". It was the duty of each individual to carry out, to the best of his ability, the task assigned to him. No one else could act as a substitute.

But this still leaves unsolved the nature of the capital crime that they would be in danger of committing. Most commentators find that the text implies, that it was the gazing on the holy things which was prohibited:

It is stated above that the sons of Kohath were only given the vessels to carry, after they had been covered. It was forbidden for them to be present when Aaron and his sons were engaged in covering them. "They shall not go in to see the holy things whilst they are being covered". We suggest that the reason for this was that the holy vessels should not be regarded simply as material articles of use. The people should realize their inner, symbolic significance. The Levites were charged with understanding the symbolic nature of the vessels that had been entrusted to their care. Had they kept their gaze directed on the holy vessels whilst they were being covered, this inner perception of their sacred purpose would have suffered, and they would have profaned their task.

(Hirsch)

Hirsch maintained that the danger which had to be guarded against, was of the symbol being accepted as its face value. They would look at the vessels as ordinary articles of use, and fail to appreciate what they really represented. Indeed, this was the fault of the Israelites, during the First Temple. The prophets denounced the insincere bringing of sacrifice, the adherence to the letter of the ritual and not to the spirit. Sacrifices were apprehended by the Israelites not as a means of bringing man closer to God but as an end in itself. Instead of stimulating the worshipper to greater loyalty to the Divine commands in every sphere of his life, the Temple service acted as a substitute for deeds and a tribute freeing the participant from responsibility. The holy vessels were not just material objects, purely ornamental in purpose. The Torah did not wish the Levites to rest content with the aesthetic enjoyment derived from handling them. They were not to gaze on the holy things in a material and profane sense. Diametrically opposed to this interpretation is Abravanel's:

"But thus do unto them" — that is to say, do on *behalf* of them that they may live and not die, by incurring the punishment of *Karet* (excision), when approaching the holy of holies, since the human soul on approaching that which is holy, naturally, yearns to see beyond the boundaries that are permitted it. Therefore you must cover up and conceal so that they shall not die, as a result of breaking through to see.

There is always a danger involved when man strives to grasp that which is beyond him, to soar higher and higher to that which is hidden and concealed. "The heavens are the heavens of the Lord but the earth hath he given to the sons of man", said the Psalmist (115,

27

16). It is sufficient for man to rest content with that which has been
granted him to understand, with that which has been entrusted to
him in his tasks, both sacred and profane. He should not strive to
"break through" to realms beyond his ken, "lest he die".

Another approach is outlined by a 16th century Italian
commentator, Moshe Ḥefez:

> I believe that the text contains a warning against the temptation of high
> office and the cure — humility. Pride and the feeling of success come before
> a fall. True contentment and happiness can only be achieved by the feeling of
> reverence and humility. The sons of Kohath were in danger of becoming
> victims of pride and vanity as a result of the privilege of carrying the ark
> which had been bestowed on them. The Holy One, blessed be He, therefore
> withheld from them one important detail. They were not allowed to carry the
> ark until Aaron and his sons had covered the holy things, so that they should
> realize that they, too, were subordinated to someone higher than themselves.
> The prohibition of touching the holy things was designed to disinflate their
> pride. They should not imagine they were in complete control and become
> overproud. This was "the burden" of the sons of Kohath. Their pride was
> meant to suffer by this burdensome provision. But it was ultimately meant
> for their benefit, that they should not be cut off and render themselves liable
> to the death penalty for lording it over their brethren. Aaron and his sons
> were charged with the responsibility of alloting each person his task.

Another commentator, Sforno, explains the text without any
resort to symbolic or homiletic treatment. The question was purely a
technical one of order and arrangement. The priests were called upon
to delegate the tasks of carrying in an orderly and prearranged
fashion, in order to avoid chaos and the resulting desecration of the
holy things. Sforno alludes to a Talmudic illustration of the dangers
to which disorder could lead. There (Yoma 23), it is related, that
during the period of the Second Temple, two youthful priests ran up
the stairs of the altar, wishing to be first to obtain the privilege of
removing the ashes. They pushed each other and one of them drew a
knife and stabbed the other. The worshippers assembled in the
Temple were shocked by this outrage and desecration of the holy

place. Only one person, it is stated, had the presence of mind to go to examine the victim to see if he was only wounded or was past remedy. His examination however was not prompted by humane motives, but in order to ascertain whether the knife had been contaminated by corpse defilement. The Talmud comments, in an outraged tone, on the fact that ritual defilement was apparently more important to them than human life.

Questions for Further Study

1. How would you explain the passage in 1 Samuel 6, 12—21, with the help of the text that we have cited from the sidra? What motives prompted the men of Beth Shemesh to violate the prohibition referred to in our sidra (read 1 Samuel Chapters 4—6).

2. What idea is symbolised by the following Midrash:

אמר משה לפני האלוקים: "רבונו של עולם! דמן של בני קהת אסור ודמן של בני אהרן
מותר?!" אמר לו הקב"ה: "לאו! אלא אהרן קדש קדשים", שנאמר (דברי הימים א,
כג): "ויבדל אהרן להקדישו קדש קדשים"; וארון קדש קדשים, ואין קדש קדשים מזיק
לקדש קדשים! אבל בני קהת אינם קדש קדשים, וארון וכל כלים הנתונים בפנים קדש
קדשים, והם מזיקים להם — לכך יתנו בני אהרן דעתם, שלא ימותו בני קהת!

"And when Aaron and his sons have made an end of covering the holy furniture, and all the holy vessels, as the camp is to set forward — after that, the sons of Kohath shall come to bear them; but they shall not touch the holy things lest they die" (Numbers 4, 15—16). Moses thus addressed God: Lord of the Universe! Is then the blood of the sons of Kohath forbidden and that of the sons of Aaron permitted? The Holy One, blessed be He, answered him: No! Aaron is most holy as it is said (1 Chronicles 23, 13): "And Aaron was separated, that he should be sanctified as most holy". The ark, too, is most holy, and things of equal sanctity cannot harm each other. The sons of Kohath, however, are not most holy, whereas the ark and all the

29

inner vessels are most holy and will cause them hurt. The sons of Aaron should therefore take care that the sons of Kohath do not die.

(Bamidbar Rabbah 4, 20)

3. Compare with Abravanel's words cited above, the following comment of *Ha'amek Davar* on Numbers 17, 3: "Who have sinned at the cost of their lives . . ."

The ones who took the firepans were really godfearing men of the highest order. The withholding of the priesthood from them which brings man close to communion and love of God, riled them like a burning fire within them. They did not seek the priesthood for the sake of personal advancement and glory but in order to become holy and achieve a higher spiritual state through the service. They likewise knew that God had spoken the truth to Moses and no doubt was cast on the authenticity of Moses' message. But they nursed a grievance against the Divine decision in their hearts and sacrificed their lives for the love of God, since "love is fierce as death". All this is explained in the Midrash cited by Rashi on Num. 16, 7: "It is enough for you, sons of Levi". The text goes on to say, "take the firepans . . . of those men who sinned at the cost of their lives (*be-nafshotam*)". What is the meaning of that curious phrase "sinned at the cost of their lives?" This text must be connected with a similar one describing the Nazirite (Num. 6, 11): "For that he sinned *al-ha-nefesh,* against his soul". There it means he deliberately deprived himself of wine in order to achieve a holier state — holy to the Lord, when this was above his merit. The proof of this was the fact that he eventually became unclean. The Torah calls the one who afflicts his soul in order to achieve a standard of holiness that is beyond his capacity — a sinner against his soul. Here also they sought to achieve a closer communion and love of God through the service, though they knew that they would not be absolved, and Moses' warning would certainly be fulfilled. In that they sinned *be-nafshotam* "against their souls".

What is common to both the transgression involved in the gazing at the vessels, according to Abravanel's explanation, and that perpetrated by the taker of the firepans, as explained in the *Ha'amek Davar*?

4. *Ha-ketav Veha-kabbalah* has a novel explanation of the word *kevala'*: He takes it as an adverb meaning "as the wink of an eye", following R. Levi's explanation in the Talmud: "That

which falls from the eye". The text means to stress that they should not see the holy things even for a split second.

(a) Does the above commentator follow Rashi's or Rashbam's interpretation or does he strike out on a new path far removed from that of his predecessors?

(b) Does his explanation appeal to you?

HAFTARAH (Hosea 2, 1—22)

וְהָיָה בַיּוֹם־הַהוּא נְאֻם־ה'
תִּקְרְאִי אִישִׁי
וְלֹא תִקְרְאִי־לִי. עוֹד בַּעְלִי:
וַהֲסִרֹתִי אֶת שְׁמוֹת הַבְּעָלִים מִפִּיהָ
וְלֹא יִזָּכְרוּ עוֹד בִּשְׁמָם:

And it shall be at that day, saith the Lord
that thou shalt call me *ishi*[1]
and shalt call Me no more *ba'ali*[2]
For I will take away the names of the Baalim out of her mouth
And they shall be no more mentioned by their name.

(Hosea 2, 18—19)

The distinction between these two terms has to be properly understood. What difference does it make what name Israel calls God? Here is Rashi's explanation:

You shall serve Me from love and not fear. *"Ishi"*: An expression of marital relationship and young love. *"Ba'ali"*: An expression of overlordship and fear.

His explanation is puzzling. Is worship of God out of fear and reverence then to be condemned? Admittedly, the one who serves God out of love is on a higher plane than the one who serves Him out of fear. But obedience to God prompted by fear is also a creditable achievement, even it is not of the highest kind. Yet the subsequent verse speaks of the complete removal of the Baalim — of pure idol worship. Radak therefore offered another explanation:

> "Baal" is a homonym. Some called the heathen idols Baal. He therefore said that you shall call Me no more Baal, in order to wean Israel away from even utterance of the term Baalim.

According to the above explanation the change of name is merely a symbol of a changeover from the worship of idols to the service of the true God.

It would seem, however, that the prophet was not accusing them of invoking the Baal in place of the true God, but rather that the people were guilty calling God by the appellation of Baal, that is, they regarded Him as the Baal. This is how Buber explains the perversion of the true faith which they practised and for which the prophet, roundly condemned Israel at the beginning of the chapter.

> The harlotries pictured by Hosea ("I am not her husband and let her put away her harlotries from her face . . . for their mother hath played the harlot, she that conceived them hath done shamefully") mean nought else but that Israel forsook the true God for God-turned-Baal. The minor Baals, the household gods were never rivals of the true God. Even the great Baal of Tyre that was imported to Samaria for political reasons was not the main target of Elijah's campaign. No god constituted as it were a danger to the place of the true God in the consciousness of Israel save the distorted image of Him.

In other words, it was not the serving of idols in place of God that was involved, but turning God Himself into Baal. The Israelites made out of their God a Baal instead of striving to know Him. In this lay their treachery. If we recall that Baal was a fertility cult, we shall understand the force of the prophet's reproof. What did the Baal worshippers expect from their gods? Verse seven of Hosea 2 explains that:

אֵלְכָה אַחֲרֵי מְאַהֲבַי
נֹתְנֵי לַחְמִי וּמֵימַי
צַמְרִי וּפִשְׁתִּי שַׁמְנִי וְשִׁקּוּיָי׃

I will go after my lovers
that give me my bread and my water
my wool and my flax, mine oil and my drink

After lovers of this nature they are ready to go, even to run after
them ("then she shall run after her lovers"). Contrast this with the
type of pursuit they indulge in in the description of their return to the
Lord:

וְנֵדְעָה נִרְדְּפָה לָדַעַת אֶת־ה׳

Let us know and run to know the Lord

(6, 3)

What do they expect from their lovers, their Baalim? First the
satisfaction of their minimal needs and their luxuries ("oil" and
"drink"). Their service is therefore prompted by ulterior motives, in
hope of a reward. But the question again arises. Admittedly,
disinterested worship prompted by no prospect of reward is more
creditable than interested worship inspired by material incentive. But
could this be called a crime? Could this be termed regarding God as
Baal, calling on him, by invoking that term of idolatrous association?
Verse ten offers us a clearer delineation of their offence:

וְהִיא לֹא יָדְעָה כִּי אָנֹכִי נָתַתִּי לָהּ הַדָּגָן וְהַתִּירוֹשׁ וְהַיִּצְהָר

For she did not know that it was I that gave her the corn, the
wine and the oil.

(2, 10)

34

They beheld the field yielding its generous crop, the vine and olive as gods liberally endowing them and enriching them; they deified nature.[3] But they failed to see the "I" who alone giveth bread to all flesh. This is the significance of the phrase: "And shalt no more call me *ba'ali*".

On the other hand the phrase "thou shalt call Me *ishi*" signifies complete identification with and cleaving to Him. Compare the archetypal description of the marital relationship in Genesis — "forsaketh man his father and mother and cleaveth to his wife".

But what is the meaning of the phrase (v. 19):

וַהֲסִרֹתִי אֶת־שְׁמוֹת הַבְּעָלִים מִפִּיהָ

For I will take away the names of the *Baalim* out of her mouth?

There is no previous allusion to Israel's role in this context nor to any Divine help. Radak gives the following explanation:

> God had dedicated the heart of Israel specifically to the purpose of fearing His Name alone. He would help them to achieve this goal in the sense of the dictum of the Sages that "He who comes to purify himself is helped from Above".

Abravanel elaborates on this theme drawing attention to the cognate idea implicit in the Pentateuchal admonition:

וּמַלְתֶּם אֵת עָרְלַת לְבַבְכֶם

Circumcise therefore the foreskin of your heart

(Deut. 10, 16)

This is followed by the corresponding Divine promise of assistance in *Niẓavim*:

35

וּמָל ה' אֱלֹהֶיךָ אֶת לְבָבְךָ וְאֶת־לְבַב זַרְעֶךָ לְאַהֲבָה לְאַהֲבָה אֶת־ה' אֱלֹהֶיךָ בְּכָל לְבָבְךָ וּבְכָל נַפְשֶׁךָ

And the Lord thy God shall circumcise thy heart and the heart of thy seed to love the Lord thy God with all thy heart and with all thy soul.

(Deut. 30, 6)

We find too in Ezekiel 18, 31:

וַעֲשׂוּ לָכֶם לֵב חָדָשׁ וְרוּחַ חֲדָשָׁה

And they shall make for themselves a new heart and a new spirit

This admonition to man is paired in a later chapter (36, 26) by a promise by God:

וְנָתַתִּי לָכֶם לֵב חָדָשׁ וְרוּחַ חֲדָשָׁה אֶתֵּן בְּקִרְבְּכֶם

And a new heart also will I give you and a new spirit will I put within you.

Similarly in our context we find:

תִּקְרְאִי אִישִׁי
וְלֹא־תִקְרְאִי־לִי עוֹד בַּעְלִי:
וַהֲסִרֹתִי אֶת שְׁמוֹת הַבְּעָלִים מִפִּיהָ
וְלֹא־יִזָּכְרוּ עוֹד בִּשְׁמָם:

Thou shalt call Me *ishi*
and shalt call Me no more *ba'ali*

**For I will take away the names of the Baalim out of her mouth
And they shall no more be mentioned by their name.**

(Hosea 2, 18—19)

In all the foregoing paired passages is exemplified the principle
alluded to by Abravanel that when the sinner forsakes his sin the
Lord shows him the way and helps him further along the path of
repentance.

If man will not regard God as a "Baal", if he does not make Him
into his idol, merely a supplier of his material wants, the Lord will
help him to see the worthlessness of all Baalim, all idols.

Saadia Gaon explains the parallel phrasing in our verse as follows:

> The missions were twofold: one concerning Israel — "And I will take away
> the names of the Baalim out of her mouth". The second concerns the nations
> of the world, that they were destined to abandon idol worship, alluded to in
> the text: "And they (the Baalim) shall no more be mentioned by their name",
> by no single person anywhere, in accordance with the prophecy of
> Zephaniah (13, 9): "For then will I turn to the peoples a pure language that
> they may all call upon the name of the Lord, to serve Him with one
> consent".

NOTES

[1] My husband.

[2] My Master.

[3] The Torah (Deut. 8, 7—11) warned Israel against this danger. The natural
bounty that would confront them on their entry into the Promised Land, its
luxuriant vegetation, the brooks, fountains and gorges would leave their impress
on the people as they settled down. "The land" which is emphasised seven times
in this passage is the source of the greatest danger intoxicating its tillers with its
plenty, inducing them to see in its fertility not the will of the Creator and His
lovingkindness but gods themselves and expressions of their orgies, the Baal and
Ashtoreth. See *Studies in Devarim*, Ekev 2.

ROBBERY OF THE PROSELYTE

This sidra from the beginning of chapter 5 presents rather a curious structure, comprising what looks, at first sight, as a jumble of subjects, with seemingly no logical connection between them. This fact has indeed been noted by our earliest authorities, and various suggestions have been advanced by both ancient and modern commentators to supply the motif linking the different items, dealt with in the sidra. To take one of the latest commentators first, let us cite the interpretation offered by Cassuto:

> Subject matter in the Bible is often arranged and linked together by a process of thought and, in particular, word association, probably originally designed as an aid to memory. This principle has not yet received sufficient recognition by modern scholars... The book of *Bamidbar* is arranged chiefly after such a fashion, various items being included because of a similarity of thought or phrase recurring in the chapters concerned.
>
> For instance, the chapters dealing with the arrangement and composition of the camp of Israel (2, 1—5, 4) are followed by that treating of the guilt offering *asham* (5, 5—5, 8) to which two verses (9, 10) concerning the priestly portions, *matnot kehunah* are appended. Then we are introduced to the laws applying to *sota — suspected adultress —* (5, 11—5, 31) succeeded by those treating of the Nazirite (6, 1—6, 21) after which is appended the formula, for the priestly blessing — *birkat ha-kohanim* (6, 22—6, 27). These, apparently, disconnected items, are indeed linked to each other in accordance with the Bible's own principles of order and arrangement. At the end of the chapters treating of the camp of Israel, it is recorded that the children of Israel were commanded to send forth from the camp every leper, etc. (5, 1). The very mention of the word leper recalls the guilt-offering he has to bring on the day of purification (Leviticus 14, 12), and this accounts for the introduction of the item on the guilt-offering, at this

juncture (*Sefer Hakinus,* p. 168, collection of lectures at World Conference of Jewish Studies, 1947).

Cassuto explains the whole arrangement of our sidra, after the same fashion. In the laws of the guilt-offering the phrase "to do a trespass against the Lord" (5, 6) occurs. A similar phrase: "If any man's wife commits a trespass against the Lord" (5, 12) is used in connection with the *sota*. The chapter of the Nazirite is linked to that on the *sota* by the almost parallel wording describing the rite of uncovering the head of the *sota* and of letting the hair of the Nazirite grow long (*para' et rosh ha-isha,* 5, 18; *gadel pera' se'ar rosho,* 6, 5). Traces of this method of interpretation are to be found in Ibn Ezra.

However, our traditional, classic commentators including the Midrash, followed by Rashi and others explain the connecting links between the various subjects in a different manner.

Taking for its text the verse (1 Samuel 2, 30): "For them that honour Me I will honour, and they that despise Me shall be lightly esteemed", the Midrash gives striking expression to the sublime ethical and moral wisdom underlying the arrangement of the sidra:

"For them that honour Me, I will honour" — this verse refers to proselytes (*gerim*) who honour the Almighty by forsaking their evil deeds and coming to take refuge under the wings of the Divine Presence (*Shekhinah*). For this reason, the Holy One recompenses them by honouring them.

"They that despise Me shall be lightly esteemed" — this part of the verse refers to the wicked who spurn the Almighty and are repaid by being lightly esteemed by Him.

Who were they that despised the Omnipotent? They that worshipped the Golden Calf. In what way did God repay them for their behaviour? He smote them with leprosy and venereal diseases and expelled them from the camp. In what way did God honour proselytes? He inserted the chapter warning us to look after the interests of proselytes after that dealing with sending the lepers out of the camp. From this you may learn that God repels the sinners of Israel, while befriending proselytes who seek Him. They are protected by the same laws as the Israelite, and whoever takes by violence from them is dealt with in the same way as if he were robbing an Israelite.

(Bamidbar Rabbah 8, 3)

The Midrash thus explains the connecting link between the subject of treatment of the lepers and that of unjust misappropriation of a proselyte (*gezel ha-ger), by way of contrast*. The question, however, that immediately springs to mind is where do we find in our sidra any mention or even suggestion of laws concerning a *ger*? If we read carefully the four verses (5, 5—8) which are given the title of *parashat azharat gerim* (chapter protecting the interests of proselytes), we shall find no hint of any such reference.

In order to understand the Midrash's justification for the title it gives this paragraph, we must compare Leviticus 5, 20—26.[1] We shall immediately perceive that the verses in our sidra are nothing more than a condensed version of what has already been said there. In accordance with the principle that the Torah never repeats itself, unnecessarily, but every repetition introduces, perforce, some new element, Rashi, following Talmudic exegesis, makes the following comment:

> The Torah repeats here the laws applicable to robbery with violence, perjury and trespass against the Lord already mentioned in Leviticus in order to introduce *two new elements*: (1) the element of confession teaching us that the offender is only liable to pay a fine of a fifth part and a guilt-offering, on the evidence of witnesses, when he himself admits the wrongdoing; (2) the case of that which has unjustly been taken from a *ger* which is restored to the priests.

The exact implications of the phrase, "If a man or woman shall commit any sin that men commit, to do a trespass against the Lord" (5, 6) are elaborated in Leviticus (5, 21) in the parallel passage, but *ger* is not mentioned anywhere. The only significant addition in our sidra is the following passage:

וְאִם אֵין לָאִישׁ גֹּאֵל

But if the man have no kinsman,

(5, 8)

40

on which Rashi makes the following comment:

> This applies to the case when the plaintiff died without heirs. Our Sages however posed the question: Is there anyone in Israel who has no next of kin nor brother, nephew or distant relation, going back to Jacob! This can only refer therefore, to a *ger* who died leaving no heirs![2]

Here at last is the clue to the reference to robbery of a *ger* contained in this item. Unjust and violent misappropriation — *gezel* — is a serious offence in Jewish law: "One who takes by violence a *peruta's (peruta* — smallest Jewish coin) worth and admits the offence, after denying it on oath, must restore it to the owner even if he has to go as far as Media to reach him" (*Bava Kamma* 103a). Media is taken as an example of a remote country and of one where money has no value, suggested by Isaiah 13, 17 where the Medes are described as not regarding "silver, and as for gold, they have no delight in it". In other words, the offence can only be expiated by restoration of the theft to the owner. The same applies to the *ger*; his violated property must be restored. But if he died leaving no heirs, then "the trespass be recompensed to the Lord, even unto the priest" (5, 8). The stolen money, termed here *asham* — trespass, which has no living master must be returned to the Master of all things, the representative of God.

Our Sages in the Midrash took the opportunity of developing this theme dwelling on the Divine love for the *ger*:

> "The Lord loveth the righteous" (Psalms 146, 8). "Thus saith the Lord: I love them that love Me" (Proverbs 8, 17).
> Why does the Holy One blessed be He love the righteous? Because they have no hereditary or family title. On the other hand, the priests and Levites constitute a father's house (a hereditary or family aristocracy), as it is written (Psalms 135, 19): "House of Aaron, bless ye the Lord, house of Levi, bless ye the Lord . . ." If a man wants to be a priest or Levite, he cannot become one, because his father wasn't a priest or Levite. But if one wants to be a righteous man, even he is a Gentile, he can be, as there is no family monopoly on it. That is why it states (Psalms 135, 20): "Those that fear the

Lord, bless ye the Lord", and not, "The *house* of those that fear the Lord . . ." Proselytes are what they are not by virtue of family title, but simply of their own free will have come to love God. He therefore responds by loving them, as it is written: "The Lord loveth the righteous".

The Holy One blessed be He bears a deep love to the *ger*. To what may this be compared? To a king who kept a flock that went to graze every day in the fields, returning in the evening. Once a stag joined the flock, grazing with them in the fields and coming home with them. The king was told about it and loved the stag, giving orders that it should have special treatment, the best pasture, etc. His shepherds said to him: O king, you have so many goats and sheep and yet you single out this stag for special treatment. The king explained his attitude as follows: My flock, whether they like it or not, graze in the field in the day and come to the pen at night. But stags, in the ordinary way, sleep in the desert and do not approach human habitation. Should we not be grateful to him for forsaking the wide open spaces with the other wild animals and coming to live with us? In the same way, should we not be grateful to the proselyte who leaves his family and people and comes to us? For this reason, God ordered special care to be taken of him, warning Israel not to cause him hurt, as it is written: "Ye shall love the *ger*" (Deuteronomy 10, 19); "Thou shalt not oppress the *ger*" (Exodus 22, 20).

The Torah laid down equal treatment for the native Israelite and proselyte, and taking by violence from either must be expiated by payment of a fine and an atonement offering, as it is written in the chapter dealing with robbery of a *ger* (Numbers 5, 6).

(Bamidbar Rabbah 8, 2)

Questions for Further Study

1.   Explain the meaning of the last Midrashic quotation above. What did our Sages wish to emphasize in the parable of the stag "leaving the wide open spaces and coming to live with us?"

2.   See 5, 7: "They shall confess their sin". The Hebrew word for confess (*hitvadeh*) is in the reflexive *hitpael* form. Give a reason for this and suggest what bearing this has on the character of Jewish confession?

3. See 5, 6: "If a man or woman shall commit any sin that men commit to do a trespass against the Lord". Note the following comment of *Sifra* on Leviticus 5, 21:

> Rabbi Akiva asked: What does the Torah mean by the words "To do a trespass against the Lord?" Because the lender and borrower and both parties to a business contract conduct their transactions only in front of witnesses and by means of a written deed. Any repudiation is a repudiation of witnesses and a written deed. But the one who deposits a bailment with his friend does not want anyone to know, except the Third Party who stands between them. When he repudiates his trust, he repudiates that Third Party.

(a) Explain the idea underlying Rabbi Akiva's words.

(b) What difficulty does he solve by means of his explanation?

4. Verse 8: "If the man have no kinsman". Compare: Leviticus 25, 26. Why cannot we ask the same question there: Is there anyone who has no next of kin?

5. Turn to the Neilah prayer in your Yom Kippur prayer-book, and find references to the demand to refrain from robbery and oppression.

NOTES

[1] Cf. also *Studies in Vayikra, Vayikra* 4.

[2] On adoption of Judaism, a *ger's* blood ties cease to exist in Jewish law. Our Sages said: One who becomes a proselyte is like a new-born babe.

GUILT-OFFERING FOR ROBBERY

דַּבֵּר אֶל־בְּנֵי יִשְׂרָאֵל
אִישׁ אוֹ־אִשָּׁה כִּי יַעֲשׂוּ מִכָּל־חַטֹּאת הָאָדָם
לִמְעֹל מַעַל בַּה׳
וְאָשְׁמָה הַנֶּפֶשׁ הַהִוא:
וְהִתְוַדּוּ אֶת־חַטָּאתָם אֲשֶׁר עָשׂוּ
וְהֵשִׁיב אֶת־אֲשָׁמוֹ בְּרֹאשׁוֹ
וַחֲמִישִׁתוֹ יֹסֵף עָלָיו
וְנָתַן לַאֲשֶׁר אָשַׁם לוֹ:

Speak unto the children of Israel;
When a man or woman shall commit any sin that men commit,
to commit a trespass against the Lord,
and that soul shall be guilty;
then they shall confess their sin which they have done;
and shall make restitution for his guilt in full,
and add unto to it the fifth part thereof,
and give it unto him in respect of whom he hath been guilty.

(5, 6—7)

Let us first examine the grammatical structure of the above passage. We have a conditional sentence with its introductory clause or protasis and the consequent main clause or apodosis. But where does the protasis end and the apodosis or main clause begin? Usually, the consequent main clause following the condition does not begin with a conjunctive "and" (*vav* — in the English version the first *vav* is translated "and": *ve-'ashma* "and that soul be guilty"; the second *vav* — *ve-hitvadu* *"then* they shall confess" and the subsequent *vavs* by "and"). Here, however, all the clauses following the introductory condition begin with a *vav* — *"and* that soul shall be guilty . . ." (The English rendering of the *vav* here is "then" — see previous parenthesis); *"and* they shall confess . . . *and* he shall make restitution"; *"and* he shall give". In other words, the question to be decided here is which of all these *vavs* is to be translated by "then", marking the turn of the sentence and the beginning of the consequent clause or apodosis and which of them are merely additional clauses continuing the protasis? Is the phrase "that soul shall be guilty" part of the protasis or the beginning of the apodosis? Let us compare a parallel passage in Leviticus (5, 21, 23). Perhaps it will throw light on our problem:

נֶפֶשׁ כִּי תֶחֱטָא וּמָעֲלָה מַעַל בַּה׳
וְכִחֵשׁ בַּעֲמִיתוֹ. . . וְהָיָה כִּי־יֶחֱטָא וְאָשֵׁם
וְהֵשִׁיב אֶת־הַגְּזֵלָה אֲשֶׁר גָּזָל
אוֹ אֶת־הָעֹשֶׁק אֲשֶׁר עָשָׁק

**If any one sin and commit a trespass against the Lord,
and deal falsely with his neighbour . . .
then it shall be, if he hath sinned and is guilty,
that he shall restore the thing he took by robbery
or the thing which he hath gotten by oppression.**

Here the Hebrew rendering clearly indicates that the guilt phrase belongs to the protasis *ve-haya ki yeheta ve-ashem* "then it shall be, if he hath sinned and is guilty . . ." and is not part of the consequence. That is also how Rashi understands it: "When the offender himself realizes the need to make amends and know and confess". The text speaks of the man who himself first acknowledged his guilt and repented of his robbery and wished to make amends. It is he who has to bring, in addition to the restitution of the theft, a fifth part thereof and an offering of a ram of atonement.

Let us continue the study of the passage:

וְהִתְוַדּוּ אֶת־חַטָּאתָם

Then they shall confess their sin

This clause begins the rulings that apply to the man who committed the trespass, who is guilty and acknowledges his guilt. The first step in making amends after acknowledging his guilt is confession — oral confession. This confession is obligatory on all transgressors.

> Regarding every command of the Torah, whether positive or negative, a man who has transgressed any one of them, deliberately or inadvertently, when he makes amends and turns away from his sin, is obliged to confess before the Lord blessed is He, as it is stated: "When a man or woman shall commit any sin ... then they shall confess". Oral confession is implied and this confession is a positive command.
>
> (Maimonides, Code, Teshuvah 1)

The reason for this command is explained as follows in the *Sefer Ha-ḥinukh:*

> The verbal confession of guilt provides an indication that the sinner truly believes that all his deeds are revealed and known to thee Lord blessed is He, and he will not deny the omnipresence of the All-seeing. Again, by verbally specifying the sin and regretting it, he will be more careful in the future not to stumble thereon. After he has said with his mouth: I did such and such a thing and was foolish in my actions, he will, as a result, become reconciled with His maker. The good God who desires the welfare of His creatures guided them in this path through which they would gain merit.

Note also the reflexive or *Hitpael* form of the Hebrew verb "to confess" *hitvadeh.* Hirsch pointed out that this indicates that the

46

confession consists of man speaking to himself, admonishing his conscience. King David advocated a similar course in his Psalms of repentance "when Nathan the prophet came unto him, after he had gone in to Bathsheba":

כִּי־פְשָׁעַי אֲנִי אֵדָע וְחַטָּאתִי נֶגְדִּי תָמִיד:

For I know my transgressions; and my sin is ever before me.
(Ps. 51, 5)

The next step is the practical making amends

וְהֵשִׁיב אֶת־אֲשָׁמוֹ בְּרֹאשׁוֹ וַחֲמִישִׁתוֹ יֹסֵף עָלָיו . . . מִלְּבַד אֵיל הַכִּפֻּרִים
אֲשֶׁר יְכַפֶּר בּוֹ עָלָיו:

And shall make restitution for his guilt in full, and add unto it the fifth part thereof... beside the ram of atonement with which to atone for him on its account.
(5, 7—8)

Here is the legal formulation of the Biblical ruling in Maimonides' Code (*Gezelah Va-avedah*):

> Whoever owes money to his fellow Jew and denies it and swears falsely is obliged to return him the amount he denied and an addition of a fifth. He is also liable for an offering called *asham gezelot* ("the guilt offering of robberies").
> The one who perjures himself to deny a monetary debt is only liable to pay a fifth part when he himself confesses his guilt, but if witnesses came and he still persists in his denial, he pays the principal only on the evidence of witnesses and not the fifth part.

Why, we may ask should the repentant sinner who confesses his guilt, on his own accord, be penalised by having to bring, in addition to the principal, a fifth and an offering, whereas the one who

47

attempts to cover up his crime, only addmitting because witnesses showed up and revealed his perjury is only liable to pay back the principal? Should the sinner be rewarded? But the explanation is quite clear if we bear in mind that the fifth part and the offering are not penalties or fines for the act of robbery and subsequent perjury but atonement.

> The guilt offering atones only for the truly repentant, but the one who spurns it is not atoned through it.
>
> (Maimonides, Code)

Without any change of heart or indication by word of mouth or deed, on the part of the wrongdoer, the offering is valueless and so is the payment of the fifth. These instructions only apply to the repentant, helping him to atone for his deeds.

The text we are studying ends with the phrase:

וְנָתַן לַאֲשֶׁר אָשַׁם לוֹ:

And give it unto him in respect of whom he hath been guilty.

This phrase comprises four Hebrew words and the object of the giving is not at all clear from them, in spite of our unambiguous English translation. First the text has already implied that he has to make restitution: "And shall make full restitution and add unto the fifth part thereof". Rashi explains the closing phrase to refer "to the one whom he owes". It is difficult to understand what Rashi meant to indicate by this piece of information, since that is already implied in the previous part of the verse. What did Rashi see in the significance of the additional words *ve-natan la-asher asham lo*?

Two supercommentators on Rashi, Mizraḥi and Gur Aryeh, give the following interpretations. First Mizraḥi's explanation:

> If A from whom the money had been stolen owed B money, the restitution should be made not to A but to B. This emerges from Rashi's wording "to

the one whom he owes it". If Rashi had meant A, he should have written "to the one from whom he had stolen it". The Talmud states the same principle: "Whence that if A owes B money and B owes C that we may directly transfer the repayment from A to C? The Torah states: *ve-natan la-asher asham lo.* Our text is interpreted to imply that the thief can sometimes be required to make restitution not to the victim but to the victim's creditor, based on the use of the word *asham* instead of *gazal.* He is required to return it not always to the one from whom he had stolen it but to the one to whom it is owing.

Gur Aryeh has a different approach:

Rashi wished to emphasise that the word *asham* in the context has not the meaning of guilt it has in the other contexts, as in "that soul shall be guilty". If that were the case the phrase would imply that the robber has to make restitution to the Almighty, "to him in respect of which he is guilty". That cannot be so since the text explicitly states that only where the man has no redeemer to whom to make restitution, only then has it to be made to the Lord, through the priest. But if the victim has a redeemer or an heir it has to be given him. We must therefore conclude that the word *asham* here has the implication of "owing".

In other words, the robber cannot make amends by dedicating the proceeds of his wrongdoing and even over and above this to a sacred cause. But he must seek out the victim of his robbery, restore it to him and add a fifth. This is the source of the ruling that "he who robs his fellow of even a *peruta's* worth and denies it on oath must go after the owner even as far as Media.[1] He shall not give it to the victim's son or his agent . . ." Rashi comments that, in such a case, when he denies it on oath and ultimately confesses his guilt, the robber can only achieve atonement by personally returning it to the owner.

Questions for Further Study

1. Compare our text with the parallel one in Leviticus 5, 20—26. Here is the Sifrei's observation on the two texts.

"And the Lord spoke unto Moses, Speak unto the children of Israel, When a man or woman shall commit any sin that men commit". What was the need for this passage when the following has already been stated "If any one sin . . . and deal falsely . . . then it shall be, if he hath sinned and is guilty, that he shall restore that which he took by robbery . . . and add the fifth part thereof" (Lev. 5, 20)? But we have not been informed of the rule applying to the robbery of a proselyte (*ger* — who on adoption of Judaism is like a new born babe. All his previous blood ties cease to exist). The Torah comes therefore to teach us that "when a man of woman shall commit any sin that men commit" referring to the one who robs a proselyte and denies it on oath and that if the proselyte dies the robber must make restitution of the principal and a fifth part thereof to the priests and a guilt-offering to the altar. This is the pattern followed by the Torah. Where there are two similar passages, one of them comes to teach us something omitted in the other.

(a) Indicate why we must presume that our sidra refers to robbery of a proselyte.

(b) Try to suggest a reason why the case of robbery from a proselyte was reserved for the passage in our sidra.

2. In what way does the text of Genesis 31, 50 help us to understand Rabbi Akiva's dictum cited in the sidra above?

3. " 'And they confess their sin' (Num. 5, 7) — whichever of them it will be, man or woman" (Ibn Ezra). What did Ibn Ezra find difficult in our text which warranted his comment?

NOTE

[1] See previous chapter, p. 41.

LAWS OF THE NAZIRITE

This sidra contains a strange chapter dealing with the laws of the Nazirite which have excited the attention and interest of many commentators.

וַיְדַבֵּר ה׳ אֶל מֹשֶׁה לֵּאמֹר:

דַּבֵּר אֶל־בְּנֵי־יִשְׂרָאֵל וְאָמַרְתָּ אֲלֵהֶם

אִישׁ אוֹ־אִשָּׁה כִּי יַפְלִא לִנְדֹּר נֶדֶר נָזִיר לְהַזִּיר לַה׳:

מִיַּיִן וְשֵׁכָר יַזִּיר חֹמֶץ יַיִן וְחֹמֶץ שֵׁכָר לֹא יִשְׁתֶּה

וְכָל־מִשְׁרַת עֲנָבִים לֹא יִשְׁתֶּה וַעֲנָבִים לַחִים וִיבֵשִׁים לֹא יֹאכֵל: ...

כָּל־יְמֵי נֶדֶר נִזְרוֹ תַּעַר לֹא יַעֲבֹר עַל־רֹאשׁוֹ

עַד־מְלֹאת הַיָּמִם אֲשֶׁר יַזִּיר לַה׳ קָדֹשׁ יִהְיֶה

גַּדֵּל פֶּרַע שְׂעַר רֹאשׁוֹ: ... כֹּל יְמֵי נִזְרוֹ קָדֹשׁ הוּא לַה׳: וְכִי יָמוּת מֵת

עָלָיו בְּפֶתַע פִּתְאֹם וְטִמֵּא רֹאשׁ נִזְרוֹ ... וּבַיּוֹם הַשְּׁמִינִי יָבֵא שְׁתֵּי תֹרִים אוֹ

שְׁנֵי בְּנֵי יוֹנָה ... וְעָשָׂה הַכֹּהֵן אֶחָד לְחַטָּאת וְאֶחָד לְעֹלָה וְכִפֶּר עָלָיו

מֵאֲשֶׁר חָטָא עַל־הַנָּפֶשׁ

And the Lord spoke unto Moses saying,
Speak unto the children of Israel, and say unto them,
When either man or woman shall separate themselves to vow a
vow of a Nazirite to separate themselves unto the Lord
He shall separate himself from wine and strong drink, and
shall drink no vinegar of wine, or vinegar of strong drink,
neither shall he drink any liquor of grapes, nor eat moist
grapes, or dried ...

51

All the days of the vow of his separation there shall no razor come unto his head:

untill the days be fulfilled, in the which he separated himself unto the Lord, he shall be holy,

and shall let the locks of the hair of his head grow...

All the days of his separation he is holy unto the Lord.

And if any man die very suddenly by him, and he hath defiled the head of his consecration...

And on the eighth day he shall bring two turtles, or two young pigeons...

And the priest shall offer the one for a sin offering, and the other for a burnt offering,

and make an atonement for him, for that he sinned by the dead.

(6, 1—11)

What is the significance of the Nazirite vow in he Torah? Rabbi Joseph Dov Soloveitchik in his treatise "איש ההלכה" ("The Halakhic Personality" published by the W.Z.O. Dept. for Torah Education, Jerusalem, 5739 in "איש ההלכה גלוי ונסתר"), describing the characteristics of the religious personality, in a general sense, states as follows:

> The aspiration to achieve a state of ecstatic transcendentalism, the negation of life and this mortal world, the annihilation of existence ahd reality, the reaching out of the religious personality to the ethereal world that stretches beyond the confines of tangible existence is embodied in many of the systems of conduct involving asceticism, vows of abstinence and withdrawal from society.
>
> The religious personality sometimes imagines that afflictions, suffering, fasts and solitude constitute the media bringing immortal happiness to man ...
> According to his outlook, the man who withdraws from the world and forgoes earthly and ephemeral pleasures is rewarded with eternal life and a sublime, spiritual existence.

Is this then the aim of the Nazirite laws in our sidra? Are they meant to embody those ascetic rites by which man is brought nearer to "a sublime, spiritual existence?"

It is possible to detect a favourable attitude to the Nazirite in our sidra (though it should be noted that the Nazirite in the Torah merely refrains from wine and grapes and any of their products from the "kernel to the husk" and his vow does not involve abstinence from other bodily pleasures). For, surely, the Nazirite is here regarded as being on a higher spiritual plane, just as "he that is the high priest among his brethren, on whose head the anointing oil was poured . . ." Like the high priest:

עַל־נֶפֶשׁ מֵת לֹא יָבֹא׃
לְאָבִיו וּלְאִמּוֹ . . . לֹא־יִטַּמָּא לָהֶם
בְּמֹתָם כִּי נֵזֶר אֱלֹהָיו עַל־רֹאשׁוֹ׃

He shall come at no dead body
He shall not make himself unclean for his father or for his mother...because the consecration of the Lord is upon his head.

(6, 6—7)

Similarly it is said regarding the Nazirite:

. . . קָדֹשׁ יִהְיֶה . . .
קָדֹשׁ הוּא לַה׳

...he shall be holy...
he is holy unto the Lord

(6, 8)

Compare the laws of the high priest (Leviticus 21, 10—12). However a closer look at the chapter will reveal that the favour with which the Nazir is viewed, is not altogether unreserved. We find that his sins are explicitly referred to:

53

וְעָשָׂה הַכֹּהֵן אֶחָד לְחַטָּאת וְאֶחָד לְעֹלָה
וְכִפֶּר עָלָיו מֵאֲשֶׁר חָטָא עַל־הַנָּפֶשׁ . . .

And the priest shall offer one for a *sin* offering and one for a burnt offering

and make an atonement for him, for that he sinned by the dead...

(6, 11)

Similarly when the days of his separation are over he has to bring his sacrifices to the entrance of the Tent of Meeting and again we read:

וְהִקְרִיב אֶת קָרְבָּנוֹ . . . לְחַטָּאת

And he shall offer his offering...for a *sin offering*

(6, 14)

What constitutes then his sin? Our Sages of old differed in their evaluation of the Nazirite in the Talmud, and two opposing schools of thought find support for their opinions in the wording of this chapter

אמר שמואל: כל היושב בתענית נקרא חוטא. סבר כי האי תנא דתניא: רבי אליעזר
הקפר ברבי אומר: מה תלמוד לומר (יא): "וכפר עליו מאשר חטא על הנפש?" וכי
באיזה נפש חטא זה? אלא — שצער עצמו מן היין. ואלא דברים קל וחומר: ומה זה
שלא צער עצמו אלא מן היין נקרא חוטא, המצער עצמו מכל דבר ודבר על אחת כמה
וכמה? ר' אלעזר אומר: נקרא קדוש, שנאמר (ב): "קדוש יהיה גדל פרע שער ראשו".
ומה זה שלא צער עצמו אלא מדבר אחד נקרא קדוש, המצער עצמו מכל דבר על אחת
כמה וכמה!... ולר' אלעזר — הא נקרא חוטא? ההוא דסאיב נפשיה (רש"י: פשט
הכתוב "מאשר חטא על הנפש" — על שנטמא במת).

Said Samuel: Whoever indulges in fasting is dubbed a sinner: This is in accordance with the view of Rabbi Eliezer Hakappar Berebi who stated: What is the implication of the phrase, "And make an atonement for him, for that he sinned by the *dead*" (Hebrew — "soul"). By which soul then did he sin? — But we must conclude that it refers to his denying himself the enjoyment of wine. If then, he that merely denied himself the enjoyment of wine is dubbed a sinner, all the more so, does this apply to the person who denies himself the enjoyment of the other pleasures of life!

Rabbi Eleazar stated: He is called "holy" as it is written: "he shall be holy, and shall let the locks of his head grow". If then this man who merely denied himself the enjoyment of wine is nevertheless called "holy", how much more does this apply to the man who denied himself enjoyment of other things? But surely how does Rabbi Eleazar explain away the fact that the Torah does call him a "sinner?" — that is because he defiled himself by contact with a dead body.

(Ta'anit 11a)

Maimonides presents Rabbi Eliezer Hakappar's view in various parts of his works. In the "Eight Chapters" *Shemonah Perakim* — (Introduction to Pirke Avot) he states:

Our Torah, about which King David stated, "The Torah of the Lord is perfect . . . Making wise the simple", advocates no mortification. Its intention was that man should follow nature, taking the middle road. He should eat his fill in moderation, drink in moderation. He should dwell amidst society in uprightness and faith and not in the deserts and mountains. He should not wear wool and hair nor afflict his body. On the contrary, the Torah explicitly warned us regarding the Nazirite.

Here the Rambam cites Eliezer Hakappar's interpretation of the chapter. Further in the Mishneh Torah, Maimonides stated (De'ot 3, 1):

שמא יאמר האדם: הואיל והקנאה והתאוה והכבוד וכיוצא בהם דרך רעה הן ומוציאין את האדם מן העולם, אפרש מהן ביותר ואתרחק לצד האחרון, עד שלא יאכל בשר ולא ישתה יין ולא ישא אשה ולא ישב בדירה נאה ולא ילבש לבוש נאה, אלא השק והצמר הקשה וכיוצא בהן, כגון כהני עכו"ם — גם זה דרך רעה היא ואסור לילך בה. המהלך בדרך זו נקרא חוטא, שהרי הוא אומר בנזיר "וכפר עליו מאשר חטא על הנפש" — אמרו חכמים: ומה אם נזיר שלא פרש אלא מן היין צריך כפרה, המונע עצמו מכל דבר ודבר — עאכו"כ. לפיכך ציוו חכמים שלא ימנע אדם עצמו אלא מדברים שמנעתו התורה בלבד ולא יהיה אוסר עצמו בנדרים ובשבועות על דברים המותרים. כך אמרו חכמים: לא דייך מה שאסר תורה אלא שאתה אוסר עליך דברים אחרים. ובכלל זה אלה

55

שמתענין תמיד אינן בדרך טובה. ואסרו חכמים שיהא אדם מסגף עצמו בתענית, ועל
כל הדברים האלה וכיוצא בהם צוה שלמה ואמר: "אל תהי צדיק הרבה ואל תתחכם
יותר, למה תשומם (קהלת ז, טו).

If man should argue: since envy, passion and pride are evil . . . then shall I
divorce and separate myself utterly from them till I eat no meat nor drink
wine, nor marry, nor reside in a comfortable dwelling nor wear fine clothes
but only wool and sackcloth after the manner of the heathen priests — this
also is an evil path and forbidden it is to walk therein, as is stated in the case
of the Nazirite (quoting Eliezer Hakappar as above).

Therefore our Sages commanded man to deny himself only the things denied
him by the Torah. He should not inflict on himself vows of abstinence on
things permitted him. Thus our Sages stated: "It is not sufficient for thee that
which the Torah hath forbidden, but thou forbiddest thyself other things
too!" This includes those who are given to fasting. Our Sages forbade a man
to mortify himself with fasting. To such things King Solomon referred when
he counselled: "Be not righteous overmuch; neither make thyself over wise;
why shouldst thou destroy thyself?" (Ecclesiastes 7, 16).

However, how is it to be explained that the Torah *does* call the
Nazirite "holy?" Naḥmanides takes a wholly different attitude in this
matter, poles apart from the middle "natural" way advocated by
Maimonides. Commenting on the Nazirites' need to bring a sin-
offering Naḥmanides adheres to the plain sense of the Scriptures
stating that:

This man sins against himself when he forsakes his vows of abstinence, when
the days of his separation are fulfilled. He had separated himself to be holy
unto the Lord and by rights he should always continue to live a life of
holiness and separation to God, in accordance with the verse: "And I raised
up your sons for prophets and of your young men for Nazirites" (Amos 2,
11). There the Nazirite is equated to the prophet. Similarly the Torah states,
"All the days of his separation he shall be holy unto the Lord". Now that he
returns to defile himself with worldly passions, he requires atonement.

How wide indeed is the chasm that separates Maimonides'
approach from Naḥmanides'! Maimonides regards the very act of
becoming a Nazirite as a sin, Naḥmanides the act of *forsaking the
Nazirite vow.*

We shall conclude here by citing a third approach from the work of Solomon Astruc: *Midreshei Hatorah*:

> "For that which he sinned"—for the fact that his passions got the better of him, till he was driven to abstain from wine to subdue his material desires and bodily wants and deny himself the legitimate enjoyment of wine that maketh glad both God and man . . .

According to the latter opinion, the sin is not in becoming a Nazirite or in ceasing to be one. The sin referred to, concerns that which preceded the Nazirite vow. Previous inability to control and discipline his desires, within the bounds imposed by the Torah, had made it necessary for the person concerned to restrict himself even further and vow himself to abstinence. The Nazirite vow was thus a necessary but extreme medicine for spiritual ills.

Questions for Further Study

1. Look up Amos 2, 11—12. What is Amos' attitude to the Nazirite? What is the meaning of, "and I raised up of your young men for Nazirites". Surely the taking up of the Nazirites' vow is a matter left to the individual, and it is not God who raises up the Nazirite?

2. Here is Ibn Ezra's definition of the Nazirite:

> "He shall not make himself unclean for his father, or for his mother, for his brother, or for his sister, when they die; because the *nezer* ("crown" or "consecration") of his God is upon his head" (Numbers 6, 7). Some maintain that the word *Nazir* is from the term *nezer*, meaning crown, adducing proof from the foregoing passage, which sounds very plausible. Know that all human beings are servants of worldly desires, and whoever is free from these desires is a king who has, indeed, a crown and royal garland on his head.

In what way does Ibn Ezra's definition deviate from the

accepted meaning of the term, "Nazirite?" What rabbinic dictum expresses this same idea?

3   "And the priest shall prepare one for a sin-offering, and the other for a burnt-offering, and make atonement for him, for that he sinned by reason of the *dead*" (literally: "soul" — *nefesh*) (Numbers 6, 11). That he was not careful not to defile himself by touching a dead body. R. Eleazar Hakappar said, that he denied himself the enjoyment of wine.

(Rashi)

The sin refers to the contact with a dead body. Compare Leviticus 19, 28: "Ye shall not make any cuttings in your flesh for the *dead*" (*nefesh*). Were the word *nefesh* to imply that he sinned against his "soul", that is, against himself (in taking up the Nazirite vow), God would not have commanded him to repeat his sin (by resuming his Nazirite vow).

(Ibn Ezra)

(a)   What difficulty does the above verse pose?

(b)   What is the difference between Rashi and Ibn Ezra's solution of this difficulty.

(c)   What explanation did Ibn Ezra rule out when he stated "Were the word *nefesh* to imply...?" What was his objection to this explanation?

4.   The Rama (R. Moses Isserles) explains the Nazirite institution as follows:

... As Maimonides stated, spiritual healing corresponds to physical. Man must divert his evil inclinations from the extreme to the middle way. This is the basic idea of the Nazirite, when he abstains, because he observes that he has a weakness for worldly pleasures. He must go to the other extreme, in order to attain the middle way. Therefore, the Torah states, "he shall be holy" (Numbers 6, 5), since the holiness of the Nazirite will only really be in evidence, later on, after he has completed the days of his Naziriteship. Only then will he have attained the middle way, not at the time of taking the vow, when he had sinned and was imperfect. This is the meaning of the statement, "and make atonement for that he sinned . . .". This is because the abstention of the Nazirite is evil in itself, since all extremes are bad. The Nazirite was only commanded to abstain in order to achieve a good purpose, the attainment of the middle way.

(a)   What difficulty does the above authority solve?

(b)   Did the Rama approve or disapprove of Naziriteship?

(c)   In what way does he differ from the other views stated in our *Studies*, particularly that of Astruc?

THE PRIESTLY BLESSING

וַיְדַבֵּר ה׳ אֶל-מֹשֶׁה לֵּאמֹר:
דַּבֵּר אֶל-אַהֲרֹן וְאֶל בָּנָיו לֵאמֹר
כֹּה תְבָרֲכוּ אֶת-בְּנֵי יִשְׂרָאֵל אָמוֹר לָהֶם:
יְבָרֶכְךָ ה׳ וְיִשְׁמְרֶךָ:
יָאֵר ה׳ פָּנָיו אֵלֶיךָ וִיחֻנֶּךָּ:
יִשָּׂא ה׳ פָּנָיו אֵלֶיךָ
וְיָשֵׂם לְךָ שָׁלוֹם:
וְשָׂמוּ אֶת שְׁמִי עַל בְּנֵי יִשְׂרָאֵל וַאֲנִי אֲבָרֲכֵם:

And the Lord spoke unto Moses, saying,
Speak unto Aaron and unto his sons, saying,
Thus ye shall bless the children of Israel, saying unto them,
The Lord bless thee, and keep thee:
The Lord make His face shine upon thee, and be gracious unto thee:
The Lord lift up His countenance upon thee,
and give thee peace,
And they shall put My name upon the children of Israel, and I will bless them.

(6, 22—27)

The priestly benedictions are familiar to every Jew who visits the synagogue, so familiar indeed that we are perhaps inclined to forget their true content and fail to appreciate their profound significance. Simple as their wording appears these benedictions have puzzled many of our classic commentators. Here is one of the difficulties involved as phrased by Isaac Arama the author of *Akedat Yiẓḥak*:

> What purpose is served by the fact that this precept enjoins that these benedictions should proceed from the priests to the people? Surely it is He on high Who blesses and what is gained or added whether the priests bless or refrain from doing so? Is it up to them to assist Him?

Indeed the very wording of the verses prompts this question. The blessings are introduced by an order addressed to the priests "thus ye shall bless" and conclude with the divine statement "And I will bless them". An easy solution to the above dilemma would be to take the object of the last phrase "I will bless *them*" as referring not to all Israel but to the priests engaged in blessing Israel, as R. Ishmael observes in the Talmud (Ḥullin 49a):

למדנו ברכה לישראל — ברכה לכהנים עצמם לא למדנו: כשהו אומר: "ואני אברכם" — הוי אומר: כהנים מברכים לישראל והקב"ה מברך לכהנים.

> We have learned regarding the blessing of Israel; but regarding a blessing for the priests themselves we have not learned. The additional phrase "And I will bless them" (repairs this omission and) implies: the priests bless Israel and the Holy One blessed be He blesses the priests.

But most of our commentators have not accepted this interpretation including the Rashbam. He explains that the priests were not commanded to bless the people as one individual blesses another but to invoke the divine blessing on them. God promised to respond to their prayer that He bless and guard Israel. A similar idea is expressed by our Sages in the Midrash Tanḥuma:

אמרה כנסת ישראל לפני הקב"ה:
רבונו של עולם, לכהנים אתה אומר לברכנו? אין אנו צריכים אלא לברכתך! "השקיפה ממעון קדשך וברך את עמך". אמר להם הקב"ה: אף על פי שאמרתי לכהנים שיהו מברכין אתכם, אני עומד עמהם ומברך אתכם!

61

Said the House of Israel to the Holy One blessed be He: Lord of the Universe, you order the priests to bless us? We need only Thy blessing. Look down from Thy holy habitation and bless Thy people. The Holy One blessed be He replied to them: Though I ordered the priests to bless you I stand with them together and bless you.

These sentiments of our Sages underline that it is not the function of the priests which is all-important. Their benedictory function is even more reduced and deprived of any independent significance in the following citation from our Sages:

מניין שלא יהיו ישראל אומרים: ברכותיהם תלויות בכהנים? והכהנים לא יהיו אומרים: אנו נברך את ישראל? ת"ל: "ואני אברכם!"

How do we know that Israel should not say: Their blessings are dependent on the priests? And that the priests should not say: We shall bless Israel? The Torah states "And I will bless them".

(Sifrei)

יכול אם רצו לברך את ישראל — הרי הם מבורכין, ואם לא — אינן מבורכין? ת"ל "ואני אברכם" — בין רוצין, בין לא רוצין, "אני אברכם" מן השמים.

You might think that if they (the priests) desired to bless Israel they would be blessed and that if they did not, they would not be blessed? The Torah states: "And I will bless them". Willy-nilly "I will bless them" from heaven.

(Sifrei Zota)

But the above statements of our Sages, careful, as they are to avoid any suggestion of the magical efficacy of the priestly blessing, do not give us a clear answer to the question of the House of Israel:

Lord of the Universe, you order the priests to bless us? We need only Thy blessing.

Since the verb ברך appears in two different contexts, first with reference to the priests and then with reference to God, it is suggested by Abravanel that there is a difference in the implications of the verb in these two contexts.

> "Blessing" is a homonym referring both to the good emanating from God to His creatures as in "And the Lord blessed Abraham with all" (Genesis 24) and the blessing proceeding from man to God above in the sense of praise, as in "And David blessed the Lord" (I Chronicles 29). Then there is the blessing given by one person to another which is neither to be compared to the abundance of grace emanating from God nor to the praise proceeding from His creatures, but rather constitutes a supplication by the author calling on God to bless the person concerned. Into this category falls the priestly blessing . . . They merely invoke the divine blessing on Israel.

Accordingly only the phrase "and I will bless them" and "the Lord bless thee" in the first section come under the category of divine blessing in the sense of an outpouring of His goodness unto man, whilst the "blessing" of human beings is nothing more than a prayer, an invocation and not a real gift. Hirsch in his comments on our subject illustrates how the Torah wished to rule out any suggestion of the creation of a priestly caste endowed with any special powers of blessing:

> The priest who blesses is but an instrument, a medium through which the benediction is expressed. The death of the two sons of Aaron (Leviticus 10) the first heirs to the priesthood emphasised the irrevocable law that only service "which God had commanded" — could be considered service. Service which "the Lord had not commanded" — human deeds and machinations constitutes something alien and the very opposite of the service desired by the Lord. This same principle applied to the priestly benediction "thus shall ye bless the Children of Israel" — only thus and no deviation whatsoever is permitted . . . Only after being summoned by the congregation do they recite the blessing, with the representative of the congregation acting as the prompter so that the congregation invokes the divine blessing through the vocal medium of the priests.

The question then arises why do we need the priest at all? This principle of enlisting human cooperation in the work of God is to be found in many places. In Deuteronomy (10, 16) we read:

63

וּמַלְתֶּם אֵת עָרְלַת לְבַבְכֶם

And *ye shall circumcise* the foreskin of your hearts.

Later we read (30, 6):

וּמָל ה' אֱלֹהֶיךָ אֶת־לְבָבְךָ

And the *Lord thy God shall circumcise* you heart.

Similarly in Ezekiel (18, 31) we read:

וַעֲשׂוּ לָכֶם לֵב חָדָשׁ וְרוּחַ חֲדָשָׁה

And *make you* a new heart and a new spirit.

whilst later (36, 26) we read:

וְנָתַתִּי לָכֶם לֵב חָדָשׁ וְרוּחַ חֲדָשָׁה...

A new heart also will *I give* you, and a new spirit...

This symbolic cooperation between God and man is referred to in the Talmud (Shabbat 89a):

כשעלה משה למרום מצאו להקב"ה שהיה קושר כתרים לאותיות. אמר לו (הקב"ה):
משה, אין שלום בעירך? אמר לפיו (משה)" רבונו של עולם, כלום יש עבד נותן שלום
לרבו? אמר לו" מכל מקום היה לך לסייעני!

When Moses ascended on high he found the Holy One blessed be He
adorning the letters (of the Torah) with crowns. The Holy One said to him:
Moses, is it not customary in your town to ask after a person's welfare?
Moses answered him: Does a slave greet his master so? The Holy One
answered him: You should at any rate have given Me a helping hand (i.e.
wished Me success in My work).

Rabbi H.Y. Pollak, one of our commentators, interprets this Midrash as follows:

> The Holy One asked Moses whether he had done all in his power as a leader to promote the welfare and moral perfection of his society. Moses however had thought that it was not within human capacity to purify and perfect human society beyond the limits set to their nature by God. To which God replied that though everything was ultimately dependent on His will it was man's duty to purify himself and society through upright conduct. Only in such a manner would they be fit to receive the blessing of God, just the same as the earth cannot profit by the rain and the dew until it is properly sown and plowed. That was the meaning of the Almighty's reply: You should at any rate have helped Me.

The human assistance that God requires is implied in the order to the priests to bless the Children of Israel and prepare their hearts — "they shall put My name on the Children of Israel", just as the ground is prepared by the farmer for the rain.

The exact formula for the benediction is laid down in the Torah and is not left to man. The blessing is divided into three parts, each one containing two verbs and the name of God in the middle.

Here is the first section of the blessing as explained by our commentators:

ר ש " י ד"ה יברכך" שיתברכו נכסיך.

"May the Lord bless thee" — that thy goods may be blessed.

(Rashi)

This implies the blessing appropriate to each person; to the student of Torah success in his studies; the businessman — in his business, etc.

(Ha'amek Davar)

וישמרך: שלא יבואו עליך שודדים ליטול ממונך, שהנותן מתנה לעבדו אינו יכול לשמרו מכל אדם וכיון שבאים ליסטים עליו ונוטלים אותה ממנו, מה הנאה יש לו במתנה זו, אבל הקב"ה הוא הנותן, הוא השומר . . .

65

"And keep thee" — that plunderers should not come and take your property. He who gives a gift to his slave cannot safeguard it from everyone and if thieves come and take it what benefit has he therefrom? But the Holy One blessed be He He both gives and stands guard . . .

(Rashi)

A blessing requires guardianship so that it should not, God forbid, be turned to a wrong purpose. The Torah scholar requires guardianship to save him from pride and bringing the name of the Lord into disrepute, and the like. The businessman requires guardianship against his wealth becoming a stumbling block to him as in the case of Korah and Naboth, and in its literal sense, against theft and loss.

(Ha'amek Davar)

Whichever interpretation we accept, the blessing referred to in the first section is material.

יאר ה׳ פניו: זה מאור תורה, שיאיר עיניך ולבך בתורה ויתן לך בנים בני תורה, שנאמר
"כי מצוה ותורה אור".

"May the Lord make His face shine upon thee, and be gracious unto thee. . . " This is the light of Torah that He should enlighten your eyes and heart in Torah and grant you children learned in Torah, as it is said: "For the commandment is a lamp and the Torah a light".

(Bamidbar Rabbah 11, 6)

The second section of the benediction refers to spiritual blessing and we may take the phrase "be gracious unto thee" to imply the good will and respect inspired by the one who engages in the study of Torah.

The third section adds to and sums up the previous:

יִשָּׂא ה׳ פָּנָיו אֵלֶיךָ וְיָשֵׂם לְךָ שָׁלוֹם:

The Lord lift up his countenance upon thee, and give thee peace.

In this connection it is fitting to quote the following dictum of our Sages in Sifra (Beḥukotai):

Peradventure you will say (in comment on the blessing in Leviticus 26, 3—6: "And ye shall eat your bread to the full . . . and I will give peace in the land") food and drink is all well and good, but without peace they are worth nothing! The Torah therefore states "and I will give peace in the land" — for peace outweighs all else.

Accordingly the three sections of the priestly benedictions illustrate an ascending order, starting with a blessing concerned with man's material needs and then dealing with his spiritual wants, and finally reaching a climax combining both these factors together, crowning them with the blessing of peace. This ascending order and increasing surge of blessing is reflected in the language and rhythm. The first phrase consists of three words, the second of five, and the third of seven:

יברכך ה׳ וישמרך

יאר ה׳ פניו אליך ויחנך

ישא ה׳ פניו אליך וישם לך שלום.

THE LORD LIFT UP HIS FACE TO YOU

<table>
<tr><td></td><td></td><td></td><td></td><td>ויברכך</td><td>ה'</td><td>יברכך</td></tr>
<tr><td></td><td></td><td></td><td></td><td>and keep you</td><td>The Lord</td><td>bless you</td></tr>
</table>

<table>
<tr><td></td><td>ויחנך</td><td></td><td>אליך</td><td>פניו</td><td>ה'</td><td>יאר</td></tr>
<tr><td></td><td>and give you grace</td><td></td><td>upon you</td><td>His face</td><td>The Lord</td><td>shine</td></tr>
</table>

<table>
<tr><td>שלום</td><td>לך</td><td>וישם</td><td>אליך</td><td>פניו</td><td>ה'</td><td>ישא</td></tr>
<tr><td>peace</td><td>you</td><td>and give</td><td>to you</td><td>His face</td><td>The Lord</td><td>lift up</td></tr>
</table>

At the end of our last chapter which was also devoted to the Priestly Blessing we drew attention to the fact that it gradually mounts to a climax, spreading itself out like an ever-flowing spring.

From the above it may be clearly seen how the number of words (in Hebrew) progressively increases from three to five and then to seven expressing ever-growing plenitude.

The same gradual progression to a climax can be seen in the content too, each blessing more generous than its precursor. The first blessing is for worldly goods, as Abravanel and others have explained it.

It is a blessing for material things — that He should send them children, life and sustenance and preserve them from want. "Keep" comes after "bless", since the former refers to wealth and material bounty. After we have it, we require a blessing to safeguard and keep us from the dangers that follow from their possession.

The second verse refers to spiritual blessing. Many commentators understand the shining of His face to refer to the granting of enlightenment in the Torah, as Sforno observes:

> May your eyes be illuminated by the light of His face to see wonders in His Torah and His works after you obtain your needs through His (first) blessing.

The third blessing, according to many commentators culminates in a merging of the two previous ones, a joint blessing of both worldly and spiritual bounty.

Let us now turn to the first section of the third verse: "The Lord lift up His face to you". What is the meaning of this blessing and in what way does it differ from the previous one: "The Lord shine His face upon you?"

If our commentators are right in asserting that each subsequent blessing transcends its precursor in the measure of its bounty, what does *yissa* ("lift up") improve on *ya'er* ("shine")? On the contrary, does not the shining of the Divine countenance symbolise greater blessing than the lifting up of His face?

Rashi following the Sifra and Midrash states: ' "The Lord lift up His face to you" — suppress His anger'. Here are the words of the Midrash:

יעביר כעסו ממך ואין "ישא" אלא לשון הסרה כמו שנאמר (בראשית מ): "ישא פרעה את ראשך מעליך". "פניו" — אלה פנים של זעם כמו שנאמר (ויקרא כ): "ונתתי את פני בנפש ההיא והכרתי אותו". כלומר אותם פנים של זעם שהיו ראויות לבוא אליך יסירם ממך.

He will remove His anger from you. *Yissa* is an expression of removal as in (Gen. 40, 19): "Pharaoh will lift up (*yissa*) your head from off you". "His face" implies a face of wrath, as it is stated (Lev. 20, 6): "I shall set my face against that soul and cut him off". In other words, He will remove that face of wrath which should have been presented to you.

(Bamidbar Rabbah 11, 14)

But if that is the meaning of the blessing, then it is certainly not superior to the blessing of "shine". The latter is wholly positive, the outpouring of Divine grace and light, whereas the former is wholly negative in nature — the removal of impending evil and misfortune. What is the basis of this unfavourable connotation of *panim* — "face". Surely the verse quoted in Leviticus derives its unfavourable connotation not from the word "face" but from the verb "set" and the preposition "against". That *panim* cannot be given an exclusively negative connotation emerges from a survey of its usage in the Bible. The Rashba (Solomon b. Aderet in his commentary to the collection of Talmudic lore *En Ya'acov*) notes that since the face portrays our feelings, both of anger and pleasure, the word "face" in the Bible can be found in all contexts expressing feeling. Thus we have (1 Sam. 1, 18): "Her face was no more sad" expressing grief and in Psalms 31, 17 expressing joy: "Make your face to shine on Your servant" or expressing compassion: "You shall not lift up the face of the poor man" (Lev. 19, 15).

Thus there is no necessity to explain *panim* in our context in an unfavourable sense, especially when the predicate is *ailekha:* "to you" and not *me-alekha*: "away from you".

We shall therefore cite here other views which explain *panim* in a different light:

שאלה בלוריאה הגיורת את ר״ג כתוב בתורתכם (דברים י): ״אשר ל א י ש א פנים ולא יקח שוחד״ וכתיב (במדבר ו): ״ י ש א ה׳ פניו אליך?״ נטפל לה ר׳ יוסי הכהן, אמר לה: ״אמשול לך משל, למה הדבר דומה? לאדם שנושה בחברו מנה וקבע לו זמן בפני המלך ונשבע לו בחיי המלך; הגיע זמן ולא נתן לו כלום. בא לפייס את המלך. אמר לו: ״עלבוני מחול לך, לך ופייס את חברך״. אף הכא נמי. כאן בעבירות שבין אדם לחברו, כאן (במדבר ו) — בעבירות שבין אדם למקום.

Bloria the proselytess asked Rabban Gamliel: In your Torah is stated: "Who will *not* respect (*yissa* — "lift up") persons (*panim* — faces) nor take bribes". It is also written: "The Lord *will* lift up His face to you?" R. Yose the priest dealt with her. He said to her: Let me tell you a parable: To what may it be compared? To a man who had a hundred zuz owing him and fixed a time for repayment in the presence of the king and he swore by the king's life to repay him. The time arrived but he gave him nought. So he came to ask the king's forgiveness. The king answered him: I forgive your insult of Me, go and appease your fellow. The same applies here. In the former case (*lo yissa panim*), transgressions between man and man are involved, in the latter case, transgressions between man and his maker are indicated.

(Rosh Hashanah 17b)

It is obvious that in our context the lifting of God's countenance towards man implies His favour and compassion. The juxtaposition of the two seemingly contradictory texts in the foregoing citation teach us the fundamental truth that God is more concerned about his creatures' honour than His own. He forgives transgressions against Himself much quicker than those committed against other men. We find another discussion on the same theme in the Midrash:

"ישא ה' פניו" — וכי הקב"ה נושא פנים? והלא כבר נאמר (דברים י): "אשר לא ישא פנים!" אמר הקב"ה: כשם שהם נושאים לי פנים, כך אני נושא להם פנים. כיצד? כתבתי בתורתי (דברים ח): "ואכלת ו ש ב ע ת וברכת" ואדם מישראל יושב, הוא ובניו ובני ביתו, ואין לפניהן כדי שביעה ונושאין לי פנים ומברכין, ודקדקו על עצמם עד כזית עד כביצה — לפיכך "ישא ה' פניו".

"The Lord will lift up His face" — Now does the Lord lift up His face (in the sense of showing partiality)? Surely it has already been stated: "Who does not lift up His face" (i.e. show partiality). The Holy One blessed be He said: Just the same as they show me partiality so shall I show them. How so? I have written in My Torah (Deut. 8, 10): "When you eat and are satisfied, then you shall bless (i.e. say Grace). Whereupon a Jew sits with his children and household even to an inadequate (not satisfying) repast, yet they show me partiality and say Grace and are meticulous even with regard to an olive's bulk or the size of an egg. Therefore "the Lord will lift up His face".

(Bamidbar Rabbah 11, 14)

Here also the expression of "lifting up the face" is taken to mean going beyond the letter of the law, forgiveness and generosity. In the first-quoted passage from the Gemara, however, this forgivingness is vouchsafed Israel in the case of offences against God. Why? Because He graciously forgives the insult involving Himself.

But in the latter passage from the Midrash, the forgiving spirit, the going beyond the letter of the law is vouchsafed Israel because they really deserve it and not as an act of grace. As it were, the Almighty observes His people, how they bear His yoke, serving and worshipping Him even in the direst of circumstances, even down to the minutest point of law. They realize that He chose them not for worldly privilege and wealth but for suffering and misfortune. In spite of this they make no complaint and do not shirk His yoke but do more than He commanded them. God had commanded them to bless him and say Grace only when they had eaten a satisfying meal, but they praise Him even on an empty stomach. They as it were lift up their face to Him, show Him favour. How can He than refrain from showing them favour!

Both interpretations, that of the Midrash and Talmud, have this in common — that they take no account of the possessive pronominal suffix in *panav*— "His face". The Tosaphists have observed this and objected that whilst the text in Deuteronomy speaks of *panim*, referring to the face of the man who is pleading for favour, the Priestly Blessing speaks of *panav*, His face, that of the Being who is showing the favour and not the object of the favour. There is therefore no contradiction between the two texts, between the partiality referred to in Deuteronomy which does not exist before God, and His showing us favour, which has the same meaning as in the blessings in Lev. 26, 9: "*I shall turn to you* (English version: "I shall have respect for you") and make you fruitful and establish My covenant with you". The Midrash explains the foregoing text thus: "He will turn His face toward you".

Hirsch regards the third and final priestly blessing of "He will lift up His face to you" as the climax of them all, since both spiritual and worldly possessions are means to an end. The third blessing of His turning His face to us is not a means to obtain any kind of worldly or material gain. The whole of life with its bustle and tumult, its material wealth and spiritual attainments are only instruments to bring us nearer to His service. The third blessing speaks of the end itself, the supreme good as the Psalmist words it:

וַאֲנִי קִרְבַת אֱלֹהִים לִי טוֹב

But, as for me, the nearness of God is my good.

(Psalms 73, 28)

PRINCES WITH A PAST

וַיַּקְרִיבוּ נְשִׂיאֵי יִשְׂרָאֵל רָאשֵׁי בֵּית אֲבֹתָם
הֵם נְשִׂיאֵי הַמַּטֹּת הֵם הָעֹמְדִים עַל הַפְּקֻדִים:

And the princes of Israel, the heads of their father's houses, offered —
these were the princes of the tribes, these are they that were over them that were numbered.

(7, 2)

The Torah evidently wishes to remind us that the princes of Israel referred to here were in some way known to us from a previous occasion. Our Sages in the Midrash discovered an allusion to the past of these princes in the additional parenthetic phrasing: "These were the princes of the tribes, these are they that were over them that were numbered".

"הֵם נְשִׂיאֵי הַמַּטּוֹת", הֵם שֶׁהָיוּ מְמֻנִּים עֲלֵיהֶם בְּמִצְרַיִם, שֶׁנֶּאֱמַר (שמות ה, יד): "וַיֻּכּוּ
שׁוֹטְרֵי בְּנֵי יִשְׂרָאֵל אֲשֶׁר שָׂמוּ עֲלֵיהֶם נֹגְשֵׂי פַרְעֹה" לֵאמֹר: "מַדּוּעַ לֹא כִלִּיתֶם חָקְכֶם
לִלְבֹּן כִּתְמוֹל שִׁלְשֹׁם?!"

"These were the princes of the tribes" — these were they who were appointed over them in Egypt, regarding whom it is stated: "And the officers of the children of Israel, whom Pharaoh's taskmasters had set over them, were beaten, saying: Wherefore have ye not fulfilled your appointed task in making bricks both yesterday and today...?" (Exodus 5, 14).

(Bamidbar Rabbah 12, 20)

Let us try to understand the role of the "officers" as pictured for us in the Midrash:

... עמדו ומנו את הלבנים ואמר להם פרעה: "כזה אתם מעמידים בכל יום ויום!"
מינה את הנוגשים של מצרים על השוטרים של ישראל והשוטרים התמנו על יתר העם,
וכשאמר להם פרעה (שמות הת ז): "לא תוסיפון לתת תבן לעם ללבן הלבנים ... הם
ילכו וקוששו להם תבן, ואת מתכנת הלבנים ... תשימו עליהם לא תגרעו ממנו", והיו
באין הנוגשים ומונין את הלבנים ונמצאו חסרות, היון מכין הנוגשים את השוטרים,
שנאמר "ויוכו שוטרי בני ישראל" והיו השוטרים מוכים על יתר העם ולא היו מוסרים
אותם בידי הנוגשים, והיו השוטרים אומרים, מוטב לנו ללקות ואל יכשל יתר העם.

They stood and counted the bricks whereupon Pharaoh said unto them: You must provide me with this number every day. He appointed the Egyptian taskmasters over the officers of the children of Israel and the latter were appointed over the people. When Pharaoh said to them (Ex. 5, 7): "Ye shall no more give the people straw to make bricks as heretofore. Let them go and gather straw for themselves, And the tale of the bricks, which they did make heretofore, ye shall lay upon them; ye shall not diminish aught thereof...", the taskmasters would come, count the bricks, finding them short. The taskmasters would then beat the officers, as it is stated: "And the officers... were beaten". Thus the officers were beaten on account of the rest of the people, but did not nevertheless inform to the taskmasters (on those who had failed to make up the necessary tale of bricks). These officers were wont to say: It is better for us to be beaten rather than that the rest of the people should suffer.

(Bamidbar Rabbah 15, 16)

The system by which Pharaoh degraded the Jewish people, setting them one against the other and appointing their own leaders to carry out his decrees is only too familiar to us in these days.

We note here how the princes who were the first to come forward here to bring offerings for the Tabernacle were identified by our Sages with those officers who sacrificed themselves to the wrath of their oppressors in place of their own brothers in Egypt. Good deeds are not forgotten, but remain to bear fruit and reap reward sooner or later.

In his important study on Rabbinic homiletics: *Darkhei Aggada*

75

(Jerusalem 5710) Y. Heinemann explains that our Sages asserted the common identity of anonymous characters of different epochs in the Biblical narrative "in order to bridge the time gap and create a closely linked historic picture easily grasped by the reader" (p. 28). This was particularly the case where the Sages wished to bring home the lesson of virtue bringing its own reward, however long the fruits thereof are deferred. Here we bring before the reader another example of this Midrashic device. It is related how Esau, breathing vengeance, came with four hundred men to meet his brother Jacob. But at the meeting Esau changed his feelings, made his peace with his brother, fell on his neck and kissed him. It is then stated:

וַיָּשָׁב בַּיּוֹם הַהוּא עֵשָׂו לְדַרְכּוֹ שֵׂעִירָה:

So Esau returned that day on his way unto Seir.

(Genesis 33, 16)

Rashi cites the following words of our Sages in this connection:

עשו לבדו; וארבע מאות איש שהלכו עמו נשמטו מאצלו אחד אחד. והיכן פרע להם הקב״ה? בימי דוד, שנאמר (שמואל א ל, יז): ״ויכם דוד . . . ולא נמלט מהם איש כי אם ארבע מאות איש נער אשר רכבו על הגמלים וינוסו״.

Esau returned alone. But the four hundred men who had accompanied him slipped away one by one. Where did the Holy One blessed be He requite them for this? In the days of David, as it is stated (1 Samuel 30, 17): "And David smote them . . . and there escaped not a man of them, save four hundred young men who rode upon camels and fled".

Our Sages thus identified the four hundred men who had accompanied Esau to wreak vengeance upon Jacob but had given up that dread design at the last moment with the four hundred men who were saved from David's sword many centuries later. Were not our Sages aware of the fact that these four hundred of Esau's retainers were not identical with the four hundred of David's enemies, the sons

of Amalek who escaped? Surely the text itself gives the reason why
they were able to escape. Those "who rode upon camels" escaped.
This was the homiletic language our Sages employed in many
Midrashim to drive home the lesson that virtue is always ultimately
rewarded, and the imprint of a good deed remains. If the reward is
not reaped by the actual commissioner of the good deed, then his
descendants will ultimately enjoy the fruits thereof in God's good
time. Esau's four hundred retainers, the taskmasters of the children
of Israel both performed a good deed and this remained to their
credit on the balance sheet of history.

On the other hand, the Torah does not confine itself to recording
the good in man. It paints with equal objectivity the bad, giving the
whole human picture with its light and shade. Those same officers of
the children of Israel who had shown such commendable self-
sacrifice in Egypt fell far beneath those heights, once the common
enemy had been defeated. As we have had occasion to note, the
princes of Israel were the last to bring their voluntary contribution
for the building of the Tabernacle, on account of their own pride and
conceit. As we read in the Midrash there,[1] they were displeased
because Moses had not made a separate and special appeal to them.
They had not wanted to be lumped together with the rest of the
public and said: "Let the people bring whatever they like; what is
lacking we shall provide" (Midrash). But the people brought so much
that there was no further need for the generosity of the princes.

> Whereupon the princes were distressed because it had not been granted them
> to contribute to the tabernacle. They said: Since it was not granted to us to
> contribute to the tabernacle we shall contribute to the garments of the high
> priest, as it is said "and the princes brought onyx stones . . ." (Exodus 35,
> 27). Said the Holy One blessed be He: My children who displayed eagerness,
> let it be recorded that they brought "too much" (ibid. 36, 7); whereas the
> princes, let there be omitted one letter from their name on account of their
> remissness, as it is written: "והנשאם" without a *yod*. As soon as the
> tabernacle was finished, they brought with alacrity an offering at the first
> opportunity that presented itself.
>
> (Bamidbar Rabbah 12, 19)

As Hirsch noted in his commentary to the Pentateuch the princes regarded the call for all the people to contribute as an insult to their lofty station.

> They looked forward to the people not being able to provide the necessary amount of offerings and they would then be able to restore their wounded pride by contributing the difference. But the generosity of the people upset their calculations, leaving them only with the opportunity of contributing the onyx stones and other articles required for the vestments of the high priest. Instead of acting as part of the people and contributing along with everyone else, they put themselves above the people and set themselves apart from the national endeavour. This undesirable trait of theirs is alluded to in the imperfect spelling of their princely title. At the moment they were not worthy of the title: "Princes of the people".

Though Ibn Ezra is no doubt correct in his insistence that the omissions and insertions of vowel letters were merely examples of variant spellings, we are, nevertheless, shown how our Sages used them to drive home a moral lesson.

Before we conclude our study, it would be useful for us to find an answer to the question why the Torah describes in so much detail the offerings of the princes, repeating in each case what they gave, despite the fact that their contributions were identical. Perhaps the Torah wished to emphasise the importance and uniqueness of the individual, repudiating the ideology that regards the human being as a cog in a vast machine and as an undistinguishable member of a mass. We may detect this emphasis in various places in the Torah as in the census taken of the children of Israel in which each one was numbered by name. Arama in his *Akedat Yizḥak* stresses this same point that each individual:

> has an importance all his own like a king or priest and this is the reason why they were all mentioned by name. They were all equal in station, but uniquely separate in their equality.

NOTE

[1] See *Studies in Shemot,* pp. 701—2.

THE LESSON OF SAMSON[1]
(Haftarah, Judges 13, 2—25)

The Israeli writer Abraham Kariv[2] regards the career of Samson as illustrating the working out of a Divine experiment to make use of the various forces within man. No two prophets deliver their message in the same way. Samson similarly exemplified the carrying out of the Divine mission in a hitherto untried way. Kariv continues:

> The Philistines had subjected the Israelites by virtue of superior arms. Providence sent His people a saviour whose unusual physical strength would render any recourse to arms unnecessary. He would need no human weapons — he himself would be the weapon — fashioned by God. Hitherto Jewish history had been distinguished for the role of the prophet who revealed the word of God. Now there appeared the seer endowed with the strength of God. But physical strength has its dangers, giving the flesh, the passions and baser instincts of man undue power. It was much more difficult for such a man to safeguard the purity of his soul, especially as the necessity of continual fighting against the enemy would bring him into overmuch contact with their idolatrous ways.
>
> Once Samson failed in his struggle with his own soul he could no longer fight the battles of the Lord. The story of Samson is the archetype of the heroic figure, blessed with unusual powers which make him an all-too-ready prey to the temptations that bring him low. On account of this, the angel gave his mother special instructions on how to bring him up, that his Nazirite vow should act as a spiritual brake on the unusual physical powers given him.

The tidings regarding the birth of the son, his mission and the restrictions governing his diet and conduct were first given to the mother not the father. This was no doubt because the primary bond both before birth and in infancy is with the mother. The mother transmitted the message to the father. But just as in all parallel passages in Scriptures we can learn volumes from a careful note of similarities and deviations, so it is worth while here to compare the words of the angel to the woman and her transmission of them to her husband:

The angel to Manoah's wife	*Manoah's wife to her husband*
Behold now, thou art barren and hath not borne	— — — — — — — — —
but thou shalt conceive and bear a son	Behold thou shalt conceive and bear a son
Now, therefore beware, I pray thee	and now
and drink no wine nor strong drink	drink no wine nor strong drink
and eat not anything unclean	and eat not anything unclean
For, lo, thou shalt conceive and bear a son	— — — — — — — — —
and no razor shall come upon his head	— — — — — — — — —
for the child shall be a Nazirite unto God from the womb	for the child shall be a Nazirite unto God from the womb to the day of his death
and he shall begin to save Israel	— — — — — — — — —

It is quite obvious why Samson's mother did not report the opening words of the angel (verse 3). Our commentators suggest why she added the words "to the day of his death". The Midrash explains that she did not know what the angel knew, that he was destined to violate his vows long before his death, succumbing to Delilah's wiles.

Abravanel maintains that she added these words to intimidate Manoah, insinuating that any deviation from the angel's instructions would meet with the babe's immediate death whilst in the womb. Abravanel also gives a reason why she concealed from her husband

81

the angel's parting message that he was destined to save Israel from the Philistines.

Since the Israelites were under their yoke, she was afraid that the prophecy would get abroad and she might be killed, if they thought she was the mother of a future saviour of her people.

But it is difficult to understand why she failed to tell Manoah about the angel's instruction that "no razor shall come upon his head". Malbim suggests it was not really omitted, but was understood in her stating that he "shall be a Nazirite of God". To the Israelite, Naziriteship implied this. Alshikh supplies a human motivation.

She did not want to offend her husband's susceptibilities, which might be wounded by the fact that the angel approached her, not him. She deliberately limited the angel's instructions to those things that applied directly to her, such as not to drink wine or eat anything unclean. The reference to "no razor shall come upon his head" did not concern her and the angel could well have told her husband.

But perhaps there is another reason for her omission of this detail connected with Samson's Nazirite vows. The very message of the angel and his insistence on Samson's Naziriteship even before his birth is puzzling. What need was there for this angelic interview, queries Abravanel. Even if Samson would not have been a Nazirite in the womb, could not the Lord have saved Israel through him? He gives three answers to his question:

First, his mother had to be vouchsafed this vision to impress upon her and her son that he was destined for greatness as a Divine instrument. It was necessary for his diet to be pure and free from taint, in order to ensure the purity of his character, to make him allergic to the depravity of the Philistine temperament debauched by wine and impurity, and make him ever ready to wreak on them the vengeance of the Lord.

Second, the Almighty knew he was destined to perform unusual things and so as not give the impression that they were prompted by drunkenness He commanded him to be a teetotaller from the womb.

Third, he was commanded not to shave his head and let his locks grow long as a sign of mourning for his people's subjection to the Philistines. This would be a further prod to his ambition to take vengeance on them.

Objection may be raised to the first reason. Surely every Israelite was in any case separated from the Gentile, Philistine included, by the numerous prescriptions of his faith, particularly the dietary laws! Similarly little significance was attached by the angel to his abstention from wine. It was the mother's abstention that the angel was specific about. The main emphasis regarding Samson was on letting his hair grow long. The third reason advanced by Abravanel that the hair was a sign of mourning for the Philistine oppression is the only one directly connected with the only prohibition imposed by the angel on Samson himself: "No razor shall come upon his head". Abravanel was evidently taking as a precedent the name given by Phineas' wife (1 Samuel 4) to the son prematurely born to her as a result of hearing the catastrophic news that the Ark of the Lord had been captured, and her father-in-law and her husband were dead. She called him Ichabod ("There is no glory") to impress upon her son the humiliation suffered by his people.

Kariv, whom we have quoted earlier gives a complete answer to Abravanel's question which also explains why the prohibition of shaving was emphasised by the angel in his message to Manoah's wife.

His Nazirite vows of abstention were to act as a spiritual brake upon him guaranteeing that his unusual physical might should be used for the purpose God had granted him it. As a Nazirite of God he would also remain a mighty man of God. He had to be sober and pure all his life, to remain true to his mission. Naziriteship was a sacred institution. The man who left his hair untouched, preserved his natural appearance, and was thereby more capable of keeping faith with the Divine.

But did Samson remain true to his Nazirite vows that were aimed at keeping him pure and capable of fulfilling his destiny? We can detec⟨ ⟩ an allusion in the text to his abstention from wine. It is related:

וַיֵּרֶד שִׁמְשׁוֹן וְאָבִיו וְאִמּוֹ תִּמְנָתָה
וַיָּבֹאוּ עַד־כַּרְמֵי תִמְנָתָה
וְהִנֵּה כְּפִיר אֲרָיוֹת שֹׁאֵג לִקְרָאתוֹ׃
וַתִּצְלַח עָלָיו רוּחַ ה׳
וַיְשַׁסְּעֵהוּ כְּשַׁסַּע הַגְּדִי וּמְאוּמָה אֵין בְּיָדוֹ
וְלֹא הִגִּיד לְאָבִיו וּלְאִמּוֹ אֵת אֲשֶׁר עָשָׂה׃

Then Samson and his father and his mother went down to Timnah;

and they came to the vineyards of Timnah.

And behold a young lion roared against him.

And the spirit of the Lord came mightily upon him

and he rent it as one would have rent a kid, and he had nothing in his hand;

but he told not his father or his mother what he had done.

(14, 5—6)

Malbim asks:

> Where were his parents all the time? Surely they were accompanying him! How could they not have known? But we must conclude that they went with him as far as the vineyard. They went through it whereas he made a detour to avoid it, in accordance with the advice given in the Talmud to the Nazirite: "Make a detour but do not go near a vineyard".

The lion confronted him when alone during his detour. Similarly he was careful not to shave his hair until he succumbed to Delilah's wiles. But with all his loyalty to his Nazirite vows he did not conduct himself like the Nazirite of God, like the man charged with the Divine mission of saving Israel. He wasted all his strength on vanities

and the repaying of personal scores. Abstention from ͨ
shaving are purely external signs of the Nazirite. But they alone
cannot make a saint. He did not rise to the height of being a Nazirite
of God even after the terrible retribution meted out to him, measure
for measure, as our Sages observed. Samson had insisted on picking
a Philistine woman for a wife in spite of his parent's protestations,
peremptorily ordering his father "Get her for me; for she is attractive
in my eyes".

> Samson followed his eyes. Therefore the Philistines gouged them out
>
> (Talmud, Sotah 9b).

Even at the great tragic moment when his hair had begun to grow
again and he felt the stirrings within him of his sense of mission, he
did not show himself completely true to his original destiny as a
saviour of Israel. In his last prayer before he broke the pillars and
destroyed the Philistines he said:

אֲדֹנָי ה׳ זָכְרֵנִי נָא וְחַזְּקֵנִי נָא אַךְ הַפַּעַם הַזֶּה הָאֱלֹהִים
וְאִנָּקְמָה נְקַם־אַחַת מִשְּׁתֵי עֵינַי מִפְּלִשְׁתִּים:

**O Lord God, remember me, I pray thee, and strengthen me, I
pray Thee,** *only this once,* **O God,**
that I may be avenged of the Philistines for my two eyes.

(16, 28)

But did not pray for vengeance for Israel. Kariv derives this moral
lesson from the tragedy of Samson:

> Unlike Greek tragedy, man is brought to destruction through no arbitrary
> decree of the gods but through his own wilfulness. God is beneficent and
> man, even the one charged with a specific mission brings his own downfall.
> The Torah gives free choice to man and that includes to the one whose
> destiny has been marked out for him. He must show himself worthy of the
> trust reposed in him by his free choice of the right path. Otherwise the

85

partnership between him and God is broken. Samson had been endowed with strength, for the purpose of harnessing it to a sacred cause by his own free choice. This he failed to do involving himself in an impure love. He forfeited his strength, his sight, freedom, life and his mission. In Greek culture it is sufficient for the mighty man to be mighty. In the world of Israel, might must be paved with holiness. The experiment to harness the two together did not succeed. The purely mighty man of the type of Samson remained a solitary character. In his place there arose one of a long line of Jewish spiritual heroes — the prophet Samuel.

Questions for Further Study[3]

1. It was patent to the Holy One blessed be He that Samson would go after his eyes (be over-susceptible to female charm). He therefore admonished him to be a Nazirite and abstain from wine because wine leads to immorality. Now if even when he was a Nazirite he still went after his eyes, had he drunk wine as well, he would have been beyond remedy from his inordinate indulgence in immorality?

(Bamidbar Rabbah 10, 16)

(a) What difficulty in the story does the above Midrash wish to solve?

(b) Does the approach outlined here fit any of the three views propounded by Abravanel?

2. In verse 10 chapter 13 it is stated that Manoah's wife "made haste and ran and told her husband". Where else do you find the Bible emphasising the haste and eagerness of the righteous in performing a good deed?

3. The Midrash asks why did the angels who came to Abraham to bring the tidings of a son to Sarah partake of food, whereas the angel here refused Manoah's invitation to dine? Can you answer this question without recourse to the Midrash?

NOTES

[1] For fuller treatment readers are referred to "Studies in the Book of Judges"
by Dr. H. Chamiel, *Mayanot* IV (Hebrew) WZO, Dept. for Torah Education,
Jerusalem 5714, pp. 75—102.

[2] In an article entitled 'From the strong goeth forth sweet", *Orot* 9, WZO,
Department of Education and Culture, Jerusalem 1953.

[3] The questions are partly taken from the article by Dr. Chamiel referred to
in note 1.

WHEN THE ARK SET FORTH

וַיְהִי בִּנְסֹעַ הָאָרֹן וַיֹּאמֶר מֹשֶׁה
קוּמָה ה'
וְיָפֻצוּ אֹיְבֶיךָ
וְיָנֻסוּ מְשַׂנְאֶיךָ מִפָּנֶיךָ:
וּבְנֻחֹה יֹאמַר
שׁוּבָה ה' רִבְבוֹת אַלְפֵי יִשְׂרָאֵל:

And it came to pass, when the Ark set forward, that Moses said,
Rise up, Lord,
and let thine enemies be scattered;
and let them that hate thee flee before thee.
And when it rested, he said,
Return, O Lord, unto the many thousands of Israel.

(10, 35—36)

These verses are enclosed both in the Sefer Torah and the printed Pentateuch by two special symbols in the form of a large inverted *nun*. The Talmud draws attention to this marking:

תנו רבנן: "ויהי בנסע הארון . . ." פרשה זו עשה לה הקב"ה סימניות מלמעלה
ומלמטה.

Our Rabbis taught: "And it came to pass, when the ark set forward, that Moses said . . .". The Holy One blessed be He made special markings above and below for this passage.

(Shabbat 115b)

What is the explanation of these markings and the meaning of the inverted *nun*? The Sifrei states that:

נקוד עליו מלמעלה ומלמטה.

It was marked with points above and below.

It may be assumed therefore that the whole of this passage was marked by points from above and below, i.e. from the beginning to the end, the same way as there are individual words in the Torah crowned by dots. This passage then was marked by symbols to denote that it should be pointed. In order that the *nun* (the first letter and abbreviation of the Hebrew verb "to point") should not be mistaken for a letter it was inverted. But what is the significance for enclosing this passage in distinctive marking?[1] We cite here the explanation of Rabbi Judah Hanasi, the editor of the Mishnah:

מפני שספר חשוב הוא בפני עצמו. דאמר ר' שמואל בר נחמני א"ר יונתן: "חצבה עמודיה שבעה" (משלי ט) אלו שבעה ספרי תורה, כמאן? כרבי.

Because it constituted a book on its own.
For R. Shemuel bar Naḥmani said in the name of R. Yohanan: "She hath hewn out her seven pillars" (Proverbs 9, 1) — these are the seven books of the Pentateuch; according to whom? According to Rabbi (Judah Hanasi).
(Shabbat 116a)

In other words, this passage constitutes a book on its own, thus dividing Bamidbar into three books, which, with the addition of the other four books of the Pentateuch makes seven. But it still remains for us to discover the reason for singling out this passage for such special distinction. Let us first study the two verses concerned more closely. Moses' invocation to the Almighty to "rise up" when the Ark moved forward and to "return" when it rested, giving the impression that it was Moses who determined the journeyings and haltings of the Ark contradicts what was previously stated that it

89

journeyed only in accordance with the commandment of the Lord. This point is made in the Sifrei on the sidra:

"ויאמר משה קומה ה' " וכתוב אחד אומר (במדבר ט): "על פי ה' יסעו ועל פי ה' יחנו'' — כיצד יתקיימו שני כתובים אלה? . . . למה הדבר דומה? למלך שהיה מתהלך בדרך ונהג אוהבו עמו; כשהוא נוסע הוא אומר: "איני חונה עד שיבוא אוהבי'', נמצא מקיים "ויאמר משה: "קומה ה' " ומקיים "על פי ה' יסעו ועל פי ה' יחנו''.

"And Moses said, rise up, Lord", and another verse says: "At the commandment of the Lord they rested and at the commandment of the Lord they journeyed". How can these two verses be reconciled? To what may this be compared? To a king who was going on a journey accompanied by his bosom friend. When he resumes his journey he says: I shall not go forward until my friend gives the order, and when he halts he says: I shall not halt until my friend comes along. This reconciles the verses "And Moses said rise up, Lord", and "At the commandment of the Lord they journeyed..."

This Midrash graphically illustrates the highest degree of communion and closeness between man and his Maker, and the complete identity of aim. Hirsch notes that Moses' invocation: "rise up" succeeds immediately the act that has been fulfilled, in accordance with the principle expressed by Rabban Gamaliel in Pirkei Avot:

Make His will thy will.

Who are the "enemies" and "them that hate Thee" that are scattered as a result of the divine "rising up?" Here is the answer given by the Sifrei:

וכי יש שונאים לפני מי שאמר והיה העולם? אלא מגיד הכתוב, שכל מי ששונא את ישראל כמו ששונא את המקום. וכיוצא בו אתה אומר (שמות טו): "וברב גאונך תהרוס קמיך'', וכי יש קמים לפני המקום? אלא מגיד הכתוב: וכן הוא אומר (תהלים ע"ד): "אל תשכח קול צורריך, שאון קמיך עולה תמיד!'' מפני מה? וכן הוא אומר (תהלים פג): "כי הנה אויביך יהמיו ומשנאיך נשאו ראש'' — מפני מה? "על ע מ ך יערימו סוד . . .'' וכן הוא אומר (זכריה ב): "כי הנוגע בכם כנוגע בבבת עינו'' — "בבבת עין'' לא נאמר אלא "בבבת עינו'' — של מקום . . .

Can there be enemies of He who spoke and the world came into being? But the verse informs us that whoever hates Israel is as if he hates the Omnipotent. Similarly, it is said (Exodus 15): "And in the greatness of Thine excellency Thou hast overthrown them that rose up against Thee". Can there be rebels against the Omnipotent? The verse informs us that whoever rises up against Israel it is as if he rose up against the Omnipotent. Similarly, it is stated (Psalms 74, 23): "Forget not the voice of Thine enemies: the tumult of those that rise up against Thee continually". Because of whom? Similarly it is stated (Psalms 83, 2): "For, lo, Thine enemies make a tumult: and they that hate Thee lift up their heads". Because of whom? "They have taken crafty counsel *against thy people*". And it is also stated (Zechariah 2): "For He that toucheth you toucheth the apple of *His* eye". It is not stated "the eye" but "His eye" — of the Omnipotent.

Accordingly the enemies of Israel are synonymous with the enemies of God. Whether we are worthy or not of this title; those bent on our destruction regard us as the standardbearers of truth and justice and the representatives of the divine Law. And it is for this reason that they persecute and hate us.

Hirsch, commenting on this passage, remarks that Moses was aware that enemies would rise up against the Torah from the moment that it was given. Its demands for justice and altruism were bound to antagonise aggressors and tyrants and stand in the way of their designs. The Torah's call to holiness would not only arouse hatred, but also active persecution.

The concluding verse: "Return O Lord unto the many thousands of Israel" presents a syntactical difficulty. The Hebrew verb: *shuv* is usually an intransitive verb implying "return", and yet it is followed by the phrase "many thousands of Israel" as a direct object. The English translation gets over the difficulty by inserting the preposition "unto" which, however, is not in the Hebrew original. Other commentators have rendered *shuv* in the transitive sense of "return" (bring back). The commentary Da'at Zekenim paraphrases our verse as follows:

יהי רצון שישובו כל האלפים והרבבות של ישראל למקומם במספרם ולא יחסר מהם
איש, ו״שובה״ כמו ״השיבה״, ודומה לו (דברים ל) : ״ושב ה׳ את שבותך״ — והשיב.

May it be granted that all the thousands and tens of thousands of Israel
return to their place according to their number with none lacking. "Return"
is here taken in the sense of "bring back" as in the verse "The Lord will bring
back thy captivity" (Deuteronomy 30, 3).

Others interpret the verb *shuv* in the sense of "causing to rest":

Give the myriads of Israel rest that they may be no more disturbed.

(Ibn Ezra)

Sforno also takes it in the sense of rest, but in an intransitive sense:

"Rest O Lord amongst the myriads of Israel"—
let Thy presence rest in our midst.

Sforno also explains the numbers, literally: "ten thousand
thousands" in its plain sense as referring to the actual figure of
Jewish men, women and children at the time. But Hirsch draws
attention to the unusual order of the Hebrew numerical description in
which the large figure "ten thousand" precedes the smaller unit
"thousand" instead of it reading "a thousand ten thousands" (cf.
Genesis 24: "Be thou the mother of thousands of millions" [i.e. ten
thousands], instead of millions of thousands). He therefore interprets
it to refer to the myriads of people who would swell the nation in
future times, in other words the tens of thousands that would be
added to the already existing thousands. The verse therefore is a
timeless invocation and not limited to the period in the wilderness.

He who rose up to scatter His enemies and remove wickedness
from the earth would dwell once more amongst the tens of thousands
of His children and followers from all peoples. This passage then
which our Sages regarded as a book on its own alludes to the period
described by the prophet Zechariah (2, 15) in the following manner:

When the ark set forth

וְנִלְווּ גוֹיִם רַבִּים אֶל־ה׳ בַּיּוֹם הַהוּא
וְהָיוּ לִי לְעָם
וְשָׁכַנְתִּי בְתוֹכֵךְ . . .

**And many nations shall be joined to the Lord in that day,
and shall be My people:
and I will dwell in the midst of thee . . .**

NOTE

[1] For a historical study of the significance of these markings cf. Lieberman S. *Hellenism in Jewish Palestine*, 'Critical Marks in the Hebrew Bible - The inverted Nuns' p. 38. New York: The Jewish Theological Seminary (Translator).

THE FISH WE ATE FOR FREE

After all the preparations recorded in the two preceding sidrot for the great trek had been concluded and the arrangements for their journeyings and encampments laid down (Numbers 9, 15—23), the Israelites were commanded to make trumpets for themselves with instructions when and how to use them (10, 1—10):

וַיְהִי בַּשָּׁנָה הַשֵּׁנִית בַּחֹדֶשׁ הַשֵּׁנִי בְּעֶשְׂרִים בַּחֹדֶשׁ נַעֲלָה הֶעָנָן מֵעַל מִשְׁכַּן הָעֵדֻת: וַיִּסְעוּ בְנֵי־יִשְׂרָאֵל לְמַסְעֵיהֶם.

On the twentieth day of the second month in the second year, the cloud was taken up from off the Tabernacle of the Testimony and the children of Israel took their journeys.

(10, 11—12)

Their whole progress in the wilderness was governed by the hand of Divine Providence and they marched forward led by their Heavenly Sovereign:

עַל־פִּי ה' יִסְעוּ בְּנֵי יִשְׂרָאֵל וְעַל־פִּי ה' יַחֲנוּ

At the commandment of the Lord, the children of Israel journeyed, and at the commandment of the Lord they pitched.

(9, 18)

Their trek through the great and terrible wilderness, "wherein were fiery serpents and scorpions and drought where there was no water"

94

(Deuteronomy 8, 15) is the story of advancement to their goal, the Land of Promise by supernatural means and accompanied by visible miracles.

The generation that went through these experiences stands revealed in our sidra, as unable to cope with these supra-human conditions, as it were, characterised by true freedom, released from outward, and inner servitude, feeding on the "corn of heaven" and the "bread of the mighty" (Psalms 78), interpreted by Rashi to imply angel's food coming directly from the Almighty's bountiful hand. Instead we are confronted by yearnings and nostalgia for a humdrum, small-time existence, a life of serfdom subject to their habits, passions and desires.

Those same longings to return to the fleshpots of Egypt came to the surface as soon as they were confronted, on their departure, by the first signs of impending danger, when they saw Egypt pursuing them, forgetful of the Divine miracles they had seen but yesterday. Demoralisation set in whenever some new obstacle appeared on the scene. Our sidra and the three subsequent ones (*Shelaḥ, Koraḥ, Ḥukkat*) in particular, constitute a record of the little faith, lack of faith and ingratitude displayed by the "generation of the wilderness" (*dor ha-midbar*), turning its back on freedom and preferring servitude. It succumbed to a rapid process of demoralization, descending from the dizzy spiritual heights of being "borne on eagles' wings" to the degenerate status of malcontents, from being nourished by the "corn of Heaven" to a gluttonous demand for onions and garlic.

The Psalmist paints a vivid picture of the spiritual backslidings of our ancestors in Psalms 106, 7—25 which we quote here:

אֲבוֹתֵינוּ בְמִצְרַיִם לֹא הִשְׂכִּילוּ נִפְלְאוֹתֶיךָ, לֹא זָכְרוּ אֶת־רֹב חֲסָדֶיךָ, וַיַּמְרוּ
עַל־יָם בְּיַם־סוּף: וַיּוֹשִׁיעֵם לְמַעַן שְׁמוֹ לְהוֹדִיעַ אֶת־גְּבוּרָתוֹ: וַיִּגְעַר בְּיַם
סוּף וַיֶּחֱרָב וַיּוֹלִיכֵם בַּתְּהֹמוֹת כַּמִּדְבָּר:
וַיּוֹשִׁיעֵם מִיַּד שׂוֹנֵא וַיִּגְאָלֵם מִיַּד אוֹיֵב: וַיְכַסּוּ־מַיִם צָרֵיהֶם, אֶחָד מֵהֶם לֹא
נוֹתָר: וַיַּאֲמִינוּ בִדְבָרָיו, יָשִׁירוּ תְּהִלָּתוֹ:

95

מִהֲרוּ שָׁכְחוּ מַעֲשָׂיו, לֹא־חִכּוּ לַעֲצָתוֹ: וַיִּתְאַוּוּ תַאֲוָה בַּמִּדְבָּר וַיְנַסּוּ־אֵל
בִּישִׁימוֹן: וַיִּתֵּן לָהֶם שֶׁאֱלָתָם וַיְשַׁלַּח רָזוֹן בְּנַפְשָׁם: וַיְקַנְאוּ לְמֹשֶׁה בַּמַּחֲנֶה
לְאַהֲרֹן קְדוֹשׁ ה': תִּפְתַּח־אֶרֶץ וַתִּבְלַע דָּתָן, וַתְּכַס עַל־עֲדַת אֲבִירָם:
וַתִּבְעַר־אֵשׁ בַּעֲדָתָם לֶהָבָה תְּלַהֵט רְשָׁעִים: . . . . וַיִּמְאֲסוּ בְּאֶרֶץ חֶמְדָּה, לֹא
הֶאֱמִינוּ לִדְבָרוֹ: וַיֵּרָגְנוּ בְאָהֳלֵיהֶם, לֹא שָׁמְעוּ בְּקוֹל ה':

**Our fathers understood not Thy wonders in Egypt; they
remembered not the multitude of Thy mercies: but provoked
Him at the sea, even at the Red Sea. Nevertheless, He saved
them for His name's sake, that He might make His mighty
power to be known. He rebuked the Red Sea also, and it was
dried up: so He led them through the depths, as through the
wilderness.**

**And He saved them from the hand of him that hated them,
and redeemed them from the hand of the enemy. And the
waters covered their enemies: there was not one of them left.
Then believed they His words: they sang His praise.**

**They soon forgot His works: they waited not for His counsel;
But lusted exceedingly in the wilderness, and tempted God in
the desert. And He gave them their request; but sent leanness
into their soul. They envied Moses also in the camp, and
Aaron the saint of the Lord. The earth opened and swallowed
up Dathan, and covered the company of Abiram. And a fire
was kindled in their company; the flame burned up the
wicked . . . Yea, they despised the pleasant land, they believed
not His word: But murmured in their tents and hearkened not
unto the voice of the Lord.**

A detailed and vivid account of these murmurings is given in our
sidra, 11, 4—6:

וְהָאסַפְסֻף אֲשֶׁר בְּקִרְבּוֹ הִתְאַוּוּ תַּאֲוָה וַיָּשֻׁבוּ וַיִּבְכּוּ גַּם בְּנֵי־יִשְׂרָאֵל וַיֹּאמְרוּ:
מִי יַאֲכִלֵנוּ בָּשָׂר:

זָכַרְנוּ אֶת־הַדָּגָה אֲשֶׁר־נֹאכַל בְּמִצְרַיִם חִנָּם
אֵת הַקִּשֻּׁאִים וְאֵת הָאֲבַטִּחִים וְאֶת הֶחָצִיר וְאֶת־הַבְּצָלִים וְאֶת־הַשּׁוּמִים:
וְעַתָּה נַפְשֵׁנוּ יְבֵשָׁה, אֵין כֹּל בִּלְתִּי אֶל־הַמָּן עֵינֵינוּ:

And the mixed multitude that was among them fell a lusting, and the children of Israel also wept again and said: Who shall give us flesh to eat?
We remember the fish, which we did eat in Egypt freely;
the cucumbers, and the melons, and the leeks, and the onions, and the garlic.
But now our soul is dried away, there is nothing at all, besides this manna before our eyes.

Note that these words were uttered by the generation of the wilderness, which had gone forth from slavery to freedom, from darkness to light, from bondage to redemption. Yet this was how they pictured their experiences in Egypt, only just over a year after that crowning act of liberation from a nightmare of persecution, hard labour and the casting of their children into the river.

Our Sages expressed astonishment at this idyllic picture of their stay in Egypt where they were fed free of charge. They said:

> "We remember the fish". Does it say that the Egyptians actually gave them fish for nought! Surely it is stated: "Now go and work; for no straw shall be given you" (Ex. 5, 18). If they wouldn't give them straw for nought, would they have given them fish for nought? How then do I explain the term *ḥinam*? — free from Divine commandments.

This explanation interpreting the Hebrew word *ḥinam* — "free" in the sense of "free from the precepts" sounds far removed from the world of their murmurings. Let us see what other commentators have to say. Ibn Ezra explains that "free" is not literally meant, but that these commodities were cheap, available, as it were, at give-away prices. Ibn Ezra often takes Biblical phraseology

97

hyperbolically. The question is whether his approach fits the picture here. Were the Israelites grumbling against the expensiveness of their food and nostalgically recalling its cheapness in Egypt? Surely not!

Other commentators strive to adhere to the literal connotation of *ḥinam* as "free" "for nothing". Naḥmanides explains:

> The Egyptian fishermen allowed them to take the fish caught in the nets as is the custom amongst fishermen. Similarly, cucumbers and leeks were so plentiful in Egypt that whenever they were employed in the vegetable gardens they were allowed to eat of them. Or perhaps the Israelite slaves of the king worked for him and were only provided with a frugal diet of bread and water. They would therefore forage for food in the fields and gardens, eat of the vegetables and no one bothered them, as is the practice where the king's slaves are concerned. Or at the river side they would be given the small fishes which have no value in Egypt, as I have already explained in Exodus.

Naḥmanides is referring to his description of the afflictions endured by the Israelites in Egypt:

> "Taskmasters to afflict them" . . . they further imposed on them hard labour with mortar and bricks. For at the beginning, the taskmasters provided them with the bricks from which the forced labour squads would build the building. But now *all* the people were put to work and ordered to bring the earth, they only being provided by the king with the straw. (i.e. Naḥmanides is here describing the situation before the decree about the straw). The bricks would then be given to the forced labour squads to build the building. All the heavy labour which Pharaoh and the Egyptians had to do such as trench digging, removal of refuse was also imposed on them accompanied by illtreatment, curses and blows to urge them on. That is the implication of the text "and all their labour which they worked them with rigour".
> The king would give them a starvation diet as is the custom with the king's workmen. This was the background to the grumblings of those who hankered after the "fish we ate in Egypt freely, the cucumbers . . ." for fish were very plentiful in Egypt and they would take from the fishermen in accordance with the command of the king and they would take cucumbers and melons from the gardens, and no one would bother them since it was the king's order.

Abravanel similarly explains *ḥinam* as literally: "free of charge". But he adds to the Sifrei's question ("if they wouldn't given them straw for nought, would they have given them fish for nought?") another:

> What was the implication of their question: "Who will give us meat to eat? We remember the fish". If they hankered after meat, then surely fish was no substitute? Admittedly, those who hankered after meat said in *Beshallaḥ* (Ex. 16, 3): "Would that we had died by the hand of the Lord sitting by the fleshpot". But here they did not speak to the point, since they began with the subject of meat and immediately shifted to the fish and other foods which were neither fish nor flesh.

He answers these two questions together as follows:

> Their statement "we remember the fish we ate in Egypt for nought" was to anticipate the argument with which Moses might have countered: Why do you grumble about the lack of meat. Did you then eat meat in Egypt? You certainly had no meat in Egypt when you were impoverished and needy and meat was very expensive.
> Therefore they said: If we didn't eat meat in Egypt, at least, we ate fish, since it was plentiful there from the waters of the Nile. We didn't even need money to buy it since it could be got free of charge since the Nile waters overflow. All one had to do was to dig a hole which was filled by the waters of the river. When the Nile receded, the fish remained in the pits and in this way they ate them free of charge. Whether we accept Abravanel's explanation that the fish were free due to the specific natural conditions which allowed everyone the opportunity to procure fish, or Naḥmanides', that it was a special privilege accorded the king's workmen, we may learn from here how powerful is the selective ability of the memory. The terrible price they had to pay for this give-away diet — slavery, suffering, persecution, murder of their children is conveniently forgotten. What remained — the fish they ate freely, without paying for them.

Pharaoh's ulterior motive in providing the fish is emphasised by Astruc in Midreshei Torah:

Rashi writes that *ḥinam* here means *ḥinam* from *miẓvot* — free of Divine precepts. The objection that "straw was not provided them, never mind fish" forced him to resort to this explanation. But perhaps straw they were not given for the express design of making them work hard, whilst food they were prepared to give them in generous amounts and free; for how could they work hard and attain good results on an empty stomach? But they certainly supplied them with food to get the most out of them.

Apt in this context is Solomon's proverb (Prov. 12, 10): "The righteous man knows the soul of his beast, but the mercies of the wicked are cruel". In other words, the really good man understands the needs of his beast that it has toiled enough and he feeds it with a measure of barley in accordance with what it requires for such labour. The wicked man, on the other hand, gives it a double or triple measure and then works it double its capacity. His mercy in giving it more food is really cruelty to drive it mercilessly and beyond its normal capacity.

Accordingly, the grumblers did not realize the full bitterness of the irony in their words. Admittedly, they had been provided with fish for nothing in Egypt, but had they not understood the real import of Pharaoh's generosity — as expressed in the rabbinic dictum (cited by Rashi) on v. 22 of our chapter *s.v.* "If flocks and herbs be slaughtered . . .": "We say to the ass: Take this measure of barley and then we shall cut off your head?"

Luzzatto bases his solution of the problem on historical proofs and considerations:

The word *ḥinam* implies nothing less than "free of charge", since the Egyptians supported the Israelites providing them with cheap items of food such as fish and cucumbers, which were plentiful in Egypt . . . We find that Herodotus informs us that, on one of the Egyptian pyramids, was an inscription reading that the king who erected it, expended 1,600 measures of garlic and onions on food for the workmen. Herodotus further states that the Egyptians did not themselves eat fish and it was therefore understandable why they gave it to the Israelites . . .

Hitherto we have cited all those who try to explain the text literally, who wish to answer the question of the Sages in terms of the tricks that memory deliberately plays with the person. They forgot the injustice they had suffered. Only pleasant memories remained of the generous helpings of food given them. The reason underlying this generosity was of no concern to them.

But it seems to us that our Rabbis evinced a profounder understanding of the Israelites' character. Was it really and truly the fish and cucumbers that prompted this outcry on the part of the Israelites? Perhaps this was merely the outward form their inner dissatisfaction took! A community will accept suffering and want with enthusiasm and eagerness, provided the ultimate aim of it all is one which appeals to them or with which they can identify themselves. No sacrifice — of convenience, property, health and even those near and dear will be too great, provided the goal is valued and sacred in their eyes. On the other hand, when discontent lurks in the heart of the public or individual, grumblings and murmurings, criticism and defamation will flare up at the slightest pretext. The most trivial difficulty will be magnified sevenfold and even the tiniest inconvenience demanded regarded as a major violation of their rights. The real motive for the inner discontent is not explicitly expressed, either because the person is unaware of its cause or because it springs from forbidden desires which have to be suppressed and concealed. Instead, the malcontents make much of trivial complaints and always have a grievance. The onlooker will be puzzled: Are these trivialities worth such an outcry? His eye will not be able to distinguish between the pretext and the real cause lurking deep down.

Our Sages detected this. When they said *ḥinam* they meant "free of *miẓvot*". Not food or drink, fish or cucumbers, whether given away or cheap, fresh or stale really concerned them, but that freedom from the irksome demands of civilization and standards of self-discipline which they had enjoyed in Egypt. The Talmud observes that "a slave enjoys his licence". The master does not interfere in the private lives of his slaves, does not bother about their moral and educational training. On the contrary the more the slave is ruled by his senses, the better for the master. Let him get drunk, fight, indulge in promiscuity and expend his superfluous energies on such outlets rather than "listen to words of falsehood" — of freedom, liberation from the toils of his bondage. Let him not think of his self-respect, of man created in the image of God daily trodden underfoot by his persecutors. It is not the master's business to teach him ethics and conduct. His slave is like his beast of burden and the slave is satisfied with that.

But when the Israelites went forth from slavery to freedom, another bondage was imposed on them, more difficult and majestic in its awesomeness — the yoke of Torah and *mizvot* imposed on them at Sinai — self-discipline in the life of the community and individual, in family life and relations with neighbours, on workdays and restdays, in matters of food and drink and clothing and, most important, in matters of sex. This yoke so dear to the one who accepts it willingly, to the one who has studied Torah and been enlightened to appreciate its lustre and experience its taste — this yoke of freedom appeared to those accustomed to slavery, as burdensome and irksome. This, in the view of our Sages, was the cause of all the grumblings about water, bread and meat and the fish they ate for nothing in Egyptian bondage. Free? Of course. Yonder, we ate fish free — free from *mizvot,* free from the yoke of Torah and *mizvot.*

This, too, is the interpretation by the Sages to the following verse which describes the behaviour of the grumblers:

"Then Moses heard the people weep throughout their families" (Num. 11, 10). R. Nehorai used to say: This indicates that the Israelites were annoyed when Moses told them to refrain from forbidden sex relations. We may understand from this that a man would marry his sister or his father's or mother's sister. When Moses ordered them to desist from such practices they were annoyed. They wept to their families — since they had become inured to sin (they had no shame about it), they vented their complaints publicly assembling their families together with them, for the purpose.

102

Rashi abbreviates the words of the Sifrei and combines the two explanations:

> "Weep throughout their families": Family after family assembled to weep and voice their grievance publicly. Our Rabbis say: "*With regard to* their families": they complained regarding family matters, regarding the sexual relationships forbidden them.

Thus in this text, too, as with the previous one of "we ate in Egypt for nothing" the literal explanation is limited to the surface meaning, whereas the homiletic exposition uncovers a deeper level of meaning. To adapt another Biblical text (1 Samuel 16, 7): the plain sense looks on the outward appearance but the homiletic sees into the heart.[1]

Questions for Further Study

1. Chapter 11 (from verse 4) treats of two subjects, that of the murmurings of the children of Israel for meat and the appointment of the seventy elders. What is the connection between them, weaving them into one organic whole?

2. Compare the murmurings of the people here (v. 4—6) with those related in the incidents recorded in Exodus 14, 11—12; 15, 22—25; why do we find that the Lord's "anger was kindled" only here, and not in the previous cases?

3. Compare Moses' reactions to their murmurings here (v. 11—15) with those in previous cases (Exodus 15, 24; 17, 4). What is the fundamental difference between his reaction here and in the previous case? Give reasons for the difference.

4. "And the anger of the Lord was kindled greatly; Moses also was displeased".

(Numbers 11, 10)

R. Isaac (of Castile, grandfather of Joseph Caro, author of the *Shulhan Arukh*) in his work, *Toledot Yizhak* states:

What is recorded in verse 4 "Who shall give us flesh to eat?" bears a twofold meaning: (1) that they had a desire to eat flesh; (2) that, in addition to their lust, they imagined that it did not lay within the power of God to provide them with flesh, as they asked: Who shall give us . . .? — in other words, no being can possibly satisfy our desire and it is not in the power of the Creator to give us flesh. The Holy One blessed be He realized the *true implications* of their words, as stated by Asaph the Psalmist (Psalms 78, 18—19) — "And they tempted God in their heart by asking meat for their lust. Yea, they spake against God; they said: Can God furnish a table in the wilderness?" But Moses and Aaron only realized their surface, obvious meaning in the sense that they lusted to eat meat.

(a)   What difficulty (in verse 10) did R. Isaac Caro wish to solve by his explanation?

(b)   What are, in his opinion, the two possible implications of the question: "Who shall give us flesh to eat?" According to which of them is the question a rhetorical one?

NOTE

[1]   Cf. Rashi on Num. 14, 4 and further, Shelaḥ, as well as the literal and homiletic explanations cited by Rashi on Num. 13, 31 and our comment to Shelaḥ 1, p. 140.

WE WANT MEAT!

Grumblings figure prominently in the history of the children of Israel's wanderings in the wilderness. These began immediately after they had witnessed the awe-inspiring miracles of God at the Red Sea, when they had attained an unprecedented level of belief in the Almighty. But the grumblings in this sidra are of a different order from those pictured in *Beshallaḥ* (Exodus 16—17). In the latter, the grumblings of the children of Israel were prompted by genuine want and danger to their lives. But it is not immediately perceptible what prompted the grumblings in our sidra. They suffered no want, since the manna, the all-purpose food, was provided for them, daily, from heaven. This fact was not indeed denied by the grumblers. There are two separate incidents described in the chapter (Numbers 11), which we shall study. The first incident briefly recorded, of Taberah, begins with the following verse:

וַיְהִי הָעָם כְּמִתְאֹנְנִים רַע בְּאָזְנֵי ה׳
וַיִּשְׁמַע ה׳ וַיִּחַר אַפּוֹ

And the people were as murmurers, speaking evil in the ears of the Lord;
and when the Lord heard it, **He was angry**

(11, 1)

The second incident described at length, begins as follows:

וְהָאסַפְסֻף אֲשֶׁר בְּקִרְבּוֹ הִתְאַוּוּ תַּאֲוָה
וַיָּשֻׁבוּ וַיִּבְכּוּ גַּם בְּנֵי יִשְׂרָאֵל וַיֹּאמְרוּ:
מִי יַאֲכִלֵנוּ בָּשָׂר:
זָכַרְנוּ אֶת־הַדָּגָה אֲשֶׁר־נֹאכַל בְּמִצְרַיִם חִנָּם:
וַיִּשְׁמַע מֹשֶׁה אֶת־הָעָם בֹּכֶה לְמִשְׁפְּחֹתָיו ... וַיִּחַר־אַף ה' מְאֹד

And the mixed multitude that was among them fell a lusting; and the children of Israel also wept on their part and said: Would that we were given meat to eat!
We remember the fish, which we were wont to eat in Egypt for nought;
Then Moses heard the people weeping family by family ... And the Lord was very angry.

(11, 4—5, 10)

How instructive is the wording of the above passages in tracing the stages by which the malady of discontent gradually spreads! First the people was "as murmurers". There is no detail of what they grumbled about. Who reacted to their grumblings? The Almighty — "The Lord heard it, and He was angry". The second incident is described in greater detail, even to the point of recording the items of diet that they maintained, that they had enjoyed in Egypt. Who reacted on this occasion? Moses — "And Moses heard the people weeping, family by family". Here is how Isaac Arama explains the development of discontent and rebellion:

"And the people were as murmurers speaking evil in the ears of the Lord". The subject of their grumblings is not revealed at this juncture, since, at the beginning, they kept it inside. Later, they clothed their discontent in the form of a hankering for meat; but though, at the beginning, their discontent smouldered within them, the Lord who knows the thoughts of man was well aware of what was going on inside their hearts — "for ye have wept in the ears of the Lord, saying: Would that we were given meat to eat!" The phrase "The Lord heard" implies that He understood the situation, though nothing

had actually been explicitly said (compare Genesis 23, 16: "and Abraham
hearkened and weighed . . .").

The text notes that the people did not learn the lesson of the punishment,
though they suffered decimation from the anger of the Lord. They reverted
to their grumblings, "and the mixed multitude that was among them fell a
lusting". They did not lust for meat or any particular item of food but simply
indulged in lusting. This is much worse than the case of a man who is
overcome by his desires. He at least has the excuse like Adam and Eve "that
the serpent seduced me". When the people saw the hankering of the mixed
multitude they began once more to weep and lust, as at the beginning. This
time, however, they expressed their discontent openly saying, "Would that
we were given meat to eat".

We have here, therefore, the story of the gradual spread of
discontent from inner to outer rebellion. Naḥmanides also sees in the
text, an allusion to the spread of the discontent from the "mixed
multitude" and the very ordinary folk, "the people", to the elite i.e.:
"The children of Israel" (11,4 end).

The question that immediately springs to mind is why Moses did
not intercede with God, just as he did when they rebelled with the
golden calf and on other occasions. Here Moses, on the contrary,
adds his own indignation at the people's behaviour to that of God's.
Evidently the nature of the grumblings here was different from what
had happened previously. We have already referred to the fact that
whereas their previous grumblings were motivated by valid causes
such as fear and want, this time, there was no real excuse. Moreover,
their demand for meat seemed to have concealed something much
more serious. Two explanations have been suggested. One is
reflected in the accepted English translation of the passage which
runs: "Would that we were given meat to eat!" But it can also be
read as a rhetoric question, "Who can give us meat to eat?" In this
sense the people would be casting doubts on the possibility of
satisfying their request. The latter interpretation is born out by the
Psalmist's version of the story:

וַיְנַסּוּ־אֵל בִּלְבָבָם לִשְׁאָל־אֹכֶל לְנַפְשָׁם: וַיְדַבְּרוּ בֵּאלֹהִים אָמְרוּ, הֲיוּכַל אֵל
לַעֲרֹךְ שֻׁלְחָן בַּמִּדְבָּר:

**And they tried God in their heart by asking food for their
craving. Yea, they spoke against God; They said: "Can God
prepare a table in the wilderness?"**

(Psalms 78, 18—19)

Their question, there, implied open repudiation of Divine
omnipotence. In the light of this, we may now understand why
Moses the faithful shepherd of his flock, changed the wording of their
complaint when he referred to it, in his dialogue with the Almighty.
The people had said: "Who can give us meat to eat?" Moses,
however, worded the matter as follows:

מֵאַיִן לִי בָּשָׂר לָתֵת לְכָל־הָעָם הַזֶּה, כִּי יִבְכּוּ עָלַי לֵאמֹר, תְּנָה־לָנוּ בָשָׂר
וְנֹאכֵלָה:

**Whence should I have meat to give unto all this people, for
they trouble me with their weeping saying: Give us meat to
eat.**

(11, 13)

We may observe that though Moses did not have the temerity to
intercede on their behalf, he nevertheless, tried his utmost to
minimise their guilt. They had not rebelled against God but had
merely complained to him. But God who sees into the hearts of men
was aware of the truth. He therefore answered Moses:

כִּי בְכִיתֶם בְּאָזְנֵי ה' לֵאמֹר, מִי יַאֲכִלֵנוּ בָּשָׂר

**For ye have wept in the ears of the Lord, saying: "Who can
give us meat to eat?"**

(ibid. 18)

It was for this reason that "the Lord was very angry".

Maimonides had observed in his *Guide for the Perplexed* that the statement, that the anger of the Lord was kindled, only occurs where the people had committed the sin of idolatry. This is a further proof that they were not really grumbling against their diet but against the authority of God, casting doubts on His power and omnipotence. God answered the twofold complaint of Moses — in respect of the bitterness of his own plight and the reporting of the people's murmurings. Moses' complaint was met in the shape of the seventy men to share his burden, and the people's demand, too, was granted.

וְאֶל־הָעָם תֹּאמַר הִתְקַדְּשׁוּ לְמָחָר וַאֲכַלְתֶּם בָּשָׂר כִּי בְּכִיתֶם בְּאָזְנֵי ה׳
לֵאמֹר, מִי יַאֲכִלֵנוּ בָּשָׂר, כִּי־טוֹב לָנוּ בְּמִצְרָיִם, וְנָתַן ה׳ לָכֶם בָּשָׂר וַאֲכַלְתֶּם:
לֹא יוֹם אֶחָד תֹּאכְלוּן וְלֹא יוֹמָיִם וְלֹא חֲמִשָּׁה יָמִים וְלֹא עֲשָׂרָה יָמִים וְלֹא
עֶשְׂרִים יוֹם: עַד חֹדֶשׁ יָמִים, עַד אֲשֶׁר־יֵצֵא מֵאַפְּכֶם וְהָיָה לָכֶם לְזָרָא, יַעַן
כִּי־מְאַסְתֶּם אֶת־ה׳ אֲשֶׁר בְּקִרְבְּכֶם, וַתִּבְכּוּ לְפָנָיו לֵאמֹר, לָמָּה זֶּה יָצָאנוּ
מִמִּצְרָיִם:

And say thou unto the people: Sanctify yourselves against tomorrow, and ye shall eat meat; for ye have wept in the ears of the Lord, saying: Would that we were given meat to eat! for it was well with us in Egypt; therefore the Lord will give you meat, and ye shall eat.

Ye shall not eat one day, nor two days, nor five days, neither ten days, nor twenty days; but a whole month, until it come out your nostrils, and it be loathsome unto you; because that ye have rejected the Lord who is among you, and have troubled Him with weeping, saying: Why, now, came we forth of Egypt?

(11, 18—20)

It is not for nothing that the formulators of our liturgy bade us pray for "a life in which the desires of our heart shall be fulfilled for good".[1]

Were God to fulfil all our desires, irrespective of whether they
were for our good, we would be in a sorry state. But, in this case,
God literally fulfilled their request just as they had demanded, when
it was not for their good. But at this juncture, Moses uttered a
statement which has confounded our commentators and Sages,
down the ages:

וַיֹּאמֶר מֹשֶׁה שֵׁשׁ־מֵאוֹת אֶלֶף רַגְלִי הָעָם אֲשֶׁר אָנֹכִי בְּקִרְבּוֹ וְאַתָּה אָמַרְתָּ
בָּשָׂר אֶתֵּן לָהֶם וְאָכְלוּ חֹדֶשׁ יָמִים: הֲצֹאן וּבָקָר יִשָּׁחֵט לָהֶם וּמָצָא לָהֶם אִם
אֶת־כָּל־דְּגֵי הַיָּם יֵאָסֵף לָהֶם וּמָצָא לָהֶם:

**And Moses said: "The people, among whom I am, are six
hundred thousand men on foot; and yet Thou hast said: I will
give them meat, that they may eat a whole month! If flocks
and herds be slain for them, will they suffice them? or if all the
fish of the sea be gathered together for them, will they suffice
them?"**

(11, 21—22)

We cite here the view of three of our ancient rabbinic authorities
on this passage, cited by Rashi, on our text.

ר' עקיבא אומר: "שש מאות אלף רגלי" — ואתה אמרת בשר אתן להם
ואכלו חדש ימים? הצאן ובקר ישחטו להם ומצא להם? הכל כמשמעו: מי יספיק להם?
ר' שמעון אומר: חס ושלום לא עלתה על דעתו של אותו צדיק כך, מי שכתוב
בו "בכל ביתי נאמן הוא" (במדבר יב) יאמר: "אין המקום מספיק לנו?" אלא כך אמר
משה: שש מאות אלף רגלי העם אשר אנכי בקרבו ואתה אמרת בשר אתן להם לחדש
ימים ואחר כך תהרוג אומה גדולה כזו?! "הצאן ובקר ישחטו להם" כדי שיהרגו ותהיה
אכילה זו מספיקתן עד עולם?! וכי שבחך הוא זה? אומרים לו לחמור: טול כור שעורים
ונחתוך את ראשך?! השיבו הקב"ה: ואם לא אתן, יאמרו שקצרה ידי? הטוב בעיניך
שיד ה' תקצר בעניהם? יאבדו הם ומאה כיוצא בהם ואל תהי ידי קצרה לפניכם אפילו
שעה אחת.
רבן גמליאל בנו של ר' יהודה הנשיא אומר: אי אפשר לעמוד על הטפל. מאחר
שאין מבקשים אלא עלילה, לא תספיק להם. סופן לדון אחריך. אם אתה נותן להם בשר
בהמה גסה, יאמרו: "דקה בקשנו". ואם אתה נותן להם דקה, יאמרו "גסה בקשנו, חיה
ועוף בקשנו, דגים וחגבים בקשנו". אמר לו: אם כן יאמרו שקצרה ידי.

R. Akiva said: "Six hundred thousand men on foot; and yet Thou hast said: I will give them meat . . . . . . If flocks . . . be slain for them . . . will they suffice them?" It is all said literally: Who can supply them with enough? R. Shimon said: Heaven forfend that such a thing should have entered the mind of that righteous man, about whom it is written, "he is trusted in all my house," that he should have said, The Omnipotent cannot supply sufficient for us. But this is what Moses implied. The people amongst whom I am are six hundred thousand men on foot, and yet Thou hast said, I will give them meat that they will eat a whole month, and then Thou wilt kill such a great nation as this? Will flocks and herds be slaughtered for them, that they should be slain, so that this eating should suffice them forever (i.e. be their last)? Will this redound then to Thy praise? Do people say to an ass: take this measure of barley and we shall cut off your head! The Holy One blessed be He, replied: If I do not grant their request they will say that My hand is grown short. Would it please you for them to imagine that the hand of the Lord has grown short? Let them and a hundred like them perish, but let not My hand appear to them to have grown short, for even a single moment! Rabban Gamliel the son of R. Judah Hanassi stated: The meaning of the text is as follows: It is impossible to take them at their word, since they are only seeking a pretext; You will never satisfy them. They will ultimately prevaricate with You. If You give them beef they will say that they asked for mutton. If You will give them mutton, they will say that they asked for beef, for fish, for grasshoppers. Thereupon He answered, in that case they will say that My hand has grown short.

It is difficult for our Sages to conceive that Moses was capable of casting doubt on the omnipotence of God. Nevertheless R. Akiva's acceptance of them at their face value seems most faithful to the text. Naḥmanides concurs with him and expresses the view that R. Shimon and R. Judah Hanassi's interpretations do violence to the text. It may be asked, why Moses was punished severely for a much smaller offence at the waters of Meribah? To this R. Akiva answers that Moses' offence was then committed in public, in front of all the Israelites, when they looked to him to set an example. He should have sanctified the name of God by speaking to the rock. Here however his offence was not so serious because it took place in private between him and his Maker. He was only responsible to himself and was not therefore punished in the same way.

Questions for Further Study

1.   Abravanel asks why the children of Israel were punished on this occasion when they asked for meat, and not on the first occasion they made this demand, when they went out of Egypt. See Exodus 16, and compare it with our context and then try to answer the question.

2.   "Now the manna was like coriander seed, and the appearance thereof as the appearance of bdellium. The people went about and gathered it" (Numbers 11, 7—8). — The Hebrew word for "went about", *shatu* is an expression of strolling without toil.

   (Rashi)

   It could have been argued that they were sick of the manna for one of the following reasons: that it did not nourish them, or was not pleasant to the eye, since nourishment which revolts one, does not appeal to the eye, or it may have been that they were sick of it because it actually came to their tent — and what a man obtains without toil is not appreciated, and he becomes sick of it. Regarding the first the Torah stated: See, now, that they are behaving maliciously and speaking falsehood. There is no sound reason for them to dislike the manna: "The manna was like coriander seed" which nourishes the body. Regarding their second complaint, it was stated that, "and the appearance thereof as the appearance of bdellium", which is like sapphire that appeals to the eye. Regarding the third, it is stated that the people "went about", it was only the righteous who had the manna sent down to them, to their tent, but this was not the case with the general populace, who lusted for food. They went about and had to search for it afar.

   (Alshikh)

(a)   What difficulty do the above two commentators find in the phrase "the people went about and gathered it?"

(b)   What is the difference in principle, between their respective answers.

NOTE

[1]   p. 154, Singer's Prayer Book.

THE MURMURINGS: A REPEAT PERFORMANCE?

Chapter 11 of our sidra opens with a description of the murmurings of the children of Israel in the wilderness against the lack of meat and the monotony of their diet of manna, grumblings which continue incessantly through the subsequent sidrot of *Shelah, Korah* and *Hukkat.* The complaints vary in details but their underlying character remains the same.

The narrative strikes a familiar note and would seem to echo the murmurings referred to in Exodus (*Beshallah*). There have indeed been commentators who have maintained that they are indeed one and the same. The passage in Ex. 16, 13: "And it came to pass at even that the quails came up and covered the camp" is taken to be an incidental reference to the quails described in Num. 11, 31—32:

> For had Moses observed that the quails had come on a previous occasion and had been sufficient for them how could he have said: "If flocks and herds be slain for them, will they suffice them?" (Num. 11, 22).
>
> (Bekhor Shor)

Bekhor Shor (medieval French) works out this approach in detail in connection with the story of Moses and the striking of the rock in the wilderness of Zin. He similarly identifies the account of the bringing forth of water from the rock at Horeb with that relating to Massah and the waters of Meribah. Num. 20, 8 is a detailed account of the reference in Ex. 17, 6, where it is also related how Moses struck the rock and water flowed forth. But there the narrative relates how God sustained Israel with the manna, quail and water

113

during their stay in the wilderness. Subsequently each particular event is described in detail in its proper context.

> Here is proof that both refer to the same event. In Exodus it is written that "he called the name of this place Massah and Meribah". In *Ve-Zot Ha-berakhah* the deed of Moses and Aaron which aroused Divine disapproval is referred to in this manner (Deut. 33, 8): "who tried Him at Massah, contended with Him at the waters of Meribah". So we see the same event is referred to. Similarly it is stated (Num. 27, 14): "They are the waters of Meribah, at Kadesh, the wilderness of Zin". There also it is written (Ex. 17, 1): "And they journeyed from the wilderness of Zin".

This commentator observes that the Torah is here true to the exegetical principle of elaborating in one context what it briefly refers to in another. But while it is common to find such duplications in the Torah where the second and more detailed treatment is designed to fill in the gaps in the earlier account, his explanation here appears improbable because of the different names given to the places where the events took place as well as to the different accounts of the events themselves.

On the other hand, we have very often in Scriptures similar accounts in which a person or group of persons experience on different occasions parallel happenings. They are to teach a specific lesson regarding their reactions. The character of the person is revealed in his success or failure, showing us the way the person or group stands up to a series of challenges. The real test of strength or weakness is in the outcome of the final challenge or trial.

The parallel accounts of David's reactions to the two opportunities given him to slay Saul (1 Samuel 24 and 26) afford ample evidence of this. In both cases Saul is out for David's blood, and Saul is apprised by informers of the former's whereabouts and reacts in a similar way.

Chapter 24

It was told him . . . David is in the wilderness of En-Gedi.

Saul took three thousand chosen men out of all Israel and went to seek David.

Chapter 26

The Ziphites came unto Saul, saying, Doth not David hide in the hill of Hacbilah.

Saul arose and went to the wilderness of Ziph, having three thousand chosen men of Israel to seek David . . .

In both cases the two meet but under odd circumstances. David is the unseen observer, Saul the unconsciously observed. In both cases David has Saul at his mercy and in both cases there are onlookers urging him to take the advantage.

And the men of David said to him, Behold the day on which the Lord hath said to thee, I will deliver thine enemy into thine hand and thou shalt do to him as it seem good to thee.

And Abishai said to David God hath delivered thine enemy into thy hand this day; now therefore let me smite with the spear to the earth at one stroke and I will not smite him a second time.

In both instances David refuses to take advantage or allow others to do so, giving the identical motivation for his conduct.

And he said to his men, The Lord forbid it me that I should do this thing unto my lord, the Lord's anointed to put forth my hand against him, seeing he is the Lord's anointed.

And David said to Abishai, Destroy him not, for who can put forth his hand against the Lord's anointed and be guiltless? . . . As the Lord liveth, nay but the Lord shall smite him, or his day shall come forth to die; or he shall fall in battle

115

and be swept away. The Lord forbid it me that I should put forth my hand against the Lord's anointed.

In both cases David took a keepsake, Saul's cruse of water or the corner of his garment to prove that he had had him in his power.

Moreover, my father, see... the skirt of thy robe in my hand; for in that I have cut off the skirt... and killed thee not, know and see that there is no evil in my hand and I have not sinned against thee though thou layest in wait for my soul to take it.

And now see where the king's spear is and the cruse of water that was at his head... behold the king's spear... forasmuch as the Lord delivered thee into my hand today and I would not put forth my hand against the Lord's anointed.

The Lord judge between me and thee and the Lord avenge me of thee; but my hand shall not be upon thee.

And behold as thy life was much set by in the eyes of the Lord and let Him deliver me out of all tribulation.

In both cases Saul speaks gently and acknowledges David's superiority, shows remorse for his acts of persecution and promises to reconcile himself with David, resign himself to the brilliant future foreshadowed him.

Thou art more righteous than I. For thou hast repaid me good whereas I repaid thee evil. And thou hast declared this day how that thou hast dealt well with me; forasmuch as when the

I have sinned; return my son David; for I will no more do thee harm because my life was precious in thine eyes this day; behold I have played the fool and erred exceedingly.

Lord delivered me up into thy
hand, thou didst not kill me.
For if a man find his enemy will
he let him go well away?
wherefore the Lord reward thee
good for that which thou hast
done unto me this day.

And now behold I know that
thou shalt surely be king and
that the kingdom of Israel shall
be established in thy hand.

Blessed be thou my son David;
thou shalt both do mightily and
surely prevail.

The parallels are striking but no one will suggest that we have here
two accounts of the same incident. The question is what prompted
the Biblical narrative to cite these two so very similar incidents in
such detail? Surely there were other more important events in their
lives which did not qualify for more than a passing mention? Here is
the answer given in Midrash Tehilim:

> "And David swore to Saul and Saul went home". As soon as Saul departed,
> the mighty men of Saul said to Saul: Do you really think that David
> refrained from slaying you out of goodness of heart? He knew that he was
> inside and we were outside and that if he dared to harm you we would have
> entered and dragged him out and torn him limb from limb. As soon as Saul
> heard that, he was convinced and pursued after him.

What does this Midrash teach us? Who are "the mighty men of
Saul?" They are none other than a personification of Saul's thoughts
and doubts which began to overcome the feelings of remorse and
reconciliation. (Cf. the Midrash of Abraham and the Satan in the
guise of an old man preventing him from going to sacrifice his son).[1]
It is natural for a person to resent the moral superiority of his

117

colleague and strive to overcome the feeling of shame and inadequacy by casting aspersions on his colleague's sincerity.

Once he begins to become susceptible to the suggestions of his instinct that his fellow's righteousness is only skin deep and is motivated by egoistical considerations, his sense of shame and remorse weakens. That was what happened to Saul. The reason for the two accounts now emerges. The second is an answer not only to the "mighty men of Saul" but also to the reader. It might be thought that David's conduct was indeed dictated on the first occasion by fear or the possibility that he might thus placate Saul. The second event is recorded for us where there was no physical danger at all confronting David (the meeting was not in a cave but in the open) where there appeared no possibility of effecting a reconciliation with Saul after he had repudiated it, on the first occasion. Furthermore, on the second occasion, David was accompanied by "every man who had a grievance" including such personalities as Abishai who were willing to do the dread deed for him, and not as previously when his followers merely tried to provoke him to doing it. David on the second occasion could even have absolved himself of all direct responsibility. Notwithstanding all this, David would not lay hands on the Lord's anointed. His sincerity could not be doubted; no ulterior motives could be attached to his gracious action. The account of the second trial of David's magnanimity proves the point.

Let us now return to our sidra. All the trials that confronted Israel and which are discussed in *Beshallaḥ* took place *before* the Giving of the Torah. Israel had not been hardened by the trials of the wilderness, they were still new to their life of freedom. Their reaction of "Would we had died by the hand of the Lord in Egypt" is understandable.

In our sidra, however, the Israelites were in their second year of wandering, the Torah had been given them, the cloud accompanied them by day and the pillar of fire by night and the manna provided their daily diet. Would they revert to their original behaviour or had they learnt their lesson? Our sidra relates how the grumblings were repeated and the nostalgia for the Egyptian fleshpots increased in intensity. Let us compare the two accounts:

Exodus 16, 3	Numbers 11, 4—6
Would that we had died . . . in Egypt when we sat by the fleshpots when we ate bread to our fill that you brought us to this wilderness, to kill all this congregation with famine.	Who will give us flesh to eat? We remember the fish we ate gratis in Egypt, the cucumbers, melons, leeks, onions and garlic, but now our soul is dried away; there is nothing at all save this manna to look at.

Obviously the situation was much worse on the second occasion, especially when they were well provided with manna. Now we can appreciate why they were not punished so direly on the first occasion in *Beshallaḥ* when in answer to their grumblings the manna and quail appeared. On the second occasion it was no longer the first offence; they had been warned; they should have known better; "so the Lord smote the people with an exceedingly great plague". The second trial, as we have noted in the case of David, is the surest test of character, indicating that the Israelites deserved beyond all doubt the punishment meted out to them. We may now understand why Moses lost his patience not on the first occasion but on the second. Only in our sidra does he give vent to his bitter complaint:

הֶאָנֹכִי הָרִיתִי אֵת כָּל־הָעָם הַזֶּה אִם־אָנֹכִי יְלִדְתִּיהוּ . . .
לֹא־אוּכַל אָנֹכִי לְבַדִּי לָשֵׂאת אֶת־כָּל־הָעָם הַזֶּה כִּי כָבֵד מִמֶּנִּי:

Have I conceived the whole of this people, have I given it birth . . .
I cannot bear alone the burden of this people because it is too heavy for me.

(11, 12, 14)

119

NOTE

[1]   See *Studies in Bereshit*, p. 195.

WOULD THE LORD'S PEOPLE WERE PROPHETS

The Torah is at pains to present both sides of the Biblical heroes, not concealing their but human faults. Even Moses is not described as the perfect man, but we see him also in his moments of impatience and weakness. Though he displayed these in reaction to the provocation of the generation of the wilderness, their grumblings and lack of faith, the Torah does not excuse them or gloss over them.

In our sidra, too, Moses is depicted in a mood of impatience, descending as it were from his perfection, denouncing the rebelliousness of the people and protesting, as it were, against the Almighty's treatment of him:

לָמָה הֲרֵעֹתָ לְעַבְדֶּךָ וְלָמָּה לֹא־מָצָתִי חֵן בְּעֵינֶיךָ לָשׂוּם אֶת־מַשָּׂא כָּל הָעָם
הַזֶּה עָלָי: לֹא־אוּכַל אָנֹכִי לְבַדִּי לָשֵׂאת אֶת כָּל־הָעָם הַזֶּה כִּי כָבֵד מִמֶּנִּי:
וְאִם כָּכָה אַתְּ עֹשֶׂה לִּי
הָרְגֵנִי נָא הָרֹג
אִם מָצָאתִי חֵן בְּעֵינֶיךָ
וְאַל אֶרְאֶה בְּרָעָתִי

...Wherefore hast Thou dealt ill with Thy servant? and wherefore have I not found favour in Thy sight, that Thou layest the burden of all this people upon me? I am not able to bear all this people myself alone, because it is too heavy for me.
And if Thou deal thus with me,
kill me, I pray Thee, out of hand,

if I have found favour in Thy sight;
and let me not look upon my wretchedness.

(11, 11, 14—15)

Isaac Arama makes an illuminating comment on Moses'
protestations in his *Akedat Yizḥak*:

> See how far removed these words of Moses are from those he uttered after
> the deed of the Golden Calf! — "Yet now, if Thou wilt forgive their sin —;
> and if not blot me, I pray Thee, out of Thy book which Thou hast written"
> (Exodus 32, 32). Here his anger brought Him to sin in that he spurned his
> mission and office over the people of the Lord with which he had been
> entrusted. This constituted somewhat presumptuous conduct vis à vis his
> Creator, for who would say to his earthly sovereign: Take your appointment
> and office in which I have no desire; all the more so in the case of the
> Sovereign Creator!

What was Moses' punishment? We do not find that Moses was
punished on account of this demand, but rather that it was acceded
to. Is then the above verdict on his conduct erroneous? Since his
request was acceded to, perhaps this is a sign that it was in order?

There are other instances in Scripture where individuals fell short
of the desired standard of conduct, and made unjust demands. But
the Almighty in acceding to their request transformed His favourable
response into a new challenge more difficult than the previous. If
they withstood the new test, their success cancelled out their previous
moral failure which ultimately proved a blessing.

This is the inner implication of the story in the first book of
Samuel (chapters 8—12) where it is related how the people requested
a king and how the Almighty, ultimately, but not willingly acceded to
their request. After Samuel had remarked that: "Your wickedness is
great, which ye have done in the sight of the Lord, in asking you a
king," he continued:

וְעַתָּה הִנֵּה הַמֶּלֶךְ אֲשֶׁר בְּחַרְתֶּם אֲשֶׁר שְׁאֶלְתֶּם
וְהִנֵּה נָתַן ה' עֲלֵיכֶם מֶלֶךְ:
אִם־תִּירְאוּ אֶת ה' וַעֲבַדְתֶּם אֹתוֹ
וּשְׁמַעְתֶּם בְּקוֹלוֹ וְלֹא תַמְרוּ אֶת־פִּי ה' וִהְיָתֶם גַּם־אַתֶּם וְגַם־הַמֶּלֶךְ אֲשֶׁר
מָלַךְ עֲלֵיכֶם אַחַר ה' אֱלֹהֵיכֶם:

**Now therefore behold the king whom ye have chosen, and
whom ye have asked for;
and, behold, the Lord hath set a king over you.
If ye will fear the Lord, and serve Him,
and hearken unto His voice,
and not rebel against the commandment of the Lord, and both
ye and also the king that reigneth over you be followers of the
Lord your God.**

(1 Samuel 12, 13—14)

Similarly, the Almighty acceded to Moses' request, providing him
with loyal helpers to assist him in his task:

וַיֹּאמֶר ה' אֶל־מֹשֶׁה
אֶסְפָה־לִּי שִׁבְעִים אִישׁ מִזִּקְנֵי יִשְׂרָאֵל אֲשֶׁר יָדַעְתָּ כִּי־הֵם זִקְנֵי הָעָם
וְשֹׁטְרָיו וְלָקַחְתָּ אֹתָם אֶל־אֹהֶל מוֹעֵד וְהִתְיַצְּבוּ שָׁם עִמָּךְ:
וְיָרַדְתִּי וְדִבַּרְתִּי עִמְּךָ שָׁם וְאָצַלְתִּי מִן־הָרוּחַ אֲשֶׁר עָלֶיךָ וְשַׂמְתִּי עֲלֵיהֶם
וְנָשְׂאוּ אִתְּךָ בְּמַשָּׂא הָעָם וְלֹא־תִשָּׂא אַתָּה לְבַדֶּךָ:

**And the Lord said unto Moses:
Gather unto Me seventy men of the elders of Israel, whom
thou knowest to be the elders of the people, and officers over
them; and bring them unto the tent of meeting, that they may
stand there with thee.
And I will come down and speak with thee there; and I will
take of the spirit which is upon thee, and will put it upon them;**

123

**and they shall bear the burden of the people with thee, that
thou bear it not thyself alone.**

(11, 16—17)

But the new situation confronts him with another challenge and
more difficult test of his sincerity. How would he regard those newly
appointed to share the burden of office and the inspiration of
leadership that had been vouchsafed him? An episode, small in the
number of verses devoted to it, but highly significant in its
implications, is recounted in the context of the execution of the
Divine command to assemble the seventy elders:

וַיֵּצֵא מֹשֶׁה וַיְדַבֵּר אֶל־הָעָם אֵת דִּבְרֵי ה': וַיֶּאֱסֹף שִׁבְעִים אִישׁ מִזִּקְנֵי הָעָם
וַיַּעֲמֵד אֹתָם סְבִיבֹת הָאֹהֶל: וַיֵּרֶד ה' בֶּעָנָן וַיְדַבֵּר אֵלָיו וַיָּאצֶל מִן הָרוּחַ
אֲשֶׁר עָלָיו וַיִּתֵּן עַל־שִׁבְעִים אִישׁ הַזְּקֵנִים וַיְהִי כְּנוֹחַ עֲלֵיהֶם הָרוּחַ וַיִּתְנַבְּאוּ
וְלֹא יָסָפוּ: וַיִּשָּׁאֲרוּ שְׁנֵי־אֲנָשִׁים בַּמַּחֲנֶה שֵׁם הָאֶחָד אֶלְדָּד וְשֵׁם הַשֵּׁנִי מֵידָד
וַתָּנַח עֲלֵיהֶם הָרוּחַ וְהֵמָּה בַּכְּתֻבִים וְלֹא יָצְאוּ הָאֹהֱלָה וַיִּתְנַבְּאוּ בַּמַּחֲנֶה:
וַיָּרָץ הַנַּעַר וַיַּגֵּד לְמֹשֶׁה וַיֹּאמַר אֶלְדָּד וּמֵידָד מִתְנַבְּאִים בַּמַּחֲנֶה: וַיַּעַן
יְהוֹשֻׁעַ בִּן־נוּן מְשָׁרֵת מֹשֶׁה מִבְּחֻרָיו וַיֹּאמַר אֲדֹנִי מֹשֶׁה כְּלָאֵם: וַיֹּאמֶר לוֹ
מֹשֶׁה הַמְקַנֵּא אַתָּה לִי וּמִי יִתֵּן כָּל־עַם ה' נְבִיאִים כִּי־יִתֵּן ה' אֶת־רוּחוֹ
עֲלֵיהֶם:

**And Moses went out, and told the people the words of the
Lord; and he gathered seventy men of the elders of the people,
and set them round about the Tent. And the Lord came down
in the cloud, and spoke unto him, and took of the spirit that
was upon him, and put it upon the seventy elders; and it came
to pass, that when the spirit rested upon them, they
prophesied, but they did so no more. But there remained two
men in the camp, the name of one was Eldad, and the name of
the other Medad; and the spirit rested upon them; and they
were of them that were recorded, but had not gone out unto
the Tent; and they prophesied in the camp. And there ran a**

young man, and told Moses, and said: "Eldad and Medad are prophesying in the camp". And Joshua the son of Nun, the minister of Moses from his youth up, answered and said: "My lord Moses, shut them in". And Moses said unto him: "Art thou jealous for my sake? would that all the Lord's people were prophets, that the Lord would put His spirit upon them!"
(11, 24—29)

What had happened here? In particular what is meant by the story of the two men of whom it is stated that they were left behind in the camp and on whom the spirit rested:

... וְהֵמָּה בַּכְּתֻבִים וְלֹא יָצְאוּ הָאֹהֱלָה ...

... And they were of them that were recorded, but had not gone out unto the Tent ...

There is a difference of opinion in the Talmud regarding the interpretation of this passage and the implication of the phrase as applied to the two men.

"וישארו שני אנשים במחנה". יש אומרים: בקלפי נשתיירו, שבשעה שאמר לו הקב"ה למשה "אספה לי שבעים איש . . ." אמר משה: "כיצד אעשה?" אברור ששה ששה מכל שבט ושבט — נמצאו שנים יתירים. אברור חמשה חמשה מכל שבט — נמצאו עשרה חסרים. אברור ששה משבט זה וחמשה משבט זה — הריני מטיל קנאה בין השבטים". מה עשה? בירר ששה ששה והביא שבעים ושנים פתקין, על שבעים כבת "זקן" ושנים הניח חלק. בלל ונתן בקלפי. אמר להם: "בואו וטלו פתקיכם!" כל מי שעלה בידו "זקן" אמר: "כבר קדשך שמים", מי שעלה בידו חלק, אמר לו: "המקום לא חפץ בך, אני מה אעשה לך? . . ."

ר' שמעון אומר: במחנה נשתיירו. בשעה שאמר לו הקב"ו למשה "אספה לי שבעים איש . . ." אמרו אלדד ומידד: "אין אנו ראויים לאותה גדולה". אמר הקב"ו: "הואיל ומיעטתם עצמכם, הריני מוסיף גדולה על גדולתכם!" ומה גדולה הוסיף להם? שהנביאים כולם נתנבאו ופסקו — והם נתנבאו ולא פסקו!

"But there remained two men in the camp..." Some maintain that they were left at the ballot boxes. For when the Holy One blessed be He said to

Moses: "Gather unto me seventy men", Moses said: How should I go about it? If I select six from each tribe there will be two too many. If I select five from each tribe there will be ten short. If I select six from one tribe and five from another, I shall sow envy between the tribes. What did he do? He selected six from each tribe and brought seventy two slips. On seventy he wrote the word "elder" and two he left blank. He shuffled them and put them in the ballot box. He said to them: Come and pick out your slips. Whoever picked out a slip marked "elder" was told by Moses: Heaven has already consecrated you. Whoever picked out a blank was told by him: The Omnipotent does not desire you, so what I can do for you?

R. Shimon said: They were left in the camp. When the Holy One blessed be He said to Moses "Gather unto me seventy men". Eldad and Medad thereupon said: We are not worthy of this honour. Said the Holy One blessed be He: Since you belittle yourselves, behold I shall add honour unto your honour. What was the honour that he added to them? That all the prophets prophesied but did so no more, whilst they prophesied but did not cease.

(Sanhedrin 17a)

Most commentators accept the view of R. Shimon that they were left in the camp. Here is how Abravanel elaborates on the view of R. Shimon:

Our Sages have already related that Moses selected six elders from each tribe making seventy two in all, in order not to sow envy between the tribes. Eldad and Medad, knowing that God had only commanded the appointment of seventy, in their humility and so as not to shame the two who would not be chosen, remained, of their own free will, in the camp and did not come to the Tent of Meeting with the rest of the elders. The Holy One blessed be He does not withhold just reward from His creatures. These two worthies were rewarded with prophetic bounty for their action in not coming to the Tent of Meeting.

If then the Almighty rewarded them for their behaviour why did Joshua want to shut them up? Joshua thought that their inspired volubility smacked of prophetic license. Only those around the Tent of Meeting on whom Moses would bestow his spirit were authorised to prophesy. But Moses did not share his opinion. Note each word of his reply:

וַיֹּאמֶר לוֹ מֹשֶׁה הַמְקַנֵּא אַתָּה לִי
וּמִי יִתֵּן כָּל־עַם ה' נְבִיאִים
כִּי־יִתֵּן ה' אֶת־רוּחוֹ עֲלֵיהֶם:

And Moses said unto him:
"Art thou jealous for my sake?
would that all the Lord's people were prophets,
that the Lord would put His spirit upon them!"

(11, 29)

Isaac Arama explains to us how Moses withstood the test of jealousy:

> In my view the prophet's words, on this occasion, constitute a remarkable
> example of humility. Apart from not envying those who were his disciples
> and the work of his own hands (as alluded to in the Talmud Sanhedrin 105b:
> "A man envies everyone except his own son and disciple"), he earnestly
> desired that all the people of God should be prophets and that the Almighty
> should bestow His spirit upon them without him. Although this was a thing
> which every other man would be jealous of, he did not display jealousy.

There is just one more detail to note, seemingly insignificant, but, in reality, profoundly instructive. Buber draws attention to the fact that Moses in his reply does not use the same form of the verb which the lad reporting the matter did when he said: "Eldad and Medad are prophesying (מתנבאים) in the camp". Moses does not answer: "Would that the Lord's people would prophesy" but rather:

וּמִי יִתֵּן כָּל־עַם ה' נְבִיאִים

Would that all the Lord's people were prophets . . .

In other words, Moses does not ask, on their account, that the spirit of the Lord should rest on them momentarily, that they should be seized by a sudden prophetic frenzy, as it were, but rather that they should attain the permanent status of prophets, the status to which he had attained, involving direct communion with God, receiving the Divine orders directly from Him (See Buber's *Moses,* p. 150).

Moses here then expresses the same desire worded by the prophet Joel, in his vision of the latter days:

וְהָיָה אַחֲרֵי־כֵן
אֶשְׁפּוֹךְ אֶת־רוּחִי עַל־כָּל־בָּשָׂר
וְנִבְּאוּ בְּנֵיכֶם וּבְנֹתֵיכֶם
זִקְנֵיכֶם חֲלֹמוֹת יַחֲלֹמוּן
בַּחוּרֵיכֶם חֶזְיֹנוֹת יִרְאוּ:

And it shall come to pass afterward,
That I will pour out My spirit upon all flesh;
And your sons and your daughters shall prophesy,
Your old men shall dream dreams,
Your young men shall see visions.

(Joel 3, 1)

Hirsch explains the significance of Moses' words as follows:

> We are shown that there is no monopoly of spiritual leadership. The spiritual powers granted by God are not the privilege of any particular office or status. The lowliest of the nation shares with the highest the opportunity of being granted Divine inspiration.

Moses' failure to rise to the occasion, in the first place, when he spurned the mission and high office of leadership bestowed on him by God is transformed into victory. His unwillingness to bear the burden of leadership alone, led the Almighty to confront him with a severer test. Moses proved however that his heart was completely untouched by envy, and that he was ready to bestow his spirit elsewhere, and even regard without envy the granting by God of His spirit directly to whomsoever He chose.

128

BLACKENING THE BEAUTIFUL

וַתְּדַבֵּר מִרְיָם וְאַהֲרֹן בְּמֹשֶׁה עַל־אֹדוֹת הָאִשָּׁה הַכֻּשִׁית אֲשֶׁר לָקָח
כִּי אִשָּׁה כֻשִׁית לָקָח:

**And Miriam and Aaron spoke against Moses because of the
Ethiopian woman whom he had married:
For he had married an Ethiopian woman.**

(12, 1)

A very puzzling situation is described in our sidra. Miriam the
prophetess committed a sin and was severely punished for it. But her
offence is not explicitly stated. What was her sin? Commentators
differ regarding the exact content of Miriam's offensive utterance
which is not recorded for us in the Torah. The only thing which is
quite clear to all of them was that her utterance was an offensive one.
This is evident from the wording of the Torah where the phrase
"speak against" or disrespectfully of Moses is used. This is implied in
the Hebrew: *dabber be* ...

A distinction must be made however, as the translators do,
between the use of *be* in the first verse: *be-Moshe* — "And
Miriam ... spoke *against*" and in the second verse where it is
rendered by: "Hath the Lord indeed only spoken *by* Moses".

There, *be* is an adverb expressing agency "by means of" as the
construction of the sentence indicates.

Both verses have formed the basis on which commentators have
built their surmises as to the exact contents of Miriam's
utterances, utilising the hints contained in verse 1 and the actual
words of Miriam and Aaron in verse 2.

129

Here are the views of some of our commentators. First Rashi:

> "And Miriam and Aaron spoke against Moses" — She started the conversation. On this account the text mentions her first. How did Miriam know that Moses had separated himself from his wife? R. Nathan answered: Miriam was with Zipporah when it was told to Moses, "Eldad and Medad are prophesying in the camp" (11, 27). When Zipporah heard this, she exclaimed, Woe to the wives of these if they have anything to do with prophecy, for they will separate from their wives just as my husband has separated from me! It was from this that Miriam learnt about it, and she told it to Aaron. Now if Miriam who had no intention of disparaging him was punished thus severely, all the more so he who deliberately speaks disparagingly of his fellow!

This account is very similar to the words of Rabbi Shimon cited in *Avot Derabi Nathan*:

> Said Miriam: The Divine word came to me, yet I separated not from my husband. Said Aaron: The Divine word came to me, yet I separated not from my wife; yea, the Divine word came to our forefathers; yet they separated not from their wives. But since he is so overweening (i.e. prides himself on the prophetic heights he has attained and withdraws from society), he separated himself from his wife.

In other words, the target of Miriam and Aaron's criticism of Moses was his excessive seclusion, self-purification and withdrawal from domestic life. Joseph Kaspi, a medieval Jewish commentator sharply criticises this explanation:

> I am suprised at the ancients, who are so much more perfect than me, to the soles of whose feet I do not reach, how it ever occurred to them to explain a text in the Torah the very reverse of its written meaning, by substituting a word or adding phrases opposite in meaning. Thus we are all familiar with Onkelos' translation, and Maimonides has asserted that Onkelos the proselyte was a great sage (in his Guide for the Perplexed). What was Onkelos' warrant for rendering the Hebrew adjective *Kushit* (Black or Ethiopian) "beautiful", the very opposite of what was stated, black being opposite to white? Furthermore, what warrant had he for adding that "he had deserted or separated himself from the beautiful woman that he had taken?" If that had been the intention of the text why did it not say so in so

many words? Why was the exact reverse recorded? Moreover, who gave us licence to tamper so with the text? Where was Onkelos' authority to do such a thing? or the Sages of the Talmud or Ibn Ezra, all of whom agreed to this explanation? Why shouldn't we do the same thing, each one doing what is right in his own eyes? till we amend the text "Thou shalt love the Lord thy God" by interpreting it to mean, Heaven forbid, "thou shalt hate the Lord," or "thou shalt hate him whom the Lord loves?" Should you argue that Moses received instruction from Sinai and handed it down to Joshua, explaining our text in this manner, our original objection is sustained. Why was not this explanation plainly indicated in the wording, instead of employing terms meaning the exact reverse? Can the substitution of words meaning the exact reverse be said to constitute an explanation? An explanation is legitimate which elaborates on the plain meaning of a text, amplifying it, revealing its profundities, within the limits imposed by the wording, particularly when no contradiction of the obvious implication is involved. Examples of this are the rabbinic explanations of the texts "Ye shall not kindle fire in all your habitations" (Exodus 36, 3), and "Ye shall not eat upon the blood" (Leviticus 19, 26). Anything else must be considered deviation, erasure and unjustified tampering with the text . . . Why should we not say that the text "and you the Lord hath *taken*" (Deut. 4, 20) means "forsaken" or "if the household will be too small for partaking of a whole lamb, then he and his neighbour shall *take*" (Ex. 12, 2) means "his neighbour shall leave". Why is this explanation inferior to the one in our text?

As the Lord liveth this mode of interpretation agreed upon by all our ancient authorities in religion and faith is beyond me and I cannot accept it.

I therefore maintain that the text bears no other interpretation but that Moses took a Cushite or Ethiopian woman. What happened was as follows. After Moses married Zipporah he took another wife, an Ethiopian woman for reasons best known to himself and it is not our business to pry into his motives. He must certainly have known what he was about. We are not told when this event happened whether at the moment of its mention during their journey in the wilderness or before. Other events too are not recorded in the Torah. Since the matter had not been mentioned hitherto, and we should not be surprised at the statement "because of the Ethiopian woman he had married", the text adds the words "for he had taken (married) an Ethiopian woman" as if to say: Know that it is true that he had married an Ethiopian woman notwithstanding it had not hitherto been recorded in the Torah, and it was regarding her that they spoke . . . Had Moses separated himself completely from woman, adopting a life of celibacy as the ancients averred, Moses would not have been the most perfect man that had ever walked the world. Our Sages have stated that "whoever is greater than his fellow, his impulses are greater than his". His natural vitality and activities had not become weakened at eighty and even at a hundred. Abraham who was inferior to him begat a son at a hundred. Accordingly we cannot accept it that Moses became a celibate since he was no Franciscan, Augustine or Carmelite monk.

Whether we accept Rashi or Ibn Kaspi's explanation it remains difficult to understand why the Torah was not more explicit about the circumstances. Evidently the Torah did not wish to prohibit merely explicit gossip about our fellowmen in general and the spiritual leaders of our generation, in particular. It wished to prohibit any kind of talk or gossip disparaging our fellowman.

What is it that prompts us to speak disparagingly of our fellowman? Bahya the author of the ethical classic *Hovot Ha-levavot* "Duties of the Heart" analyses human motives in this context with deep psychological insight:

> Should one of your colleagues be superior to you in the service of God and his deeds be better than yours and he tries harder than you to draw nearer to Him, your evil inclination will seduce you and say to you: His greater efforts to achieve moral perfection only throw into relief your faults. If not for him you would be considered by everyone the most righteous in your generation. Stir up opinion against him, envy him and hate him! Find fault with him, and if you can spread an evil report of him, in order to lessen his reputation, do so! Then you reply thus to him (the evil inclination): How can I despise him whom the Lord loveth, condemn whom the Lord praiseth? It sufficeth not that I am slothful in carrying out His service like him, but I add insult to injury by hating him who serves Him. This is not the recompense that I am obliged to render to the Creator. On the contrary, I am commanded to love Him and honour those that honour Him, as it is written in the Psalms (15, 4): "He shall honour they that fear the Lord". You already know what happened to Miriam regarding the matter "And Miriam and Aaron spoke against Moses".

The desire to make the great man small, to blacken the reputation of the famous, to belittle the character of the good man and minimise any symptom of human greatness is prevalent among the small-minded, those a prey to human weaknesses, those who themselves fail to achieve any heights of greatness or heroism. It was such greatness of mind that was displayed by Moses on hearing that two other prophets were abroad, besides those on whom the spirit had been bestowed by Moses. He did not display anger but, on the contrary, exclaimed:

וּמִי יִתֵּן כָּל־עַם ה' נְבִיאִים כִּי־יִתֵּן ה' אֶת רוּחוֹ עֲלֵיהֶם:

Would that all the Lord's people were prophets and that the Lord would bestow His spirit on them!

(11, 29)

Questions for Further Study

1. Ibn Kaspi adds, in explanation of the sin of Miriam and Aaron, the following:

   Miriam and Aaron criticised Moses for taking another wife because they were ignorant of his motives in doing so. They said: "Hath the Lord indeed spoken only by Moses?" They did not take into account Moses' superior wisdom, and that what they could not understand was plain to Moses — the motives leading him to taking another wife and the secret of his wisdom in taking this step. They should have said: He knew what he was doing and if it is a vain thing, it is only so to us. But they equated themselves with him in general, because they were equal in prophecy, not regarding the fact that though they shared the prophetic gift, it was by no means on the same level but on a much inferior plane.

   What was the additional offence of Miriam and Aaron according to the above?

2. Abravanel asks what was the point of the Torah informing us that God "heard it". Do we not know that there is One above who sees and hears all? He answers that the words "And the Lord heard it" (Num. 12, 2 end) are also part of Miriam's and

Aaron's complaint — "... hath He not spoken also to us and the Lord has heard our words and if we speak unto Him and He hears us without this separation, why should Moses separate from his wife?"

In what way does Abravanel's explanation deviate from the accepted interpretation and how can you answer his question in another way?

FACT AND OPINION IN THE SPIES' REPORT

In the previous sidra we were treated to an account of the backslidings of the children of Israel, their lack of faith, their preference for "onions and garlic" rather than the sustenance afforded them by Divine Providence. Similarly, rather than be borne on "eagles' wings" to the Promised Land, they preferred to be guided by the report of spies and secret agents. God does not prevent man from going his own way, even if it be an evil one. Our Sages said: "Man is led on by the path he wishes to pursue".[1] This is what the Torah meant to imply when it stated:

שְׁלַח לְךָ אֲנָשִׁים

Send thou men

(13, 2)

אני איני מצוה, אם תרצה שלח; אני אמרתי להם שהיא טובה, שנאמר אעלה אתכם
מעני מצרים...אל ארץ זבת חלב ודבש

I (i.e. God) Myself have not given you such an order but if you want, send . . . I told them it was good, as it is written: "I shall bring you up from Egyptian affliction to a land flowing with milk and honey".

But the Israelites preferred to rely on the reports brought by their spies rather than on the Almighty's word. However, although man is given free will to follow his own devices, he is nevertheless afforded the opportunity to mend his ways and help to steer him clear of pitfalls. Consequently, the men chosen to spy out the land were those specially suited to the task, the elite of Israel, the leaders of the people. So we must understand the verse which states:

וַיִּשְׁלַח אֹתָם מֹשֶׁה . . . עַל־פִּי ה׳ כֻּלָּם אֲנָשִׁים רָאשֵׁי בְנֵי־יִשְׂרָאֵל הֵמָּה:

And Moses by the commandment of the Lord sent them... all those men who were heads of the children of Israel.

(13, 3)

The correct policy would have been for them to have relied on Divine Providence, but since they wished to send in advance men to scout the territory, God would not interfere with their design, but on the contrary, help them to carry it out, in the best manner possible. The initiative however was theirs, not His.

The questions to which Moses charged them to bring clear and precise answers are six in all:

וּרְאִיתֶם אֶת־הָאָרֶץ מַה־הִוא
וְאֶת־הָעָם הַיֹּשֵׁב עָלֶיהָ הֶחָזָק הוּא הֲרָפֶה הַמְעַט הוּא אִם־רָב:
וּמָה הָאָרֶץ אֲשֶׁר־הוּא יֹשֵׁב בָּהּ
הַטוֹבָה הִוא אִם רָעָה
וּמָה הֶעָרִים אֲשֶׁר הוּא יוֹשֵׁב בָּהֵנָּה
הַבְּמַחֲנִים אִם בְּמִבְצָרִים: וּמָה הָאָרֶץ הַשְּׁמֵנָה הִוא אִם־רָזָה
הֲיֵשׁ בָּהּ עֵץ אִם־אַיִן:

And see the land what it is;
and the people that dwelleth therein, whether they be strong or weak, few or many.
What the land is that they dwell in,
whether it be good or bad;
and what cities they be that they dwell in,
whether in tents or in strongholds;

136

**And what the land is, whether it be fat or lean,
whether it be wooded or not.**

(13, 18—20)

Their terms of reference were clearly defined and they came back and gave their answers. The spies unburdened themselves on three occasions. Let us study their words carefully.

Immediately on their return they reported as follows:

בָּאנוּ אֶל־הָאָרֶץ אֲשֶׁר שְׁלַחְתָּנוּ וְגַם זָבַת חָלָב וּדְבַשׁ הִוא וְזֶה פִּרְיָהּ:
אֶפֶס כִּי־עַז הָעָם הַיּשֵׁב בָּאָרֶץ וְהֶעָרִים בְּצֻרוֹת גְּדֹלֹת מְאֹד
וְגַם יְלִדֵי הָעֲנָק רָאִינוּ שָׁם: עֲמָלֵק יוֹשֵׁב בְּאֶרֶץ הַנֶּגֶב...

**We came unto the Land whither thou sent us, and it does
indeed flow with milk and honey and this is the fruit of it.
Nevertheless, the people be fierce that dwell in the land, and
the cities are very strongly fortified;
moreover, we saw the children of Anak there. Amalekites live
in the south...**

(13, 27—28)

The second occasion was in reply to Caleb's soothing words of encouragement:

עָלֹה נַעֲלֶה וְיָרַשְׁנוּ אֹתָהּ כִּי־יָכוֹל נוּכַל לָהּ:

**Let us go up at once and possess it; for we are well able to
overcome it** (v. 30).

To which they replied:

לֹא נוּכַל לַעֲלוֹת אֶל־הָעָם כִּי־חָזָק הוּא מִמֶּנּוּ:

137

We be not able to go up against the people; for they are stronger than we.

(13, 31)

On the third occasion they unburdened themselves not to Moses who sent them nor to their colleague, Caleb, but:

וַיֹּצִיאוּ דִּבַּת הָאָרֶץ אֲשֶׁר תָּרוּ אֹתָהּ אֶל בְּנֵי־יִשְׂרָאֵל לֵאמֹר
הָאָרֶץ אֲשֶׁר עָבַרְנוּ בָהּ לָתוּר אֹתָהּ אֶרֶץ אֹכֶלֶת יוֹשְׁבֶיהָ הִוא וְכָל־הָעָם
אֲשֶׁר־רָאִינוּ בְתוֹכָהּ אַנְשֵׁי מִדּוֹת:

They brought up an evil report of the land which they had explored unto the *children of Israel saying***:**
The land, which we have thoroughly explored, is a land that eateth up the inhabitants thereof, and all the people that we saw in it are men of great stature.

(ibid. 32)

What characteristics distinguish their words on these three different occasions and how do they combine to culminate in sin and rebellion against the Lord?

Superficially their words on the first occasion constitute nothing more than an objective report, answers to the question asked by Moses. They gave the desired information on the land, its inhabitants and their cities. Indeed, Ramban (Naḥmanides) asks what was wrong with their report. He makes the point that the spies only carried out their instructions. What was their crime in simply proffering the information that "the people who live there are a fierce lot". Had they been sent out to bring back false reports?

However, if we examine their words closely, we shall notice that they were not really so objective. A subjective tinge can be detected in their reply, when they contended that all the good points of the Promised Land would avail them nothing, because the inhabitants were too powerful and their strongholds too formidable.

138

This is indeed how one of our Spanish commentators, Isaac Arama interprets their behaviour in his classic work *Akedat Yizhak*. Their crime, he avers, lay in the fact that instead of acting as neutral observers contenting themselves with the facts, they gave their opinions on the matter.

Isaac Arama brings home his point by the following parable —

> It can be compared to a man who says to his agent: Go to the warehouse and have a look at a *tallit* the merchant has in stock, examine it carefully for the quality of the wool and linen, for size, appearance and price and let me know, as I wish to purchase it. If the agent returns and says: I had a look at it and the wool is pure, it is long and wide, greenish and reddish in colour and the price a hundred gold pieces, he has carried out his mission correctly. But if he said: I had a look at it, the wool is pure, it is long and wide, but it is reddish and greenish in colour and it is very dearly priced at 100 gold pieces, then he has exceeded the bounds of his mission and become instead an adviser. This is as a result of inserting the qualifying word "but".

Similarly the spies qualified their description of the conditions they saw by the significant word: "nevertheless",[2] the people are fierce. In their report there was already a nuance of their own subjective feelings, regarding the possibilities of conquering the land which came out in the open after Caleb's spirited reply to their mutiny, inspired by their tendentious report:

לֹא נוּכַל לַעֲלוֹת אֶל הָעָם כִּי חָזָק הוּא מִמֶּנּוּ

We be not able to go up against the people for they are stronger *than we.*

(13, 31)

Here it is interesting to note the differing midrashic and literal approaches to the interpretation of the word *mimenu,* which in Hebrew can refer to either the first person plural or third person singular, either "than we" or "than him".

139

The plain meaning of the text is obviously "they are stronger than we" (*mimenu*). We cannot conquer the inhabitants of the land because "they are stronger than we". However, the Midrash cited by Rashi states: "they meant it in reference to Him that is Above". In other words, they implied that the people of the land were stronger than Him, than God, interpreting *mimenu* in the third person.

What prompted the Midrash to adopt such an explanation which seems so far removed from the plain meaning of the text? The Midrash, apparently, aims to bring out not merely what was on their lips, but at probing deeper and unfolding their inner thoughts. In verse 29, they had already made the point that their cities were heavily fortified and that the people were strong, a fact that Caleb had not denied. He merely encouraged the people, by telling them that in spite of these obstacles, they were well able to overcome them. Caleb does not explain how they were going to achieve this and by whose aid; but, presumably, implies that they should rely on Divine help. It was this trust in God which the spies were repudiating. They said: "For they are stronger than we", but repudiation of Divine Providence was implicit in their behaviour. What they really meant was, therefore, "they are stronger than Him, than God" — in whom Moses and Aaron, Caleb and Joshua ultimately placed their confidence.

As is often the case, the homiletical and literal meaning of the text do not contradict, but rather complement each other, revealing different levels and shades of meaning.

On the third occasion, the spies make no bones about the matter, and unrestrainedly reveal their feelings, casting to the winds all pretence of objectivity!

וַיֹּצִיאוּ דִּבַּת הָאָרֶץ אֲשֶׁר תָּרוּ אֹתָהּ אֶל בְּנֵי־יִשְׂרָאֵל לֵאמֹר
הָאָרֶץ אֲשֶׁר עָבַרְנוּ בָהּ לָתוּר אֹתָהּ אֶרֶץ אֹכֶלֶת יוֹשְׁבֶיהָ הִוא וְכָל־הָעָם
אֲשֶׁר־רָאִינוּ בְתוֹכָהּ אַנְשֵׁי מִדּוֹת:

They brought up an evil report of the land which they had explored unto the children of Israel saying,
The land, which we have thoroughly explored, is a land that eateth up the inhabitants thereof;
and all the people that we saw in it are men of a great stature.

(13, 32)

Here we are faced by an obvious contradiction in their statement. If the land consumed its inhabitants, how did there exist men of great stature? Two explanations are advanced by commentators, one by Sforno, who suggests that what they meant was, that the land and climate were so detrimental to health, that only the fittest, the strongest could survive, only giants and men of extraordinarily physical resistance could live, after the manner of natural selection.

Other commentators, however, explain that their report was a mixture of fact and fiction. Like all propagandists aiming at giving a false and distorted picture of events, they were not aware of the tendentiousness of the picture they painted or of the contradictions it contained.

As Isaac Arama points out it was not just a case of cowardice. They had actually rejected the Promised Land, as stated in 14, 31:

וְטַפְּכֶם אֲשֶׁר אֲמַרְתֶּם לָבַז יִהְיֶה וְהֵבֵיאתִי אֹתָם וְיָדְעוּ אֶת־הָאָרֶץ אֲשֶׁר
מְאַסְתֶּם בָּהּ׃

But your little ones which ye said would be a prey, them will I bring in, and they shall know the land *which ye have rejected.*

Arama concludes:

It is this rejection of Eretz Israel which is responsible for our tribulations and exile, for our being a reproach to our neighbours and a scorn and derision unto them that are round about us. We shall never recover our spiritual and physical equilibrium until we return to it.

Questions for Further Study

1. Our Sages enunciated in the Midrash the principle: "A lie to succeed must contain a grain of truth".

   To which verse in the sidra can this principle be applied?

2. The spies said: "We were as grasshoppers in our eyes and so we were in their sight!" How did the spies know how they appeared in the sight of the inhabitants of the land?

3. On the passage: "And all the congregation lifted up their voice, and cried; and all the people wept that night" (Numbers 14, 1) our Sages in the Talmud made the following comment:

   אתם בכיתם בכייה של חנם ואני קובע לכם בכייה לדורות.

   The Holy One blessed be He said unto them: Ye wept without cause: I shall give you a lasting cause for weeping.

   (Ta'anit 29a)

   To which weeping does this dictum of our Sages allude?

NOTES

1. בדרך שאדם רוצה לילך מוליכין אותו.
2. אפס.

A REASON TO WEEP

וַתִּשָּׂא כָּל־הָעֵדָה וַיִּתְּנוּ אֶת־קוֹלָם
וַיִּבְכּוּ הָעָם בַּלַּיְלָה הַהוּא:

And all the congregation lifted up their voice, and cried; and the people wept that night.

(14, 1)

In the previous chapter we focussed on the offence of the spies. On this occasion we shall devote our attention to the sin of the children of Israel for which they were punished by dying in the wilderness. After Moses' intercession in which he succeeded in averting the decree of complete destruction, it is stated:

בַּמִּדְבָּר הַזֶּה יִפְּלוּ פִגְרֵיכֶם וְכָל־פְּקֻדֵיכֶם לְכָל־מִסְפַּרְכֶם מִבֶּן עֶשְׂרִים שָׁנָה
וָמָעְלָה . . .

Your carcasses shall fall in this wilderness, and all that were numbered of you, according to your whole number, from twenty years old and upward . . .

(Ibid. 29)

Rashi, following the Sages in the Talmud, maintains that Israel sinned through the very act of sending the spies. The generation that had been brought out of Egypt with a strong hand and outstretched arm through direct Divine intervention, which journeyed by the mouth of the Lord and encamped by the mouth of the Lord, was not

143

inspired with implicit faith and trust in the Almighty. Instead they preferred to put their trust in spies to reconnoitre the land, despite the fact that they had been given the cloud by day and the pillar of fire by night to lead them.

According to this view, the sin lay in the rebellious conduct that had prompted the people to ask that spies be sent. This is borne out by the fact that Scripture dwells on the incidents that *preceded* the sending of the spies and the assembling of the people against Moses not in this sidra, which merely gives an historical account, but in Deuteronomy, where Moses is striving to teach the people the moral lesson of their history.

Naḥmanides however prefers another explanation:

> The Israelites wished to adopt orthodox military strategy in sending men to reconnoitre the highways and approaches to the towns in order, on their return, to be able to lead the army. Cf. (Judges 1, 24): "Show us, we pray thee, the entrance into the city . . ." and give advice on the strategy of conquering the land. This is stated explicitly: "And bring us back word of the way by which we must go up, and the cities unto which we shall come" (Deuteronomy 1, 22). This is indeed sound advice for all conquerors. Moses himself followed it, as it is stated (Numbers 21, 32): "And Moses sent to spy out Jazer . . ." Joshua son of Nun did the same (Joshua 2). For this reason Moses approved of the idea, since the Torah does not intend man to depend on miracles, but demands that those who fight, help themselves, keeping guard and laying ambush. Cf. the battle of Ai (Joshua 8) which was in accordance with the commandment of the Lord, as also in many other cases.

Naḥmanides thus did not consider that the action of the people in demanding spies betrayed any lack of trust in the Almighty. There was no contradiction between the Almighty's supernatural leadership of the people in the wilderness and the taking of the necessary mortal measures to prepare for war. Their sin therefore lay in what was related *after* the return of the spies:

וַתִּשָּׂא כָּל הָעֵדָה וַיִּתְּנוּ אֶת־קוֹלָם
וַיִּבְכּוּ הָעָם בַּלַּיְלָה הַהוּא: וַיִּלֹּנוּ עַל־מֹשֶׁה וְעַל אַהֲרֹן כֹּל בְּנֵי יִשְׂרָאֵל

וַיֹּאמְרוּ אֲלֵהֶם כָּל־הָעֵדָה
לוּ מַתְנוּ בְּאֶרֶץ מִצְרַיִם אוֹ בַּמִּדְבָּר הַזֶּה לוּ־מָתְנוּ:
וְלָמָה ה' מֵבִיא אֹתָנוּ אֶל־הָאָרֶץ הַזֹּאת לִנְפֹּל בַּחֶרֶב
נָשֵׁינוּ וְטַפֵּנוּ יִהְיוּ לָבַז
הֲלוֹא טוֹב לָנוּ שׁוּב מִצְרָיְמָה:
וַיֹּאמְרוּ אִישׁ אֶל־אָחִיו נִתְּנָה רֹאשׁ וְנָשׁוּבָה מִצְרָיְמָה:

**And all the congregation lifted up their voice, and cried;
and the people wept that night.
And all the children of Israel murmured against Moses and
against Aaron;
and the whole congregation said unto them:
Would that we had died in the land of Egypt! or would we had
died in the wilderness.
And wherefore doth the Lord bring us unto this land, to fall by
the sword?
Our wives and our little ones will be a prey;
were it not better for us to return into Egypt?
And they said one to another:
Let us make a captain, and let us return into Egypt.**

(14, 1—4)

Their sin is alluded to in the above passage particularly in its last
verse. Two offences can be detected in the people's grumblings, both
of which are noted by Isaac Arama in his *Akedat Yizhak*:

They rejected the Land of Divine promise. It is this rejection of the land
which has been our undoing throughout the ages. On account of it, we were
exiled from our country, divorced from our soil, and became a reproach to
our neighbours, a scorning and derision to those round about us. There is
absolutely no other way of restoring our integrity than by returning unto it.

Isaac Arama elaborates further on their sin as follows:

145

What was the reason for the terrible wrath of the Almighty in giving forth this irrevocable decree? What should it matter to the Holy One blessed be He that they rejected a goodly land, a land flowing with milk and honey? Surely all these good things are only transitory! But the truth is that it was not these earthly things that they rejected but they forsook the Lord, they despised the Holy One of Israel who granted them life and its joys, circumscribed by the precepts of His law ... They retreated saying "We cannot go up" implying that they did not desire to scale the heights of *spiritual* perfection, the ladder to which was the Holy Land itself, but preferred to choose a captain and go back to Egypt, descending to an impure land. "Why did God bring us to that land that we should fall by the sword in occupying a land for our wives and young ones. Let Him rather leave us in this wilderness. If the lives of our wives and children are thereby endangered, we prefer that, rather than to die in the fight to conquer habitations not our own. If we weigh up all the issues involved, it becomes transparent that it is better to go back to Egypt, the bondage being a lesser evil".

In other words, their sin lay in making their own selfish calculation of the material prospects ahead of them. They were afraid of the responsibilities of freedom, the dangers involved in securing it. Far better it was to wander in the wilderness and even to return to Egyptian bondage. The slave has no responsibility and his fate is decided by others. They spurned the opportunity to lead their own lives, foster their own economy and govern themselves. The congregation which wept on that night set the pattern for future generations, characterized by the search for security, the flight from responsibility and independence. Their motto was, "let us go back to our place of bondage". This formula has been echoed even in our own day, and on it our Sages made the following comment:

הם בכו בכייה של חינם, ואני אקבע להם בכייה לדורות.

They wept for no reason, but I shall give them a reason to weep for generations.

146

BACK TO EGYPT!

The spies knew their job well, first singing the praises of the Promised Land, aware that a lie to succeed must have a modicum of truth in it, to give it an appearance of objectivity. They knew how to pass from an apparently objective report (13,27—29) to a subjective expression of opinion (verse 31).[1] They knew what could be said to Moses and Aaron, in their presence, and what had to be voiced behind their back, in the tents of Israel. Then all pretence of objectivity could be set aside; they could give full rein to their imagination:

וַיּוֹצִיאוּ דִּבַּת הָאָרֶץ אֲשֶׁר תָּרוּ אֹתָהּ אֶל־בְּנֵי יִשְׂרָאֵל לֵאמֹר
הָאָרֶץ אֲשֶׁר עָבַרְנוּ בָהּ לָתוּר אֹתָהּ אֶרֶץ אֹכֶלֶת יוֹשְׁבֶיהָ הִוא
וְכָל־הָעָם אֲשֶׁר־רָאִינוּ בְתוֹכָהּ אַנְשֵׁי מִדּוֹת:
וְשָׁם רָאִינוּ אֶת־הַנְּפִילִים . . . וַנְּהִי בְעֵינֵינוּ כַּחֲגָבִים וְכֵן הָיִינוּ בְּעֵינֵיהֶם:

And they spread an evil report of the Land which they had explored *unto the children of Israel, saying,*
The land which we have thoroughly explored, is a land that eateth up the inhabitants thereof;
and all the people we saw in it are men of great stature.
There we saw the Nephilim...
and we were in our sight as grasshoppers
and so we were in theirs.

(13, 32—33)

147

That they continued with their incitement behind Moses' back is apparent from the text recapitulating the same incident in Deuteronomy 1, 27: "They murmured in their tents". The murmurers succeeded in their evil intent and their audience grumbled, rebelled and wept:

לוּ־מַתְנוּ בְּאֶרֶץ מִצְרַיִם

אוֹ בַּמִּדְבָּר הַזֶּה לוּ־מָתְנוּ:

וְלָמָה ה' מֵבִיא אֹתָנוּ אֶל הָאָרֶץ הַזֹּאת לִנְפֹּל בַּחֶרֶב

נָשֵׁינוּ וְטַפֵּנוּ יִהְיוּ לָבַז

הֲלוֹא טוֹב לָנוּ שׁוּב מִצְרָיְמָה:

וַיֹּאמְרוּ אִישׁ אֶל־אָחִיו

נִתְּנָה רֹאשׁ וְנָשׁוּבָה מִצְרָיְמָה:

Would that we had died in the land of Egypt!
or would we had died in the wilderness!
And wherefore doth the Lord bring us unto this land, to fall by the sword?
Our wives and our little ones will be a prey;
were it not better for us to return to Egypt.
And they said one to another,
Let us appoint a leader, and let us return to Egypt.

(14, 2—4)

Their murmuring passed through two stages. First (vv. 2—3) regret for the past, for the Exodus, the signs and wonders, the division of the sea, the Divine revelation, the manna and quail, the sweetening of the bitter water, drawing of water from the rock, the Sabbath, the giving of the Law — all these had not been worth it. The land which the Lord had promised to give them and which even the spies had termed a land flowing with milk and honey was referred to as "this land" (13, 27), distinguished for its death-dealing qualities. But no practical alternative had as yet emerged for the future, merely

148

a repudiation of the past. The next stage reflects progress, "They said one to the other" — a kind of mutual incitement. What no one had dared to utter publicly, was whispered in each other's ears:

נִתְּנָה רֹאשׁ וְנָשׁוּבָה מִצְרָיְמָה:

Let us appoint a leader and let us return to Egypt.

(14, 4)

At last we have an alternative plan of action, not merely grumblings and bitterness. Rashi gives two explanations of the phrase *nitnah rosh* "let us appoint a leader". He gives first the literal explanation of: "Let us make a king over us" and then refers to the Midrashic explanation that it is "an expression of idol worship". What clue in the text affords ground for the latter explanation? Why should their fear of the dangers of conquering the land, their wish to return to Egypt be interpreted to imply idolatry, the gravest of sins?

Naḥmanides comes to our help in his comment on our text in connection with another passage in the sidra. This passage (15, 22, 31) describes the offerings brought by the inadvertent offender:

וְכִי תִשְׁגּוּ וְלֹא תַעֲשׂוּ אֵת כָּל־הַמִּצְוֹת הָאֵלֶּה אֲשֶׁר־דִּבֶּר ה' אֶל מֹשֶׁה:
אֵת כָּל־אֲשֶׁר צִוָּה ה' אֲלֵיכֶם בְּיַד־מֹשֶׁה
מִן־הַיּוֹם אֲשֶׁר צִוָּה ה' וָהָלְאָה לְדֹרֹתֵיכֶם:
וְהָיָה אִם מֵעֵינֵי הָעֵדָה נֶעֶשְׂתָה לִשְׁגָגָה וְעָשׂוּ כָל הָעֵדָה פַּר בֶּן־בָּקָר אֶחָד
לְעֹלָה לְרֵיחַ נִיחֹחַ לה' וּמִנְחָתוֹ וְנִסְכּוֹ כַּמִּשְׁפָּט וּשְׂעִיר עִזִּים אֶחָד לְחַטָּת:
וְכִפֶּר הַכֹּהֵן . . . וְנִסְלַח לְכָל עֲדַת בְּנֵי יִשְׂרָאֵל וְלַגֵּר הַגָּר בְּתוֹכָם כִּי לְכָל
הָעָם בִּשְׁגָגָה:
וְאִם־נֶפֶשׁ אַחַת תֶּחֱטָא בִשְׁגָגָה וְהִקְרִיבָה . . .
וְהַנֶּפֶשׁ אֲשֶׁר תַּעֲשֶׂה בְּיָד רָמָה מִן הָאֶזְרָח וּמִן־הַגֵּר, אֶת־ה' הוּא מְגַדֵּף
וְנִכְרְתָה הַנֶּפֶשׁ הַהִוא מִקֶּרֶב עַמָּהּ: כִּי דְבַר־ה' בָּזָה, וְאֶת מִצְוָתוֹ הֵפַר, הִכָּרֵת
תִּכָּרֵת הַנֶּפֶשׁ הַהִוא, עֲוֹנָה בָהּ:

And when ye shall err, and fail to observe all these commandments, which the Lord hath spoken unto Moses,
even all that the Lord hath commanded you by the hand of Moses,
from the day that the Lord gave commandment, and onward throughout your generations;
then it shall be, if it be done in error by the congregation, it being hid from their eyes, that all the congregation shall offer one young bullock for a burnt-offering, for a sweet savour unto the Lord — with the meal-offering thereof, and the drink-offering thereof, according to the ordinance, and one he-goat for a sin offering.
And the priest shall make atonement . . .
and all the congregation . . . shall be forgiven; and the stranger that sojourneth among them, for in respect of all the people it was an error.
And if one person sin through error then he shall offer . . . But the soul that doeth aught with a high hand, whether he be homeborn or a stranger,
the same blasphemeth the Lord; and that soul shall be cut off from among his people.
Because he hath despised the word of the Lord and hath broken his commandment,
that soul shall be utterly cut off, his iniquity shall be upon him.

(15, 22—31)

This passage is full of difficulties, all of which Naḥmanides answers. First, what is a passage dealing with sacrifices doing in our sidra dealing with the spies? The proper context would be Leviticus. Second, the offering of the inadvertent sinner is dealt with in Leviticus. What is added in this passage? Let us compare both passages:

150

Numbers 15	Leviticus 4
(22) And when ye shall err	(13) And if the whole congregation of Israel err, the thing being hid from the eyes
and not observe all these commandments, which the Lord hath spoken unto Moses.	of the assembly, and do any of the things which the Lord hath commanded not to be done, and are guilty
(23) Even all that the Lord hath commanded you by the hand of Moses, from the day that the Lord gave commandment, and onward throughout your generations (24) then it shall be, if it be done in error by the congregation, it being hid from their eyes,	
that all the congregation shall offer *one young bullock for a burnt-offering* and a he-goat for a *sin-offering.*	then the assembly shall offer *a young bullock for a sin-offering.*

One important difference between the two texts may be noticed. Leviticus speaks of he who errs with respect to "any of the things the Lord hath commanded not to be done", of one who transgresses a negative precept (the punishment for deliberate violation of which is excision) in error — he brings a sin-offering for his atonement. Our text speaks of one who leaves undone, but inadvertently, "all these commandments which the Lord hath spoken unto Moses", which is rather a puzzling statement. Has one who neglects *all* the commandments to bring a sin-offering? Naḥmanides corrects us in this respect and shows that the text cannot mean that one who fails to perform *all* the commandments of the Torah has to bring an

151

offering just the same as the offender with respect of but one commandment. He shows that the text really speaks of one who transgresses any one negative precept and cites this text in his support: "If any one shall sin through error in any of the things which the Lord hath commanded not to be done". The "all" should be rendered "any of".

Nahmanides then explains the distinction between the two texts. The sacrifice in respect of the error of the congregation is different from that in Leviticus. In the latter, the offender has but to bring a bullock for a sin-offering whereas here he has to bring a bullock for a burnt-offering and a he-goat for a sin-offering. Our Sages therefore interpreted the latter to refer to an offering brought in respect of inadvertent idolatry.

> The Torah states: "And when ye shall err and not observe all these commandments". Which commandment is equal in weight to *all* the commandments? It can only be idol worship.

That explains the deviation in our text from the usual wording. "All the commandments" refers to a sin which is tantamount to repudiation of the whole Torah — idolatry. But the question remains how is it possible for a person to repudiate the whole Torah in error, inadvertently? Nahmanides states:

> For example one who joins another people, accepts their way of life and does not desire to remain a part of the Jewish people — all this being done in error.

But again, we may wonder how such an act of disassociation could be done in error? There can be nothing more deliberate than a repudiation of one's nationality and peoplehood. Nahmanides however proceeds to explain how it could happen in terms of contemporary history. It could happen with respect to an individual, in the case of a Jew who had been brought up from childhood by heathens; many such children had been secreted in non-Jewish homes to save them from death. Others had been brought up in Jewish homes but in ones divorced from Jewish tradition. In this manner they lead a life quite inadvertently violating all the precepts of Judaism. They cannot be blamed since they had no chance of knowing what was required of them. This can be true both of individuals and a whole congregation. Naḥmanides cites the case of the Israelites in the times of Jeroboam who had become estranged from Judaism by the king's propagation of idolatry or the Jews in the days of Ezra, when it is stated that the people read the Torah and found written therein that the children of Israel dwelt in booths in the seventh month (Nehemiah 8, 13). Evidently there were many people who had completely forgotten the cardinal precepts of Judaism. Similarly, in our day, whole Jewish communities have forgotten their traditions as a result of divorcement from Jewish learning and their remoteness from centres of scholarship.

Naḥmanides brings yet another example of inadvertent divorcement from the practices of Judaism. He cites the elders who came to Ezekiel as elaborated in the Midrash Tanḥuma to the text Deuteronomy 29, 13—14: "Not with you alone have I made this covenant but with those who are here with us standing today before the Lord our God and with those who are not here with us today". Here are the words of the Midrash (see also Ezekiel 20, 1 ff.):

So you find when they sought to release themselves from the yoke of His oath in the days of Ezekiel (after they were told of the destruction of the Temple). What is written there? "There came men of the elders of Israel to seek the Lord". What did they say to him? Son of man, a priest who acquires a slave, may the latter partake of *terumah*? He answered: He may. They further asked: If the priest disposes of the slave to an Israelite, has he not left his possession? He answered them: He has. They retorted: We too have already left the possession of the Holy One blessed be He; we will be like all the nations of the world. Ezekiel answered them: "And that which cometh into your mind shall not be at all; in that ye say: We will be as the nations, as the families of the countries, to serve wood and stone. As I liveth, saith the Lord God, surely with an outstretched arm, and with fury poured out, will I be king over you". He said to them: As long as he has not sold him (i.e. the priest his slave) he remains in his possession. You too have not been sold . . . for I shall not go back on the oath I swore to their fathers: "Not with you alone have I made this covenant" but with the generations destined to come forth who were also present at that moment, as it is written: "But with those who are here with us standing today before the Lord our God and with those who are not here with us today".

Naḥmanides thus regards those who imagine that by accepting an alien way of life and joining another people and faith that they have absolved themselves from the obligation to observe the precepts of Judaism — inadvertent sinners. The text therefore singles out one error which is tantamount of violating all the commandments of the Torah, and that is the repudiation of God and acceptance of idol worship, of another faith and way of life.

The reason why the passage on the sacrifices to be offered up for such inadvertent alienation from Judaism is included in our sidra becomes apparent. Naḥmanides observes that the spies too were guilty of this error when they proclaimed: "Let us appoint a (new) leader, and let us return to Egypt" by which they implied, repudiation of the Torah and the whole of Judaism and a reversion to their heathen way of life in Egypt. The passage therefore assures us that the embracing of idolatry, if prompted by error, is forgivable, can be atoned for. "But the soul that doeth aught with a high hand . . . shall be utterly cut off".

We see now the logic of the interpretation of our Sages, when they understood the aspiration of the people to return to Egypt in the sense of an abandonment of Judaism, in the sense of idolatry. The deification of our selfish desires, the repudiation of a will outside ourselves is idolatry too. The spurning of the miracles of their past, of the pillar of cloud, of the Promised Land, the preference for human slavery to freedom under the constitution of the Torah spelt nothing less than idolatry. Isaac Arama too in his *Akedat Yizḥak* equates the spurning of the Promised Land with idolatry. Why should the Almighty care, he asks, if the Israelites rejected the land flowing with milk and honey? Why was the sin of the spies and people in this connection regarded as such a terrible one?

> But the truth of the matter is that it wasn't the Land they were rejecting, but God Himself; they were retreating from the heights of spiritual glory. "We cannot go up". They did not desire to possess the land of the living. "Let us appoint a new leader, and let us return into Egypt", they said, for that was a descent into an impure land.

Questions for Further Study

1. *"And all the congregation* lifted up their voice and the people wept that night" — the heads of the Sanhedrin (Rashi).

(a) What prompted Rashi to give this explanation?

(b) Why did Rashi not make the same point in Ex. 12, 3 where the same word "congregation" is used and why did he again comment that the Sanhedrin is meant in the text in Leviticus 4, 13?

2. "And Moses and Aaron fell on their faces" (14, 5). When they saw the people were ready to throw off the yoke of the Lord and His prophet, they understood that if they spoke, the people would silence them and not listen at all to their words. They therefore fell on their faces as a request for permission to speak, so that they should not be interrupted in their address. They asked a favour to be given a hearing. But when Joshua and Caleb saw Moses and Aaron humiliating themselves before the people, the fire of the Lord burned within them, and they rent their garments and did not let them speak but spoke on their behalf.

(S.D. Luzzatto)

(a) What difficulties does Luzzatto wish to solve?

(b) Can you suggest an alternative reason for their falling on their faces?

(c) Compare: "And Moses heard and fell on his face" (Num. 16, 4); "And Moses and Aaron came before the assembly at the

155

entrance of the tent of meeting and fell on their faces" (Num. 20, 6).

Is the falling on their faces mentioned in either of the above passages to be compared with the one in our context or are they different?

NOTE

[1] See Shelaḥ 1, p. 136 for more detailed treatment.

MOSES' INTERCESSION AFTER THE
SIN OF THE SPIES

וְאָמְרוּ הַגּוֹיִם אֲשֶׁר־שָׁמְעוּ אֶת־שִׁמְעֲךָ לֵאמֹר:
מִבִּלְתִּי יְכֹלֶת ה' לְהָבִיא אֶת־הָעָם הַזֶּה אֶל־הָאָרֶץ . . .
וַיִּשְׁחָטֵם בַּמִּדְבָּר:

Then the nations will speak saying,
Because the Lord was not able to bring this people unto the land . . .
Therefore hath He slain them in the wilderness.

(14, 15—16)

A similar intercession, that of Moses after the sin of the Golden
Calf is recalled in Psalms 106, 23:

וַיֹּאמֶר לְהַשְׁמִידָם
לוּלֵי מֹשֶׁה בְחִירוֹ עָמַד בַּפֶּרֶץ לְפָנָיו
לְהָשִׁיב חֲמָתוֹ מֵהַשְׁחִית:

Therefore he said that he would destroy them,
had not Moses His chosen stood before him in the breach,
to turn away His wrath, lest He should destroy them.

Moses found himself very frequently in this position of interceding
on behalf of his people to avert the dread decree of divine wrath. In
our sidra he again had to plead for his people after the Almighty had
threatened:

157

אַכֶּנּוּ בַדֶּבֶר וְאוֹרִשֶׁנּוּ וְאֶעֱשֶׂה אֹתְךָ לְגוֹי־גָּדוֹל וְעָצוּם מִמֶּנּוּ :

I will strike them with the pestilence, and disinherit them, and will make of thee a nation greater and mightier than they.
(14, 12)

Let us compare side by side the two prayers of intercession made by Moses, the one subsequent to the sin of the golden calf, the other, in our sidra, to avert the punishment for their little faith and grumblings after the spies had brought their evil report:

Exodus 32, 11—13	Numbers 14, 13—19
And Moses besought the Lord his God and said,	And Moses said unto the Lord, Then the Egyptians shall hear that thou broughtest up this people in thy might from among them;
Lord, why doth thy wrath wax hot against thy people, which thou hast brought out of the land of Egypt with great power, and with a mighty hand? Wherefore should the Egyptians speak, and say, For mischief did he bring them out, to slay them in the mountains, and to consume them from the face of the earth?	And they will tell it to the inhabitants of this land: For they have heard that thou Lord art among this people, that thou Lord art seen face to face, and that thy cloud standeth over them, and that thou goest before them, by day time in a pillar of a cloud, and in a pillar of fire by night. Now if thou shalt kill all this people as one man, then the nations which have heard the fame of thee will speak, saying, Because the Lord was not able to bring this people into the land

158

which he sware unto them, therefore he hath slain them in the wilderness.

And now, I beseech thee, let the power of my Lord be great, according as thou hast spoken saying,

The Lord is longsuffering, and of great mercy, forgiving iniquity and transgression, and by no means clearing the guilty, visiting the iniquity of the fathers upon the children unto the third and fourth generation. Pardon, I beseech thee, the iniquity of this people according unto the greatness of thy mercy and as thou hast forgiven this people from Egypt even until now.

Turn from thy fierce wrath, and repent of this evil against thy people.

Remember Abraham, Isaac, and Israel, thy servants, to whom thou didst swear by thine own self, and saidst unto them, I will multiply your seed as the stars of heaven, and all this land that I have spoken of will I give unto your seed, and they shall inherit it for ever.

Moses advanced three arguments to influence the Almight to show mercy to the people after they had sinned with the Calf. First, he called on the Almighty's proverbial love for His people "why doth Thy wrath wax hot against Thy people?"

The second argument which Moses employs is that of *ḥillul ha-shem* — the bringing of the Divine Name into disrepute among the nations of the world.

לָמָּה יֹאמְרוּ מִצְרַיִם לֵאמֹר
בְּרָעָה הוֹצִיאָם לַהֲרֹג אֹתָם בֶּהָרִים

159

Wherefore should the Egyptians speak and say,
For mischief did He bring them out to slay them in the
mountains?

(Ex. 32, 12)

The third plea advanced by Moses was the merit of the Patriarchs
and the covenant made with them.

In contrast to this, the long intercession in our sidra contains only
one single argument — that of bringing the name of the Lord into
disrepute "the Egyptians will hear and say because the Lord was not
able". This same argument is found in Joshua's dialogue with the
Almighty after Israel had suffered their first defeat in the Promised
Land:

וּמַה תַּעֲשֶׂה לְשִׁמְךָ הַגָּדוֹל

What wilt Thou do for the sake of Thy great name.

(Joshua 7, 9)

The difference between the argument contained in Moses'
intercessions may be explained in the light of the divergent situations
to which they applied. After the Jewish people had proved so
faithless preferring the tendentious reports of the spies, despite all the
miracles they had been granted in Egypt and the wilderness, Moses
had no more the heart to call them "Thy people" but merely refers to
them by the distant appellation of "this people". In the face of their
ingratitude and lack of faith only one argument remained for him. He
could not plead that they or the merit of their fathers should be taken
into consideration but only that God should have regard, as it were,
for the repute of His name, that the nations should not say that the
Lord is unable to bring the people to the land.

But even this argument seems to have a flaw in it which is pointed
out by Arama in his Akedat Yiẓḥak:

"Wherefore should the Egyptians say" — is no plea. Should then justice be perverted for the sake of fools?

Abravanel expands on this theme:

How could Moses have conceived that the Judge of all the earth should refrain from administering strict justice for fear of what the Egyptians in their foolishness would argue? Surely the Holy One blessed be He has no fear of the multitudes of peoples. What does it profit Him whether the Egyptians honour Him or otherwise, that He should refrain from dealing justly in His world and with His people?

The concept of *ḥillul ha-shem*, the bringing of the Divine Name into disrepute, constituting a factor causing the Almighty to waive His retribution is elaborated by the Prophet Ezekiel (36, 17—36). Here we quote some of the relevant verses:

בֶּן־אָדָם בֵּית יִשְׂרָאֵל יֹשְׁבִים עַל־אַדְמָתָם וַיְטַמְּאוּ אוֹתָהּ
וָאֶשְׁפֹּךְ חֲמָתִי עֲלֵיהֶם עַל הַדָּם אֲשֶׁר־שָׁפְכוּ עַל־הָאָרֶץ ...
וָאָפִיץ אֹתָם בַּגּוֹיִם וַיִּזָּרוּ בָּאֲרָצוֹת כְּדַרְכָּם וְכַעֲלִילוֹתָם שְׁפַטְתִּים:
וַיָּבוֹא אֶל־הַגּוֹיִם אֲשֶׁר־בָּאוּ שָׁם וַיְחַלְּלוּ אֶת־שֵׁם קָדְשִׁי בֶּאֱמֹר לָהֶם עַם־ה'
אֵלֶּה וּמֵאַרְצוֹ יָצָאוּ: ...
לָכֵן אֱמֹר לְבֵית־יִשְׂרָאֵל כֹּה אָמַר אֲדֹנָי ה' לֹא לְמַעַנְכֶם אֲנִי עֹשֶׂה בֵּית
יִשְׂרָאֵל כִּי אִם לְשֵׁם־קָדְשִׁי אֲשֶׁר חִלַּלְתֶּם בַּגּוֹיִם ...
וְקִדַּשְׁתִּי אֶת־שְׁמִי הַגָּדוֹל הַמְחֻלָּל בַּגּוֹיִם אֲשֶׁר חִלַּלְתֶּם בְּתוֹכָם וְיָדְעוּ הַגּוֹיִם
כִּי־אֲנִי ה' נְאֻם אֲדֹנָי ה' בְּהִקָּדְשִׁי בָכֶם לְעֵינֵיהֶם:
וְלָקַחְתִּי אֶתְכֶם מִן־הַגּוֹיִם וְקִבַּצְתִּי אֶתְכֶם מִכָּל־הָאֲרָצוֹת וְהֵבֵאתִי אֶתְכֶם
אֶל אַדְמַתְכֶם ...
וְיָדְעוּ הַגּוֹיִם אֲשֶׁר יִשָּׁאֲרוּ סְבִיבוֹתֵיכֶם כִּי אֲנִי ה' בָּנִיתִי הַנֶּהֱרָסוֹת נָטַעְתִּי
הַנְּשַׁמָּה אֲנִי ה' דִּבַּרְתִּי וְעָשִׂיתִי:

Son of man, when the house of Israel dwelt in their own land, they defiled it ...
Wherefore I poured my fury upon them for the blood they had shed upon the land ...

161

And I scattered them among the heathen, and they were dispersed through the countries: according to their way and according to their doings I judged them.

And when they entered unto the heathen, whither they went, they profaned my holy name, when they said to them, These are the people of the Lord, and are gone forth out of his land. Therefore say unto the house of Israel, Thus saith the Lord God; I do not this for your sakes, O house of Israel, but for mine holy name's sake, which you have profaned among the heathen . . .

And I will sanctify my great name, which was profaned among the heathen, which ye have profaned in the midst of them; and the heathen shall know that I am the Lord, saith the Lord God, when I shall be sanctified in you before their eyes.

For I will take you from among the heathen, and gather you out of all countries, and will bring you into your own land.

Then the heathen that are left round about you shall know that I the Lord build the ruined places, and plant that that was desolate:

I the Lord have spoken it, and I will do it.

Ezekiel here reveals another side of the picture which should answer the question posed by Abravanel and Arama. The Almighty is interested in the welfare of all His creatures. He is both transcendent and immanent, towering as it were above His world and His creatures, but at the same time providentially concerned with their interests. "Wherever you find His greatness, there you find His meekness" is a Talmudic dictum originating with R. Yoḥanan. The Almighty wishes the whole world to acknowledge Him and, for this reason even the meting out of His justice and retribution is suspended in order to further this exalted aim. Naḥmanides, commenting on our sidra, aptly sums up this conception:

God created humanity to acknowledge and give thanks to His name. When mankind sinned there only remained this people (i.e. Israel) to publicise His oneness and that He is the God of the universe. Were He then to destroy Israel, the peoples of the world would forget His deeds and the whole intention of human creation would be completely defeated. It was only logical therefore that the Divine Will that had willed the creation of the world should desire the continued existence of the people since they were nearer to Him and knew him more than all the nations. Moses therefore advanced this argument in his intercessory prayer and God accepted it — "And the Lord said: I have forgiven in accordance with thy words".

Perhaps Naḥmanides' words will become clearer to us after noting the employment of this same concept by a modern Israel author, the renowned S.Y. Agnon[1] in his prologue to the *kaddish* recited on the martyrs of Eretz Israel (in *Samukh Venir'eh,* last page).

... O our King, the King of the kings of kings, the Holy One blessed be He, the King Who desireth life, loveth peace and pursueth peace, loveth His people Israel and hath chosen us from all other peoples; not because we are many did the Lord desire us, for we are the fewest of all the peoples. But because of His love with which He loved us though we are but few, each one of us is of account unto Him as a whole legion since He has not many like us to put in our place. Should God forbid, but a single individual be missing from the ranks of Israel there is a gap in the legions of the King leading to a weakening, as it were, in His kingdom, blessed be He, since His kingdom lacks one member of its legions, and, God forbid, His greatness blessed be He has suffered a diminution.

Therefore we pray and recite concerning every deceased of Israel: *Yitgadal Veyitkadash* ... May His great name be magnified and sanctified — May the power of the Name be magnified and that there should not arise as a result of this any weakening before Him, blessed be He, and that He be sanctified in the worlds that He has created in accordance with His will and that we should only stand in awe of the majestic excellency of His exalted holiness. And cause His kingdom to reign supreme — that His kingdom should be revealed and displayed in perfection and not, God forbid, suffer any diminution whatsoever — in your life and in your days and in the life of all the House of Israel speedily and at hand; for if His kingdom is revealed in the world, there is peace in the world and song in the world and abundance of praise in the world and great consolation in the world ...

163

NOTE

[1] The citation in this connection was brought to my notice by Rabbi Dr. Meir Weiss of Jerusalem.

HAD GOD CHANGED HIS MIND?

In this chapter we shall deal with the end of the section on the spies — with the last verse. Their punishment had already been explained to them and been given added force by being worded in the form of an oath:

חַי־אָנִי נְאֻם־ה׳ אִם לֹא כַּאֲשֶׁר דִּבַּרְתֶּם בְּאָזְנָי כֵּן אֶעֱשֶׂה לָכֶם:

As I live, saith the Lord, surely as you have spoken in My ears, so will I do to you.

(14, 28)

They had "begged": "Would that we had died in the land of Egypt, or would that we had died in this wilderness". Accordingly:

בַּמִּדְבָּר הַזֶּה יִפְּלוּ פִגְרֵיכֶם וְכָל־פְּקֻדֵיכֶם לְכָל־מִסְפַּרְכֶם מִבֶּן עֶשְׂרִים שָׁנָה
וָמָעְלָה אֲשֶׁר הֲלִינֹתֶם עָלָי:

Your carcasses shall fall in this wilderness from twenty years old and upward, you that have murmured against Me.

(14, 29)

וּבְנֵיכֶם יִהְיוּ רֹעִים בַּמִּדְבָּר אַרְבָּעִים שָׁנָה וְנָשְׂאוּ אֶת־זְנוּתֵיכֶם עַד־תֹּם
פִּגְרֵיכֶם בַּמִּדְבָּר:
בְּמִסְפַּר הַיָּמִים אֲשֶׁר־תַּרְתֶּם אֶת־הָאָרֶץ אַרְבָּעִים יוֹם יוֹם לַשָּׁנָה יוֹם לַשָּׁנָה
תִּשְׂאוּ אֶת־עֲוֹנֹתֵיכֶם אַרְבָּעִים שָׁנָה וִידַעְתֶּם אֶת־תְּנוּאָתִי:

165

**And your children shall be wanderers in the wilderness forty
years and shall bear the brunt of your strayings until your
carcasses be consumed in the wilderness.
After the number of the days in which you spied out the land,
shall you bear your iniquities, even forty years, and you shall
know My displeasure.**

(14, 33—34)

The punishment was immediately felt when death overtook the evil
congregation of the ten spies (14, 37):

וַיָּמֻתוּ הָאֲנָשִׁים מוֹצִאֵי דִבַּת־הָאָרֶץ רָעָה בַּמַּגֵּפָה לִפְנֵי ה':

**And these men that brought an evil report of the land died by
the plague, before the Lord.**

After all this the people mourned. On the morrow (14, 40):

וַיַּשְׁכִּמוּ בַבֹּקֶר וַיַּעֲלוּ אֶל־רֹאשׁ־הָהָר לֵאמֹר הִנֶּנּוּ וְעָלִינוּ אֶל־הַמָּקוֹם
אֲשֶׁר־אָמַר ה' כִּי חָטָאנוּ:

**They rose up early in the morning and went up to the top of
the mountain saying, Lo we are here and we will go up to the
place which the Lord has promised; for we have sinned.**

The reaction to this was (vv. 41—43):

לָמָּה זֶּה אַתֶּם עֹבְרִים אֶת־פִּי ה' וְהִיא לֹא תִצְלָח:
אַל־תַּעֲלוּ כִּי אֵין ה' בְּקִרְבְּכֶם . . . :
. . . וַיַּעְפִּלוּ לַעֲלוֹת אֶל־רֹאשׁ הָהָר וַאֲרוֹן בְּרִית־ה' וּמֹשֶׁה לֹא־מָשׁוּ מִקֶּרֶב
הַמַּחֲנֶה:

**Why do you now transgress the commandment of the Lord
seeing it shall not prosper?**

166

Go not up for the Lord is not among you.
... But they insisted on going up to the top of the mountain;
nevertheless the ark of the covenant of the Lord and Moses did
not budge from the camp.

The result of this behaviour of theirs (14, 45):

וַיֵּרֶד הָעֲמָלֵקִי וְהַכְּנַעֲנִי הַיֹּשֵׁב בָּהָר הַהוּא וַיַּכּוּם וַיַּכְּתוּם עַד־הַחָרְמָה׃

The Amalekite and the Canaanite who dwelt in that hill
country descended and fell upon them and crushed them even
to Hormah.

Our commentators have been puzzled by this. Arama thus words
the difficulty in his *Akedat Yizḥak*:

> After they had presumed to go up to the top of the mountain, why did not
> the ark of the Lord and Moses move from the camp and why were the gates
> of repentance shut against them? Does not this story violate the golden rule
> that he who acknowledges his sin and forsakes it shall find grace? Was it not
> the Lord's desire that they should overcome their fear, that they should not
> be afraid of the people of the land and go up and fight? Were they not
> bidden: "Go up! Be not afraid, neither be dismayed" (Deut. 1, 21). Was not
> their action in ascending the mountain what was expected of them? Or had
> the Lord changed His mind?

We find a similar problem in the messages of two great Hebrew
prophets. Isaiah called on his brothers:

הִשָּׁמֵר וְהַשְׁקֵט אַל־תִּירָא וּלְבָבְךָ אַל־יֵרַךְ

Keep calm and be tranquil; fear not nor let your heart be faint.
(Isaiah 7, 4)

He demanded resistance to the enemy and promised that salvation
would come. But when Jeremiah saw his king rising up and the
people enthusiastic for rebellion, he prophesied catastrophe and

167

destruction, demanded immediate surrender and acceptance of the overlordship of the king of Babylon, even himself bearing the yoke on his own neck as a symbol of the humbling that had been ordained. Had God changed His mind?

This is not the case. Not the God who defends His city unconditionally, who does not allow the stranger and enemy to enter its gates is the living God in whom we are to put our trust. Nor is the God who destroys and overturns, the God of retribution, the living God in whom we are to believe. Buber thus explained it in his work on *The Teaching of the Prophets:*

> It is immaterial whether the prophecy involves salvation or catastrophe. What matters is that the prophecy, irrespective of its content, should fit in with the Divine demand at that particular historic moment. In times of unjustified complacency, a message of shattering catastrophe is called for, the finger pointing at impending destruction in history. On the other hand, in times of great tribulation, from which deliverance is still possible, in times of remorse and repentance an encouraging message of salvation is in keeping.

When Jeremiah called for surrender and acceptance of the yoke of the king of Babylon, he knew that the people could no longer be purified and restored to the true path except through arduous sufferings involving the destruction of the Temple and the yoke of exile. It was no longer possible "to build and to plant" without fulfilling the message of "to root out and pull down, to destroy and overthrow" (Jer. 1, 10). The work of rebuilding could not be contemplated before the process of destruction and uprooting had been endured.

The same applies to our subject. Their inability to go and occupy the land became clearly manifest in the statement: "Let us appoint a leader and let us return to Egypt", in that weeping that they wept on that night. Now matters could not be remedied without them accepting what had been imposed on them. Their words: "Lo we are here and we will go up" constituted no repentance unless they accepted their sentence, humbled themselves and bore their punishment. Divine punishment is itself the cure for their ills, the path of repentance. So Maimonides explains the purpose of their wanderings in the wilderness:

> Man cannot be expected suddenly to leave the state of slavery and toiling in bricks and straw and the like, wash his soiled hands at the spur of the moment and fight with giants . . . It was therefore part of the Divine wisdom to make them wander around the wilderness until they had become schooled in courage. For, as is well known, a nomadic existence under spartan conditions breeds courage, and the reverse, cravenness. In addition a new generation of people grew up who had known no humiliation and bondage.

Questions for Further Study

1. "וּפִגְרֵיכֶם אַתֶּם": כתרגומו "דִילְכוֹן". לפי שדיבר על הבנים להכניסם לארץ וביקש לומר: ואתם תמותו, נופל לשון זה כאן לומר: אתם.

> "But, as for you, your carcasses shall fall in the wilderness" (14, 32), as the Targum has it: "Yours". Since he had spoken of the children, of their entry into the Land and He wished, in contrast to say: But you shall die; the text employs the expression *atem* "you" (English Version: "But as for you".)
> (Rashi)

(a) Why does Rashi quote Targum Onkelos?

(b) Why did he not rest content with the Targum, but added his own words: "since He had spoken . . ." What did he wish to achieve by this?

2. "After the number of days in which you spied out the land, even forty days, for every day a year, shall you bear your iniquities, even forty years".
Isaac Arama in his *Akedat Yiẓḥak* asks:

> What reason was there in His debiting them a whole year for each day? Surely it is not the Almighty to behave thus and it was sufficient to mete out to them punishment, measure for measure! Far be it from Him to mete out a greater punishment than the sin?

169

(Malbim adds that we know that in the ordinary way God's dealing of reward is more generous than his dealing out of punishment).[1]

Try to answer his question on the basis of what is discussed in this chapter.

3. Compare the words of the Israelites in our text: "Lo we are here and we will go up; for we have sinned" with Saul's words (1 Samuel 15,24—25): "I have sinned, for I have transgressed the word of the Lord and your words . . . and now I pray you forgive my sin and return with me and I shall bow down to the Lord".
What is the difference between our text and the one in Samuel?

NOTE

[1] Cf. *Studies in Vayikra*, Beḥukotai, p. 304.

THE PRECEPT OF ẒIẒIT

דַּבֵּר אֶל־בְּנֵי יִשְׂרָאֵל וְאָמַרְתָּ אֲלֵהֶם וְעָשׂוּ לָהֶם צִיצָת עַל־כַּנְפֵי בִגְדֵיהֶם
לְדֹרֹתָם וְנָתְנוּ עַל־צִיצָת הַכָּנָף פְּתִיל תְּכֵלֶת: וְהָיָה לָכֶם לְצִיצָת . . .

**Speak unto the children of Israel, and bid them make fringes
on the borders of their garments throughout their generations,
and that they put upon the fringes of the borders a thread of
blue. And it shall be to you for a fringe...**

(15, 38—39)

The sidra concludes with the chapter on *ẓiẓit,* which every Jew is
obliged to recite twice daily, "when thou liest down and when thou
risest up". Our Sages stated regarding this precept that:

שקולה מצוה זו כנגד כל המצוות כלן.

This precept is equal in weight to all the precepts.

(Talmud, Menaḥot, 43b)

Wherein lies the supreme importance of this precept and in what
way is it equal in weight to all the precepts in the Torah? Before we
proceed to answer this question, let us make a closer study of the
first verses of the chapter concerned.

ועשו להם ציצית על כנפי בגדיהם לדורותם ונתנו על ציצית הכנף פתיל תכלת והיה
ל כ ם לציצית.

...*them* make *ẓiẓit* on the borders of their garments ... and that *they* put
upon the *ẓiẓit* ... a thread of blue, and it shall be to *you* for *ẓiẓit* ...

171

Two unusual features are to be detected here: (1) the switchover from the third to the second person, — from "*them* make" "*they* put" to "it shall be to *you*" (2) the tautological repetition of *zizit*. What does the verse achieve by stating that the *zizit* shall be to you for *zizit*?

The *Biur* explains the changes from the third to second person as follows. According to this commentary, the actual obligation to wear *zizit* is derived from Deut. 22, 12:

גְּדִלִים תַּעֲשֶׂה־לָּךְ עַל־אַרְבַּע כַּנְפוֹת כְּסוּתְךָ אֲשֶׁר תְּכַסֶּה־בָּהּ:

Thou shalt make thee fringes upon the four corners of thy vesture wherewith thou coverest thyself.

The purpose of the passage in our sidra is not to announce the precept but to explain its underlying intention and aim. The first two clauses mentioning the precept are here subordinate, and the passage should read as follows:

> Then they (i.e. children of Israel) make them *zizit* on the corners of their garments and put upon the *zizit* . . . a thread of blue (as commanded in Deut.). Then tell them: And it shall be to you for *zizit* . . .

In other words, the fringes and blue thread shall constitute *zizit* for you. But what is the implication of the word *zizit*?

Rashi offers two explanations:

על שם הפתילים התלויים בה כמו (יחזקאל ח): ״ויקחני בציצית ראשי״. ד״א:
״ציצית״ על שם ״וראיתם אותם״, כמו (שיר השירים ב): ״מציץ מן החרכים״.

> Alluding to the threads — compare: And he took me by a lock (*zizit*) of mine head (Ezekiel 8, 3). Another explanation: alluding to "and ye shall look upon it" compare: "*looking* through (*meziz*) the lattice" (Song of Songs 3, 9).

Why was not Rashi satisfied with one explanation? Rashbam

throws light on this generosity of his grandfather, when he interprets the first mention of *zizit* in verse 38 in accordance with Rashi's first explanation to mean a lock, "fringes", whilst the second mention in verse 39 "And it shall be to you for *zizit*" alludes to the idea of "looking", cited by Rashi as an alternative:

The *zizit* shall be for a witness, that you may look upon it...

The *zizit* are not commanded merely to be made and worn on the four corners of one's garments, but also *to be seen*. What are the implications of this seeing? This the verse proceeds to explain:

וּרְאִיתֶם אֹתוֹ וּזְכַרְתֶּם אֶת־כָּל־מִצְוֹת ה' וַעֲשִׂיתֶם אֹתָם

And you shall see it and *remember* **all the commandments of the Lord and** *do* **them.**

Regarding this, our Sages commented in Menahot (43b):

... Teaching that seeing leads to remembering, remembering to doing.

How does seeing the *zizit* lead to remembering all the *mizvot* in the Torah? Nahmanides explains this by pointing to the fact that the object of the seeing is not the *zizit* but the thread of blue. (The accusative pronoun "it" — *oto* is masculine, referring to the *petil*, thread of blue, and not to *zizit,* which is feminine).

What memories does gazing at the blue thread stir up? Nahmanides and Rashbam, in answer, refer us to the dictum of Rabbi Meir (Menahot ibid.):

מה נשתנה התכלת מכל הצבעים? מפני שהתכלת דומה לים וים לרקיע ורקיע לכסא הכבוד.

What distinguishes blue from all other colours? Blue is like the sea, the sea is like the sky and the sky like the Throne of Glory.

The blue thread reminds man of his Creator and his obligation to carry out His will, through the medium of the precepts of the Torah.

The author of the commentary *Kli Yakar* develops this idea further, basing himself also on a quotation from Sifrei:

> Said the Holy One blessed be He to Moses: Look up at the heavens I have created to minister to you. Peradventure they have changed their nature? Or peradventure the orb of the sun has risen in the west? On the contrary; they rejoice to do My will. Thus he said also regarding the sea: "Fear ye not me? saith the Lord: will ye not tremble at my presence, which have placed the sand for the bound of the sea by a perpetual decree: and though the waves therefore toss themselves, yet can they not prevail; though they roar yet can they not pass over it" (Jeremiah 5). Peradventure it (the sea) has changed its nature? On the contrary, it strains itself to do so but cannot, as it is written: "though the waves... toss themself, yet can they not prevail".
> From here we see that the sea does not change its nature, out of *fear* (it is cowed into submission), since it strains to do so — but is not permitted, whilst the heavens change not their nature, out of *love*. (They rejoice to do the Divine will). Now, our Rabbis likened the blue thread to the sea, by which the Jew will call to mind the action of the sea which deviates not even a hairbreadth from its nature. So he should not budge one iota fom the command of God. But we can only learn obedience through fear from the sea, which is prevented in spite of itself from overstepping its bounds... But he that observes the word of God out of *love* is on a higher plane than he who merely *fears* Him. Therefore, our Rabbis added, "the sea is like the sky or heavens"... Just as the sky does not change its nature but, on the contrary, rejoices to serve, so he should serve God with joy, out of love. Should you ask, what advantages has he who serves God through love, over the person who serves Him through fear, the answer given is, "the sky is like the Throne of Glory". Love of God will lead him to cleaving to the Divine presence... since he that stands in awe, keeps his distance from the object of his fear, but he that loves, endeavours to draw closer to the object of his love.

The main objection to the above interpretation is the emphasis placed on the blue thread, which is, according to our sources, merely a secondary detail of the precept of *ẓiẓit*. Today we wear no *tekhelet*, in accordance with the dictum of the Sages in Menaḥot:

The lack of blue (thread) does not preclude (the wearing of) the white (one on its own).

Sforno's explanation therefore would seem to be more acceptable. He states as follows:

Remember that you are servants of the Almighty, from whom you received commandments on oath. This you will do when you see the *zizit* which is the seal of the King on his servants.

The chief purpose of the precept, would, therefore, seem to be, to act as a device for aiding the memory, just as a person ties a knot on his garment to remember something. We shall conclude by quoting Ibn Ezra who has something pertinent to say to those who imagine that *zizit* should chiefly be worn during prayers on the *tallit*.

Ibn Ezra states:

This precept applies to everyone who has a four-cornered garment, that he should wear it continually and not take it off, in order to remember. Those who wear a *tallit* during prayers, do so because they recite the *shema* which contains the chapter on *zizit*. But, in my opinion, it is much more necessary for him to wear *zizit* during the rest of the day and not merely during prayers, in order to remember not to err and commit a sin *at all times,* since during prayers he will in any case do no sin.

Questions for Further Study

1. "...that ye may look upon it, and remember all the commandments of the Lord, and do them ... that ye may remember and do all my commandments".

(Numbers 15, 39—40)

Commentators have been puzzled by the apparently tautological repetition "and remember" "that ye may remember". Can you explain the reason for this repetition?

175

2. "That ye go not after your own heart and your own eyes" — indicating that the eyes follow the heart. Or perhaps the heart follows the eyes? But don't you find a blind man who commits every conceivable abomination? What then is the implication of the text "that ye go not after your own heart and your own eyes?" To indicate that the eyes follow the heart.

(Sifrei)

On this Malbim comments:

If visual impressions of desire are first to lead the human heart astray, man would not be moved by them. The demoralising effect of visual impressions indicates that the heart has previously been affected by immoral desire and that it has already been preoccupied with ways of casting off the fear of heaven.

Here by way of comparison is Rashi's comment on the same theme:

The heart and the eyes are the spies of the body and act as procurers; the eye sees and the heart desires, whilst the body commits the transgression.

(a) What is the difference between the comment of Sifrei and that of Rashi?

(b) The above two views are based on divergent psychological conceptions. What are they?

THE ROVING EYE

וְלֹא תָתוּרוּ אַחֲרֵי לְבַבְכֶם וְאַחֲרֵי עֵינֵיכֶם אֲשֶׁר־אַתֶּם זֹנִים אַחֲרֵיהֶם:

You shall not rove after your heart and your eyes after which you are wont to go astray.

(15, 39)

We devoted the last chapter to understanding the essential character of the precept to wear ẓiẓit, endeavouring to answer the question: How does the sight of the ẓiẓit prompt us to remember all the precepts. On this occasion we shall try to understand the purpose of the precept, as it is expressed in the Torah in our introductory text:

> The heart and eyes are the spies of the body acting as procurer for its transgressions. The eye sees, the heart covets and the body commits the transgression.
>
> (Rashi)

The foregoing is rather a strange statement. After all the Torah did not forbid man to behold reality, to direct his heart and eyes at the world of the Deity. On the contrary, it is precisely a drinking in of the beauty and wonder of the universe that is likely to draw us closer to God and love and fear Him. This is what Baḥya observes in his *Duties of the Heart*:

Are we obliged to contemplate all created things or not? Both Reason and Tradition (written and oral) oblige us to contemplate creation and learn from it the wisdom of the Creator . . .

With respect to written tradition it is stated in the Bible (Isaiah 40, 26): "Lift up your eyes on high and *behold* who created these" and (Psalms 8, 4—5) "when I behold Thy heavens, the work of Thy fingers, the moon and the stars which Thou hast established, what is man that Thou art mindful of him?"

Maimonides places an even greater emphasis on the duty of contemplating and studying the beauty of the universe in his *Code*:

The Almighty has commanded us to love and fear Him, as it is written: "Thou shalt love the Lord thy God"; "thou shalt fear the Lord thy God". What is the way to love Him and fear Him? When man reflects on His wonderful creatures and works and perceives therefrom His matchless and infinite wisdom, he immediately loves, praises, glorifies Him and is seized with an overwhelming desire to know His great name, as king David stated in Psalms 42, 3: "My soul thirsteth for God, for the living God". When he ponders on these very things, he immediately recoils in fear and dread, realizing he is but a puny, wretched, lack-lustred mortal, standing with his despicably insignificant intelligence before the perfect in knowledge, as David pointed out (Psalms 8, 4—5): "When I behold the heavens . . . what is man that Thou art mindful of him?" On the basis of this approach I present general rules regarding the works of the Almighty, so that they will afford an opening for the intelligent person to love God. As our Sages observed regarding Love: "Through this you come to acknowledge He-who-spoke-and-the-world-came-into-being".

Let us study the two passages we have cited. The contemplation referred to is that of one who seeks with his eyes and heart a predetermined goal. In both, the contemplator has already found the goal of his life and existence — the service of God. He is simply looking for authentication of what he already knows, of ways of attaining a purpose clear to him before he began to reflect. Maimonides' ruling opened with the precept to love and fear God and his comments are in answer to the question. The advice to man to open his eyes and contemplate the great and wonderful works and creatures of God are an answer to the question how to love Him.

On the other hand, the text with which we headed the chapter speaks of the roving eye and heart that is still seeking in the world around a purpose. As soon as it finds it, it will forthwith go astray after it and deify it.

The distinction between these two kinds of seeing has been observed by Baḥya in his *Duties of the Heart*:

> Try after that to shut your eyes and spare your senses from beholding that which you have no need of or that which will disturb your heart from thinking on what will be of benefit to you and shun superfluous spectacle as much as you can.
>
> Our Sages stated: "The eyes and heart are the two procurers of sin". Use your sight rather to contemplate the works of the Creator, to study them and reflect on them and understand thereby the power and bounty of the Creator, as David observed: "When I behold Thy heavens, the works of Thy fingers . . ."

We may detect an allusion to this distinction even in the very wording of our text. It does not state "you shall not *walk* (i.e. purposefully) after your eyes and heart" but "you shall not *rove*". Malbim has pointed this out:

> Man's soul and capacities have been created in an upright manner. The heart is naturally attracted to good. Man spoils his nature and introduces into his heart evil thoughts. The text could not then say "you shall not walk after your heart". For if man walked in the path mapped out for him by nature he would follow the good and upright path.

We are bidden therefore not to rove. But what type of roving is referred to in the text, against which the precept of *ẓiẓit* is to guard us? Opinions differ. First Maimonides:

179

It is not only to idolatry that we are forbidden turn our thoughts, but we are warned never to call to mind or divert our attention to any thought which may lead man to uproot any of the fundamentals of the Torah and be drawn after the promptings of our hearts. This is because man's mental capacities are limited and not every intellect is capable of grasping the truth in its totality. If ever man allows himself to be led by the promptings of his heart he will come, in his own shortsightedness, to destroy the world. How so? At one time he will dabble in idolatry and at another ponder on the unity of the Creator, postulating His existence and non-existence, questioning what is above and what is below and debating whether prophecy is true and false. He does not have the mental apparatus for judging these things in order eventually to arrive at the real truth. As a result he is misled into heresy. Against this the Torah warned us when it stated "you shall not rove after your heart . . .". In other words, no one should be led after his own limited intelligence and imagine that his mind has attained the truth. Our Sages commented on the text "after your heart" — this implies heresy . . .

(Code, Idolatry)

"You shall see it and remember all the precepts of the Lord . . ." — you will remember that you are slaves of the Lord whose precepts you accepted — by beholding the *ẓiẓit* which is like the seal of the master on his slaves. Through this you will cease going astray after your own hearts to satisfy the whims of your heart for the sake of wealth and honour even if it involves robbery.

"After your eyes" — to attain the lusts that you set your eyes on. "After which you go astray" — diverting your intellectual soul from the ways of eternal life to those of destruction and death.

(Sforno)

Question for Further Study

Explain the difference between the approaches of Maimonides and Sforno to the text "after your own heart".

AN UNHOLY CONTROVERSY

כל מחלקת שהיא לשם שמים, סופה להתקיים ושאינה לשם שמים אין סופה להתקיים.
איזו היא מחלקת שהיא לשם שמים? מחלקת הלל ושמאי, ושאינה לשם שמים זו
מחלקת קרח וכל עדתו (פרקי אבות).

Every controversy that is pursued in a heavenly cause, is destined to be
perpetuated; and that which is not pursued in a heavenly cause is not
destined to be perpetuated. Which can be considered a controversy pursued
in a heavenly cause? This is the controversy of Hillel and Shammai. And
that not pursued in a heavenly cause? This is the controversy of Koraḥ and
his congregation.

(Ethics of the Fathers 5, 17)

Malbim draws an interesting and penetrating distinction between
these two kinds of controversies:

Our Sages wished to point out that in a holy or heavenly cause both sides
are, in fact, united by one purpose, to further unselfish, Divine ends.
However, in a controversy pursued for unholy ends, for personal
advancement and the like, then even those who have come together on one
side are not really united. Each are governed by their own calculations of
what they stand to gain and are ready to cut each others' throats, if it so
serves their interests. This was the case as far as the controversy of Koraḥ
and his congregation. Koraḥ was interested in the High Priesthood, since he
contended that Amram had received the firstborn share as the eldest son of
Kehat, in the fact that his son, Moses, had been appointed leader and king
over the people. It was therefore only right, so Koraḥ claimed, that the High
Priesthood be given to himself as the son of Yitzhar, the next in line of
succession. Dathan and Abiram and On ben Peleth, on the other hand, were

181

animated by other considerations, in their opposition to Moses. Their grievance lay in the fact that they belonged to the tribe of Reuben who, as the firstborn son of Jacob, was entitled to all the highest offices, that of spiritual and political leadership. Instead, they complained, the priesthood and Divine service had been given to the tribe of Levi and leadership of the tribes to Judah and Joseph. Similarly, the two hundred and fifty men contended that, as they were "princes of the assembly, famous in the congregation, men of renown", they should be accorded the priesthood. They were against conferring a hereditary title on a tribe but asserted that individual prestige and distinction should be considered. Ibn Ezra suggests that these 250 rebels were in actuality firstborn who considered that the priesthood was their natural privilege.

The above analysis of Malbim explains in quite a compelling fashion why the Mishnah was not worded as we might have expected it to be "A controversy pursued in a Heavenly Cause . . . that is the controversy of Hillel and Shammai. That not pursued in a Heavenly cause is the controversy of *Korah and Moses*". Instead it reads: "Korah and his congregation". As he explains, Korah's followers were simply a band of malcontents, each harbouring his own personal grievances against authority, animated by individual pride and ambition, united to overthrow Moses and Aaron and hoping thereby to attain their individual desires. What would really happen, however, would be that they would quarrel amongst themselves, as each one strove to attain his selfish ambitions. The controversy therefore was rightly termed "between Korah and his congregation". They would ultimately fight among themselves.

Let us now study their grievances as recorded in the words of the Torah:

רַב־לָכֶם כִּי כָל־הָעֵדָה כֻּלָּם קְדֹשִׁים וּבְתוֹכָם ה' וּמַדּוּעַ תִּתְנַשְּׂאוּ עַל־קְהַל
ה':

Ye take too much upon you, seeing all the congregation are holy, every one of them, and the Lord is among them:

wherefore then lift ye up yourselves above the congregation of the Lord?

(16, 3)

Note that they do not say: "All the congregation *is* holy" — as a unit but: "All the congregation *are* holy", "every one of them" — each one taken, individually. The assertion of individual, selfish ambitions outweighs their group feeling as a "kingdom of priests and holy nation". They interpreted the mission of holiness, the role of "chosen people" with which they had been charged by God, in the sense of conferring on them superiority and privilege, rather than as constituting a call to shoulder extra duties and responsibilities. God demanded of them: "Ye shall be holy" that is to say: Show yourselves holy by your deeds! "For thou art an holy people unto the Lord thy God: and the Lord has chosen thee to be a special people unto Himself". The titles of "special people", "holy people" were in the nature of demand notes presented by the Almighty for them to honour by deeds of holiness. Instead they took them to be titles of distinction conferring privileges on them. Instead they clamoured for rights, they presented the Almighty with a demand note, as it were. This is a far cry from the Divine call to Israel: "Ye shall be holy to Me" (Leviticus 19, 2) charging Israel with a spiritual mission to perfect herself by carrying out the Divine commandments. Instead we are faced by the brazen assertion: "The whole congregation are holy, everyone of them", so unsupported by realities as we know it only too well from the previous sidrot.

Now let us turn our attention to the wording of Moses' reproof to Koraḥ and his followers in verses 8-11.

As we have noted on previous occasions, the Torah is meticulously careful in choice of words, and every turn of phrase is significant, and is not employed merely for ornament.

Isaac Arama points to the impudent, mocking tone employed by the rebels in their retorts to Moses. To Moses' opening phrase "Seemeth it but a small thing to you", and closing phrase "Ye take

183

too much upon you, ye sons of Levi" which is itself an echo of their
opening words against Moses (16, 3), they reply, "Is it a small thing
that thou hast brought us out of a land flowing with milk and
honey". Just as Moses ended with a rhetorical question "And ye seek
the priesthood also?" so they concluded "except thou make thyself a
prince over us?" Moses had promised to bring them out of Egypt the
land of bondage to a land flowing with milk and honey. They twist it
round and accuse Moses of bringing them out of a land flowing with
milk and honey.

Only after their refusal to come and meet Moses and discuss
matters with him and argue them out is Moses angry. Only when
they said "we will not go up" and not before. Let us quote the
Midrash Tanḥuma on this point:

נצטער מאד. למה הדבר דומה: לאדם הדן עם חברו ומתווכח עמו. אם משיבו — יש
שם נחת רוח ואם אינו משיבו יש בו צער גדול.

Moses was very displeased. To what can this be compared; to one who
debates and argues with his colleague. If his colleague replies to him — he is
pleased, if he does not reply, he is deeply annoyed.

There is no greater annoyance than when one party to a dispute
refuses to sit down and talk things out with the other side. In such a
situation lies little hope of a peaceful settlement. It was therefore only
at this point that Moses became really angry . . .

Questions for Further Study

1. If, as Malbim suggests, the grievance of the sons of Reuben lay
    in the fact that they claimed for their tribe the birthright and
    priesthood, why had they waited so long till after the incident
    of the spies to vent it, when Reuben's birthright had been
    forfeited to Joseph as far back as Jacob's lifetime and the

priesthood transferred from the first born to the Levites, after the worshipping of the Golden Calf?

2. Rashi basing himself on the Midrash comments on 16, 15: "I have not taken one ass from them" as follows:

מה שהיה דרכי ליטול, לא נטלתי מהם. בנוהג שבעולם אדם שהוא עושה בהקדש, נוטל שכרו מן ההקדש, ואני בשעה שהייתי יורד ממדין למצרים, בדין היה לי ליטול חמור מהם שבשביל צרכיהם ירדתי — ולא נטלתי.

What was my legal due I did not take from them. In the ordinary way, whoever works for a sacred cause takes his payment from sacred property. When I went down from Midian to Egypt, I should have taken for myself an ass from them, as I went down for their sakes — but I did not take.

How does this explanation differ from the plain sense of the verse and what prompted Rashi to offer this explanation?

3. (16, 22):
Shall one man sin, and wilt thou be wroth with all the congregation?

Isaac Arama poses the following question:

What was the point of their question? Surely, in the case of the Golden Calf, not all of them sinned and yet Scripture states: "Let me alone . . . that I may consume them" (Exodus 32, 10). The same applied at Shittim (Numbers 25), when God waxed wroth against the whole of Israel and with Achan (Joshua 22, 20): "Did not Achan . . . commit a trespass . . . and wrath fell on all the congregation of Israel? and that man perished not alone in his iniquity". It was considered as if "Israel hath sinned . . ." (*ibid.* 7, 11). This also follows reasonably from the fact that the whole is made up of the part. Indeed, if only one part of the body is suffering from a malady, one nevertheless generalizes and says that the whole body is sick.

(a) Elaborate the question.
(b) Can you suggest a straightforward answer to this query?

THE GRIEVANCES OF KORAḤ AND COMPANY

וַיִּקַּח קֹרַח בֶּן־יִצְהָר בֶּן־קְהָת בֶּן־לֵוִי וְדָתָן וַאֲבִירָם בְּנֵי אֱלִיאָב וְאוֹן בֶּן־
פֶּלֶת בְּנֵי רְאוּבֵן:
וַיָּקֻמוּ לִפְנֵי מֹשֶׁה וַאֲנָשִׁים מִבְּנֵי־יִשְׂרָאֵל חֲמִשִּׁים וּמָאתָיִם נְשִׂיאֵי עֵדָה
קְרִאֵי מוֹעֵד אַנְשֵׁי־שֵׁם:
וַיִּקָּהֲלוּ עַל־מֹשֶׁה וְעַל־אַהֲרֹן וַיֹּאמְרוּ אֲלֵהֶם רַב־לָכֶם כִּי כָל־הָעֵדָה כֻּלָּם
קְדֹשִׁים וּבְתוֹכָם ה' וּמַדּוּעַ תִּתְנַשְּׂאוּ עַל־קְהַל ה':

Now Koraḥ, the son of Izhar, the son of Kehath, the son of
Levi, and Dathan and Abiram, the sons of Eliab, and On, the
son of Peleth, sons of Reuben took men:
And they rose up before Moses, with certain of the children of
Israel, two hundred and fifty princes of the assembly, famous
in the congregation, men of renown.
And they gathered themselves up against Moses and against
Aaron, and said unto them, ye take too much upon ye, seeing
all the congregation are holy, every one of them, and the Lord
is among them: wherefore then lift ye up yourselves above the
congregation of the Lord?

(16, 1—3)

Who were the two hundred and fifty men who followed Koraḥ,
Dathan and Abiram to rebel against Moses who led the children of
Israel out of Egypt through the desert, the prophet of the Lord who
received the Torah at Sinai? What was their grievance?

According to Ibn Ezra, this rebel band contained grumblers and malcontents of all kinds. Included were Levites who felt aggrieved at being appointed to minister to the priests, Reubenites who considered they had been deprived of the birthright which had been transferred to the tribe of Joseph. According to Ibn Ezra they suspected Joshua (an Ephraimite) of using his influence to favour his own tribe over others. Then there were the firstborn of Israel who felt aggrieved because the privilege of priesthood had been taken from them and granted to the Levites who had not served the golden calf. It is easy to fan the flame of discontent and such a procedure would be made unusually easy if we accept Naḥmanides' timing of the rebellion straight after the incident of the spies. Naḥmanides states:

> Were anyone to have questioned Moses' authority at any other time, the people would have stoned him outright, since they ardently loved Moses their leader and obeyed him. Consequently Koraḥ put up with the high office filled by Aaron, the firstborn with the lofty station of the Levites and all Moses' deeds. But when they arrived at the wilderness of Paran and the Israelites were burnt at Taberah (Num. 11, 1—3) and died at Kibrot Hataavah (verses 33—34) and sinned with the spies, the princes of the tribes being killed by the plague and the people condemned to die in the wilderness, then the people became bitter and some began to doubt the wisdom of Moses' leadership. It was this moment that Koraḥ found opportune to start his mutiny and this was the significance of his reference to them being brought to be killed in the wilderness.

Koraḥ wished to channel all this smouldering discontent to his own benefit. But the Torah does not afford us details of the way he went around fanning their discontent against Moses. This our Sages reconstructed for us applying the following verses to the situation.

אַשְׁרֵי־הָאִישׁ אֲשֶׁר לֹא הָלַךְ בַּעֲצַת רְשָׁעִים
וּבְדֶרֶךְ חַטָּאִים לֹא עָמָד
וּבְמוֹשַׁב לֵצִים לֹא יָשָׁב:

187

Happy is the man who hath not walked in the counsel of the wicked
and in the way of the sinners hath not stood
and in the seat of scorners hath not sat.

(Psalms 1, 1)

Commenting on this verse the Midrash (Shoḥer Tov) states:

"ובמושב לצים . . .". זה קרח, שהיה מתלוצץ על משה ועל אהרן. מה עשה קרח? כנס כל הקהל, שנאמר "ויקהל עליהם קרח את כל העדה". והתחיל לומר להם דברי לצנות, ואומר להם: "אלמנה אחת היתה בשכונתי והיו עמה שתי נערות יתומות, והיתה לה שדה אחת. באה לחרוש — אמר לה משה (דברים כב): "לא תחרוש בשור וחמור יחדיו". באה לזרוע — אמר לה (ויקרא יט, יט): "שדך לא תזרע כלאים". באה לקצור ולעשות ערמה, אמר לה: "הניחי לקט שכחה ופאה". באה לעשות גרן, אמר לה: "תני לי תרומה ומעשר ראשון ומעשר שני". הצדיקה עליה את הדין ונתנה לו. מה עשתה עניה זו? עמדה ומכרה את השדה וקנתה שתי כבשות כדי ללבוש מגזותיהן ולהנות מפרותיהן. כיון שילדו — בא אהרן ואמר לה: תני לי את הבכורות, שכך אמר לי הקב״ה (דברים טו, יט): "כל הבכור אשר יולד בבקרך ובצאנך הזכר — תקדיש לה׳ אלוקיך". הצדיקה עליה את הדין ונתנה לו את הולדות. הגיע זמן גזירה וגזרה אותן — בא אהרן ואמר לה: תני לי ראשית הגז שכך אמר הקב״ה (דברים יח, ד): "ראשית דגנך תירושך יצהרך וראשית גז צאנך תתן לו". (לכהן) אמרה: "אין בי כח לעמוד באיש הזה, הרי אני שוחטת אותן ואכלתן". כיון ששחטה אותן בא אהרן ואמר לה: "תני הזרוע והלחיים והקיבה". אמרה: "אפילו ששחטתי אותן, לא נצלתי מידו — הרי הן עלי חרם!" אמר לה אהרן: אם כן — כולה שלי הוא, שכך אמר הקב״ה (במדבר יח, יד): "כל חרם בישראל לך יהיה". נטלן והלך והניחה בוכה היא עם שתי בנותיה. כך עלתה לעלובה זו! "כל כך הם עושים ותולים בקב״ה?!"

"In the seat of scorners..." this refers to Koraḥ who made scorn of Moses and Aaron. What did Koraḥ do? He assembled all the congregation as it said: "And Koraḥ gathered all the congregation against them". He began to speak to them words of scorn, saying: There was once a widow in my neighbourhood who had two fatherless daughters and one field. When she came to plough, Moses said to her: "Thou shalt not plough with an ox and an ass together" (Deut. 22, 10). When she came to sow, he said to her "Thou shalt not sow thy field with divers seeds" (Leviticus 19, 19). When she came to reap and stack the corn, he said to her, Leave gleanings (*leket*) the forgotten sheaf (*shikheḥah*) and the corner of the field (*pe'ah*) for the poor. When she came to thresh, he said to her, Give tithes, priestly dues, the first

188

and second tithes. She justified heaven's pronouncement and gave him. What did this poor woman do? She went and sold her field, and purchased with the proceeds two lambs, to clothe herself from its shearing and enjoy its products. As soon as they gave birth, Aaron came and said to her: Give me the firstborn, since the Holy One blessed be He hath said: "Every firstborn that shall be born of thy herd and flock, the male one, shalt thou consecrate to the Lord thy God". She justified heaven's pronouncement and gave him the offspring. The time came for shearing and she sheared them — came Aaron and said to her, Give me the first of the shearing since the Holy One blessed be He said (Deut. 18, 3): "The first of thy grain, thy wine and oil and the first of the shearing of thy flock shalt thou give to him".

Thereupon she said: Since I have no more strength to withstand this man, I shall slaughter them and eat them. As soon as she had slaughtered them, Aaron came and said to her: Give me the shoulder, two cheeks and maw (Deut. 18, 3). Whereupon she said: Even after I have slaughtered them I am not delivered from his hand. Let them then be forbidden (*herem*) my use. Said Aaron to her: In that case it is all mine since the Holy One said: "Every devoted thing (*herem* — expression of prohibition, exclusion from ordinary usage) in Israel shall be thine" (Num. 18, 14). He took them, departed and left her weeping with her two daughters. Such was the lot that befell this unfortunate woman! So much they do in the name of the Holy One blessed be He!

In the above excerpt, the Torah, whose ways are the ways of peace is seen through distorted spectacles. All Korah's ranting contains the familiar rabble-rousing ingredients of demagogy.

In the first place, there is no constructive criticism of the law, no reasoned argument but merely a hardship story containing personal details regarding how a particular person suffered from the rigours of the law. Naturally, the hero of the story has to be someone whose very name will excite compassion, a widow. Whose heart would not melt at the sight of a widow's suffering? Yet the Torah's decree knows no mercy!

Second, the story omits to mention that that same oppressed and wronged widow victimised, as it were, by the cruel decrees of the

189

Torah is together with the orphan and stranger, the subject of very special concern and protective legislation —

וְלֹא תַחֲבֹל בֶּגֶד אַלְמָנָה

Thou shalt not take a pledge of a widow's garment.
(Deut. 24, 17)

כָּל אַלְמָנָה וְיָתוֹם לֹא תְעַנּוּן

Thou shalt not afflict any widow and the fatherless.
(Exodus 22, 21)

The very same widow who when she owns property is obliged to give *leket, shikhehah* and *pe'ah,* is entitled to them, when in need.

כִּי תִקְצֹר קְצִירְךָ בְשָׂדֶךָ וְשָׁכַחְתָּ עֹמֶר בַּשָּׂדֶה לֹא תָשׁוּב לְקַחְתּוֹ לַגֵּר לַיָּתוֹם
וְלָאַלְמָנָה יִהְיֶה . . .
כִּי תַחְבֹּט זֵיתְךָ לֹא תְפָאֵר אַחֲרֶיךָ לַגֵּר לַיָּתוֹם וְלָאַלְמָנָה יִהְיֶה:

When thou reapest thy harvest and hast forgotten a sheaf in the field, thou shalt not go again to fetch it. It shall be for the stranger, fatherless and widow.
When thou beatest thine olive tree, thou shalt not go over the boughs again: it shall be for the stranger, the fatherless and widow.
(Deut. 24, 19—20)

Like any demagogue, Korah stresses the obligations rather than the privileges. Just as the taxpayer only sees the burden imposed on him and not the benefits in the way of health, education, public security and other public services that he enjoys in return, so Korah depicts the Torah to the malcontents as demanding, extorting and giving nothing in return.

Third, Koraḥ's speech does not lack the familiar stock-in-trade of the demagogue, the weapon of personal abuse. Aspersions are cast on the legislator bringing the law or its executor into disrepute.

So much they do in the name of the Holy One . . .

Accordingly, not the Torah was to blame but rather its administrators, Moses and Aaron who had disorted its regulations to suit their own needs, and that of their officials and minions.

This was how our Sages pictured Koraḥ's methods of misleading the people, of the way he "took" implying as Rashi explains "took with words", that is, seduced the people. Many will ask how is it possible to conceive that the people who had been redeemed from slavery, for whom the waves of the sea had parted, who had received the Torah at Sinai, amidst thunders and lightnings, led by the cloud by day and pillar of fire by night — how was it conceivable that a people vouchsafed such miracles could succumb to the guile and abuse of one such as Koraḥ?

This was indeed the case. Though two hundred and fifty officially took the plunge and went over to Koraḥ, many more were influenced by his words, as the succeeding chapters indicate. True:

פִּקּוּדֵי ה׳ יְשָׁרִים מְשַׂמְּחֵי־לֵב מִצְוַת ה׳ בָּרָה מְאִירַת עֵינָיִם:

**The precepts of the Lord are upright — making glad the heart.
The commandment of the Lord is pure, enlightening the eyes.**
(Psalms 19, 9)

But the heart of man is crooked and there is no light which man through his stupidity and shortsightedness, cannot succeed in .dimming and darkening.

191

Questions for Further Study

1. "Now Koraḥ ... and Dathan and Abiram ... and On took,
    And they rose up before Moses with certain of the children of
    Israel, two hundred and fifty men ..."

    (Numbers 16, 1—2)

    The author of *Tzedah La-derekh* queries the odd word order
    in the above two verses. Why does it not say simply that
    Koraḥ, Dathan, Abiram, On, took certain of the children of
    Israel, two hundred and fifty princes and they rose up against
    Moses? Can you suggest an answer?

2. "Ye take too much upon you, seeing all the congregation,
    every one of them, are holy ..."

    (Ibid. 3)

    Why does not the text read "all the congregation is, all of it, is
    holy" in the singular, as the grammar would dictate; *edah*
    being singular?

3. Koraḥ jumped up and said to Moses: Is a *tallit* completely blue free from the
    requirement of *ẓiẓit*? Moses replied: it still requires *ẓiẓit*. Whereupon Koraḥ
    retorted: A *tallit* that is all *ẓiẓit* (i.e. blue) still requires them and yet four
    threads free an ordinary *tallit* from the requirement of *ẓiẓit*? He then asked:
    Does a house full of Torah scrolls require a *mezuzah*? Yes! replied Moses.
    Whereupon Koraḥ retorted: The whole Torah with its 278 chapters does not
    free the house, yet the two chapters inside the *mezuzah* do? You were never
    given such ordinances. You fabricated them yourself!

    (Midrash Tanḥumah)

    "And Dathan and Abiram". What did Koraḥ do? He assembled 250 heads
    of the sanhedrins mostly from the tribe of Reuben, his neighbours,
    ... clothed them each with a *tallit* completely blue and presented them to
    Moses. They asked: Does a *tallit* completely blue require *ẓiẓit* or not? It
    does! replied Moses. Whereupon they began to mock him: Is it conceivable

that a *tallit* of another type only requires one thread of blue, yet a *tallit* wholly blue still requires a blue thread?

(Rashi)

(a)   Why did our Sages above put a question on the subject of *zizit* in the mouth of Koraḥ? In what way is it appropriate as the pretext for his rebellion?

(b)   Why did Rashi in citing from the Midrash omit the question relating to the house full of Torah scrolls, resting content with the first question?

THE ISRAELITES' ROLE IN THE KORAḤ MUTINY

In the previous chapter we discussed the respective grievances — of "Koraḥ's congregation". We shall devote ourselves on this occasion to one passage in the story which is simple in its wording but difficult to understand.

In the first half of the chapter the struggle involves Moses, on the one hand, and Koraḥ and his congregation, on the other. The whole of this congregation airs its views:

רַב־לָכֶם כִּי כָל־הָעֵדָה כֻּלָּם קְדֹשִׁים וּבְתוֹכָם ה'
וּמַדּוּעַ תִּתְנַשְּׂאוּ עַל־קְהַל ה':

You take too much upon yourselves; all the congregation is holy, every one of them and the Lord is among them; why do you then lord it over the assembly of the Lord?

(16, 3)

Moses replied, harangued, reproved, strove to placate them. They retorted, Dathan and Abiram with greater impudence than the rest, till Moses made his final proposition regarding the firepans "for the morrow". Where were the rest of the Israelites? On whose side did they range themselves? Were they swept along in the murky current of the malcontents, joining Koraḥ's hand or did they remain loyal to Moses their teacher and prophet? The text has hitherto paid no attention to them.

In verse 19 we do have an allusion to an attempt by Koraḥ to influence them to join forces with him:

וַיַּקְהֵל עֲלֵיהֶם קֹרַח אֶת כָּל־הָעֵדָה אֶל־פֶּתַח אֹהֶל מוֹעֵד

And Koraḥ assembled all the congregation against them (i.e. Moses and Aaron) to the door of the tent of meeting.

Rashi observes:

> With words of scorn. The whole of that night he repaired to the tribes and seduced them: Do you imagine that I am concerned only for myself, I am concerned for you all. They are monopolising all the high offices: him the kingship, his brother, the priesthood! — till all of them were won over.

But we are still uninformed as to the extent of their acceptance of Koraḥ's point of view. Did they merely agree to come to the the tent of meeting and watch the proceedings to see how things would work out or did they share his views? Perhaps subsequent verses will clarify matters:

וַיַּקְהֵל עֲלֵיהֶם קֹרַח אֶת־כָּל־הָעֵדָה־אֶל־פֶּתַח אֹהֶל מוֹעֵד
וַיֵּרָא כְבוֹד־ה׳ אֶל־כָּל־הָעֵדָה:

And Koraḥ assembled all the congregation against them to the door of the tent of meeting
Whereupon the glory of the Lord appeared to all the congregation.[1]

The suddenness of this Divine revelation portrayed His indignation. Let us study the contents of the message accompanying the Divine revelation:

וַיְדַבֵּר ה׳ אֶל מֹשֶׁה וְאֶל־אַהֲרֹן לֵאמֹר:
הִבָּדְלוּ מִתּוֹךְ הָעֵדָה הַזֹּאת
וַאֲכַלֶּה אֹתָם כְּרָגַע:

And the Lord spoke unto Moses and Aaron saying:
Separate yourselves from this congregation
that I may consume them in a moment.

(16, 20)

This verse raises many problems. First of all, who is the congregation? Who were faced with the threat of retributive extinction? Our commentators differ. Naḥmanides cited the view of Rabbenu Ḥananel only to repudiate it, prefacing first another question:

> It may be asked, if the Israelites had in no way sinned or rebelled against their master why the anger against them and the threat to consume them in an instant? If they too had rebelled like Korah and his band how could Moses and Aaron say: "Shall one man sin and wilt Thou be wrath with the whole congregation?"
>
> Rabbenu Ḥananel explained the demand to "separate from the congregation" to refer to the congregation of Korah and not that of the children of Israel. "And they said. O God, the God of all spirits . . ." Whereupon the Almighty immediately informed Moses that he had intended to consume not all the children of Israel but merely the congregation of Korah. For this reason the Almighty clarified His original message. When I said "separate yourselves", I meant "Get you up from about the dwelling of Korah" (v. 24).

According to this interpretation, Korah only succeeded in winning over his own immediate followers, his congregation, whereas Moses had misunderstood the Divine threat to refer to the whole people. The second message of God in verse 24 is merely a clarification of the first one. Shadal (Luzzatto) takes a similar attitude — the congregation referred to by God were the incense offerers whom God did not wish Aaron to join because they would not wait for the morrow. Moses, on the other hand, had thought that God had meant to involve the whole or the major part of the people.

But besides the difficulty of attributing to Moses such a mistake in understanding the prophetic message, Naḥmanides objects to R. Ḥananel's interpretation on other grounds.

196

He is not correct since the term "congregation" could not be applied to three individuals — Koraḥ, Dathan and Abiram, since they did not constitute a congregation and the Israelites were not with them, whereas Aaron was with the congregation of incense offerers. Further, the command "separate yourselves" referred to Moses and Aaron alone, as in 17, 10: "Get you up". The threat to consume them in a moment alluded to the plague which would consume a great multitude in an instant. Far be it for Moses to misunderstand a prophecy and be misled.

But this is the true explanation. At the beginning all the people supported Moses and Aaron. It was only when Koraḥ and his band assembled with their firepans at the entrance of the tent of meeting with Moses and Aaron and told the people that he was fighting not for himself but for their rights, that they began to be won over and imagined that perhaps it would please God to restore the priesthood to their firstborn. This is the force of "And Koraḥ assembled all the congregation against them". By this they all merited destruction since they had doubted their leader which was tantamount to doubting the Divine Presence, repudiating the message of the prophet in their heart, making themselves liable to death at the hands of Heaven.

Moses and Aaron defended them by arguing that they had not sinned in deed, but that Koraḥ was to blame for seducing them. He alone should die as a public example. This is the way of the intercessor to extenuate the sin as regards the community, as a whole, and place the blame on the individual who is, on all counts, guilty. Compare David's plea: "Behold I have sinned and done perversely, but these sheep, what have they done? let thy hand, I pray Thee be against me and against my father's house" (2 Sam. 24, 17).

According to Naḥmanides the Almighty had meant to consume the whole congregation who were guilty of inner rebellion against Moses His prophet, but the latter had endeavoured to extenuate their conduct. But Moses's intercession raises another problem alluded to by Isaac Arama in his *Akedat Yiẓḥak*.

"Shall one man sin and will Thou be wroth with all the congregation?" What was unusual in this? Surely not all of them had sinned with the Calf, yet it is stated (Ex. 32, 10): "Leave Me and let My anger be kindled against them that I may consume them". Similarly with Achan it is stated (Joshua 22, 20): "Did not Achan commit a trespass concerning the devoted thing and wrath fell upon all the congregation of Israel? and that man perished not alone in his iniquity?" The individual is a part of the whole just as the whole man is sick even when only one part of the body is affected.

197

The voice of Koraḥ is heard no more after this. He has no rejoinder to Moses' retort neither to his words of reconciliation or reproof. Our Sages remarked on Koraḥ's silence during the whole chapter and explained it as follows:

''ויאמר משה אל קרח: שמעו נא בני לוי!'' כל הדברים האלה פייס משה לקרח ואין אתה מוצא שהשיבו דבר, לפי שהיה פקח ברשעתו. אמר: אם אני משיבו, יודע אני בו שהוא חכם גדול, עכשו יקפחני בדבריו ומקלקלני ואני מתרצה לו בעל כרחי, מוטב שלא אזקק לו.

"And Moses said to Koraḥ: Hear now, O sons of Levi!": Moses uttered all these words in an endeavour to appease Koraḥ but you do not find that he gave answer. That was because he was clever in his wickedness. He said: If I answer him I know that he being a wise man will outwit me in his arguments and I will be forced to become reconciled to him. Better I should not enter into argument with him.

(Tanḥuma)

Dathan and Abiram, on the other hand, answer him explicitly. Their words repay careful study:

לֹא נַעֲלֶה:
הַמְעַט כִּי הֶעֱלִיתָנוּ מֵאֶרֶץ זָבַת חָלָב וּדְבַשׁ לַהֲמִיתֵנוּ בַּמִּדְבָּר כִּי־תִשְׂתָּרֵר
עָלֵינוּ גַּם הִשְׂתָּרֵר:
אַף לֹא אֶל אֶרֶץ זָבַת חָלָב וּדְבַשׁ הֲבִיאֹתָנוּ וַתִּתֶּן לָנוּ נַחֲלַת שָׂדֶה וָכָרֶם:
הַעֵינֵי הָאֲנָשִׁים הָהֵם תְּנַקֵּר:
לֹא נַעֲלֶה:

We shall not come up;
Is it a small thing that you have brought us up out of a land
flowing with milk and honey to kill us in the wilderness but
you must needs make yourself a prince over us?

Moreover you have not brought us to a land flowing with milk
and honey, nor given us an inheritance of fields and vineyards;
will you put out the eyes of these men.
We shall not go up.

(16, 12—14)

separate themselves and get away physically from the vicinity of Korah? But, as Arama has emphasised Malbim likewise points out, they were bidden to perform a public act of disassociation from Korah's acts:

> God answered him that his wrath was caused by the fact that their standing near the wicked implied that that they condoned their actions. They had to show by keeping away that they did not share their views.
>
> (Malbim)

According to the foregoing commentators, the Israelites were in the dangerous situation characteristic of many people to this day.* They neither agreed with Korah nor actively opposed him, but stood aside to see how things would work out. (Our Sages condemned this attitude and regarded Abraham's brother, Haran, as the archetype of the opportunist. In a well known Midrash they describe how Haran debated with himself whether to follow Abraham into the furnace to which Nimrod had resolved to cast him as punishment for his iconoclastic activities. He said, If Abraham comes out alive I shall proclaim my monotheism like Abraham. If not, I shall support Nimrod. Abraham came out unscathed but when Haran was thrown into the furnace, he was burnt). The Almighty therefore demanded that the congregation get up from about the dwelling of Korah, Dathan and Abiram. But again the question arises, why did Moses the faithful mediator between God and Israel not transmit the Divine order in exactly the same words as he had received it? Instead he said:

סוּרוּ נָא מֵעַל אָהֳלֵי הָאֲנָשִׁים הָרְשָׁעִים הָאֵלֶּה
וְאַל־תִּגְּעוּ בְּכָל־אֲשֶׁר לָהֶם
פֶּן תִּסָּפוּ בְּכָל־חַטֹּאתָם:

---

* [Cf. Bunyan's Mr. Facing-both-ways] T.

**Depart, I pray you, from the tents of these wicked men
and touch nothing of theirs,**
lest you be swept away in all their sins.

(16, 26)

Alshikh suggests that Moses' substitution of the phrase *suru na*
(depart I pray you) for *he'alu* (get you up) implied a softening of the
Divine order. He tried to persuade them for their own good, in order
to placate them.

> I am not asking you to get away from them completely but just to move
> away a little. The succeeding verse states, "they got them up" implying that
> they left unwillingly, as if they had been forced to leave, shamed by Moses.
> For this reason, Moses had himself gone to the place and stood by Korah,
> Dathan and Abiram to make sure they would be shamed into moving, and
> did not communicate the Divine message through an intermediary.
>
> (Alshikh)

On the other hand, another commentator gives the very opposite
explanation. *He'alu* implies merely to move away a little, whereas
Moses, who understood the Divine intention gave it greater force by
asking them to depart or turn aside completely, both physically and
spiritually, from all connected with Korah and his evil doctrines. The
Israelites however contented themselves with moving away —
physically — from the place from fear of the immediate
consequences, but inwardly did not repudiate Korah's evil path and
the material greed symbolised by it. In proof of this, we may cite
what happened immediately after the miracle and dreadful
punishment meted out to Korah and his followers:

וַיִּלֹּנוּ כָּל־עֲדַת בְּנֵי־יִשְׂרָאֵל מִמָּחֳרָת עַל־מֹשֶׁה וְעַל־אַהֲרֹן לֵאמֹר אַתֶּם
הֲמִתֶּם אֶת־עַם ה' :

Arama's answer explains the connection between verse 22 — Moses' intercession — and verse 23 — the Divine answer and reaction:

> Divine anger is directed against the community for the sin of the individual as in Achan's case when the individual is knit to his group and is identified with it (since in such a case we blame the community for not having warned him or disassociated itself from his acts. Further if the community is all of one mind, it is more likely they will be influenced by the misdeeds of the guilty person. They are indeed like the body which is affected by the sickness of one of its limbs — it quickly spreads further — Commentary of Haim Joseph Falk). But when the sinner has separated himself from the community and taken himself to one side to take issue with them, the burden of sin is already removed from them. We no longer hold the public guilty then for the misdeed of the individual. It is like a limb that has been severed from the living body, having no further connection with it.

We may now understand Moses's plea: "Shall one man sin and wilt Thou be wroth with all the congregation". For according to Arama, Korah did not succeed in winning over all the Israelites. On the contrary he separated himself from the congregation to dispute with Moses (as Rashi explains, the first words of our sidra: "And Korah took . . ." — he took himself to one side to dispute the priesthood.) Now we may understand how apt is the Divine reply in the next verse:

> God rightly demanded that just as Korah and his band had separated themselves from the rest of the congregation so should the congregation actively separate and disassociate themselves from Korah.
>
> (Akedat Yizhak)

This also solves another difficulty raised by Ibn Atar (*Or Hahayyim*). Why should the Israelites merit instant destruction even if they happened to be standing among Korah's band. Surely Aaron who was with them was unharmed when the ground opened underneath them. What was the purpose of the Divine demand to

2. Proof that the punishment for the seducer is not the same as that of his victim is brought from *Beha'alotkha*. Where?

3. In what way does *Kli Yakar* deviate from the usual interpretation in his understanding of the term "God of all spirit?"

4. In what way does he deviate from the usual sense in his understanding of the word "saying?"

NOTE

1   The appearance of the Divine glory was evidently a sign of His indignation. Ḥizkuni explains: Moses told Koraḥ in the name of God: "Turn up before the Lord you and Aaron on the morrow". Koraḥ did otherwise, "assembled all the people" (i.e. did not wait for the morrow). On account of this he was angry with them, immediately.

DATHAN AND ABIRAM

In the previous chapter we dwelt on the content of the grievances aired by Koraḥ and his company, the causes of the rebellion, its timing and the attitude of the people. This time we shall endeavour to get to know the persons who headed it.

Four of them are named:

קֹרַח . . .וְדָתָן וַאֲבִירָם . . .וְאוֹן בֶּן־פֶּלֶת

Korah, Dathan and Abiram and On the son of Peleth...
(16, 1)

The last-mentioned is referred to but once in the account, and nothing more is heard of him. As for Koraḥ himself — his words are recorded for us on one occasion only, and then not as the only spokesman, but as one of the whole company of malcontents, together with Dathan, Abiram and others.

רַב־לָכֶם כִּי כָל־הָעֵדָה כֻּלָּם קְדֹשִׁים
וּבְתוֹכָם ה'
וּמַדּוּעַ תִּתְנַשְּׂאוּ עַל־קְהַל ה':

You take too much upon yourselves, seeing all the congregation are holy, every one of them, and the Lord is among them; why then do you lord it over the assembly of the Lord?
(16, 3)

On the morrow all the congregation of the children of Israel murmured against Moses and against Aaron saying, You have killed the people of the Lord.

(17, 6)

Questions for Further Study

It is reasonable to assume that the Almighty had never intended to punish these who had not sinned but only referred to the congregation of Korah, whereas Moses understood that He referred to the whole congregation of Israel since it is stated that "Korah assembled against them all the congregation". Moses imagined the Almighty assumed that the whole of Israel had followed Korah, and for this reason threatened to destroy them in a moment. Moses therefore interceded "God, God of all spirits . . ." since he saw nothing criminal in the conduct of the people. The fact that Korah had assembled them did not mean that they had all been won over by his words. But he understood from the fact that God wished to destroy them that in their hearts they really had been influenced by Korah, since God is the God of all spirits and knows what is going on in men's minds.

Nevertheless Moses placed the chief blame on Korah who had misled them. God should therefore not be angry with the whole congregation. He defended them on the grounds that they had not spontaneously committed his sin but had been misled into it. They did not merit being destroyed in a moment in the same way as the misleader himself.

"Speak unto the congregation, Get you up from about the dwelling of Korah". It never entered My mind to punish all the congregation. On the contrary, I know that they were not won over by Korah. When I said separate yourselves from the congregation, I meant that all Israel should separate themselves from the congregation of Korah. This is indicated by the wording of the text "And God spoke to Moses and Aaron, *saying*". What is the force of the word *saying*? To whom should they say? But God wanted them to instruct all the Israelites to separate themselves. Moses however misunderstood the Divine message.

(Kli Yakar)

1. Does the *Kli Yakar* follow Rabbenu Ḥananel or Naḥmanides or elaborate a third interpretation?

It is no accident that they opened and closed with the identical words: "We shall not go up". Their wickedness lies in this, that they were not even prepared to reason. Their impudence becomes even more obvious when we contrast their words with Moses', and the latter's second statement with their first words. In this way we shall be able to read between the lines of Scriptures

Moses' Words	*The Words of Korah, Dathan and Abiram*
	They assembled against Moses and Aaron and they said to them, *You take too much upon you*, seeing all the congregation are holy . . .
Moses heard and fell on his face. Then he spoke to Korah and all his company . . . *you take too much upon you* O sons of Levi . . . *is it but a small thing to you that* the God of Israel has separated you from the congregation of Israel to bring you near to Himself . . . and that He has brought you near and all your brethren the sons of Levi with you and will you seek the priesthood *also*? (vv. 4—10)	*Is it a small thing that you* have brought us out of a land flowing with milk and honey to kill us in the wilderness but you must needs make yourself *also* a priest over us? (vv. 3, 13)

We have often drawn attention in our Studies[1] to the significance of recurring words and phrases in the Bible, in the course of the same chapter (key or motif words[2]). Our Sages pointed this out too. Of particular importance is the recurrent word or phrase in a duologue.

The word bandied to and fro between speaker and respondent emphasises some lesson, agreement or acceptance[3] or perhaps, on the other hand, contrariness, mockery and opposition. It is the latter in our context. Isaac Arama has pointed this out in *Akedat Yizḥak*:

> Their impudence is reflected both in the form and trend of their utterance. Moses had begun by saying, "Is it but a small thing" and ended with "You take too much upon yourselves O sons of Levi" which were the words they had used to him in their utterance: "You take too much upon yourself seeing all the congregation are holy". So they deliberately began their words now with: "Is it a small thing that you brought us up". In other words: "You seized on the first words of our utterance at the end of your argument. We shall similarly seize on, at the beginning of our utterance, your opening expression. We are capable of answering in just the same way as you". They were certainly employing a deliberately mocking and offensive tone.

It should be noted that this mocking is not just in the repetition of the phrases "is it but a small thing" and "you take too much upon you" but also in the resemblance between the whole structure of the last verse of their utterance and that of Moses' first verse:

הַמְעַט מִכֶּם כִּי הִבְדִּיל אֱלֹהֵי יִשְׂרָאֵל . . .

וּבִקַּשְׁתֶּם גַּם כְּהֻנָּה:

הַמְעַט כִּי הֶעֱלִיתָנוּ . . .

כִּי־תִשְׂתָּרֵר עָלֵינוּ גַּם־הִשְׂתָּרֵר:

Is it a small thing that God has separated . . .
will you seek *the priesthood also*?
Is it a small thing that you have brought us up...
that you must *make yourself also a prince* **over us.**

(vv. 9, 10, 13)

They meant: You concluded with a rhetoric question up-braiding us for our ambition. We too conclude with a rhetoric question which denounces your uppertiness.

206

But their impudence reached a climax in the use they made of the description applied to the Promised Land "a land flowing with milk and honey". When was this description first applied to the Land? Surely it was the crux of God's revelation of Moses at the burning bush, when he was first apprised of the message of redemption:

וַיֹּאמֶר ה׳

רָאֹה רָאִיתִי אֶת־עֳנִי עַמִּי אֲשֶׁר בְּמִצְרָיִם וְאֶת־צַעֲקָתָם שָׁמַעְתִּי מִפְּנֵי נֹגְשָׂיו

כִּי יָדַעְתִּי אֶת מַכְאֹבָיו:

וָאֵרֵד לְהַצִּילוֹ מִיַּד מִצְרַיִם

וּלְהַעֲלֹתוֹ מִן־הָאָרֶץ הַהוּא אֶל־אֶרֶץ טוֹבָה וּרְחָבָה

אֶל־אֶרֶץ זָבַת חָלָב וּדְבָשׁ

And the Lord said:

I have surely seen the affliction of My people who are in Egypt and have heard their cry by reason of their taskmasters; for I know their pains.

I shall come down to deliver them out of the hand of the Egyptians

and to bring them unto a good and spacious land,

to a land flowing with milk and honey.

(Ex. 3, 7—8)

לֵךְ וְאָסַפְתָּ אֶת־זִקְנֵי יִשְׂרָאֵל

וְאָמַרְתָּ אֲלֵהֶם

ה׳ אֱלֹהֵי אֲבֹתֵיכֶם נִרְאָה אֵלַי . . .

וָאֹמַר אַעֲלֶה אֶתְכֶם מֵעֳנִי מִצְרַיִם

אֶל אֶרֶץ הַכְּנַעֲנִי וְהַחִתִּי . . .

אֶל אֶרֶץ זָבַת חָלָב וּדְבָשׁ:

Go and gather the elders of Israel

and say to them:

The God of your fathers appeared to me...
and I have said: I will bring you up out of the affliction of
Egypt
to the land of the Canaanite and Hittite...
to a land flowing with milk and honey.

(Ex. 3, 16—17)

This was the message imparted by Moses to the elders of Israel
when he returned from Midian.

Again, before their departure from Egypt, when the Lord imparted
to the Israelites the precepts of the Passover they were told:

וְהָיָה כִי־יְבִיאֲךָ ה׳ אֶל־אֶרֶץ הַכְּנַעֲנִי . . .
אֲשֶׁר נִשְׁבַּע לַאֲבֹתֶיךָ לָתֶת לָךְ
אֶרֶץ זָבַת חָלָב וּדְבָשׁ
וְעָבַדְתָּ אֶת הָעֲבֹדָה הַזֹּאת

And it shall come to pass when the Lord will bring you to the
land of the Canaanite...
which He vowed to your fathers to give you
a land flowing with milk and honey,
then you shall perform this service.

(Ex. 13, 5)

Then, even after the sin of the calf and Moses' intercession and the
averting of the retribution, when the Lord became reconciled to His
people and re-accepted them, they were again promised:

לֵךְ עֲלֵה מִזֶּה אַתָּה וְהָעָם
אֲשֶׁר הֶעֱלִיתָ מֵאֶרֶץ מִצְרָיִם . . .
וְשָׁלַחְתִּי לְפָנֶיךָ מַלְאָךְ . . .
אֶל־אֶרֶץ זָבַת חָלָב וּדְבָשׁ

**Depart and go up hence you and the people
you have brought up out of the land of Egypt...
and I will send an angel before you...**
to a land flowing with milk and honey.

(Ex. 33, 1—3)

Even the spies, with all their malicious intent, could not deny,
though but weakly, grudgingly admitting:

בָּאנוּ אֶל־הָאָרֶץ אֲשֶׁר שְׁלַחְתָּנוּ
וְגַם זָבַת חָלָב וּדְבַשׁ הִוא

We came to the land to which you despatched us, *and it does
indeed flow with milk and honey.*

(13, 27)

This description of the promised land, the land "which I swore to
give to Abraham, Isaac and Jacob" is applied by Dathan and
Abiram to the land of abominations, the house of bondage, the iron
furnace — to Egypt.

הַמְעַט כִּי הֶעֱלִיתָנוּ מֵאֶרֶץ זָבַת חָלָב וּדְבַשׁ

**Is it but a small thing that you have brought us up out of a
land flowing with milk and honey?**

(16, 13)

It is again evident here that the literalists (Ibn Ezra and Rashbam)
out of their slavish adherence to the wording have not plumbed the
depths of its real and profounder meaning in their comment: "Who
brought us forth from a goodly place". By this all the sting is taken
out of Dathan and Abiram's words. The Israelites had already
lauded Egypt as the place of "the fleshpot" as the place where they
had eaten "fish for nothing". They had wistfully yearned for it even

209

before this. But here is something new and unprecedented — a complete reversal of values, calling black white and white black. What was slavery is termed freedom, the land of uncleanness is given the title exclusively applied to the holy land. It is a symbol for all time to all those who in the lands of their dispersion proclaim: Here is our Jerusalem!

Questions for Further Study

1. "We shall not go up".
    Their mouths were their own undoing, for theirs was indeed only a descent.

    (Rashi)

    ### Cf. Rashi with the following expositions:

    Rashi on Gen. 43, 20 s.v. *yarod yaradnu* ("we came indeed down"): It was a comedown for us. We were used to supporting others; now we are reduced to depending on you.

    Rashi on Ex. 32, 7 s.v. *lekh red* ("go, get down"): Get down from your greatness; I gave you greatness only on account of them. At that moment Moses was banned from the heavenly court!

    Rashi on Deut. 1, 42 s.v. *lo ta'alu* ("you shall not go up"): You shall experience no uplift but a comedown.

    In all these four places, in what way does the exposition deviate from the literal meaning of the text and in what sense is it true to its profounder meaning?

2. "We shall not go up".
    The tent of meeting may conceivably have been in the middle of the camp, on an eminence, and that is why the text states: "Get you *up* from around the tabernacle of Koraḥ, Dathan and Abiram" (16, 24). Or, perhaps, he who goes to perform the service of God or to the chosen place of worship is described as "going up".

    (Ibn Ezra)

(a) Explain the difference between his explanation and that of Rashi.

210

(b)   Explain the difference between the two explanations of Ibn Ezra.

3.   Rashi s.v. *ha-anashim ha-hem* ("those men"): like a man who attributes his own curse to another (i.e. a euphemistic avoidance of applying an unpleasant fate to themselves.

Ibn Ezra: s.v. *ha-anashim ha-hem*: do you wish to pluck out the eyes of those persons —meaning all those who left Egypt as if it said: do you wish to pluck out the eyes that they should not see; for what you have done to us is plain for all to see. Figuratively we say: "So-and-so's eyes are closed; therefore he cannot see". Therefore we shall not go up. Others explain: Do you wish to blind us that we should not see, i.e. you are trying to deceive us (cf. "pull the wool over our eyes"). We shall not go up! . . . The expression "those men" is an example of a euphemism — the vulgar do not like to apply anything bad to themselves. But the correct explanation is, in my view, that "those men" refers to the elders who were with Moses, as it is stated: "And the elders of Israel went after him".

(a)   Explain the difference between the two explanations of Ibn Ezra to the phrase: "Will you pluck out the eyes of those men". Which sounds more plausible?

(b)   What is the difference between him and Rashi in the explanation of "those men". Which sounds more plausible?

(c)   Where do we find in the Torah an expression that can likewise be explained "like a man who attributes his own curse to another" as Rashi explains here?

NOTES

[1] See *Studies in Devarim*, Ki Tavo; Niẓavim-Vayelekh; *Studies in Shemot*, Beshallaḥ.

[2] See Buber-Rosenzweig: *Die Schrift und ihre Verdeutschung* (Schocken Verlag, Berlin 1936).

[3] See *Studies in Bereshit*, Mikeẓ, pp. 439 ff.

SIN IS A KILLER

The children of Israel followed their leader Moses and the pillar of cloud, "according to the commandment of the Lord they journeyed and according to the commandment of the Lord they encamped". The Ark stood in the centre of the camp; they were encircled by clouds of glory protecting them and driving away the serpents and the scorpions; water was provided for them from the flinty rock and food from the heavens. Divine providence miraculously and immanently accompanied them:

> ‏. . .כִּי־אַתָּה ה׳ בְּקֶרֶב הָעָם הַזֶּה אֲשֶׁר־עַיִן בְּעַיִן נִרְאָה ה׳ וַעֲנָנְךָ עֹמֵד
> עֲלֵהֶם
> ‏וּבְעַמֻּד עָנָן אַתָּה הֹלֵךְ לִפְנֵיהֶם יוֹמָם
> ‏וּבְעַמּוּד אֵשׁ לָיְלָה:

... that thou Lord art seen face to face, and that thy cloud standeth over them,
and that thou goest before them, by day time in a pillar of a cloud,
and in a pillar of fire by night.

(14, 14)

But the generation of the wilderness was not able to live on the lofty plane of closeness to the Almighty and descended into its own petty world of jealousies and empty prestige, slandering their peerless leader Moses, of whom it was said that he was "the most unassuming of all men upon the face of the earth". "Wherefore then lift. ye up yourselves above the congregation of the Lord" was the accusation they hurled against the man with whom the Lord had spoken face to face. He who had givem them the Torah had to justify his conduct in the face of their slanders and prove that "hereby ye shall know that the Lord has sent me to do all these works for I have not done them of my own mind". How did he demonstrate that he was the accredited emissary of the Almighty? — By the following miracles:

וַתִּפְתַּח הָאָרֶץ אֶת־פִּיהָ
וַתִּבְלַע אֹתָם וְאֶת בָּתֵּיהֶם. . .
וְאֵשׁ יָצְאָה מֵאֵת ה'
וַתֹּאכַל אֵת הַחֲמִשִּׁים וּמָאתַיִם אִישׁ. . .

And the earth opened her mouth,
and swallowed them up, and their houses . . .
And there came out a fire from the Lord,
and consumed the two hundred and fifty men . . .

(16, 32, 35)

As a result of this the Children of Israel ran away in terror "lest the earth swallow us up". But what was the outcome of all these miracles and the quelling of the mutiny? Everything returned to its previous order. The fire disappeared, the earth closed its mouth and the people reverted to their grumblings and lack of faith and limited conceptions:

וַיִּלֹּנוּ כָּל־עֲדַת בְּנֵי־יִשְׂרָאֵל מִמָּחֳרָת עַל־מֹשֶׁה וְעַל־אַהֲרֹן לֵאמֹר
אַתֶּם הֲמִתֶּם אֶת עַם ה':

But on the morrow all the congregation of the children of
Israel murmured against Moses and against Aaron, saying,
Ye have killed the people of the Lord.

(17, 6)

213

It is an astonishing fact that the Children of Israel immediately reverted to their grumblings after having witnessed such striking divine intervention. However, we meet the same situation at other times in Jewish history. When Elijah stood on Mount Carmel and faced the 400 prophets of Baal he similarly demonstrated the supremacy of the true God by the invocation of His help:

> Then said Elijah unto the people, I, even I only, remain a prophet of the Lord; but Baal's prophets are four hundred and fifty men. Let them therefore give us two bullocks; and let them choose one bullock for themselves, and cut it in pieces, and lay it on wood, and put no fire under: and I will dress the other bullock, and lay it on wood, and put no fire under: And call ye on the name of your gods, and I will call on the name of the Lord: and the God that answereth by fire, let him be God. And all the people answered and said, It is well spoken. And Elijah said unto the prophets of Baal, Choose you one bullock for yourselves, and dress it first; for ye are many: and call on the name of your gods, but put no fire under. And they took the bullock which was given them, and they dressed it, and called on the name of Baal from morning even until noon, saying, O Baal, hear us. But there was no voice, nor any that answered. And they leaped upon the altar which was made. And it came to pass at noon, that Elijah mocked them, and said, Cry aloud: for he is a god; either he is talking, or he is pursuing, or he is in a journey, or peradventure he sleepeth, and must be awaked. And they cried aloud, and cut themselves after their manner with knives and lancets, till the blood gushed out upon them. And it came to pass, when midday was past, and they prophesied until the time of the offering of the evening sacrifice, that there was neither voice, nor any to answer, nor any that regarded. And Elijah said unto all the people, Come near unto me. And all the people came near onto him. And he repaired the altar of the Lord

that was broken down. And Elijah took twelves stones, according to the number of the tribes of the sons of Jacob, unto whom the word of the Lord came, saying, Israel shall be thy name: And with the stones he built an altar in the name of the Lord: and he made a trench about the altar, as great as would contain two measues of seed. And he put the wood in order, and cut the bullock in pieces, and laid him on the wood, and said: Fill four barrels with water, and pour it on the burnt sacrifice, and on the wood. And he said, Do it the second time. And they did it the second time. And he said, Do it the third time. And they did it the third time. And the water ran round about the altar; and he filled the trench also with water. And it came to pass at the time of the offering of the evening sacrifice, that Elijah the prophet came near, and said, Lord God of Abraham, Isaac and of Israel, let it be known this day that thou art God in Israel, and that I am thy servant, and that I have done all these things at thy word. Hear me, O Lord, hear me, that this people may know that thou art the Lord God, and that thou has turned their heart back again. Then the fire of the Lord fell, and consumed the burnt sacrifice, and the wood, and the stones, and the dust, and licked up the water that was in the trench. And when all the people saw it, they fell on their faces: and they said, the Lord, he is the God; the Lord, he is the God. And Elijah said unto them, Take the prophets of Baal; let not one of them escape. And they took them: and Elijah brought them down to the brook Kishon, and slew them there.

(I Kings 18, 22—40)

But did the people learn a permanent lesson from this? By no means. On the next day the true prophets were slaughtered, Jezebel and the followers of Baal remained alive, and Elijah who had triumphed in the contest fled to the wilderness of Sinai.

A miracle cannot serve either to accredit the emissary or his mission. Whoever is consumed by doubts and scepticism will always find an

215

explanation of the miracles. Just the same as he does not acknowledge the Almighty as the guiding power behind his servants and prophets so he will not detect the workings of Providence behind the wonders of the creation, both in its natural and supernatural aspects. Our Sages have already drawn attention to this:

ויגש אליהו הנביא ויאמר: "ענני ה' ענני! "ענני" — שתרד אש מן השמים ו"ענני" שלא יאמרו מעשה כשפים הם. —

"Hear me O Lord, hear me" — twice; the first time for fire to come down from heaven and the second "hear me" that the Children of Israel should not regard it as mere sorcery.

(Berakhot 6b)

In our sidra therefore, it is equally understandable that the miraculous opening of the earth and the burning of two hundred and fifty people would not convince the mutineers. Ibn Ezra phrases the reaction of the people as follows:

> What proof is it that it is the tribe of Levi which is chosen and that Aaron is the truly elected high priest? Perhaps through your prayers or through some trick you burnt those who brought the sacrifices!

Instead of repenting of their ways the people looked for a natural, mechanical explanation of the miracle. Magic and sorcery were the primitive equivalent of modern science which worked in accordance with its own laws and from which no power could deliver. So thought the ancients. Thus Moses' desire to stir the people to an acknowledgement of their sin and return to God was not achieved by the miracles. Perhaps now the following verses describing a strange and mysterious incident in our sidra will be more understandable:

וַיֹּאמֶר מֹשֶׁה אֶל אַהֲרֹן קַח אֶת־הַמַּחְתָּה וְתֶן־עָלֶיהָ אֵשׁ מֵעַל הַמִּזְבֵּחַ וְשִׂים קְטֹרֶת וְהוֹלֵךְ מְהֵרָה אֶל הָעֵדָה וְכַפֵּר עֲלֵיהֶם כִּי־יָצָא הַקֶּצֶף מִלִּפְנֵי ה' הֵחֵל הַנָּגֶף: וַיִּקַּח אַהֲרֹן כַּאֲשֶׁר דִּבֶּר מֹשֶׁה וַיָּרָץ אֶל תּוֹךְ הַקָּהָל וְהִנֵּה הֵחֵל הַנֶּגֶף בָּעָם וַיִּתֵּן אֶת הַקְּטֹרֶת וַיְכַפֵּר עַל־הָעָם: וַיַּעֲמֹד בֵּין הַמֵּתִים וּבֵין הַחַיִּים וַתֵּעָצַר הַמַּגֵּפָה:

**And Moses said unto Aaron, Take a censer, and put fire
therein from off the altar, and put on incense, and go quickly
unto the congregation, and make an atonement for them: for
there is wrath gone out from the Lord; the plague is begun.
And Aaron took as Moses commanded, and ran into the midst
of the congregation; and, behold, the plague was begun among
the people: and he put on incense, and made an atonement for
the people. And he stood between the dead and the living; and
the plague was stayed.**

(17, 11—13)

Rashi basing himself on the words of our Sages, comments on this
verse as follows:

למה בקטורת? לפי שהיו ישראל מליזין ומרננים אחר הקטורת, לומר: "סם המות
הוא" . . .
אמר הקב"ה: תראו שעוצר המגפה הוא והחטא הוא הממית.

Why with incense? Because the Israelites were denouncing the incense
saying: It is a deadly poison. Said the Holy One blessed be He: You will see
that it is an antidote to the plague and that on the contrary, it is sin which
kills.

The above quotation is characteristic of a number of rabbinic dicta
designed to counter the belief in magic and its supernatural powers,
and to discredit the role of chance and fate in the conducting of
human affairs. Rather they wished to emphasise the hand of
Providence everywhere. We shall conclude by quoting from the
Mishnah of Rosh Hashanah (III, 8) on this theme:

"והיה כאשר ירים משה ידו וגבר ישראל" (שמות יז, יא). וכי ידיו של משה עושות
מלחמה או שוברות מלחמה! אלא לומר לך: כל זמן שהיו ישראל מסתכלין כלפי מעלה
ומשעבדים את ליבם לאביהם שבשמים — היו מתגברים, ואם לאו היו נופלים.

"And it came to pass when Moses held up his hand that Israel prevailed, and
when he let down his hand Amalek prevailed" (Exodus 17, 11). — But could

the hands of Moses make or break the battle! — it is rather to teach thee
that such time as the Israelites directed their thoughts on high and kept their
hearts in subjection to their Father in heaven, they prevailed, otherwise they
suffered defeat.

כיוצא בדבר אתה אומר: "עשה לך שרף ושים אותו על נס, והיה כל נשוך וראה אותו
וחי" (במדבר כא, ח). וכי נחש ממית או מחיה? אלא שבזמן שישראל מסתכלים כלפי
מעלה ומשעבדים את ליבם לאביהם שבשמים — היו מתרפאים, ואם לאו — היו
נמוקים.

In like manner thou mayest say: "Make thee a fiery serpent and set it upon a
standard, and it shall come to pass that everyone that is bitten when he seeth
it shall live" (Numbers 21, 8). But could the serpent slay or keep alive! — it
is rather to teach that such time as the Israelites directed their thoughts on
high and kept their hearts in subjection to their Father in heaven, they were
healed, otherwise they pined away.

THE FIREPANS

וַיְדַבֵּר ה' אֶל מֹשֶׁה לֵּאמֹר:
אֱמֹר אֶל־אֶלְעָזָר בֶּן־אַהֲרֹן הַכֹּהֵן
וְיָרֵם אֶת הַמַּחְתֹּת מִבֵּין הַשְּׂרֵפָה וְאֶת־הָאֵשׁ זְרֵה־הָלְאָה
כִּי קָדֵשׁוּ: אֵת מַחְתּוֹת הַחַטָּאִים הָאֵלֶּה בְּנַפְשֹׁתָם
וְעָשׂוּ אֹתָם רִקֻּעֵי פַחִים צִפּוּי לַמִּזְבֵּחַ
כִּי־הִקְרִיבֻם לִפְנֵי־ה' וַיִּקְדָּשׁוּ וְיִהְיוּ לְאוֹת לִבְנֵי יִשְׂרָאֵל:

And the Lord spoke unto Moses, saying,
Speak unto Eleazar the son of Aaron the priest,
that he take up the firepans out of the burning
and scatter thou the fire yonder;
for they are become holy;
even the firepans of these men who have sinned at the cost of
their lives,
and let them be made beaten plates for a covering for the altar
—
for they are become holy, **because they were offered before the**
Lord,
that they may be a sign unto the children of Israel.
(17, 1—3)

Our commentators have been puzzled by the above ordinance to
make the firepans into "beaten plates for a covering for the altar"
and by the yet more mystifying testimony of the Torah that "they
are become holy". At the same time, the text emphasises the origins

219

of the firepans and refers directly to the ones who used them in the words, "even the firepans of these men who sinned with their souls" (or "at the cost of their lives"). The *Akedat Yizhak* observes:

> On the contrary, the firepans, as the objects with which a heinous crime against God had been committed, should have been banished from the sanctuary. To serve as a solemn warning to future wrongdoers to beware of the command forbidding a stranger to set foot in the sanctuary it would have sufficed to hang the offending firepans in the courtyard of the Tabernacle or in any other public place. It would have been much more fitting to have used Aaron's firepans and his alone to serve as a sign of holiness to the Lord!

Various answers have been propounded to this admittedly very difficult problem. First Rashi. He observes:

> The use of the firepans was strictly forbidden since they had already served as holy vessels for ministering purposes.

But this is purely a formal reason which Nahmanides has questioned:

> I do not know the reason for such a prohibition since, after all, they offered up strange incense, and a holy vessel made by one who is not a priest to offer up incense outside, in violation of the Torah does not become sanctified.

In other words, a ritually irregular action cannot result in the consecration of a vessel. But Nahmanides characteristically tries to meet the objections he himself has raised against Rashi's explanation. He observes:

> In this case the vessels became holy because, after all, they sanctified them at the bidding of Moses, imagining that God would vindicate them through the fire, and the firepans would accordingly become permanently consecrated, as holy vessels for use in the tent of meeting.

The important fact was not the holy use to which the firepans were put but the fact that they were so used at the bidding of Moses and that the users were under the impression that God would answer them through fire. But Naḥmanides himself rejected this explanation on the grounds that the whole purpose was to attack Aaron and satisfy the selfish ambitions of the officiants. What intention was there then to consecrate the vessels? Naḥmanides therefore propounds another solution:

> The text states that they became holy to become a sign to the children of Israel because they were offered before the Lord. God made the vessels holy from the moment they were offered before Him to serve as a sign to the children of Israel.

The holiness of the vessels did not originate in the action of these who sinned, but God had them sanctified to serve as a lesson to the people, to remind them of the fate that befell those who aspired to a greatness that did not become them.

In the *Ha'amek Davar* we find a different answer to this question:

> The men who offered the firepans were not sinners but saintly persons, for whom the deprivation of priestly office spelt the forfeiting of a coveted opportunity for closer communion with the Creator. They harboured no illusory worldly ambitions, nor hankered after the sweets of office but longed to sanctify themselves and achieve greater spiritual heights through the sacred service. They were well aware of the authenticity of the Divine message through Moses and that none dare gainsay it. In spite of that, they longed to do the will of God and gave their lives for the love of God; for love is stronger than death.

The *Ha'amek Davar* reads his interpretation into the words "these men who have sinned against their souls". This phrase has been the subject of many explanations. This commentator connects it with a parallel phrase in Num. 6, 11 which speaks of the Nazirite's atonement for breaking his vow.

> Just as there, it has been interpreted to mean that the Nazirite has to atone "for sinning against his soul" for trying to be holier than he was capable by

abstaining from wine — and failing, so here the ones who strove to attain a sanctity that was beyond them were guilty of sinning against their souls, against themselves, against their own personalities, knowing full well that their aspirations however worthy and spiritual could not be attained and that Moses's word would be fulfilled.

Nevertheless the explanation of the *Ha'amek Davar* hardly fits the text which paints a vivid picture of the pettiness, the mutinousness of the rebels, especially when we recall that the two hundred and fifty who joined Korah were malcontents. They included Reubenites aggrieved at being deprived of the firstborn right, the Israelite firstborn at forfeiting the priesthood in favour of the Levites, and Levites such as Korah who were annoyed at the entrusting of the priesthood to the sons of Aaron. Although it might be maintained that all these sections were really interested in the spiritual and not material implications of the priesthood, it is difficult not to accept the opinion of our Sages that here we have a classic example of an unworthy controversy, not inspired by unworldly considerations, as they put it, "a controversy not for the sake of Heaven".

The *Akedat Yizhak* advances another explanation for the reason for the consecration of the firepans.

They symbolised the victory over falsehood. They were used, admittedly, by sinners, but served to vindicate, in the end, the cause of truth and were therefore sanctified to become a sign to the children of Israel. Whatever counters and abrogates the enemy of holiness is certainly holy — there is none better than he who vanquishes the enemy and there is no vessel holier than that which vindicates the cause of the saint.

The text itself supports this explanation, emphasising, as it does that the purpose of the beating of the firepans into holy vessels was to be a sign to Israel, presumably of the triumph over evil and calling them to distinguish between the worthy and unworthy cause, between right and wrong.

וְיִהְיוּ לְאוֹת לִבְנֵי יִשְׂרָאֵל: . . . זִכָּרוֹן לִבְנֵי יִשְׂרָאֵל
לְמַעַן אֲשֶׁר לֹא־יִקְרַב אִישׁ זָר אֲשֶׁר לֹא מִזֶּרַע אַהֲרֹן הוּא לְהַקְטִיר קְטֹרֶת
לִפְנֵי ה'
וְלֹא־יִהְיֶה כְקֹרַח וְכַעֲדָתוֹ

**That they may be a sign unto the children of Israel . . . to be a
memorial unto the children of Israel,**
**to the end that no layman that is not of the seed of Aaron,
draw near to burn incense before the Lord;**
that he fare not as Koraḥ, and as his company.

(17, 3—5)

What does the last clause imply? Does it mean as the English
rendering (Jewish Publication Soc.) seems to indicate, that it is a
warning against suffering the fate of Koraḥ or is it rather as its more
literal translation (as the Authorised Version) would have it, a
warning that "he should not be as Koraḥ and his company", that he
should not commit the same evil deeds, not be guilty of the same
sinful and selfish behaviour? Rashi takes it to mean that "he should
not behave as Koraḥ"; the *Biur*: "That he should not meet the same
punishment".

We may however assume that the passage bears more than one
meaning and implied both things, alluding to the sin and its
punishment. The man who imagines himself to deserve the status of
Koraḥ, who aspires to ambitions that suit him as ill as they did
Koraḥ will ultimately meet with a similar end.

Questions for Further Study

1.   Abravanel asks why the command to beat the firepans into
covers for the altar was addressed to Eleazar and not Aaron
who, as the object of Koraḥ's conspiracy, should have been
the natural choice?

223

2.   "These men who have sinned in their souls" (17, 3) — who *became transgressors* by their own souls, taking issue with the Holy One blessed be He.

(Rashi)

Perhaps God meant to set Moses and Aaron's mind at rest, that they should not imagine that they were in any way responsible for the fate of the sinner, and that the Israelites too should not think so. The text therefore emphasises that "these men who have sinned in their own souls" i.e. they brought it on themselves . . . nevertheless we find that the Israelites were not aware of God's intention.

(Or Ha-ḥayyim)

(a)   What difficulty did Rashi find in the text and how does his comment solve it?

(b)   What difficulty does the Or Ha-ḥayyim find in the text?

(c)   On what does he base his assumption that the "Israelites were not aware of God's intention?"

3.   "That he should not be as Korah". Said Rav: Whoever perpetuates controversy violates a negative precept, as it is stated; "that he should not be as Koraḥ and his company".

Explain in what way the above interpretation of our Sages to the text differs from the various explanations we have cited.

THE PROMPTING OF THE HOLY SPIRIT

Our Sages accorded Moses the title of "Father of the Prophets".
Maimonides explained in his *Guide for the Perplexed* (I, 63) that the
Patriarch Abraham was not, in the strict sense, a prophet of the
same calibre as Moses:

> Prior to the advent of Moses, no man had laid claim to the title of prophet in
> the sense of maintaining that God had spoken to him or sent him. Do not be
> misled by the statements that God spoke to the Patriarchs or had appeared
> to them. Abraham, Isaac or Jacob or any of their predecessors did not tell
> the people: "God said to me, Do this thing", or "God has sent me to you".

Maimonides explains that the Patriarchs had never been entrusted
with a mission to other people, which is the essence of the prophetic
calling. They had merely received Divine communication regarding
things concerning themselves. It is no accident therefore that Moses'
chief argument against the rebels in our sidra, against Koraḥ,
Dathan and Abiram is formulated as follows:

ה׳ שְׁלָחַנִי לַעֲשׂוֹת אֵת כָּל־הַמַּעֲשִׂים הָאֵלֶּה כִּי־לֹא מִלִּבִּי:

**The Lord hath sent me to do all these works, I have not done
them of mine own mind.**

(16, 28)

In the light of this, it is puzzling to note that there are several
places in the Pentateuch, particularly in our sidra, where Moses gave
orders to the children of Israel, without it being recorded, that he had

225

been specifically commanded to do so by the Almighty, without the accustomed introductory phrase: "And the Lord spoke unto Moses . . ."

We may note the following:

זֹאת עֲשׂוּ קְחוּ־לָכֶם מַחְתּוֹת
קֹרַח וְכָל עֲדָתוֹ:
וּתְנוּ בָהֶן אֵשׁ
וְשִׂימוּ עֲלֵיהֶן קְטֹרֶת לִפְנֵי ה׳ מָחָר
וְהָיָה הָאִישׁ אֲשֶׁר יִבְחַר ה׳ הוּא הַקָּדוֹשׁ . . .

**This do: take ye censers,
Korah, and all his company;
and put fire therein,
and put incense upon them before the Lord tomorrow; and it
shall be that the man whom the Lord doth choose, he shall be
holy . . .**

(16, 6—7)

Similarly, it is not recorded, in the following instance, that God had instructed him to speak so:

. . . בְּזֹאת תֵּדְעוּן כִּי־ה׳ שְׁלָחַנִי לַעֲשׂוֹת אֵת כָּל־הַמַּעֲשִׂים הָאֵלֶּה
כִּי לֹא מִלִּבִּי:
אִם־כְּמוֹת כָּל הָאָדָם יְמֻתוּן אֵלֶּה
וּפְקֻדַּת כָּל הָאָדָם יִפָּקֵד עֲלֵיהֶם
לֹא ה׳ שְׁלָחָנִי:

**. . . Hereby ye shall know that the Lord hath sent me to do all
these works,
and that I have not done them of mine own mind.
If these men die the common death of all men,
and be visited after the visitation of all men,
then the Lord hath not sent me.**

(16, 28, 29)

Various answers are propounded by our commentators. Here is Naḥmanides' who makes three suggestions:

> There are some who explain that the phrase "And Moses heard and fell on his face" (Ibid. 4) implied that he went to inquire of the Lord regarding what he should do, and the statement: "In the morning the Lord will show who are His, and who is holy, and will cause him to come near unto Him" refers to the results of that meeting with God, which is now reported in Moses' instruction to the people. I have shown you many examples of this. Sometimes the original Divine instruction is elaborated on, and Moses' execution briefly reported, and at other times, the reverse is true. Sometimes one of these stages will be entirely omitted, as in the case of the story of the sons of Gad and Reuben (Numbers 32) which attributes the steps taken, to Moses himself when they were, of course, actually prompted by the Almighty. The two and a half tribes allude to this, in their statement: "That which *the Lord hath spoken* to thy servants, so we shall do" (Ibid. 31).

According to this view, everything that Moses did was prompted by a specific instruction of the Almighty. The instruction itself was sometimes omitted for the sake of brevity and left to be understood. In this case he was briefed by God, during the time he lay prostrate "on his face". But is this the implication of the passage: "Moses heard and fell on his face?" Rashi differs in his explanation of the meaning of this phrase. This was not a description of his communion with the Almighty, but he fell on his face:—

> טז, ד ד״ה ״ויפול על פניו״: מפני המחלוקת, שכבר זה בידם סרחון רביעי. חטאו בעגל — (שמות לב, יא): ״ויחל משה״; במתאוננים, (במדבר יא, ב) — ״ויתפלל משה״; במרגלים — (במדבר יד, יח) — ״ויאמר משה אל ה׳ ושמעו מצרים . . .״; במחלוקתו של קרח נתרשלו ידיו. משל לבן מלך שסרח על אביו, ופייס עליו אוהבו פעם, שתים ושלש; כשסרח רביעית, נתרשלו ידי האוהב ההוא. אמר: ״עד מתי אטריח על המלך? שמא לא יקבל עוד ממני!״.

On account of the dissension, since this was already the fourth case of misconduct to their discredit. They sinned with the Calf (Exodus 32, 11) — "And Moses interceded"; with the grumblings (Numbers 11, 2) — "And Moses prayed"; with the spies (Numbers 14, 11) — "And Moses said unto the Lord if the Egyptians shall hear . . .". In the case of the strife of Korah,

227

his nerve failed him. This may be compared to a prince who misbehaved, towards his father. His friend interceded for him on one, two and three occasions, but when he misbehaved a fourth time, his friend's nerve failed him. He said: How much longer can I bother the king? Perhaps he will no longer listen to me!

Naḥmanides himself was evidently not completely satisfied with his own explanation and he suggests another approach:

Moses himself was responsible for this idea but was confident that the Lord "confirmeth the word of His servant, and performeth the counsel of His messengers" (Isaiah 44, 26).

Naḥmanides does not elaborate on whether Moses did rightly or wrongly in making his own decision. Albo, however, elaborates on Naḥmanides' explanation in his *Sefer Ha-ikkarim* (IV, 22):

It is a fundamental of Judaism that God subjects nature to the needs of the faithful. This idea is expressed in Psalm 91 where the Psalmist avers that God will deliver him from pestilence, and will cause him to tread upon the lion and the asp, etc. If this is true of the righteous, how much more so in the case of actual prophets . . . Moses himself asserted this when he said: "If these men die the common death of all men . . . then the Lord hath not sent me. But if the Lord make a new thing . . . And it came to pass, as he made an end of speaking . . . that the ground did cleave asunder that was under them. And the earth opened her mouth . . ." (Numbers 16, 29—32). In this instance, we do not find that God had actually apprised Moses beforehand of all this. But here we have an example of Isaiah's statement that the Lord "confirmeth the word of His servant, and performeth the counsel of His messengers".

According to this view, it is to Moses' credit that he placed his life in jeopardy and trusted in God to vouchsafe him a sign and sanctify His name. But this view did not satisfy Naḥmanides and he adds yet another suggestion — his last one, and his own personal view:

My view in this matter and in the case of the instruction that Moses gave to Aaron: "Take thy fire-pan . . . and lay incense thereon" (Numbers 17, 11), was that the hand of the Lord was upon them. They were inspired by what is known as the holy spirit. Cf. the statement that King David and King Solomon were inspired by the holy spirit in their writings, as seen in the following allusion: "These are the words of David . . . the spirit of the Lord spoke through me and His word was upon my tongue" (2 Samuel 23, 1—2). This must be true also in the case of Moses who "is trusted in all My house" (Numbers 12, 7) . . .

This stage of prophecy is closely akin to the lowest grade of prophecy described by Maimonides in his *Guide for the Perplexed* (II, 45). According to him, the lowest degree of prophecy consists in the Divine assistance given to a person to encourage him to do something good.

"To deliver a congregation of good men from the hands of evil doers . . ." The individual himself is prompted to the deed. This degree of Divine influence is called "the spirit of the Lord". Of such a person we say that the spirit of the Lord came upon him, or rested upon him, or that the Lord was with him, etc. This was the case with the judges of Israel (Cf. Judges 11, 29; 14, 19; 1 Samuel 11, 6; 1 Chronicles 12, 19). Moses too was always distinguished by this prophetic spirit. It prompted him to slay the Egyptian, to prevent injustice between the two men who quarrelled, and at Midian, at the well. Whenever he saw wrong being done, he could not restrain himself, as it is said: "And Moses rose and saved them" (Exodus 2, 17).

The above view is then a compromise between the first one, according to which, Moses was actually instructed by God, Moses not saying anything not explicitly imparted to him by the Almighty, and the second view that he acted completely on his own initiative.

Whether we accept the second or third interpretation, in which case Moses had not acted on an explicit Divine instruction, the following difficulty arises. By striving to authenticate his Divine mission by recourse to a miracle from God, he was surely violating an express command of the Torah, which prohibits such a test.[1]

Signs and miracles cannot authenticate a prophet's mission. Our commentators, however, explained that this ruling applied after the Torah had been given and the people had reached a higher stage of

229

consciousness of the Divine. Before that, however, in Egypt and at the Red Sea, God had utilised miracles in order to set in motion the redemption, whilst the people were still sunk in Egyptian depravity, and could only be aroused in this manner. In that case, what right had Moses after the people had accepted the Torah, to prove his case by means of miracles? If he did indeed act wrongly, why did God accede to his request and perform the miracle?

But we may suggest that the Almighty wished to teach Moses and the Jewish people, for all time, the real value of miracles. When the earth opened its mouth:

וְכָל־יִשְׂרָאֵל אֲשֶׁר סְבִיבֹתֵיהֶם נָסוּ לְקֹלָם

And all Israel that were round about them fled at the cry of them.

(16, 34)

The next day, however, all had been forgotten:

וַיִּלֹּנוּ כָּל־עֲדַת בְּנֵי־יִשְׂרָאֵל מִמָּחֳרָת עַל־מֹשֶׁה וְעַל־אַהֲרֹן לֵאמֹר
אַתֶּם הֲמִתֶּם אֶת־עַם ה':

But on the morrow, all the congregation of the children of Israel murmured against Moses and against Aaron saying: Ye have killed the people of the Lord.

(17, 6)

The same thing happened even after the great miracle at the Red Sea:

וַיַּרְא יִשְׂרָאֵל אֶת הַיָּד הַגְּדֹלָה
אֲשֶׁר עָשָׂה ה' בְּמִצְרַיִם,
וַיִּירְאוּ הָעָם אֶת ה', וַיַּאֲמִינוּ בַּה'
וּבְמֹשֶׁה עַבְדוֹ

And Israel saw the great work which the Lord did upon the Egyptians, and the people feared the Lord; and they believed in the Lord, and in His servant Moses.

(Exodus 14, 31)

But on the morrow, the people that had proclaimed the sovereignty of God for evermore, are reported as saying:

‎. . . מִי־יִתֵּן מוּתֵנוּ בְיַד־ה׳ בְּאֶרֶץ מִצְרַיִם בְּשִׁבְתֵּנוּ עַל־סִיר הַבָּשָׂר בְּאָכְלֵנוּ
‎לֶחֶם לָשֹׂבַע
‎כִּי־הוֹצֵאתֶם אֹתָנוּ אֶל־הַמִּדְבָּר הַזֶּה לְהָמִית אֶת־כָּל־הַקָּהָל הַזֶּה בָּרָעָב:

. . . Would that we had died by the hand of the Lord in the land of Egypt, when we sat by the flesh-pots, when we did eat bread to the full;
for ye have brought us forth into this wilderness, to kill this whole assembly with hunger.

(Ibid. 16, 3)

Miracles cannot change men's minds and hearts. They can always be explained away. Some argue, in our own day that if only the Almighty had vouchsafed us miracles, people would immediately repent and acknowledge His sovereignty. But in the absence of miracles, religious faith is also absent. Isaiah refers to this delusion in the following words:

‎לָמָּה תַתְעֵנוּ ה׳ מִדְּרָכֶיךָ
‎תַּקְשִׁיחַ לִבֵּנוּ מִיִּרְאָתֶךָ . . .
‎לוּא־קָרַעְתָּ שָׁמַיִם יָרַדְתָּ
‎מִפָּנֶיךָ הָרִים נָזֹלּוּ:

O Lord, why dost Thou make us to err from Thy ways,
And hardenest our heart from Thy fear...

231

If only Thou wouldest rend the heavens, that Thou wouldst come down,
That the mountains might quake at Thy presence.

(Isaiah 63, 17—19)

Our sidra demonstrates that this is not so. Miracles convince only those who can and are prepared to see them. Lack of faith points to a lack of will.

NOTE

[1]   See Deut. 13, 2—6; discussed in our *Studies in Devarim, Re'eh* 2.

MYSTERY OF THE RED HEIFER

The chapter on the Red Heifer with which our Sidra begins is one of the most mystifying in the Torah. Our Sages observed that it was one of the matters which even the wisdom of the wisest of men failed to fathom:

> "This is the statute of the Torah". R. Isaac opened with the text: "All this I have tried (to fathom) by wisdom; I said, I will get wisdom; but it was far from me" (Ecclesiastes 7, 23). Thus spoke Solomon: I succeeded in understanding the whole Torah, but, as soon as I reach this chapter about the Red Heifer, I searched, probed and questioned, "I said I will get wisdom, but it was far from me".
>
> (Yalkut Shimoni 759)

We shall similarly not pretend to fathom it completely but shall present some of the observations of our commentators and Sages thereon.

R. Joseph Bechor Shor (one of the Tosaphists) adopts a completely rational approach:

> The rites pertaining to the Red Heifer were designed to discourage association with the dead, prompted by the bereaved's love for the departed, and excessive grief. Alternatively, that people should not make a practice of consulting the dead or familiar spirits, the text pronounced the defilement of the dead person as more contaminating than all other defilements, making it the prime source of uncleanliness, defiling both man and vessels and defiling as well through overhanging (ohel).
>
> Also on account of human respect, that people should not come to using human skin for coverings and human bones for articles of use just as we use

the skin of animals; it is disrespectful of humanity. Our Sages made a similar point (Ḥullin 122a): "Why has the skin of a corpse been declared unclean? That a person should not use his parent's skin for coverings". The greater the love, the greater the defilement. The text likewise went to the strictest lengths in its requirements, demanding the ashes of a red heifer which are an expensive item.

The foregoing exposition would seem to be an oversimplification, not in keeping with the mysterious irrational character of the whole chapter and certainly does not afford an explanation of the strange details of the rite.

Others have adopted an allegorical, homiletic approach. Here is an extract from Sforno's elaborate explanation:

> The crux of the mystery is its property of contaminating the pure and purifying the contaminated. Perhaps we may catch a little of its significance in our attempt to understand the observance ... one of the fundamental requirements is that the heifer had to be completely red. The prophet has explained that sin is described as red; cf.: "though your sins be as scarlet, they shall be white as snow" (Isaiah 1, 18).
>
> We should bear in mind that the Torah recommends the golden mean — all extremes are undesirable ... there is no better way of rectifying misdoing (the crooked) regaining the middle way than by veering to the other extreme. The cedar symbolises pride, the hyssop, the opposite. The scarlet thread between symbolises that both are sinful. It has been said that Saul was punished for not caring about his own dignity (erring on the side of humility).
>
> Thus though this precept is a statute which has not to be questioned, possessing without doubt a sublime meaning known to the King who commanded it, it contains an allusion to the way of repentance to be followed by every sinner — that he should tend to the other extreme in order to regain the middle path and be purified. But while this corrective measure is beneficial and purifying for the sinner, it is wrong and defiling for every pure heart.

But the Talmudic sage Rabbi Yoḥanan ben Zakkai adopts an entirely different approach, far removed from the allegorical. His words are highly instructive for us today.

A certain heathen asked R. Yoḥanan ben Zakkai: The rites you perform in connection with the Red Heifer smell of witchcraft! You bring a heifer, burn it, grind it and take its ashes. You sprinkle two or three drops on one of you who is contaminated with corpse defilement and say to him, You are clean. Said R. Yoḥanan b. Zakkai to him: Have you never been possessed by a demon? He answered: No. — Have you never seen a man possessed by a demon? He answered: Yes. — And what do you do for him? — We bring herbs and make them smoke beneath him, and throw water on him and the demon is exorcised. He answered: Let your ears hear what your mouth has spoken. The spirit of defilement is the same as your demon. We sprinkle on it the waters of purification and it is exorcised.

After the heathen had left, R. Yoḥanan's disciples said to him: Him you have put off with a straw, but what answer will you give us? He replied to them. By your life, neither does the dead defile nor the water purify, but the Holy One blessed be He said: It is a statute I have laid down, a decree that I have decreed and you are not authorised to violate my decree.

The heathen required a rational explanation, appealing to his common sense. The Torah's defilement is a kind of disease or evil spirit. The red heifer's ashes are no more than a kind of cure for the disease, a demon-repellent. But he could tell his disciples, students of the Torah and who accepted its yoke, the truth. Uncleanliness is not an integral part of nature, neither in the corpse nor in the one who comes in contact with it. It is not a demon or pest originating in the corpse itself. The ashes of the heifer and the waters of the sin-offering have no intrinsic purificatory properties. It is a Divine commandment. That alone determines the defilement of the corpse and the purificatory properties of the ashes. It is the commandments that refine the human soul.

Let us not be among those who seek for rational explanation for those things, to which the laws of reason do not apply. May we be like the disciples of Rabbi Yoḥanan ben Zakkai who accept the yoke of the statutes (*ḥukkim*), just as they do the yoke of the other commandments of the Torah.

MOSES' SIN

What was Moses' sin? The Torah refers to it on four different occasions. Twice in our sidra:

וַיֹּאמֶר ה׳ אֶל מֹשֶׁה וְאֶל־אַהֲרֹן
יַעַן לֹא־הֶאֱמַנְתֶּם בִּי לְהַקְדִּישֵׁנִי לְעֵינֵי בְּנֵי יִשְׂרָאֵל
לָכֵן לֹא תָבִיאוּ אֶת־הַקָּהָל הַזֶּה אֶל הָאָרֶץ אֲשֶׁר־נָתַתִּי לָהֶם:
הֵמָּה מֵי מְרִיבָה אֲשֶׁר־רָבוּ בְנֵי־יִשְׂרָאֵל אֶת־ה׳ וַיִּקָּדֵשׁ בָּם:

And the Lord said unto Moses and Aaron,
Because ye believed not in Me, to sanctify Me in the eyes of
the children of Israel,
therefore ye shall not bring this assembly into the land which I
have given them.
These are the waters of Meribah, where the children of Israel
strove with the Lord, and He was sanctified in them.

(20, 12—13)

וַיֹּאמֶר ה׳ אֶל־מֹשֶׁה וְאֶל־אַהֲרֹן בְּהֹר הָהָר . . . יֵאָסֵף אַהֲרֹן אֶל־עַמָּיו
כִּי לֹא יָבֹא אֶל הָאָרֶץ אֲשֶׁר נָתַתִּי לִבְנֵי יִשְׂרָאֵל
עַל אֲשֶׁר־מְרִיתֶם אֶת־פִּי לְמֵי מְרִיבָה:

And the Lord spoke unto Moses and Aaron on mount Hor . . .
Aaron shall be gathered into his people;
for he shall not enter into the land which I have given unto the
children of Israel,
because ye rebelled against My word at the waters of Meribah.

(20, 23—24)

Again in a later sidra, *Pinḥas,* evidently in order to arouse Moses
to the need for a successor, after Aaron was no longer with him:

וַיֹּאמֶר ה' אֶל מֹשֶׁה
עֲלֵה אֶל־הַר הָעֲבָרִים הַזֶּה וּרְאֵה אֶת־הָאָרֶץ אֲשֶׁר נָתַתִּי לִבְנֵי יִשְׂרָאֵל:
וְרָאִיתָה אֹתָהּ וְנֶאֱסַפְתָּ אֶל־עַמֶּיךָ
גַּם אָתָּה כַּאֲשֶׁר נֶאֱסַף אַהֲרֹן אָחִיךָ:
כַּאֲשֶׁר מְרִיתֶם פִּי בְּמִדְבַּר־צִן בִּמְרִיבַת הָעֵדָה
לְהַקְדִּישֵׁנִי בַמַּיִם לְעֵינֵיהֶם

And the Lord said unto Moses,
Get thee up into this mountain of Abarim, and behold the land
which I have given unto the children of Israel.
And when thou hast seen it, thou also shalt be gathered unto
thy people
as Aaron thy brother was gathered;
because ye rebelled against My commandment in the
wilderness of Zin, in the strife of the congregation,
to sanctify Me at the waters before their eyes.

(27, 12—14)

And on the fourth occasion near the end of the Torah on the eve
of Moses' death in *Ha'azinu*:

וַיְדַבֵּר ה' אֶל מֹשֶׁה בְּעֶצֶם הַיּוֹם הַזֶּה לֵאמֹר:
עֲלֵה אֶל־הַר הָעֲבָרִים הַזֶּה הַר־נְבוֹ אֲשֶׁר בְּאֶרֶץ מוֹאָב אֲשֶׁר עַל־פְּנֵי יְרֵחוֹ
וּרְאֵה אֶת אֶרֶץ כְּנַעַן אֲשֶׁר אֲנִי נֹתֵן לִבְנֵי יִשְׂרָאֵל לַאֲחֻזָּה:
וּמֻת בָּהָר אֲשֶׁר אַתָּה עֹלֶה שָׁמָּה
וְהֵאָסֵף אֶל־עַמֶּיךָ
כַּאֲשֶׁר־מֵת אַהֲרֹן אָחִיךָ בְּהֹר הָהָר וַיֵּאָסֶף אֶל עַמָּיו:
עַל אֲשֶׁר מְעַלְתֶּם בִּי בְּתוֹךְ בְּנֵי יִשְׂרָאֵל
בְּמֵי־מְרִיבַת קָדֵשׁ מִדְבַּר־צִן
עַל אֲשֶׁר לֹא־קִדַּשְׁתֶּם אוֹתִי בְּתוֹךְ בְּנֵי יִשְׂרָאֵל:

237

And the Lord spoke unto Moses that selfsame day, saying,
Get thee up into this mountain of Abarim, unto Mount Nebo,
which is in the land of Moab, that is over against Jericho;
and behold the land of Canaan, which I give unto the children
of Israel for a possession;
and die in the mount whither thou goest up
and be gathered unto thy people;
as Aaron thy brother died in mount Hor, and was gathered
unto his people.
Because ye trespassed against Me in the midst of the children
of Israel
at the waters of Meribah-Kadesh, in the wilderness of Zin;
because ye sanctified Me not in the midst of the children of
Israel.

(Deuteronomy 32, 48—51)

The accusations levelled against Moses were grave indeed:

יַעַן לֹא־הֶאֱמַנְתֶּם בִּי לְהַקְדִּישֵׁנִי לְעֵינֵי בְּנֵי יִשְׂרָאֵל . . .

מְרִיתֶם אֶת־פִּי . . .

מְרִיתֶם פִּי . . . לְהַקְדִּישֵׁנִי . . . לְעֵינֵיהֶם

מְעַלְתֶּם בִּי . . .

לֹא קִדַּשְׁתֶּם אוֹתִי בְּתוֹךְ בְּנֵי יִשְׂרָאֵל.

Because ye believed not in Me, to sanctify Me in the eyes of
the children of Israel,
ye rebelled against Me,
ye rebelled against My commandment... to sanctify Me...
at their eyes
ye trespassed against Me...
ye sanctified Me not in the midst of the children of Israel.

The place where the sin occurred is clearly located in our text —
at the waters of Meribath-Kadesh in the wilderness of Zin. The

actual incident is recorded in our sidra 20, 2—11. But even a close study of the text fails to detect the exact nature of the sin. Isaac Arama devoted considerable attention to this problem in striving to find an answer. Recalling a Talmudic dictum he notes that we have everything,

> A table, meat and a knife before us but no mouth to eat with — the commandment of God is clearly outlined, the deed that was performed is not concealed from us and the subsequent wrath of God astonishes us, but no satisfactory explanation emerges.

We shall do what he advises, survey the numerous explanations advanced and note how they fit in with the texts we have quoted. Maimonides devoted a section of his *Shemonah Perakim* to this point, in illustration of his principle of the golden mean between the two extremes. Where man errs to one extreme he should go to the other in order to redress the balance. Maimonides then cites the texts bearing on Moses' sin at the waters of Meribah and concludes:

> His whole sin lay in erring on the side of anger and deviating from the mean of patience, when he used the expression "hear ye now ye rebels!" The Holy One blessed be He censured him for this, that a man of his stature should give vent to anger in front of the whole community of Israel, where anger was not called for. This behaviour in such a man constituted a profanation of the Name (*ḥillul ha-shem*), since he was the model of good conduct for all the people, who aspired to find their worldly and other-worldly happiness in emulating him. How would they regard anger in him, when as we have explained, that it is an evil springing from an evil side of one's character. The text "Ye have rebelled against My commandment" implies that Moses was not just addressing anyone, but an assembly the most ignorant housewife of which was reckoned as the prophet Ezekiel, as our Sages observed. Whatever he did or said would be subject to scrutiny. When they saw him thus in anger, they must certainly have concluded that he was not displaying personal animus or pique but, on the contrary, had not God been angry with them at their demand for water, Moses would not have been provoked. Yet we do not find that God was angry or showed disapproval when he told Moses to take the staff and assemble the people. We have thus in digressing

from our main topic succeeded in solving one of the obscurities of Scripture
— the nature of Moses' sin.

Maimonides refers to two sins — one a personal one of Moses in
inclining to anger. But since this could not be read into the text "ye
have rebelled against My commandment" he emphasises another
offence, that of misleading the people by his display of anger with
regard to the nature of the Deity. They would imagine that God was
angry with them for demanding water and the All-Merciful was
wrathful even when the occasion did not warrant it. They would
imagine the Deity was a cruel forbidding God and not the
Compassionate Father of all, hastening to quench the thirst of His
people by commanding water from the flinty rock. In this sense
Moses and Aaron had rebelled against God's commandment.

Naḥmanides takes Maimonides to task and refutes his arguments,
citing the wording of the text.

> The Torah speaks of Moses not believing in God and nowhere mentions that
> Moses was angry or waxed wroth. Aaron was never guilty of anger — his
> whole life was one of peace-making and yet both Moses and Aaron were
> guilty of the same sin.

Naḥmanides concludes:

> We must admit that God was angry with His people for their disbelief
> "because ye despised the word of the Lord in your midst and wept before
> Him saying, Why did we leave Egypt?" Other texts refer directly to the
> Israelites striving with God "they are the waters of Meribah wherein the
> children of Israel strove with the Lord". What greater transgression could
> there be than this? Moses also remarked that the Lord was angry with him
> "for your sakes, saying, Thou also shalt not come there". How can
> Maimonides therefore maintain that God was not angry with them and it
> was Moses who gave the wrong impression?

Naḥmanides also rebuts the argument based on the fact that no
allusion is made to God's anger in His command to Moses to speak
to the rock and satisfy the people's thirst. He observes:

Know that when men are in dire need of sustenance, even if they murmur and sin against Him, He the All-Merciful forgives iniquity and does not give vent to all His displeasure, does not refer to it but accedes to their request. The same happened on the first occasion when He answered calmly "Pass in front of the people . . . and smite the rock that water should go forth from it and the people may drink" (Ex. 17, 5), although the demand was accompanied by trials and strivings which were an example for all time.

Naḥmanides notes too that God did not show his anger with regard to the manna but sent it, in spite of His displeasure, merely informing them of their sin:

"I have heard the grumblings of the children of Israel". But when they grumbled for no cause whatever, then he poured out His anger on them. There was a difference between the Divine displeasure at complaints which had some basis and the anger at arbitrary grumblings as in the case of Korah and the spies.

Naḥmanides ends his attack on Maimonides' explanation with a triumphant quotation from the Psalms:

"And they angered Him at the waters of Meribah, and it went ill with Moses for their sakes" (Ps. 106, 32). The text thus includes this sin under the great trials with which they tried God in the wilderness.

Naḥmanides offers therefore another explanation citing Rabbenu Ḥananel.

Moses made the fatal mistake of saying, "Shall *we* bring you forth water", instead of saying "Shall *God* bring you forth water", as in all the other miracles where the authorship of God is always explicitly stressed (cf. Ex. 16, 8 "when the Lord giveth you meat in the evening to eat"). The people might have been misled into thinking that Moses and Aaron had extracted the water for them, by their own skill. Thus they failed to "sanctify Me in the midst of the children of Israel".

This explanation gains in plausibility when we recall that the children of Israel had, but a short while previously, left a land of

241

enchantments and sorcery and were very likely to attribute the production of water to Moses and Aaron's magical skill. Thus the two great leaders of Israel were liable to defeat the purpose of the whole Torah by their sin of omission. Their whole life was directed at propagating the idea of the omnipotence and providence of God and here was another golden opportunity of driving the lesson home. It may be argued, however that the people had been shown the hand of God on so many previous occasions that there was no reason to doubt that they would fail to discern the hand of God on this one. Nahmanides anticipates this argument and endeavours to show that, on all other occasions, the hand of God was plainly visible. The last occasion on which they had been provided with water was accompanied by the appearance of the pillar of cloud standing over the rock (Ex. 17, 6). But here they saw nothing and by this the people were misled.

Nahmanides adduces further proof for his explanation from the phrase: "Because ye trespassed against Me", since whoever benefits from holy things is called a trespasser. Moses and Aaron had benefited from a kind of misrepresentation, by not making clear that it was God who brought the water out of the rock. They arrogated to themselves something belonging to God.

How does Nahmanides explain the other passages about "rebelled against Me", "did not believe Me?" —

> They violated the express command of God to "speak to the rock before their eyes" in order to sanctify Him publicly thereby. They rebelled in the sense of deviating from the command of God in not taking every step that was necessary to publicise the power of God. Or perhaps the phrase "because you did not believe Me" refers to the children of Israel.

Ibn Ezra takes a different view and sees the fault of Moses and Aaron not in their actions at the rock or in any deviation from the Divine instruction but in their undignified reaction to the people's grumblings and threatenings. He comments that "Moses and Aaron came before the assembly (verse 6) — "as fugitives" instead of sanctifying the name of God and showing initiative. There was no greater desecration of God's name than this. Joseph Albo reinforces this explanation, similarly taking issue with Maimonides and not accepting that the sin lay in the anger displayed by Moses, but rather in his display of lack of faith stressing the text, "because ye did not believe in Me".

A fundamental principle of the Torah and the root of faith emanating from the belief in His providence is that He subjugates nature to the will of the faithful, a thought which occurs in the Psalm to Moses (Ps. 91), the man of God that "He who dwelleth in the shelter of the Most High and sheltereth in the shadow of the Almighty" promises to deliver him from all snares, from all natural plagues, even to the extent of treading on the adder, viper, whelp and dragon. This is true of some righteous people, and how much more so of the prophets, for whose benefit miracles were constantly performed at their bidding! Elijah said: "As the Lord liveth surely there shall be no dew or rain these years except according to my word" (1 Kings 17, 1) . . . Moses himself said, "If like the common death of all men . . . but if the Lord will create a new thing . . . and it came to pass when he had finished speaking all these words that the ground beneath them did cleave asunder and the earth opened its mouth" (Num. 16, 29 ff.). Yet we do not find that God had previously given him command regarding this matter. Thus said Isaiah (44, 26) "He establisheth the word of His servant and the counsel of his messengers perfecteth".

Whoever doubts that the Lord will implement the word of the prophet casts doubts, as it were, on the Torah, especially where sanctification of the Lord is involved, when it is proper to publicise that nature is subjugated to the will of those who observe the Law. The failure of a prophet to perform miracles to save the nation is liable to make people doubt the truth of the text that the Lord establishes the words of His servants, especially when the prophet through whom the Torah was given, would not rely on the efficacy of his own faith to invoke a miracle, changing the order of nature . . . this is the implication of the text "because ye did not believe in Me . . ." had Moses and Aaron invoked a miracle to cleave the rock, the Lord would have undoubtedly established the word of his servant and been sanctified in the eyes of all the people. As it was, they appeared as fugitives at the entrance to the tent of meeting, as Ibn Ezra observes, as if they were at a loss what to do. This certainly profaned the name of God and caused a diminution of faith. Ye did not believe, in the sense of you had not sufficient faith to invoke a change in the natural order. Aaron and Moses acted, as they did, out of a sense of their own unworthiness; they did not wish to usurp such authority. Nevertheless it was accounted an iniquity and a symptom of lack of faith because it gave rise to a profanation of the name of God . . . You will find that Joshua, in similar circumstances did not wait for God to give him authority but relied on Him to do his will, and on his own initiative said, "sun stand still at Gibeon", and the Lord established his word. The Torah thus ascribes to Moses and Aaron the sin of insufficient faith, condemning them for not acting on their own initiative, without God.

Arama is thoroughly disgusted with this explanation and notes how what Rabbenu Ḥananel regards as trespass and rebellion is held by Albo to be desirable and creditable.

Moses never did anything except at the express bidding of God who never once disapproved of such obedience. Cf. "And the Lord said unto Moses, Behold I shall rain down on you bread from the heavens". The Almighty showed no disapproval of the fact that Moses had not produced, on his own initiative, bread and meat from heaven and earth. Afterwards at Rephidim the people asked for water — the same thing that happened in our context. Moses said: "Why do you strive with me and Moses cried unto the Lord saying, What wilt thou do unto this people? a little longer and they will stone me". By rights God should have been very angry at Moses' frenzied and impotent reaction. Yet God took no offence but said, "Pass before the people . . . behold I stand before thee there on the rock and thou shalt smite the rock and water shall flow therefrom that the people may drink".

(Akedat Yizḥak)

Arama likewise disposes of the argument that Moses and Aaron were perhaps prompted by a sense of their own unworthiness, by observing that it would have been the height of impertinence and folly for them to have desisted from sanctifying the name of God out of such considerations. Indeed, Moses and Aaron were perfectly correct in not anticipating a miracle from God. Arama is at pains to show that Moses had never acted on his own initiative not even in the case of Korah where the text explicitly notes that "it was not from my heart". Even the most trivial matter required a prior command of

244

God, "The Lord shall command thee and thou shalt be able to stand up" (Ex. 18, 23). Joshua also had not ordered the sun to stand still, but had previously prayed to God for help, and it was only when he was answered, that he acted and spoke as he did. It distinctly says that the Lord hearkened to the voice of man (Joshua 10, 14) and not that the sun hearkened to the voice of man, as Albo would have it.

It is highly significant for us to observe how the approach of humility and discipline reflected in the *Akedat Yizhak* triumphs over the ecstatic miracle-working approach of Albo. We have to obey the commands and precepts of God and must certainly avoid any resort to miracles, to a revolution in nature. Even the greatest prophet has but to carry out the commands of His creator.

If Moses was neither guilty of arrogating to himself too much or not showing enough initiative wherein had he sinned? We are thus left in the position of the commentator (*Or Ha-hayyim*) who, having exhausted all the original explanations, decided to revert to the simplest one known to every child, that Moses struck the rock instead of speaking to it, as the Midrash explains:

> Four sins are referred to: "Ye did not believe" — wherein I did not tell you strike, yet you did strike; "Ye did not sanctify" to bring forth water from *any* rock they desired"; "ye trespassed" — that you said "Shall we bring forth from *this* rock"; "ye rebelled" — wherein I told you to speak to the rock, yet you violated my words.

Nahmanides who refuses to accept all the other explanations we have outlined likewise attacks this one. He regards the approach of the Midrash as purely homiletical and not at all supported by the plain sense of the text. Since God had explicitly bidden Moses to "take the staff" that itself implied that he should strike the rock. Had He insisted on him speaking to the rock, there would have been no need for the staff. Nahmanides cited Moses' carrying out the bidding of God in sending the plagues in Egypt, where he was ordered to take his staff and always for the purpose of striking with it. The text doesn't have to be so explicit but leaves it to be understood that he

245

was to strike the rock. In any case, the miracle gained nothing by consisting of speaking rather than striking.

Naḥmanides also observes that the text itself records that Moses spoke in the hearing of the rock regarding the bringing forth of water from it. Moses' action could therefore not be termed trespass. He did speak to the rock. In spite of all this, the simple explanation is the most plausible and is accepted by one our later commentators Luzzatto:

> Moses our teacher committed one sin, but our commentators have heaped on him thirteen and more, each one of them having invented a fresh one . . . I have therefore hitherto refrained from going into this problem for fear I might attribute a new sin to Moses!

Luzzatto remarks that he had accepted for fifteen years the explanation that Moses and Aaron had acted like cowards and failed to sanctify the name of God by prompt and courageous action but in the end had to admit that it did not fit the text, which speaks of rebellion and not of cowardice. He therefore accepted the interpretation of Rashi that Moses should have spoken to the rock. Admittedly, as far as the rock was concerned, it was all one whether he addressed it or struck it. But to the ordinary folk it certainly seemed more miraculous if the rock gushed water at Moses' oral command rather than at his physical blow, and the name of God would have been accordingly sanctified to a greater extent. It but remains for us to refer to the ingenious interpretation advanced in *Ha-ketav Ve-hakabbalah* based on the text, "speak ye unto the rock *before their eyes*" (20, 8). ,

> It should really have said "their ears" since speech is apprehended by the organ of hearing. We must therefore conclude that not external sight is meant but rather insight — the mind's eye, just as the phrase "And their eyes were opened" in the case of Adam and Eve implied that they became conscious inwardly of a new state of affairs, and not that any physical blindness of theirs was suddenly cured. Moses and Aaron were bidden to act

246

in a way calculated to impress the people with the omnipotence of God —
appeal to their insight, that they should be made aware of God's providence.
Rashi's comment, in the light of this becomes clearer: "Had you spoken to
the rock to bring forth water I would have been sanctified in the eyes of the
congregation who would have argued, If this rock which can neither speak
nor hear yet fulfils the word of the Omnipotent, how much more so we".

We have cited many different explanations of the problem of
Moses' sin. We can do no better than conclude with Maimonides'
own closing words to this subject:

> Set what we have said, against what has already been said about it, and let
> the truth have its way.

THE DEPUTATION TO EDOM

The subject of study we have chosen is the deputation sent to Edom (20, 14—21) by Moses to petition for the right of way through its territory. This event is described in our sidra as immediately succeeding the sin of Moses at the waters of Meribah and the announcement of his punishment: "Because you believed not in Me, to sanctify Me in the eyes of the children of Israel, therefore you shall not bring this assembly into the land which I have given them" (ibid. 12). Immediately after this personal setback, it is recorded that:

וַיִּשְׁלַח מֹשֶׁה מַלְאָכִים מִקָּדֵשׁ אֶל מֶלֶךְ אֱדוֹם

Moses sent messengers from Kadesh unto the king of Edom.
(20, 14)

The Midrash comments that this juxtaposition reflects great credit on Moses' character:

"וישלח משה מלאכים": זה שאמר הכתוב (תהלים טו): "לא רגל על לשונו, לא עשה לרעהו רעה, וחרפה לא נשה על קרובו". בנוהג שבעולם אדם עוסק בפרקמטיא עם חברו והקפידו (= והקניטו), פורש הימנו ואינו רוצה לראותו; ומשה — אף על פי שנענש על ישראל, שנאמר (תהלים קו): "ויקציפו על מי מריבה וירע למשה בעבורם" — לא פרק משאן מעליו, אלא: "וישלח מלאכים".

"And Moses sent messengers". To this may the following text be applied: "That hath no slander upon his tongue, nor doeth evil to his fellow, nor taketh up a reproach against his neighbour" (Psalms 15, 3). In the usual way, when a man is slighted by his business partner, he wishes to have nothing more to do with him; whereas Moses, though he was punished on account of Israel, as it is stated: "They angered him at the waters of Meribah, and it went ill with Moses because of them", did not rid himself of their burden but: "sent messengers".

(Bamidbar Rabbah 19, 7)

An allusion to this idea can be detected in the text itself. Why does the text in verse 1 stress the locality from which Moses sent the messengers? It was obvious that he had sent them from where he was stationed at that moment:

וַיָּבֹאוּ בְנֵי־יִשְׂרָאֵל . . . מִדְבַּר־צִן . . . וַיֵּשֶׁב הָעָם בְּקָדֵשׁ

And the children of Israel . . . came into the wilderness of Zin . . . and the people abode *in Kadesh.*

(20, 1)

Furthermore, wherever no change of locale is recorded in the text, it is presumed that the event described took place at the last mentioned place. Why then did the Torah repeat here "Kadesh?" Obviously to emphasise Moses' adherence to his mission of bringing the people to the land, even after his rebuff, in spite of the fact that he had been explicitly excluded from it. He sent messengers a second time, when the first deputation failed. Let us compare the messages of the two deputations:

The First Deputation	*The Second Deputation*
(verses 14—17)	(verse 19)
Thus saith thy brother Israel: Thou knowest all the travail that hath befallen us, how our fathers went down into Egypt, and we dwelt in Egypt a long time; and the Egyptians dealt ill	

with us, and our fathers, and when we cried unto the Lord, He heard our voice, and sent an angel, and brought us from Egypt; and, behold, we are in Kadesh, a city in the uttermost of thy border.

Let us pass, I pray thee, through thy land; we will not pass through field or through vineyard, neither will we drink of water of the wells; we will go along the king's highway, we will not turn aside to the right hand nor to the left, until we have passed thy border.

We will go up by the highway and if we drink of thy water, I and my cattle, then will I give the price thereof, let me only pass through on my feet; there is no hurt.

Common sense dictates that the second proposition in a diplomatic exchange will be less demanding than the first one which met with refusal. Rashi makes this point in his comment on Genesis 24, 55: "A few days, at least ten".

אין דרך המבקשים לבקש דבר מועט ואם לא תרצה, תן לנו מרובה מזה.

It is not the custom of a petitioner to demand the minimum and then, if refused, to demand more.

This principle is adhered to in our text too, as can be seen from the above comparison. Of course the preamble is omitted on the second occasion, since that is already understood. But the actual proposition has been whittled down. Moses no longer demanded the "king's highway". Perhaps this would be inconvenient. He merely requests the right of way, even if only by a sidetrack. Some commentators understand the word *mesilah* (translated "highway" by the accepted

250

renderings) as referring to a track skirting the borders in a meandering fashion. They point to Edom's reply in this case. This time Edom did not say, "Thou shalt not pass *through me*" but simply, "thou shalt no pass through", by whatever route, even if it only skirts my territory. Moses further added, in his second proposition, that he would go beyond taking care not to trespass on the king's property, fields and vineyards and wells. He would bring them positive gains, would pay for whatever they needed.

Let us now return to the preamble to the first proposition, cited above (verses 14—16). What was the point of referring to all their "travail?" Did Moses wish to arouse their compassion? Let us note Rashi's cryptic comment to one phrase:

"And the Egyptians dealt ill with us" — We suffered many misfortunes.

Rashi's comment is to say the least singularly uninformative, merely paraphrasing the text. One of Rashi's supercommentators enlightens us.

When a man relates his misfortunes, he has three possible aims in mind; to discredit the perpetrator or simply to make known his own suffering or both. Rashi wishes to emphasise that Moses merely wished to publicise the suffering and travail of his people and nothing more.

(Sefer Zikkaron)

In other words, Moses' preamble must not be regarded as a denunciation of Egyptian villainy but as the story of their suffering. But the question still remains to what purpose? Rashi asks in this vein:

"Thus saith thy brother Israel". What was his point in alluding to their brotherhood?

But the common sense answer would seem to be, as Abravanel states, that the allusion to their blood relationship and the story of

251

their suffering was designed to excite compassion. The objection to this approach is that Esau might well retort that if they were brothers, both had been promised the holy land. Here is the answer of the Midrash which is echoed in Rashi:

"אתה ידעת . . ." אמרו לו: אתה ידעת, כשאמר הקב״ה לאברהם (בראשית טו): "ידע תדע כי גר יהיה זרעך . . . ועבדום וענום . . ." — אנו נשתעבדנו ואתה בן חורין "וירדו אבותינו" וכל אותו ענין. משל למה הדבר דומה? לשני אחים שיצא שטר חוב על זקניהם, פרע אותו אחד אחד מהם. לימים התחיל לשאל חפץ מאחיו א״ל: אתה יודע שאותו חוב שפרעתי על שנינו היה, ואני הוא שפרעתיו, לכך אל תחזירני מן חפצי שאני שואל״.

"Thou knowest..." (Numbers 20, 15). Thou knowest that when the Holy One blessed be He said unto Abraham (Genesis 15, 13), "Know of surety that thy seed shall be a stranger... and shall serve them; and they shall afflict them", *we* were enslaved and *you* remained free and "our fathers went down into Egypt" and all that story. To what may this be compared? To two brothers who were presented with a bill of debt on their father. One of them paid it up. Subsequently the latter went to ask his brother a favour. He said, You remember I paid up the debt which was really on both of us. Do not therefore refuse me the favour that I request of you.

(Tanḥuma)

In other words, it was the suffering of the bondage, the refining effect of the iron furnace of serfdom in Egypt which alone gave title to the land. This idea is also embodied in another Midrash:

The Lord endowed Israel with three bountiful gifts and he bestowed them all, only at the price of suffering ... The Torah, Eretz Israel and the Hereafter. The Torah as it is stated: "Happy is the man whom thou chastiseth, O Lord and teachest out of Thy Torah" (Psalms 94, 12); Eretz Israel, as it is stated: "And thou shalt consider in thy heart, that, as a man chasteneth his son, so the Lord thy God chasteneth thee" (Deuteronomy 8, 5). What is stated thereafter? — "For the Lord thy God bringeth thee into a good land..." (ibid. 7). The Hereafter, as it is stated (Proverbs 6, 23): "For the commandment is a lamp, and Torah is a light, and the reproofs of instruction are the way of life (i.e. the other life).

(Tanḥuma)

252

Questions for Further Study

1. Compare Moses' deputation to Edom with that dispatched to Sihon, king of the Amorites:

   To Edom
   "Let us pass, I pray thee, through thy land".

   To Sihon
   "Let me pass through thy land".

   What is the difference for the change in phraseology?

2. The following text has given rise to a well known question:

   "And I sent messengers out of the wilderness of Kedemoth unto Sihon king of Heshbon with words of peace, saying: Let me pass through thy land; I will go along by the highway, I will neither turn unto the right hand nor to the left. Thou shalt sell me food for money, that I may eat; and give me water for money that I may drink, only let me pass through on my feet; as the children of Esau that dwell in Seir".

   (Deuteronomy 2, 26—29)

   Can you explain the question and suggest answers?

3. "Thus saith thy brother Israel" (20, 14).

   Commentators ask why Moses does not employ the name Jacob (as in Malachi 1, 2: "Was not Esau Jacob's brother?")

4. "Lest I come out with the sword against thee".

   (Numbers 20, 18)

   Sforno comments on the above text:

   This implies that the Edomites are bloodthirsty and quick to anger. On the smallest pretext they are likely to attack those passing through.

(a)   In what way does Sforno deviate from the accepted sense of the verse?

(b)   What linguistic anomaly prompted his explanation?

WHAT MADE THE KING OF ARAD FIGHT?

וַיִּשְׁמַע הַכְּנַעֲנִי מֶלֶךְ־עֲרָד יֹשֵׁב הַנֶּגֶב כִּי בָּא יִשְׂרָאֵל דֶּרֶךְ הָאֲתָרִים וַיִּלָּחֶם
בְּיִשְׂרָאֵל וַיִּשְׁבְּ מִמֶּנּוּ שֶׁבִי:

**And the Canaanite, the king of Arad, who dwelt in the South,
heard tell that Israel came by the way of Atharim; and he
fought against Israel, and took some of them captive.**

(21, 1)

The above verse is puzzling on two counts, first with regards to its
own immediate significance and second to that attributed to it by our
Sages. Let us first examine the initial difficulty. The Canaanite king's
conduct here contradicts the assertion made in the Song of the Red
Sea that all the nations of the world were terror-struck by the Divine
miracles and dared not interfere with Israel:

שָׁמְעוּ עַמִּים יִרְגָּזוּן
חִיל אָחַז יֹשְׁבֵי פְּלָשֶׁת:
אָז נִבְהֲלוּ אַלּוּפֵי אֱדוֹם
אֵילֵי מוֹאָב יֹאחֲזֵמוֹ רָעַד
נָמֹגוּ כֹּל יֹשְׁבֵי כְנָעַן:

**The peoples have heard, they tremble;
Pangs have taken hold on the inhabitants of Philistia.
Then were the chiefs of Edom affrighted;
The mighty men of Moab, trembling taketh hold upon them;
all the inhabitants of Canaan are melted away.**

(Exodus 15, 14—15)

255

The terror inspired by the children of Israel is graphically described by Rahab of Jericho in the book of Joshua:

יָדַעְתִּי כִּי־נָתַן ה׳ לָכֶם אֶת הָאָרֶץ . . .
וְכִי־נָפְלָה אֵימַתְכֶם עָלֵינוּ
וְכִי נָמֹגוּ כָּל־יֹשְׁבֵי הָאָרֶץ מִפְּנֵיכֶם:
כִּי שָׁמַעְנוּ אֵת אֲשֶׁר־הוֹבִישׁ ה׳ אֶת־מֵי יַם־סוּף מִפְּנֵיכֶם . . .
וַאֲשֶׁר עֲשִׂיתֶם לִשְׁנֵי מַלְכֵי הָאֱמֹרִי . . .
וַנִּשְׁמַע וַיִּמַּס לְבָבֵנוּ
וְלֹא־קָמָה עוֹד רוּחַ בְּאִישׁ מִפְּנֵיכֶם

...I know that the Lord hath given you the land,
and that your terror is fallen upon us,
and that all the inhabitants of the land melt away before you.
For we have heard how the Lord dried up the water of the Red Sea before you...
And what ye did unto the two kings of the Amorites...
And as soon as we had heard it, our hearts did melt, neither did there remain any more spirit in any man, because of you...

(Joshua 2, 9—11)

How came the King of Arad to be an exception to this rule? What had given him the audacity to attack Israel. Before we attempt to solve this question let us turn our attention to our Sages' comment on the passage:

מה שמועה שמע? שמע שמת אהרן ונסתלקו ענני הכבוד, וכסבור נתנה לו רשות להלחם.

What tidings did he hear? He heard that Aaron had died and that the clouds of glory had dispersed. He imagined, therefore, that permission had been granted him to fight.

(Rosh Hashanah 3a)

This Rabbinic comment poses another puzzle. Surely Scripture
itself states what the king of Arad had heard — "that Israel came by
the way of Atharim". — The criticism of the following commentator
would seem to be well-directed:

> Why should we look for what is already there? It is like the rider of an ass
> who goes in search of it, taking with him provision for several days journey
> and going from town to town when he is all the time astride it. Surely the text
> explicitly states what it was that the Canaanite had heard. Why should we
> then look any further?

> (Ibn Kaspi, *Meẓaref La-kesef*)

But if we study the comment of our Sages a little more closely, we
shall see that even Ibn Kaspi's shafts of criticism are not so well
directed. First let us compare a similar comment of theirs on the first
verse of *Yitro*:

"וישמע יתרו" — מה שמועה שמע ובא? מלחמת עמלק שמע ובא . . . דברי ר'
יהושע. ר' אלעזר אומר: מתן תורה שמע ובא, שבשעה שנתנה תורה לישראל, זעו כל
מלכי האדמה בהיכליהם . . .

"Now Jethro heard" — what tidings did Jethro hear that he came? He heard
of the battle of Amalek and came. These are the words of R. Joshua. R.
Eliezer said: He heard of the giving of the Law and came; for when the
Torah was given Israel all the kings of the earth trembled in their temples.

(Mekhilta)

Another version in the Talmud, *Zevaḥim* 116a reads:

מה שמועה שמע ובא? ר' יהושע אומר: מלחמת עמלק שמע ובא . . . ר' אלעזר
המודעי אומר: מתן תורה שמע ובא, וכשנתנה תורה לעם ישראל, היה קולו הולך מסוף
העולם עד סופו; ר' אליעזר בן יעקב אומר: קריעת ים סוף שמע ובא, שנאמר (יהושע
ה): "ויהי כשמע כל מלכי האמורי את אשר הוביש ה' את מימי . . .

R. Eliezer the Modi'ite said: He heard of the giving of the Law and came; for
when the Torah was given to the children of Israel, His voice went from one
end of the earth unto the other. R. Eliezer ben Yaacov said: He heard of the

257

crossing of the Red Sea and came, as it is said: "And it came to pass when all the kings of the Amorites had heard that the Lord had dried the waters . . ."

In the above case, Ibn Kaspi's objection still holds good. Why should the Sages ask what Jethro heard when the text itself states that "he heard all that God had done for Moses and for Israel His people?" The answer is immediately apparent, if we read the comment of the Sages carefully. They did not simply ask what Jethro heard, but what did he hear *that he came.* What event or events had *prompted* him to come? Which of the many occurrences that had happened, at the time, had moved him more than anything else? We must similarly understand the Rabbinic comment on the passage in our sidra. What had prompted the King of Arad to attack Israel, when all the nations had stood in awe of the people chosen by God? To understand this, we must bear in mind the sequence of events in the narrative. What had immediately preceded the attack of the King of Arad? — The story of the spies. Naḥmanides, therefore, explains the aggression in the light of this:

> The reason for it was that the Israelites had come by way of Atharim. When the spies travelled through the Negev and returned, the inhabitants of the country — the Canaanites — noted their presence and followed them back to the camp of Israel.

Naḥmanides thus understands the word "Atharim" to connote "spies" from a Hebrew root meaning "to spy". Ibn Ezra also states that the word means spies and the phrase should be translated: "the way of the spies".

What connection then was there between the incident of the spies and this attack on the children of Israel? The latter had shown their lack of confidence and fear of the future, by sending the spies. The Canaanites fortified themselves with the knowledge of Israel's sense of weakness and inferiority. The lowering of the Israelites' morale was followed, automatically, by the rising morale of their enemies.

The spies had said:

וַנְּהִי בְעֵינֵינוּ כַּחֲגָבִים וְכֵן הָיִינוּ בְּעֵינֵיהֶם:

... And we were in our own sight as grasshoppers, and so we were in their sight.

(13, 33)

Perhaps Naḥmanides noted a concealed allusion in our passage to this increase of courage that fed on the Israelites' lack of faith. The passage states that the Canaanite king had heard that Israel came *by the way of the spies*. He drew courage from the *way* or manner in which the spies had acted or from the Israelites' resort to spies to explore the country.

The Midrash relates that the Emperor Hadrian said to R. Joshua:

אדרינוס אמר לר׳ יהושע: גדולה הכבשה העומדת בין שבעים זאבים, אמר לו: גדול הוא הרועה שמצילה ושומרה, ושוברן מפניה.

Great is the lamb that stands amongst seventy wolves. Said he to him: Great is the Shepherd who rescues and guards her and rends them in front of her.

Only if the lamb is aware of the omnipotence of the Shepherd in rescuing and guarding her, can she, indeed, withstand the seventy wolves.

We may therefore regard this as the lesson of the story of the King of Arad. The children of Israel showed their lack of trust in God by sending the spies. The result was that the Canaanite inhabitants lost their dread of the Chosen People and attacked them at the first opportunity.

THE COPPER SERPENT

The sidra tells us how the children of Israel persisted in their murmurings, even after the Almighty had extracted water for them from the stony rock. We have seen from what has gone previously how miracles, signs and wonders — manna from Heaven, meat from above could not change human nature. Again we hear the familiar complaint:

לָמָה הֶעֱלִיתֻנוּ מִמִּצְרַיִם לָמוּת בַּמִּדְבָּר

Wherefore have ye brought us up out of Egypt to die in the wilderness . . . ?

(21, 5)

But note the change in the wording of their complaint as compared with previous occasions. When they stood at the Red Sea with Egypt pursuing them, they said: "Wherefore hast *thou* dealt thus with us, to carry us forth out of Egypt?" or in the case of Dathan and Abiram: "Is it a small thing that *thou* hast brought us out of a land flowing with milk and honey" (16, 13). They employed the singular form: "thou". This time, however — "the people spake against God and against Moses: "Wherefore have *ye* brought us up out of Egypt?" (21, 5) using the plural form to include both the Almighty and Moses — as Rashi states:

השוו עבד לקונו, שניהם שווים! מיד: "וישלח ה' בעם את הנחשים השרפים וינשכו את
העם . . .".

260

They equated the servant with his Master; both of you are on the same footing. Forthwith, "the Lord sent fiery serpents among the people and they bit the people".

The Midrash cited by Rashi with reference to the verse (Exodus 17, 8): "Then came Amalek, and fought with Israel at Rephidim", is equally appropriate in our context. Rashi, commenting on the juxtaposition of this verse with the previous one, which reads: "He called the name of the place Meribah ... because they tempted the Lord saying, Is the Lord among us or not?" states:

תמיד אני ביניכם ומזומן לכל צרכיכם ואתם אומרים "היש ה' בקרבנו אם אין?!"
חייכם שהכלב בא ונושך אתכם ואתם צועקים לי, ותדעו מי אני! משל לאדם שהרכיב
בנו על כתפו ויצא לדרך, היה אותו בן רואה חפץ ואומר: "אבא טול זה ותן לי!"
והוא נותן לו, וכן שנית, וכן שלישית. פגעו באדם אחד — אמר לו אותו הבן: "ראית
את אבא?" אמר לו אביו: "אינך יודע היכן אני?" השליכו מעליו ובא הכלב ונשכו!

I (i.e. the Lord) am always among you and ready to serve your needs; yet you say, Is the Lord among us or not? By your lives! A dog will come and bite you, and then you will cry unto Me and know My whereabouts. This may be compared to a man who carried his son on his shoulder and went on a journey. The son catching sight of an object on the road said: Father, pick it up and give it me. His father gave it him. This happened on a second and third occasion until they met someone on the way. The son said to him: Have you seen father? His father answered: So you don't know where I am? Thereupon his father threw him down and a dog came and bit him.

Similarly, the serpents came and bit the people. Let us now examine the wording of the verse closely, the verb *va-yeshalaḥ* in particular. There is an important difference between *va-yishlaḥ*[1] in the *kal* form and *va-yeshalaḥ*[2] in the *pi'el*. In the former, the meaning is always "sent", in the sense of sending on a mission as illustrated by the following examples: "And Jacob sent messengers" (Genesis 32, 4) or "Jacob sent him (Joseph) out of the vale of Hebron" (*ibid.* 31, 14). In the latter, however, the implication is, "setting free", "letting go" and the opposite of forcible restraint as in: "Let my people go" (Exodus 5, 1), or "When Pharaoh had let the people go"

261

(Exodus 13, 17), or on the subject of freeing slaves: "In the seventh year thou shalt let him go free..." (Deuteronomy 15, 12), the sending away of the mother bird: "thou shalt in any wise let the dam go and take the young..." (Deuteronomy 22, 7).

Now that this distinction is clear, let us study the verse in our sidra. It is not stated "And the Lord *sent (va-yishlah)* fiery serpents" (although the King James version wrongly translates it as if it was so written) but: "He *let go* the serpents" (*va-yeshalah*). (Actually only Hirsch has noted this in his German translation[3]). The reason for the Torah saying: "And the Lord set free" or let go the serpents and not merely sent them, should become quite clear, when we recall that the wilderness they were travelling through was a place of "fiery serpents and scorpions and drought..." If the serpents had not bitten them till now, it was only thanks to Divine Providence which had been watching over them, leading them through that great and terrible wilderness and not allowing the serpents to touch them, just as He did not allow the drought to overcome them with thirst, but drew them out water from the rock. The children of Israel, however, had spurned the Almighty's supernatural intervention, not wishing to live on the bread He provided, the manna ("our soul loathed this light bread"), but aspiring to lead a more normal "natural" existence. Accordingly, the Lord let things go their ordinary, normal way. He allowed the serpents to behave in their natural manner, in the great and terrible wilderness, which was to bite anyone crossing their path. Therefore:

וַיְשַׁלַּח ה' בָּעָם הַנְּחָשִׁים הַשְּׂרָפִים וַיְנַשְּׁכוּ אֶת־הָעָם וַיָּמָת עַם־רָב מִיִּשְׂרָאֵל:

The Lord *let the serpents go* against them and they bit the people and large numbers of the people of Israel died.

(21, 6)

It was not therefore the attack of the serpents, but rather their absence during the whole of their wanderings till then, that constituted the miracle.

After the people had admitted their guilt and said:

חָטָאנוּ כִּי־דִבַּרְנוּ בַה' וָבָךְ
הִתְפַּלֵל אֶל־ה' וְיָסֵר מֵעָלֵינוּ אֶת־הַנָּחָשׁ

We have sinned, for we have spoken against the Lord and thee; pray unto the Lord, that he take away the serpents from us,

(21, 7)

Moses was advised to heal the victims in a somewhat strange fashion.

וַיֹּאמֶר ה' אֶל־מֹשֶׁה
עֲשֵׂה לְךָ שָׂרָף וְשִׂים אֹתוֹ עַל־נֵס
וְהָיָה כָּל־הַנָּשׁוּךְ וְרָאָה אֹתוֹ וָחָי:

**And the Lord said unto Moses,
Make thee a fiery serpent, and set it upon a pole:
and it shall come to pass that every one that is bitten, when he looketh upon it, shall live.**

(21, 8)

This verse has puzzled many commentators and the Mishnah (*Rosh Hashanah* 3, 5) asks:

וכי נחש ממית או נחש מחיה? אלא בזמן שישראל מסתכלין כלפי מעלה ומשעבדין את לבם לאביהם שבשמים היו מתרפאים, ואם לאו, היו נימוקים.

But could the serpent slay or the serpent keep alive It is rather to teach thee that such time as the Israelites directed their thoughts on high, and kept their hearts in subjection to their Father in Heaven, they were healed; otherwise they pined away.

Another answer is tendered in the *Zohar (Shelah,* 175):

"Everyone that is bitten, when he looketh upon it, shall live". Why? As soon as he (the victim) turns his eyes and sees the likeness of the serpent, he forthwith becomes filled with awe and prays to the Lord, knowing that this was the punishment that he deserved. As long as the son sees his father's strap, he is afraid of his father... Regarding this it is stated: "When he looketh upon it, he shall live". He saw the strap with which He struck—and this led to him being redeemed.

Hirsch explains:

The serpents were sent to show the people that danger beset their every step and it was only thanks to the miraculous and perpetual intervention of Divine Providence that they were able to proceed, unharmed. Their path was so smooth that they failed to perceive the constant miracle in their unmolested progress. Every victim of the serpents' venom had to concentrate his attention on the image of the brazen serpent, to enable him to realise that, even after God had delivered him from the serpents, there lay ahead of him fresh dangers. He had to thank Divine Providence for every minute of security granted him. Nothing is more calculated to make man more satisfied with his lot than the knowledge of the chasm that ever yawns beneath him, and that it is only Divine mercy that bears him safely over, as if on eagles' wings. Happy is he who takes note of the unseen "fiery serpents" that beset his path, put to flight by the Almighty... In this lies the healing power of the serpent. Every victim had always to bear in mind the bite of the serpent "and everyone that is bitten, when he looketh upon it, he shall live".

Questions for Further Study

1. Explain whether the following verses bear out or contradict the principle laid down regarding the difference between *shalah* in the *kal* and *shilah* in the *pi'el* form: "He sent forth (*va-yeshalah*) a dove from him" (Genesis 8, 8); "He cast upon (*yeshalah*) them, the fierceness of His anger, wrath and indignation"

(Psalms 78, 49 — this passage is cited in the Passover Haggadah).

2. Compare in chapter 21, verse 8 with verse 9. Can you suggest a reason for the variation in the wording, in the substitution of *ve-ra'ah* — "When he looketh upon it" in verse 8, for *ve-hibit* — "when he beheld it", in verse 9. Try to discover the difference in implication between the Hebrew words *hibit* and *ra'ah*.

3. In what way do the interpretations given to the word "shall live" (*va-ḥai*) by Hirsch and the *Zohar* deviate from the literal meaning of the word?

4. The Mishnah *Rosh Hashanah* cited above asks the same question and gives the same answer regarding the lifting up of Moses' hand in the battle of the Amalekites (Exodus 17, 8—13). In what way are these cases similar?

NOTES

[1] וַיִּשְׁלַח.

[2] וַיְשַׁלַּח.

[3] Da *liess* Gott wider das Volk die Giftschlangen *los*.

FEAR HIM NOT

The Israelites had begun the invasion of the approaches to the Promised Land vanquishing in the process the mighty Sihon king of the Amorites:

וְהוּא נִלְחַם בְּמֶלֶךְ מוֹאָב הָרִאשׁוֹן וַיִּקַּח אֶת־כָּל־אַרְצוֹ מִיָּדוֹ עַד־אַרְנֹן׃

Who had fought against the former king of Moab, and taken all his land out of his hand, even unto Arnon.

(21, 26)

Our Sages described the king of Moab and his kingdom as presenting a most difficult problem of conquest to the Israelites. But they succeeded in overcoming him and occupying his land from Arnon to Jabbok. Then they turned their attention to the north:

וַיִּפְנוּ וַיַּעֲלוּ דֶּרֶךְ הַבָּשָׁן
וַיֵּצֵא עוֹג מֶלֶךְ־הַבָּשָׁן לִקְרָאתָם
הוּא וְכָל־עַמּוֹ לַמִּלְחָמָה אֶדְרֶעִי׃
וַיֹּאמֶר ה׳ אֶל מֹשֶׁה
אַל־תִּירָא אֹתוֹ.

**And they turned and went up by the way of Bashan:
And Og the king of Bashan went out against them,
he, and all his people, to the battle at Edrei.
And the Lord said unto Moses,
Fear him not.**

(21, 33—34)

The divine exhortation to Moses not to fear presents some difficulty. Where do we find any hint in our chapter that Moses was afraid? Should it then be argued that the Torah would not wish to record Moses' but mortal fears of flesh and blood out of respect for him, this suggestion is ruled out by the fact that we do have earlier on in the Pentateuch the following statement describing Moses' state of mind after he had slain the Egyptian:

וַיִּירָא מֹשֶׁה וַיֹּאמַר אָכֵן נוֹדַע הַדָּבָר:

And Moses feared, and said, surely this thing is known.

(Exodus 2, 14)

Why then did not the Torah reveal Moses' natural fears of the mighty kings of Canaan in our sidra? It may be argued, of course, that the revelation of Moses' fears in Egypt applied to the period in his life before he had been spoken to by God. But after Moses had been entrusted with the divine mission and attained unprecedented prophetic heights, his character changed and he was no more subject to such fears. Presumably then we may argue that, at the outset of his prophetic career, when he "hid his face for he was afraid to look upon God", he was still subject to mortal weaknesses and feared for his life, but after attaining the prophetic heights of —

פֶּה אֶל־פֶּה אֲדַבֶּר בּוֹ
וּמַרְאֶה וְלֹא בְחִידֹת
וּתְמֻנַת ה׳ יַבִּיט

With him will I speak mouth to mouth,
even apparently, and not in dark speeches;
and the similitude of the Lord shall he behold —

(12, 8)

he would no more know fear for flesh and blood. However, the Torah records explicitly in our sidra that God exhorted him not to fear, implying that he was still subject to mortal apprehensions of superior might. Why then did not the Torah record for us the fact that Moses was indeed afraid? It would seem that the Torah wished to teach us that human fears cannot be completely eradicated and that though the prophet overcomes and suppresses them from the eyes of the onlooker and even possibly from himself, the all-knowing God sees into the innermost recesses of his mind. Though it was not therefore plainly evident that Moses was afraid, God Himself, aware of Moses' innermost feelings, exhorted him not to fear. Nevertheless, it is still surprising that this exhortation was necessary. Surely Moses who had brought the Torah down from Mount Sinai neither eating bread nor drinking water for forty days, and who had experienced the closest divine communion and triumphed over his mortal desires to such an extent should not still have been subject to such apprehensions! Let us quote here in explanation of this phenomenon the story retold by Rabbi Israel Lifshitz in his famous commentary to the Mishnah, *Tiferet Yisrael* at the end of Kiddushin IV:

When Moses brought the children of Israel out of Egypt all the peoples of the world trembled and were astonished at the greatness of the man Moses, through whom all these miracles had been performed. Thereupon one Arabian king sent one of his most distinguished painters to paint a likeness of this great leader and bring it to him. The painter executed the portrait and brought it to the king. The king called together all his wise men and asked them to draw conclusions regarding the character and nature of Moses from his portrait. To which the wise men replied: If we are to judge by the likeness portrayed in this picture we must conclude that he is wicked, proud, covetous and perverse, indeed characterised by the worst of human faults. The king was very wroth and indignant and said: "What is this? Do you mock me? Have you not heard about the fame of this great man from all corners of the earth!"

Thereupon the king took his chariot and horsemen and set forth for the camp of Israel ... where he was astounded to see Moses looking exactly as the painter had portrayed him. The king entered the tent of the man of God and bowed and prostrated himself before him and told Moses all that his wise men had said. And Moses answered and said: Know that all the faults which your wise men ascribed to me are indeed a part of my nature and perhaps in greater measure than ascribed to me by your wise men. But through perseverance I have triumphed over them and suppressed them and for this reason I have become honoured in the world.

Every man, however perfect, is subject to weaknesses and frailties and his greatness lies rather in his measure of control over them. Moses thus triumphed over his but mortal fears. However, the phrase alluding to his fears will repay closer study. It is evident that it is no ordinary fear that is referred to in our sidra. Here the Hebrew verb "to fear" is used in a transitive sense with a direct object "him" אותו and not intransitively with the indirect object "because of him" מפניו which we may translate as "be not afraid of him" (cf. Deuteronomy 20, 3 "fear not neither be ye terrified *because of* them"). Our commentators have explained that "fear" in the intransitive sense implies physical terror of the might of the enemy whilst "fear" in the transitive sense implies "to stand in awe". It is usually used with reference to the fear of God ("Thou shalt fear the Lord thy God") and the respect due to parents which is compared by the Torah to the fear of heaven ("Each man shall fear his father and mother"), and with regard to man and his neighbour when respect is mixed with fear. Rashi points this out in his comment on the verse "fear him not":

"אל תירא אותו": שהיה משה ירא להלחם, שמא תעמוד לו (= לעוג) זכותו של אברהם
שנאמר (בראשית יד): "ויבא הפליט ויגד לאברהם", הוא עוג . . .

Moses was afraid of doing battle, peradventure he (Og) might be protected by the merit of (his services to) Abraham, as it is written (Genesis 14, 13): "And there came one that had escaped and told Abraham" — that is Og.

We are not here concerned with the identification by the Midrash of the survivor that came to tell Abraham of the plight of Lot, with Og, but with the concept of the meritorious actions that may stand to the credit of even a wicked man. Though he may seem to us to be completely devoid of good deeds the Almighty who sees into the human heart may find even in such a man merit and will not begrudge him his reward. It is impossible therefore for one human being to judge the character of another and appraise his moral worth. This only the Almighty can do. Our Sages stated:

והוה דן כל האדם לכף זכות.

Judge every man charitably.

(Pirke Avot I, 6)

Maimonides in the Laws of Teshuva III 2, speaks in the same strain:

אדם שעונותיו מרובים על זכויותיו — מיד הוא מת ברשעו . . . וכן מדינה שעונותיה מרובין — מיד היא אובדת; שנאמר (בראשית יח): "זעקת סדום ועמורה כי רבה", וכן כל העולם כולו, אם היו עונותיהם מרובים מזכויותיהן מיד הן נשחתים, שנאמר (בראשית ו): "וירא ה' כי רבת רעת האדם". ושקול זה אינו לפי מניין הזכויות והעוונות אלא לפי גודלם. יש זכות שהיא כנגד כמה עוונות שנאמר (מלכים א יד, יג): "יען נמצא בו דבר טוב". ויש עון שהוא כנגד כמה זכויות שנאמר (קהלת ט, יח): "וחוטא אחד יאבד טובה הרבה". ואין שוקלין אלא בדעתו של אל דעות והוא היודע היאך עורכין הזכויות כנגד העוונות.

A person whose iniquities outweigh his meritorious deeds dies forthwith on account of his wickedness[1]... so it is with the city whose iniquities are excessive — forthwith it is destroyed, as it is stated (Genesis 18, 20): "The cry of Sodom and Gomorrah is great" (literally "much" implying that their sins were more than their good deeds); and so it is with the whole of mankind, if their iniquities exceeded their meritorious actions — forthwith they are destroyed, as it is stated: "And the Lord saw that the wickedness of man was great" (Genesis 6). This calculation is not based on a quantitive reckoning of good and bad deeds but on a qualitative reckoning. One meritorious action may outweigh many iniquities, as it is stated: "Because there was found in him one worthy deed" (with reference to Jeroboam's son — I Kings 14, 13). On the other hand, one iniquity may outweigh many meritorious deeds as it is stated "One sinner (or "sin") destroyeth much good"[2] (Ecclesiastes 9, 18). But the reckoning is made in accordance with the judgement of the Divine Arbiter and only He knows how the balance sheet of merits and iniquities is drawn up.

NOTES

[1] Should it be argued that we witness so many wicked men who live long and prosperous lives, we should realize, as Maimonides remarks, subsequently, that the account of good and evil is not calculated mathematically and that the evildoer concerned may have had some hidden merit to his credit (Kesef Mishneh). Another explanation suggested is that Maimonides refers to the reckoning made at man's death. If his sins outweigh his merits, then his soul does not enjoy eternal life in the Hereafter but "dies forthwith on account of his wickedness". Death here means spiritual not physical death (Leḥem Mishneh).

(Translator's note)

[2] הרי שהיו ישראל מחצה צדיקים ומחצה רשעים ובא אחד וחטא ועשאן מרובים — נמצא שהכריע את כלם לחובה.

"Suppose the righteous and wicked of Israel were exactly equal in number and there came along one man and committed a sin making them (i.e. the wicked) the majority. This one sinner would then be responsible for weighting down the scales on the side of evil to the disadvantage of all" (Rashi).

(Translator's note)

JEPHTHAH'S VOW[1]
(Haftarah, Judges 11,1-33)

The connection between the Sidra and the Haftarah is obvious. The conquest of Sihon's kingdom, part of which he had previously wrested from Ammon and Moab constitutes the historical basis for the diplomatic negotiations conducted between Jephthah and the king of Moab. The Ammonite king argued that:

כִּי־לָקַח יִשְׂרָאֵל אֶת־אַרְצִי בַּעֲלוֹתוֹ מִמִּצְרַיִם
מֵאַרְנוֹן וְעַד־הַיַּבֹּק וְעַד־הַיַּרְדֵּן

**Israel took away my land when he came up out of Egypt,
from the Arnon even unto the Jabbok and unto the Jordan.**

(Judges 11, 13)

This is exactly what is alluded to in our sidra:

וַיַּכֵּהוּ יִשְׂרָאֵל לְפִי־חָרֶב
וַיִּירַשׁ אֶת־אַרְצוֹ
מֵאַרְנֹן עַד־יַבֹּק עַד־בְּנֵי עַמּוֹן

**Israel smote him with the edge of the sword
and possessed his land
from the Arnon unto the Jabbok even unto the children of
Ammon.**

(Num. 21, 24)

But we shall not, this time, deal with the diplomatic finesse of

Jephthah in his desire to avoid war by political negotiation, nor with his military prowess, but with that one point for which he is most famous — his vow:

וַיִּדַּר יִפְתָּח נֶדֶר לַה׳ וַיֹּאמַר
אִם־נָתוֹן תִּתֵּן אֶת־בְּנֵי עַמּוֹן בְּיָדִי:
וְהָיָה הַיּוֹצֵא אֲשֶׁר יֵצֵא מִדַּלְתֵי בֵיתִי לִקְרָאתִי
בְּשׁוּבִי בְשָׁלוֹם מִבְּנֵי עַמּוֹן
וְהָיָה לַה׳ וְהַעֲלִיתִהוּ עוֹלָה:

Jephthah vowed a vow to the Lord, and said:
If you indeed deliver the children of Ammon into my hand,
then whatever issues forth from the doors of my house,
when I return in peace from the children of Ammon
shall be the Lord's,
and I will offer it up for a burnt-offering.

(Judges 11, 30—31)

What actually was the content of this vow? Two approaches to understanding the drift of his vow and deed he committed in its fulfillment can be discerned in the comments of our Sages and commentators. We shall first cite our Sages who clothed the trend of his thoughts and even his debate with his daughter in dramatic and pictorial form (Tanḥuma Yashan, Buber Beḥukotai 7):

״אִישׁ כִּי יַפְלִא נֶדֶר בְּעֶרְכְּךָ נְפָשֹׁת לַה׳״ (וַיִּקְרָא כז, ב): זֶה שֶׁאָמַר הַכָּתוּב (מִשְׁלֵי יא, ל):
״פְּרִי צַדִּיק עֵץ חַיִּים וְלוֹקֵחַ נְפָשׁוֹת חָכָם״, אִם יִהְיֶה אָדָם צַדִּיק, וְאַף עַל פִּי שֶׁהוּא צַדִּיק
אִם אֵינוֹ עוֹסֵק בַּתּוֹרָה אֵין בְּיָדוֹ כְּלוּם אֶלָּא פְּרִי צַדִּיק עֵץ חַיִּים זוֹ הַתּוֹרָה שֶׁמִּתּוֹךְ שֶׁהוּא בֶּן
תּוֹרָה הוּא לוֹמֵד הֵיאַךְ לוֹקֵחַ נְפָשׁוֹת שֶׁנֶּאֱמַר: ״לוֹקֵחַ נְפָשׁוֹת חָכָם״.

"When a man shall clearly utter a vow of persons to the Lord . . ." (Leviticus 27, 2). Regarding this the text (Prov. 11, 30) observes: "The fruit of a righteous man is a tree of life making him wise to win souls". If a man is righteous, though he is righteous, if he does not engage in Torah he has nothing. But the fruit of the righteous is a "tree of life", meaning the Torah. As a result of becoming a Torah scholar he learns how to win souls, as it is stated: "Making him wise to win souls".

וכן אתה מוצא ביפתח הגלעדי, מפני שלא היה בן תורה — אבד את בתו. אימתי? בשעה שנלחם עם בני עמון ונדר, שנאמר: "וידר יפתח נדר לה' ויאמר: אם תתן את בני עמון בידי, והיה היוצא אשר יצא מדלת ביתי לקראתי, בשובי בשלום מבני עמון והיה לה' והעליתיהו עולה". באותה שעה כעס עליו הקב"ה, אמר הקב"ה: "אלו יצא מביתו כלב או חזיר או גמל — יקריב לפני?!"...

So you find with Jephthah the Gileadite; because he was no Torah scholar he lost his daughter. When? When he fought Ammon and vowed, as it is stated: "Whatever issues forth from the doors of my house when I return in peace from the children of Ammon shall be the Lord's and I will offer it up for a burnt-offering". At that moment the Holy One blessed be He became angry with him. The Holy One blessed be He said: Had a dog, swine or camel issued forth from his house he would have offered it to me!?

"והנה בתו יוצאת לקראתו..." "ויהי כראותו אותה ויקרע את בגדיו ויאמר... "ואנכי פציתי פי אל ה' ולא אוכל לשוב". והלא פנחס היה שם והיה אומר "ולא אוכל לשוב?" אלא פנחס אמר: "אני כהן גדול בן כהן גדול — אשפיל עצמי ואלך אל עם הארץ?!" ויפתח אמר: "אני ראש שבטי ישראל, ראש הקצינים, אשפיל עצמי ואלך אצל הדיוט?!" מבין שניהם אבדה ההיא העלובה.

"Behold his daughter came out to meet him ... and it came to pass when he saw her that he rent his clothes and said ... for I have opened my mouth unto the Lord and I cannot take it back". Surely Phinehas was (as a priest he was authorised to absolve him from his vow) there? Yet he said: "I cannot take it back?" But Phinehas said: Should I a high priest, the son of a high priest lower myself and go to that boor!? Jephthah said: Should I, the head of tribes of Israel, general of the officers stoop to go to that civilian? Between them both that unfortunate girl perished.

(בראשית רבה ס: "בין חייתא למחבלתא אזל ברא דעלובתא") ושניהם נתחייבו בדמיה...

(In Bereshit Rabbah: Between the midwife and mother the unfortunate child perished). And both of them were to blame for her death.

כיון שבקש לקרבה, היתה בוכה לפניו, אמרה לו בתו: "אבי יצאתי לקראתך בשמחה, ואתה שוחט אותי?!".

When he sought to sacrifice her she wept before him. His daughter said to him: Father, I came to meet you full of joy, now you would slaughter me?

אמרה לו בתו: "אבי! שמא כתוב בתורה שיקריבו נפשות בניהם על גבי המזבח?!"
והלא כתיב (ויקרא א, א): "אדם כי יקריב מכם קרבן לה' מן הבהמה מן הבקר ומן
הצאן". מן הבהמה — ולא מבני האדם!" אמר לה: "בתי, נדרתי והיה היוצא אשר
יצא מדלתי ביתי... והיה לה". שמא כל הנודר יכול הוא שלא לשלם נדרו?!"

His daughter said to him: Father! Is it perhaps written in the Torah that people should offer the lives of their children on the altar!? Surely, is it not written (Leviticus 1, 2): "If a person wishes to offer sacrifice to the Lord from the cattle or the herd or the flock" — from the cattle and not from man! He answered her: I have vowed that whatever issues forth from the doors of my house shall be the Lord's.

כל הדברים האלה אמרה לו ולא שמע לה... עד ושחטה לפני הקב"ה, ורוח הקודש
צווחת: נפשות הייתי מבקש שתקריב לפני?! (ירמיהו יט, ה): "אשר לא צויתי ולא
דברתי ולא עלתה על לבי". לא צויתי לאברהם שישחוט בנו, אלא אמרתי (בראשית כב,
יב): "אל תשלח ידך אל הנער" — בשביל להודיעך היאך היה אברהם עושה רצוני,
שהיו אומות העולם אומרים: למה הקב"ה מחבב לאברהם הרבה? לכך אמר לו "קח נא
את בנך". הוי אשר לא צויתי לאברהם לשחוט את בנו ודאי.

She spoke all these words but he paid no heed until he slaughtered her before the Holy One blessed be He. The Holy Spirit cried out: Did I ask you to make human sacrifice to Me? — "which I commanded not nor spoke nor entered My mind" (Jeremiah 19, 5). I did not command Abraham to slaughter his son but I said (Genesis 22, 12): "Lay not your hand on the lad" — in order to publicise how Abraham performed My will. For the nations of the world were wont to say: Why is the Holy One blessed be He so fond of Abraham? On this account He told him to "take now your son". Thus in the final outcome I did not command Abraham to slaughter his son.

"ולא דברתי" ליפתח להקריב לי את בתו. "ולא עלתה על לבי" שיפול מלך מואב ביד
מלך ישראל ויקריב לי בנו בכורו שנאמר (מלכים ב ג, כז): "ויקח את בנו בכורו אשר
ימלוך תחתיו ויעלהו עולה על החומה".

"Nor spoke" to Jephthah that he should offer up his daughter to Me. "Nor did it enter My mind" that when the King of Moab fell into the hand of the king of Israel that he should offer his firstborn son to Me, as it is stated (2

Kings 3, 27): "He took his firstborn son who was to succeed him and offered him up as a burnt-offering on the wall".

מי גרם ליפתח לאבד את בתו? על שלא קרא בתורה שאלו קרא בתורה לא אבד את בתו, שכתוב (ויקרא כז, ב): "איש כי יפליא נדר... ואם נקיבה היא...".

What caused Jephthah to take the life of his own daughter? Because he failed to read the Torah. Had he read the Torah he would not have done his daughter to death. For it is written: "When a man shall clearly utter a vow ... it be a female ..." (i.e. a vow of human beings is rendered in monetary terms).

But most of our commentators understood the vow and its fulfillment quite differently:

"And I will offer it up for a burnt-offering". The view of our rabbis on this is wellknown, but my late father explained that *vav* "and" is to be translated "or", the verse running as follows: "... shall be the Lord's if it is not suitable for a burnt-offering; or I will offer it up for a burnt-offering. Cf. Ex. 21: "He that strikes his father *and (ve)* his mother shall surely be put to death" where the "and" obviously means "or". His explanation is indeed apt.
So it emerges from the text that he did not kill her. For she said: "And bewail my virginity" — he did not kill her. But she remained celibate as it is stated: "She had not known man" (v. 39). Again the fact that the text states: "He did with her according to his vow" and not "and he offered her up as a burnt-offering" indicates that she remained celibate and that was the vow he had vowed that "... shall be the Lord's". This seems to be the plain sense of the text. As for the words of our Sages, if that was the tradition they had received, we have no option but to accept it.

(Radak)

Radak explains the following verses too according to his conception:

"And he did with her according to his vow he had vowed". He prepared her a house and placed her there to be separate from people and divorced from society. It became a statute in Israel that every year, the daughters of Israel would make pilgrimage to her, *litnot*, to weep and lament with her to the

276

Lord on account of her virginity. Or perhaps the word *litnot* means, to comfort her and converse with her for four days, since for the whole year she lived in complete seclusion like a hermit and anchorite. This custom they kept during the whole of her life.

Radak's rejection of the view of the Sages was apparently prompted not by the need to tone down the horrible nature of the deed. He felt that the wording of the text supported his contention. First, his daughter did not say: "and bewail my *life*" but "bewail my *virginity*". Second, the text did not say; "And he offered her up for a burnt-offering" as it does in those cases where human sacrifice is involved, as in the case of the king of Moab (2 Kings 3): "And he took his firstborn son ... and offered him up as a burnt-offering upon the wall". The same applies to God's trial of Abraham (Gen. 22): "And offer him up to me as a burnt-offering". We do not find this expression here, but it merely notes that "he did with her according to his vow which he had vowed". Third, it concludes with the statement: "She had not known man". Had he killed her — what point would there be in telling us that she had never had relations with a man?

Ralbag takes a similar view to Radak, though he does not base it on the wording of the text.

> "Whatever issues forth from the doors of my house" — this must refer to an animal. But if it would be a human being then it shall be the Lord's — exclusively dedicated to the service of the Lord. If a male, he would not need to be celibate since he would be dedicated to the Lord's service without that, as you have with the levites and priests. Compare the case of Samuel whose mother gave him to the Lord (1 Sam 1, 11) He married and had children.
> But if it would be a woman she would have to be celibate. For if she married she would not be exclusively dedicated to God but would also serve her husband like all married women.
> It was because of this that Jephthah rent his garments when he saw his daughter, since his vow necessitated that she should not marry. Evidently he built her a house in an isolated spot away from man or woman and she dwelt there ... except for four days a year when the daughters of Israel came to visit her.

277

Abravanel shares the same approach — that Jephthah did not kill her, except that he suggests a different reason for her betaking herself to the mountains for two months:

"You have brought me very low" (v. 35). The Ammonites did not succeed in overcoming or subduing me yet you my daughter brought me low for I have opened my mouth to the Lord and have vowed that you shall never marry. She answered him that he should stand by his vow but begged him to let her bewail her virginity with her companions: "and go down upon the mountains", as if to say: "I am distraught in my complaint and will moan" (Psalms 55, 3). Because she was destined to be cooped up in one house and not leave if for the rest of her life she begged to be allowed to wander where she desired, and have her fill of wandering and travelling, since she would have no further opportunity to do so and would never marry, and also to choose her place of seclusion.

I imagine that the Christians learnt from this to make convents into which women enter and never leave and see no man.[2]

Naḥmanides is one of the few of our commentators who explains the text as our Sages have done, as implying actual killing. He says:

"None devoted that may be devoted of men . . ." (Leviticus 27, 29) . . . this was the mistake of Jephthah with his daughter. He imagined that if he vowed in a time of war to sacrifice a person or persons, the vow is valid. He did not know that it is impossible for a vow to make a burnt offering to apply to something that, God forbid, is not suitable for the Lord.

Do not be misled by the empty talk of R. Abraham (Ibn Ezra)[3] who maintains that "and I will offer it up for a burnt-offering" of Jephthah implies that if a man or woman issues forth from the doors of my house then he or she shall be the Lord's in the sense of separated from the ways of the world to stand and minister to the Lord in prayer and thanksgiving; but if the thing be suitable to be sacrificed then I shall offer it up as a burnt-offering. And he made a house for his daughter outside the city and she lived in seclusion there, never getting married and leading a hermit's existence. All this is quite baseless but dedicating something by vow to the Lord does not imply complete celibacy but that he should be like Samuel whose mother promised to give him to the Lord and he ministered to the Lord without becoming a recluse.

Further according to the laws of the Torah no man can bind by his vow those who come forth from his house to become hermits, just as he may not offer them up as a burnt-offering.

Had Ibn Ezra's approach been correct (that she was condemned to be a recluse and celibate) his daughter and her companions weeping for her virginity would be like harlots. For they fixed four days a year to bewail the daughter of Jephthah because she did not marry. God forbid that there should be such a law in Israel. For it was still possible for her to serve the Lord in purity.[4] But we must conclude that the text literally means he actually sacrificed his daughter as a burnt-offering and his mistake was as we have explained.

But whether we accept the view of the Sages and Naḥmanides that Jephthah sacrificed his daughter or that of Radak, Ralbag and the commentators who share their approach, we cannot ignore the serious criticism which emerges from the words of them all.

Jephthah is not to be regarded as a national hero. His deed is not to be admired as one of self-sacrifice and greatness prompted by patriotic feeling. It was a cruel and unwarranted deed. We may rely on our Sages who saw him as an ignorant and unlettered person, a boor, empty and rash. Enthusiasm by itself is no guarantee of the desirability of a cause. Enthusiasm that is not backed by conscience and the self-discipline of Torah is liable to bring disaster.

What caused Jephthah to take the life of his own daughter? His failure to read the Torah.

Questions for Further Study

1. Segal in his studies in Judges, *Tarbiz*, vol. 2, p. 6 states:

According to the tactical situation we may assume that Jephthah preferred to find a peaceable way out of the quarrel with Ammon and avoid war. For the text indicates that Ammon was the stronger and war would have constituted a very risky thing for the Gileadites.

(a) What verses in our chapter and the immediate ones indicate this?

279

(b)   Further, Segal cites a proof from 2 Kings 3, 27. What proof is there from there?

2.   Which verses in our sidra serve as a proof of the justice of Jephthah's arguments in his negotiations with the king of Ammon?

3.   On the verse: "Israel did not take the land of Moab and the land of the sons of Ammon", Abravanel asks:

> If these enemies were the sons of Ammon and it was to them that Jephthah sent messengers and they answered that "Israel took my land when they went up from Egypt" then why did Jephthah answer: "Israel did not take the land of Moab?" What reason had he to mention the land of Moab?

Try to answer his question, with the help of our sidra.

4.   "And Israel sent messengers to the king of Edom . . . but the king of Edom would not listen to them". What was the purpose of Jephthah's reference to this mission to the king of Edom, in his negotiations with the king of Ammon?

NOTES

[1]   For the nature of vows and the views of our Sages and commentators on their value and the character of those who make them see *Studies in Devarim*, Ki Teze 3.

[2]   Segal in his long article on Abravanel observes that the latter often solves obscurities in the Bible by reference to practices he noted in his countries of domicile (which we have noted, though rarely, in Rashi) such as his comment on the custom of anointing the Israelite kings with oil by the prophet. He suggests that the French custom of anointing their kings with oil was copied from the Biblical custom (See Segal, *Massoret Ubikoret*, Jerusalem 1957). Of course it is hardly necessary to point out that Abravanel's tracing the origin of the catholic convents to Jephthah's vow is questionable, since celibacy and asceticism were familiar phenomena, in the ancient world. See also *Hazon Hamikra*, I, Jacobson (part 1, p. 402).

3   Chavel in his edition of Naḥmanides' commentary (Mossad Harav Kook
    Jerusalem, 5720, vol. 2) observes: "I do not know the source, for no
    commentary by Ibn Ezra to Judges is extant!

4   Naḥmanides here is true to his approach to the Nazirite vows of abstention. He
    regards them as constituting the highest stage of holiness and purity in contrast
    to most of our Sages and commentaries. Cf. his words here with his comment
    above *Naso* 3, pp. 51ff. Of course Naḥmanides is not trying to extenuate
    Jephthah's conduct but merely rejects the rival explanation which tones down
    the extreme nature of the vow.

PROPHET OR SORCERER?

What sort of man was Balaam whose curses God turned into blessings? Was he indeed a prophet who, according to his testimony, "Heard the words of the Lord", or was he merely just a "sorcerer", as he is termed in Joshua 13, 22 — "Balaam the son of Beor the Sorcerer?"

Let us first compare the language describing the receiving of the prophetic call, in the case of the prophets of Israel, with the phraseology in which the coming of the word of the Lord to Balaam is couched.

Regarding the prophets of Israel, the following is recorded:

וַיְהִי דְבַר-ה׳ אֵלַי לֵאמֹר:

Then the word of the God came unto me saying
(Jeremiah 1, 4)

הָיֹה הָיָה דְבַר-ה׳ אֶל יְחֶזְקֵאל

The word of the Lord came expressly unto Ezekiel
(Ezekiel 1, 3)

דְּבַר-ה׳ אֲשֶׁר הָיָה אֶל-הוֹשֵׁעַ

The word of the Lord that came unto Hosea
(Hosea 1, 1)

דְּבַר־ה׳ אֲשֶׁר הָיָה אֶל־יוֹאֵל

The word of the Lord that came unto Joel

(Joel 1, 1)

Even more emphatic and vivid is the phrase recurring in Ezekiel (cf. 1, 3): "And the hand of the Lord was there upon him". Now, let us contrast the above with the verses in our sidra, recounting the preliminaries preceding Balaam's communion with the Almighty.

וַיֹּאמֶר בִּלְעָם אֶל־בָּלָק
בְּנֵה־לִי בָזֶה שִׁבְעָה מִזְבְּחֹת
וְהָכֵן לִי בָּזֶה שִׁבְעָה פָרִים וְשִׁבְעָה אֵילִים:
וַיַּעַשׂ בָּלָק כַּאֲשֶׁר דִּבֶּר בִּלְעָם . . . וַיֹּאמֶר בִּלְעָם לְבָלָק הִתְיַצֵּב עַל־עֹלָתֶךָ
וְאֵלְכָה אוּלַי יִקָּרֵה ה׳ לִקְרָאתִי
וּדְבַר מַה־יַּרְאֵנִי וְהִגַּדְתִּי לָךְ וַיֵּלֶךְ שֶׁפִי:

And Balaam said unto Balak,
build me here seven altars,
and prepare me here seven oxen and seven rams.
And Balak did as Balaam had spoken...
And Balaam said unto Balak,
stand by thy burnt offering, and I will go, peradventure the
Lord will come to meet me,
and whatsoever he showeth me I will tell thee — and he went
solitary.

(23, 1—3)

Similar preliminaries accompanied the second time he heard the word of the Lord:

וַיִּקָּחֵהוּ שְׂדֵה צֹפִים אֶל־רֹאשׁ הַפִּסְגָּה
וַיִּבֶן שִׁבְעָה מִזְבְּחֹת . . . וַיֹּאמֶר אֶל־בָּלָק
הִתְיַצֵּב כֹּה עַל־עֹלָתֶךָ וְאָנֹכִי אִקָּרֶה כֹּה: וַיִּקָּר ה׳ אֶל־בִּלְעָם

283

And he brought him unto the field of Zophim, to the top of Pisgah,
and he built seven altars ...
and he said unto Balak:
Stand by the burnt offering, whilst I meet the Lord yonder.
And the Lord met Balaam.

(23, 14—16)

In what lies the contrast in the above comparison? The prophets of Israel do not themselves run after prophecy. On the contrary, a glance at Exodus 3—4 or Jeremiah 1 reminds us that they objected, as a rule, to this sudden imposition of responsibility from On High. Far from seeking it, it was thrust on them. Balaam, on the other hand, hankers after prophecy, and strives, through magical means, to obtain such power, to force it down from Heaven, as it were, through the medium of seven altars, seven bullocks, enchantments and solitude. As Naḥmanides observed in respect of sacrifices, the person bringing them, wishes, through their medium, to achieve closer communion with God, elevating human nature to a Divine level, whilst Balaam wanted to mould, as it were, the Divine will to his own nefarious ends, bringing the Divine down to mortal level.

What did he achieve through his sorcery? What are the implications of the phrase: "And the Lord put a word into Balaam's mouth" (23, 5). This has already formed the subject of a Talmudic discussion in Sanhedrin 105b.

> "And the Lord put a word in Balaam's mouth" — Rabbi Eliezer said: an angel, Rabbi Yoḥanan said: a hook.

According to Rabbi Eliezer, Balaam was merely guided from above to bless and not to curse. He had been intellectually enlightened to face the true facts. According to Rabbi Yoḥanan, however, he uttered the blessings in spite of himself, forced against his will, struggling and in distress like a fish that is hooked, to do the bidding of his master.

A similar idea is expressed in the Midrash:

עיקם את פיו ועקמו כאדם שקובע מסמר בלוח.

He (God) twisted his mouth (as with a bit) and pierced it like a man who drives a nail into a board.[1].

(Bamidbar Rabbah 20, 16)

A less extreme opinion is voiced by Naḥmanides who explains the phrase: "And the Lord put a word in Balaam's mouth", not as implying external compulsion, in which Balaam played no part, but rather as denoting that God taught him *by rote* what he should say, so that he should not forget. Maimonides in his *Guide for the Perplexed* (Chapter 45, p. 242, Friedlander edition) in the course of his essay on the different levels of prophetic inspiration defines one of the lower grades of prophecy, as being in the nature of a new power inspiring a human being to utter words of wisdom, Divine praises or moral reproof. "Regarding such as these, it is said that their speech is inspired with *ruaḥ ha-kodesh* — the Holy Spirit". Maimonides adds that Balaam belonged to this class "when he was good", as it is written: "And God put a word in Balaam's mouth". Whatever the case may be, Balaam apparently knew quite well that his intentions and preparations did not meet with Divine approval. The situation is appropriately summed up in the Midrash:

"ויקר אלוקים אל בלעם ויאמר אליו: את שבעת המזחות ערכתי". "ויקר אלוקים אל בלעם". אמר לו: "רשע! מה אתה עושה?" אמר לו: "את שבעת המזבחות ערכתי". משל לשולחני המשקר במשקלות, בא בעל השוק והרגיש בו. אמר לו: "אתה משקר במשקל". אמר לו: "כבר שלחתי דורון לביתך!" אף כך בלעם. רוח הקודש אומרת לו: "רשע מה אתה עושה?" אמר לו: "את שבעת המזבחות ערכתי".

"And God met Balaam": He said to him: What are you doing? Said he: "I have prepared Thee seven altars". This is like the case of a money-changer who falsified his weights. The inspector of the market came and detected him. You are, he said, falsifying the weights! The other replied: I have already sent a gift to your house! Balaam also acted in like manner. The

Holy Spirit said to him: Villain! What are you doing? He replied: "I have
prepared Thee seven altars".

(Bamidbar Rabbah 20, 15)

Another difference between Balaam and the true prophets has
been noticed by our commentators. The prophets of Israel
continually emphasise the Divine authority for their utterances, as
expressed in the phrase: "Saith the Lord" which recurs like a refrain
in their prophecies. Only this gives them the right to prophesy and
justifies their claim to be heard. "For it is the mouth of the Lord
which hath spoke"; "for it is not of my heart". Balaam, on the other
hand, prefaces his two latter utterances with the introduction: "Saith
Balaam son of Beor and the man whose eyes are open" (24, 3—16).

His utterances he attributes to himself, his family antecedents and
his own powers. However, whether we understand the phrase: "And
God put a word in Balaam's mouth", uttered on the earlier
occasions, in the sense of a "hook" or an "angel", there is no doubt
that a change takes place on the third occasion, in his attitude and
preparations and the quality of his inspiration.

וַיַּרְא בִּלְעָם כִּי טוֹב בְּעֵינֵי ה' לְבָרֵךְ אֶת־יִשְׂרָאֵל
וְלֹא־הָלַךְ כְּפַעַם־בְּפַעַם לִקְרַאת נְחָשִׁים וַיָּשֶׁת אֶל־הַמִּדְבָּר פָּנָיו:
וַיִּשָּׂא בִלְעָם אֶת־עֵינָיו וַיַּרְא אֶת־יִשְׂרָאֵל שֹׁכֵן לִשְׁבָטָיו
וַתְּהִי עָלָיו רוּחַ אֱלֹהִים:

**And when Balaam saw that it pleased the Lord to bless Israel,
he went not, as at other times to meet with enchantments, but
he set his face toward the wilderness.**
**And Balaam lifted up his eyes and he saw Israel abiding tribe
by tribe.**
And the spirit of God came upon him.

(24, 1—2)

Rashbam, elaborating on this verse, explains that Balaam did not
this time seek after enchantment and try to find a suitable location

from which he would be able to curse them, but meant, ungrudgingly to bless them. Consequently, "the spirit of the Lord came upon him", the Divine presence rested on him, out of love.

Hirsch dwells at greater length on the change that came over Balaam.

> "Balaam saw" — the veil had been lifted from his eyes, as he began to realize that the will of God could not be influenced by means of sorcery. The sentiments he had uttered on the two earlier occasions in 23,9, 20 now became his own inner conviction. He set his face toward the wilderness waiting to act as a vehicle for the will of God and he saw Israel "abiding in his tents according to his tribes", arranged according to their families, and forthwith, "the spirit of God came upon him". Now it was not a question of God putting a word into his mouth against his will, *in spite of himself,* as heretofore, but of the spirit of unconstrained prophecy informing his utterances.

Nevertheless it is only right to cite here the opinions of a number of our Talmudic authorities who detected, even in Balaam's final utterances, a false note:

מאי דכתיב (משלי כז): "נאמנים פצעי אוהב ונעתרות נשיקות שונא". טובה קללה
שקלל אחיה השילוני את ישראל שברכם בלעם הרשע. אחיה השילוני קללם בקנה, אמר
להם לישראל (מלכים א יד): "והכה ה׳ את ישראל כאשר ינוד הקנה במים". מה קנה זה
עומד במקום מים וגזעו מחליף ושרשיו מרובים ואפילו כל הרוחות שבעולם באות
ונושבות בו — אין מזיזות אותו ממקומו, אלא הולך ובא עמהן, דממו הרוחות —
עמד הקנה במקומו; אבל בלעם הרשע ברכן בארז שנאמר (במדבר כד, ו): "כארזים".
מה ארז זה . . . אפילו כל הרוחות שבעולם נושבים בו אים מזיזין אותו ממקומו, כיון
שנשבה רוח דרומית עוקרתו והופכתו על פניו.

What is the meaning of the verse (Proverbs 27, 6): "Faithful are the wounds of a friend; but the kisses of an enemy are importunate?" This implies that the curse uttered by Achijah the Shilonite against Israel was better than the blessing given them by the wicked Balaam. Achijah the Shilonite cursed them by comparing them to a reed; now the reed rises in water, always drives young shoots and has many roots, so that even if all the winds of the world come and blow against it, the reed will move with the wind hither and thither, and when the winds have subsided, the reed stands firm in its place.

287

No so wicked Balaam. He blessed them by comparing them to a cedar tree, as it is said (24, 6): "As cedars beside the waters". Now the cedar tree does not grow in the water, does not drive young shoots, and its roots are not many and when the winds come and blow against it, it does not yield to them; hence when a strong southern wind springs up, it uproots it and overturns it.

(Ta'anit, 20a)

However, in spite of this, Balaam's blessings have earned pride of place at the beginning of our prayer book, distinguished for their poetic beauty and purity of their sentiments.

Questions for Further Study

1. What is unusual in the phrasing of verse 4, prompting *Bamidbar Rabbah* to adopt the interpretation we have cited?
2. Kalish in his *Prophecies of Balak* suggests that the third utterance of Balaam constitutes a synthesis of the two preceding ones. Explain.
3. The verse: "How goodly are thy tents O Jacob, thy habitations O Israel", is explained by most commentators as exemplifying the principle of a parallelism — a poetic repetition often found in the Bible. Suggest an alternative explanation justifying both clauses not merely on the basis of poetic repetition.
4. In Balaam's third utterance, 24, 3—9, note the frequent use of figurative language. In verse 6 alone, four consecutive similes occur. What common idea pervades all the figures of speech employed in the first part of his utterance (3—7), uniting them into one whole?

NOTE

[1] According to this interpretation, Balaam can take no credit at all for the blessings he uttered. Far from being responsible even for reciting them, he could not even be compared to the musical instrument which responds to the touch of the player.

ANATOMY OF BLESSING

In this chapter we follow Balaam's ascent from common sorcerer to a prophet "who hears the words of God" and may note how these changes in his character and mood are reflected in the preparations attending each poetic effusion of his. His first endeavours are directed at invoking divine aid through magical means,[1] striving to accommodate the divine will to his interests rather than to achieve closer communion with Him. Only after the first two perorations in which he blessed Israel against his will, his tongue being bridled by the Almighty, did he leave all his wiles and whole-heartedly give himself up to the divine prophetic urge:

וַיַּרְא בִּלְעָם כִּי טוֹב בְּעֵינֵי ה׳ לְבָרֵךְ אֶת־יִשְׂרָאֵל
וְלֹא־הָלַךְ כְּפַעַם־בְּפַעַם לִקְרַאת נְחָשִׁים
וַיָּשֶׁת אֶל־הַמִּדְבָּר פָּנָיו:
וַיִּשָּׂא בִלְעָם אֶת־עֵינָיו וַיַּרְא אֶת־יִשְׂרָאֵל שֹׁכֵן לִשְׁבָטָיו
וַתְּהִי עָלָיו רוּחַ אֱלֹהִים:

**And when Balaam saw that it pleased the Lord to bless Israel,
he went not, as at the other times, to meet with enchantments,
but he set his face toward the wilderness.
And Balaam lifted up his eyes, and he saw Israel dwelling tribe
by tribe;**
and the spirit of God came upon him.

(24, 1—2)

Let us compare here the content of Balaam's three poetic musings regarding Israel. (1) Numbers 23, 7—10; (2) 18—24; (3) 24, 5—9.

The first blessing of Balaam constitutes a prologue in which the prophet introduces his theme and mission. He has been charged with a mission and he explains what a mortal king has demanded of him and what, in contrast, the King of Kings, the Almighty, desires of him. But he is not only prevented from cursing by the promptings of the divine spirit, but also by the spectacle of the holy people itself spread out before him. He is forced to appreciate their unique character in spite of himself, as Rashi observes:

"כי מראש צורים אראנו": אני מסתכל בראשיתם ובתחילת שרשיהם ואני רואה אותם מיוסדים וחזקים כצורים וגבעות הללו על ידי אבות ואמהות.

"For from the *top* of the rocks I see him, and from the *hills* I behold him":I look at their beginnings and their first origins and see them firmly founded and as strong as these *rocks* and *hills* through their forefathers.

Balaam was impressed by the historic continuity of the Jewish people, the vigour and firm foundations of its traditions initiated by the Patriarchs and Matriarchs.

In his second blessing Balaam replies to the arguments and importunings of the king who had engaged his services, countering Balak's indignant ranting:

מֶה עָשִׂיתָ לִי
לָקֹב אֹיְבַי לְקַחְתִּיךָ וְהִנֵּה בֵּרַכְתָּ בָרֵךְ:

What hast thou done unto me? — I took thee to curse mine enemies, and, behold, thou hast blessed them with a vengeance!

(23, 11)

Balaam in his retort no longer addresses Balak by his kingly title as at the beginning, neither quotes his sovereign orders, but merely refers to him as just another mortal. In contrast to the transitory nature of human desires caught in the toils of its own falsehood, he cites the unchanging standards of his true Provider and Guardian, the Holy One blessed be He Who is affected by no charms and Who accompanies His people in triumphant sovereignty.

In the third blessing there is, however, no hint of any polemic. Balak disappears completely from the picture along with his demands, machinations and arguments. Without any preliminary invocation the prophet plunges into his panegyric of Israel. We have here neither vindication nor denunciation but pure prophecy. This third blessing is characterised by a more sublime note, richer and more imaginative language than the previous ones. From the linguistic point of view we may note that there are no figures of speech in the first blessing and there is only one taken from the animal kindgom in the second. The third is rich in figurative description, beginning with the vegetable and ending with the animal kingdom.

The three blessings are also differentiated in their relation to the time factor; the first one refers to the immediate present, to the generation of the wilderness facing him, the second to the immediate future, to the generation which would conquer the land, whilst the third concerns the distant future, to an era when wars and conquests will be no more and when the lion will lie down to rest after it has finished its task.

Let us study the third blessing a little closer. It begins with a reference to the ideal picture of Jewish life in the Promised Land "how goodly are thy tents". According to the Midrash the adjective "goodly" refers to moral, ethical goodness:

‏"מה טובו" — על שראה פתחיהן שאינם מכוונים זה מול זה.

"How goodly" — that he saw that the doors of their tents were not directly facing each other.

(Rashi)

According to Rashi, Balaam, who had been reared amongst the idolatrous and immoral practices of his home country, is here praising the purity and chastity characteristic of the Jewish people. But the plain meaning of the term "goodly" is perfection in all respects — beauty and charm, simplicity and purity.

In verses 6—7 we may also note the recurring of the "water" motif. This is a favourite symbol in the Bible for abundance, freshness and vital life. The simile of the water is followed by the plants with which it is integrally connected. We may recall in this context the employment of a similar figure in the Bible as a symbol of upright living:

וְהָיָה כְּעֵץ שָׁתוּל עַל־פַּלְגֵי מָיִם

And he shall be like a tree planted by streams of water . . .
(Psalms 1, 3)

וְהָיָה כְּעֵץ שָׁתוּל עַל־מַיִם
וְעַל־יוּבַל יְשַׁלַּח שָׁרָשָׁיו

For he shall be as a tree planted by the waters,
and that spreadeth out its roots by the river . . .
(Jeremiah 17, 8)

וְהָיִיתָ כְּגַן רָוֶה
וּכְמוֹצָא מַיִם אֲשֶׁר לֹא־יְכַזְּבוּ מֵימָיו:

And thou shalt be like a watered garden,
and like a spring of water, whose waters fail not.
(Isaiah 58, 11)

וְהָיְתָה נַפְשָׁם כְּגַן רָוֶה
וְלֹא־יוֹסִיפוּ לְדַאֲבָה עוֹד:

And their soul shall be as a watered garden,
and they shall not pine any more at all.

(Jeremiah 31, 11)

The plants and the water similes are followed by a reference to fragrant spices:

כַּאֲהָלִים נָטַע ה׳

As the tree of aloes which the Lord hath planted

(24, 6)

which led naturally to the association of the divine planting of a garden at the creation of the world:

וַיִּטַּע ה׳ אֱלֹהִים גַּן בְּעֵדֶן . . .
וַיַּצְמַח ה׳ אֱלֹהִים מִן־הָאֲדָמָה כָּל־עֵץ נֶחְמָד לְמַרְאֶה . . .

And the Lord God planted a garden . . . in Eden . . .
And out of the ground made the Lord God to grow every tree
that is pleasant to the sight . . .

(Genesis 2, 8—10)

The prophet after recalling the pristine purity of the perfect world in the Garden of Eden proceeds to dwell on the theme of abundance. But we are not treated here to a description of artificial riches, palaces, urban magnificence, but rather to natural abundance of fields and vineyards.

The blessing then abruptly switches to another aspect of good — that which emerges from the freedom of the people from bondage and its impending conquest of the land. The people stand on the threshold of gaining their patrimony and aspire to inherit a fertile and well watered land, each man under his vine and fig tree. The final

294

verse conjures up a picture of peace using the figure of the lion lying down to rest. This same blessing is referred to directly and without recourse to figurative illustration in the blessing at the end of Leviticus:

וְנָתַתִּי שָׁלוֹם בָּאָרֶץ
וּשְׁכַבְתֶּם וְאֵין מַחֲרִיד

And I will give peace in the land,
and ye shall lie down, and none shall make you afraid ...
(Leviticus 26, 6)

This is indeed a universal aspiration expressed in modern parlance as the "freedom from fear". But the blessing does not conclude with this negative assurance of security against sudden disturbance but rather on the positive note of perfect blessing for all who bless us, in accordance with the divine promise to Abraham:

וַאֲבָרְכָה מְבָרְכֶיךָ
וּמְקַלֶּלְךָ אָאֹר
וְנִבְרְכוּ בְךָ כֹּל מִשְׁפְּחֹת הָאֲדָמָה:

And I will bless them that bless thee,
and him that curseth thee will I curse;
and in thee shall all the families of the earth be blessed.
(Genesis 12, 3)

These same sentiments are repeated in the following words by one of the last in the line of the Hebrew prophets, Zechariah (8, 13):

וְהָיָה כַּאֲשֶׁר הֱיִיתֶם קְלָלָה בַּגּוֹיִם
בֵּית יְהוּדָה וּבֵית יִשְׂרָאֵל
כֵּן אוֹשִׁיעַ אֶתְכֶם וִהְיִיתֶם בְּרָכָה

295

אַל־תִּירָאוּ
תֶּחֱזַקְנָה יְדֵיכֶם:

And it shall come to pass that, as ye were a curse among the nations,
O house of Judah and house of Israel,
so will I save you, and ye shall be a blessing;
fear not,
but let your hands be strong.

NOTE

[1]   See previous chapter.

BALAAM AND HIS ASS

This sidra abounds in difficult passages but undoubtedly the most puzzling is Balaam's encounter with the ass and its vocal performance. The ass' opening of its mouth to speak has provided an easy target for scoffers and sceptics. It is an extreme instance of deviation from the laws of nature, in which speech which was exclusively bestowed on man, is here granted to the beast.

Our Sages in the Ethics of the Fathers included the "mouth of the ass" among those things which were created "on the Sabbath eve at twilight" (Avot 5, 6). What is the meaning of this Rabbinic dictum? The author of the Mishnaic commentary *Tiferet Israel* makes the following comment:

This was on the first Sabbath eve after the Creation. But this does not imply that they were actually created then. It cannot be assumed that the ram for the sacrifice of Isaac discovered by Abraham and Balaam's ass existed, on the basis of this, for thousands of years and that Scriptures would not even mention this great miracle. What is meant is that creation had been invested by God with the power of bringing forth these wonders at the appropriate time.

This approach is based on Maimonides' explanation of miracles, which he himself refers to, in the same context:

We have already mentioned that our Sages did not believe in the continued operation of Divine creativity. Rather they maintained that He implanted in nature, as the very beginning, the potential power of bringing forth all that was necessary, whether the event was something continuous which we call natural, or something of rare occurrence, which we term a miracle.

297

> Therefore they said that on the sixth day . . . God endowed the ass with the power of speech.

In other words the wonders and miracles that take place in history are in the nature of a delayed action fuse prepared at the time of Creation. God set in motion the natural order of things at Genesis and also took into account events of unusual occurrence. All this was done at the moment when His creative activity was finished, on the Sabbath eve at twilight. All that happened after that was based on the properties with which the Almighty endowed the universe during the period of Creation.

Other approaches to this question have also been suggested. Maimonides himself in his *Guide for the Perplexed* finds no difficulty, since he assumes that the whole encounter between Balaam and the ass, till it opened its mouth, took place in a prophetic vision as in similar instances of visions recorded in Scriptures. Ibn Kaspi in his comment on this passage scoffs in his usual way at the literalists:

> Regarding the ass there is no need for me to say anything at all. It is sufficient what the author of the *Guide for the Perplexed* stated(that the ass did not really speak but it was seen in a dream). However, let me tell you what happened to me not many years ago. Someone asked me — one of those who looks for faults in others without seeing his own — whether I believed that the ass really spoke and I answered him without looking him in the face and said, As the Lord liveth, I believe in all that is written in the Torah. Why should I not then believe in the verse which states "and the ass said . . ." and the verse "a donkey spoke".[1]

S.D. Luzzatto has a somewhat different explanation:

> The usual specific Hebrew root connoting human speech (*daber*) is not used here. This may indicate that the Torah implies that the ass did not actually utter any words, but made a plaintive sound which implied protest, as if it had really said: "What have I done unto thee". Balaam in his anger answered the ass, much as any man might shout at his beast of burden. The ass made a responsive sound to this abuse as if to say "Am not I thine ass . . .". Then Balaam softened and said, No. As if to say it is not like my

ass to defy me thus. The Almighty did indeed open the mouth of the ass and it brayed in an unusual manner... There was a miracle but it was a hidden one...

We have often referred to Naḥmanides' definition of the distinction between hidden and open miracles:

From a recognition of the large-scale historic miracles, man is led to acknowledge the hidden ones, which constitute the foundation of the whole Torah. For no man has any portion in the law of Moses our teacher, until he is convinced that all our affairs and chance occurrences and the routine workings of the universe, both in the private and public field, are miracles and are not to be attributed merely to nature.

The only reason why these miracles are termed hidden ones is because they are not obvious to the onlooker, and are considered to be just nature. But they are not the less miraculous for that.

But this discussion of the nature of the miracle in the opening of the mouth of the ass does not answer the real problem which is: What is the lesson and significance of this dialogue between man and beast? Why was it recorded in the Torah? Professor Y. Kaufmann in his work on the history of the Israelite Religion devotes a special chapter to this subject which takes its title from the phrase "For there is no enchantment in Jacob" in our sidra. He shows that this enchantment is not just connected with idolatry, since the diviners and sorcerers did not resort only to the gods and demonic forces. The Torah was not concerned only with fighting magical practices, but:

The opposition between God and the sorcerer is the opposition between the Deity and mortal wisdom. Sorcery is one of the forms of heathen "wisdom" which misleads man into believing in his own powers and causes him to throw off the yoke of God . . . Babylon trusts in her enchantments, in her wisdom and science and not in the power of God . . . In the story of Balaam too we see these two domains. On the one side the power of Balaam, the enchantments, divinations and altars. On the other, the Deity and His message. The vanquishing of Balaam constitutes the triumph of the Divine message over mortal enchantments. The sorcerer wishes to curse but he is forced to submit to the power of the Divine.

(page 463)

What is the Scriptures' definition of enchantment? Enchantment is a kind of wisdom or science of omens by which man can foretell the future in magic. The understanding of these omens and the wizard's art is a kind of heathen science and "counsel". Balaam's prophecy is also "counsel" (Numbers 24, 14): "Come now, I will counsel thee". He advises the Midianites on how to mislead the Israelites.

Divination is an abomination of the Lord because its purpose is to reveal the secrets of God in an ungodly way. The heathen consults the dead, idols, oracles, his rod, his cup, arrows, the liver, and heavenly omens in order to foretell the future. It is one of the forms of heathen pride, self-confidence, wisdom and ambition to be like the gods (cf. the serpent's words to Eve, Genesis 3). The Israelite must be perfect with the Lord his God and only consult Him (cf. Deuteronomy 18, 13).

(page 497)

This is the profound implication of Balaam's unwilling and awed admission that: "For there is no enchantment with Jacob, neither is there any divination with Israel" (Numbers 23, 23).

Our Sages express the philosophic ideas of this modern thinker in their own concrete dramatic language:

''ותרא האתון את מלאך ה' '' — והוא לא ראה, שנתן הקב״ה לבהמה רשות לראות יותר מן האדם.

"And the ass saw the angel of the Lord"—that he (Balaam) did not see, since the Holy One blessed be He endowed the beast with greater farsightedness than man.

(Rashi)

''ויפתח ה' את פי האתון'' — להודיע שהפה והלשון ברשותו, שאם ביקש לקלל — פיו ברשותו.

"And the Lord opened the mouth of the ass"—to teach him that the mouth and the tongue are in His power; that if he sought to curse—his mouth was in His power.

(Bamidbar Rabbah 20, 12)

300

"ויאמר בלעם לאתון": כך אמרה האתון לבלעם: "אני אין אתה יכול להרגני אלא אם
כן חרב בידך — והיאך אתה רוצה לעקור אומה שלמה?" שתק ולא מצא תשובה . . .
חס הקב"ה על כבודן של בריות ויודע צרכן וסתם פי הבהמה שאילו היתה מדברת —
לא היו יכולים לשעבדה. שזו הטפשה שבבהמה וזה החכם שבחכמים, כיון שדברה לא
היה יכול לעמוד בפניה.

"And Balaam said to the ass"—Thus said the ass to Balaam, me thou canst
not slay except that thou hast a sword in thy hand. How then dost thou
propose to uproot an entire nation? Balaam held his peace and found no
answer. The Holy One blessed be He, out of respect for His creatures and
understanding of their needs, closed the mouth of the beast. For had it been
given the power of speech, man would not have been able to subject it. Here
was the most foolish of beasts and the wisest of sorcerers—as soon as it
spoke he could not withstand it.

(Bamidbar Rabbah 20, 12)

"ויגל ה' את עיני בלעם וירא" — וכי סומא היה? להודיע שאף העין ברשותו.

"And the Lord opened the eyes of Balaam that he saw" — was he then
blind? But this is to teach that even the eye is in His power.

(Bamidbar Rabbah 20, 13)

This then is the lesson of the story of Balaam's ass and the
threefold repetition of the phrase: "And the ass saw the angel of the
Lord". We may now the more readily appreciate the view of those of
our commentators, who interpreted the dialogue between the man
and the ass, as the Torah's scornful commentary on the imaginary
powers ascribed to sorcerers, its mockery of human gullibility, in
believing in the power of the magician to curse and subject the
supernatural to his will. Balaam was the most renowned sorcerer of
history. Balak, King of Moab, sent him this message:

כִּי יָדַעְתִּי אֵת אֲשֶׁר תְּבָרֵךְ מְבֹרָךְ וַאֲשֶׁר תָּאֹר יוּאָר

**...For I know that he whom thou blessest is blessed, and
he whom thou cursest is cursed.**

(22, 6)

But even his wisdom, powers, his eyes and tongue were subject to the authority of Him who is the unique source of blessing, and to whom is entrusted the soul of every living thing.

NOTE

[1] The latter quotation is of course Kaspi's own invention and is said ironically.

THE IMPACT OF CURSE AND BLESSING

The story of Balaam presents a number of difficulties, some of which we have dealt with on previous occasions. We shall devote our *Studies* this time to discussing the following question asked by Abravanel:

> Why did God prevent Balaam from cursing the Israelites? Why should they have cared about his curse, as long as the Lord blessed His people with peace?

The Torah places no faith in divination and magic. Only the heathen deities were limited in their powers which were circumscribed by occult laws. They were powerless to break a spell or dissolve the potency of a malediction. But such was not the portion of Jacob. Even Balaam had to admit that "there was no divination in Jacob". The whole of our sidra is concerned with discrediting superstition and belief in magical practices. This is the aim of the story of the ass. Balaam was proceeding to curse a whole nation with his mouth. He, the seer and prophet, who claimed to probe the mysteries of time could not even see what his ass beheld.

שזו הטפשה בבהמות וזה חכם שבחכמים, כיון שדברה — לא היה יכול לעמוד בה.

The most foolish of animals confronted the wisest of men. Yet the moment it spoke, he was confounded.

(Bamidbar Rabbah 20, 12)

In that event, greater force is added to our original question. What significance, indeed, could be attached to the curse of such a personality and why was it necessary to turn it into blessing? Some commentators suggest that this was done to teach Balaam a lesson, that he was not his own master. No magic rites (build me seven altars etc.) could prevail over the Supreme Master. He had no choice but utter the words the Almighty had put into his mouth ("And the Lord put a word in the mouth of Balaam" 23, 5), even if they were the opposite to what he wished to say.

Others however maintain that the curses were turned into blessings not so much as to teach Balaam a lesson as to benefit Israel. Did Israel need his blessing? Surely the Almighty was the true source of all blessing and it was He who blessed Israel? The answer given to this is that Balaam's words objectively speaking, maledictory or otherwise, were of no effect. It depended on the Almighty to do good or evil. But subjectively, from the point of view of the Israelies themselves who had been reared in Egypt on magic and superstition, his utterances as sorcerer-in-chief of the nations, were bound to have a considerable impact. This is the explanation outlined by Joseph Ibn Kaspi:

> The curse of Balaam had no objective potency neither in terms of the author or the deed. Its effect must only be considered from the point of view of those at the receiving end, i.e. the Israelites. Balaam, was a renowned sorcerer and people were impressed both then and now by sorcerers and diviners. There is no point in asking the reason for the belief of Balak and his company just as there is no reason for doing so in the case of Jacob and Esau, who attached such importance to their father's blessing. If they did, how much more so the Israelites of those days, in particular the women and children, who would be greatly affected by the maledictions of such a renowned sorcerer!
>
> A true friend will save his colleague any pain, even if he knows that no danger will ensue. Similarly the Almighty, out of the abundance of His love for Israel prevented Balaam from cursing them, though He was aware that his curses were impotent. But the Almighty did not rest content with this. He went so far as to make Balaam bless the people to give them pleasure, as it is stated: "The Lord thy God would not hearken unto Balaam" (Deuteronomy

23, 6) ... The reason for this was "because the Lord loveth thee". Similarly it is recorded in Joshua (24, 9—10): "Balak called Balaam to curse you. But I would not hearken to Balaam; therefore he even blessed you; so I delivered you out of his hand". This means that God delivered the Israelites out of his hand, according to his idea of the power of his own words and that of some of the children of Israel. At any rate, He delivered them from hearing his curse — all out of love for His people.

(Tirat Kesef)

Abravanel makes a similar point:

Balaam's sorcery was world famous. Balak referred to his renown when he said: "For I know he whom thou blessest is blessed, and he whom thou cursest is cursed". Had Balaam cursed Israel, the surrounding nations would have plucked up courage and gone to do battle with Israel on the strength of his curses. But when they heard how God had turned them into blessings, they would then realize who was Master . . . and would lose all desire to fight His people. From this point of view, the turning of Balaam's words into blessing served a very useful purpose. This same psychological warfare is referred to by Joshua (2, 9): "I know that the Lord hath given you the land, and that your terror is fallen upon us". How did Rahab know all this if not from Balaam's prophetic blessings?

There are other authorities however who maintain that neither Balaam's nor Israel's good was exclusively involved. The Almighty was concerned to protect all his creatures from error. He does not want to be instrumental in bolstering superstition. Had Balaam cursed, the Moabites would certainly have assumed that the reason why the Israelites refrained from attacking them was due to their effect, and not because the Almighty had forbad them to "be at enmity with Moab neither contend with them" (Deuteronomy 2, 9). This explanation closely follows Luzzatto's:

Israel had been forbidden to attack Moab. Had Balaam cursed, the latter and Balak would have boasted that they had succeeded in warding off the Israelites. They might even have gone forth to fight them like the Edomites did. Israel would have retreated and the name of God would have been discredited.

305

A similar explanation involving the consideration of *hillul ha-shem* is advanced by Anselm Astruc:

> The Almighty's warning "thou shalt not curse the people" was given not because Balaam was capable of doing harm, since "the guardian of Israel neither slumbers nor sleeps". But this was done to preclude the inhabitants of the land from ascribing any retribution the Israelites might suffer for their sins to the effect of Balaam's curses. The Almighty wished to bring home to His people their disobedience, immediately, as a father chastiseth his son. He wished too to preclude misguided talk impugning His omnipotence. Compare Numbers 14, 14 and Exodus 22, 12.
>
> That was the reason why "God's anger against Balaam was kindled because he went" (Numbers 22, 22), not that he would do any damage, but because some of his hearers would ascribe any retribution they might suffer for their sins to the effect of his curse.
>
> (Midreshei Torah)

There is a difference between the two latter approaches. Luzzatto regards the Divine action against Balaam as an expedient of temporary effect only, to weaken the morale of Israel's enemies, as well as to sanctify the name of God publicly. Whereas Astruc regards it as an expedient with a long-term effect, to preclude Israel attributing all their sufferings, in their future history, to the effect of Balaam's curse, instead of to the incurring of Divine displeasure through their disobedience. This would be a *hillul ha-shem*, a desecration of the Divine name.

The Almighty turned Balaam's curses into blessings not to save Israel from their hurt but all the peoples from being led further into superstitious beliefs.

Questions for Further Study

1. Astruc compares our context with the intercession of Moses after the misconduct of the spies (Numbers 14) and the golden calf (Exodus 32). Explain the connection.

2.   "And Balak... saw all that Israel had done to the Amorites" (22, 2). The two kings on whom we relied were not able to withstand them. How much less will we be able to! Consequently "Moab was sore afraid".

                                                        (Rashi)

What is the point of Rashi's explanation and what impression does he correct? What prompted his comment? In answering, compare Rashi's comment to Genesis 18, 3 on the first word to the sidra.

3.   "And he sent messengers unto Balaam to call him saying, Behold, there is a people come out of Egypt; behold, they cover the face of the earth, and they abide over against me" (22, 5). A nameless people who have broken out like slaves to carve out estates for themselves and dwell in a land not their own.

                                            (Ha'amek Davar)

What textual variation prompted the foregoing explanation?

MAN LEADS HIMSELF DOWN THE GARDEN PATH

Our commentators, ancient and modern have been concerned with
the apparent *volte face* in the response of the Almighty to Balaam's
request to be allowed to accompany the princes of Moab. At first the
Almighty refused, but on the second occasion He agreed.
Nevertheless His anger was kindled when Balaam arose to go.
Abravanel has thus worded the difficulty:

> If the Almighty had indeed permitted Balaam to go, why, after he went, is it
> stated, "the anger of the Lord kindled". Surely he had only gone with His
> permission?

Nahmanides gives a detailed answer to this problem:

> In my view, the Lord had stopped him, at the beginning, from going to curse
> the people, since they were blessed. Why should he go with them, if he were
> not to curse them. They were interested in no other course of action. To this
> eventuality the text "thou shalt not go with them" refers, to curse the people,
> for they are blessed. Of course, Balaam informed them of the Divine
> message and then Balak sent another mission to him, since he did not believe
> what he was told. He added more honour to him and sent more distinguished
> princes than the previous time, and promised to reward him even more
> munificently. Balaam, however, answered them that it did not depend on
> money or on him but only on God, and that he would once again consult
> Him. In this he behaved correctly; for what could he know of the Almighty's
> intentions? The counsel of the Lord is always good, instructing the sinners in
> the way and giving us to know what the messengers of the nations shall
> answer,[1] or telling them what shall befall them in the future.
> Now the Lord told him, I have already informed you that the people are
> blessed and you cannot curse them, and the emissaries have just come back

again. The text "if the men have come to call thee" implies "if they have come solely for the purpose of inviting you, and will be content if you accompany them on condition you do not curse the people, as I forewarned you", then, "rise up, go with them; but only the word which I speak unto thee, that shalt thou do". Even if I command you to bless them, you shall not be afraid of Balak. This is the sense of "if the men are come to call thee".

It was therefore the original desire of the Almighty that Balaam accompany them after he had informed them he would do no cursing but follow the instruction of the Almighty. For it was His wish, blessed be He that Israel should be blessed by a prophet of the nations.

Balaam should have said as much to Balak's emissaries, telling them, Behold God has permitted me to accede to your invitation to go with you and that is all, but on condition not to curse the people but to bless them, if He should so command me. If they would not agree to this, they would then leave him, just as Balak on the second occasion said "Come now, curse for me this people" (Num. 22, 17). He did not want him to foretell the future but to do nothing else but curse the people.

Now Balaam, out of his eagerness to accompany them did *not* tell them this, said nothing to them, but "rose up in the morning, and saddled his ass, and went with the princes of Moab" as if he was willing to do just what they wanted. The Lord was therefore angry for his going. For had he told them the whole truth, he would not be going. Moreover a profanation of the Divine name was involved, since his going, without specifying any conditions, might be interpreted to mean that God had given him permission to curse the people, contradicting the original message of "thou shalt not curse the people for they are blessed". When they would see that he did not curse them they would assume that God had changed His mind and was fickle; far be it from the Lord to do such a thing, for the Eternity of Israel will not lie or repent.

Nahmanides' explanation solves, too, another problem, that of the general purpose of the whole chapter, furnishing a reason for the turning of the curses into blessings. Compare our Sages on the text: "Blessed shalt thou be more than all the peoples" (Deut. 10, 14):

> Said R. Hiyya bar Abba: The praise of a woman is not when she is extolled by her friends but when she is extolled by her rivals.
>
> (Devarim Rabbah 3, 6)

God's purpose in guiding Balaam was to promote brotherhood and friendship between peoples and displace the hatred and rivalry. Nevertheless, Nahmanides' approach finds no support in the wording of the text itself. Balaam's alleged malicious intentions, accompanying the princes in all eagerness, "as if he was willing to do just what they wanted" is not referred to in the text which simply states that "Balaam rose up and went with the princes of Mcab, and the anger of the Lord was kindled against him because he went".

The text affords no conclusive proof that he had accompanied them without any intention of fulfilling the other part of the Divine message, "but only the word which I speak unto thee, that thou shalt do". Nahmanides' argument is based not on what is in the text but on what is not. The same objection applies to Sforno who shares Nahmanides' approach. Balaam accompanies them not to carry out God's wish but as a party interested in furthering their designs, in defiance of God's wish. Both commentators have penetrated into the real motives of Balaam's actions but without distilling them from the wording of the text itself. This is achieved by two later commentators who have noted a subtle difference in the wording of the text. God had told Balaam originally, "thou shalt not go *along* with them (*imahem*), thou shalt not curse the people, for blessed are they". Again the Lord warned Balaam on the second occasion, "if but to call thee, the men have come, rise up and go with them (*itam*), but only the word which I speak unto thee, that thou shalt do". But what did Balaam do? — "And Balaam rose up in the morning, and saddled his ass and went *along* with (*im*) the princes of Moab".

Two 19th century commentators elaborate on this distinction between the use of the preposition *im* and *et*. *Ha-ketav Veha-kaballah* explains:

> The Divine instruction expressly forbade *active* going with them, sharing their designs, but did not forbid Balaam merely passively accompanying them, did not rule out the purely physical travelling with them back to Balak. "Go with them" (*itam*) implied a formal accompanying of the princes out of

respect, without any purpose or benefit. But Balaam went along with them, deliberately and for the purpose of carrying out their wishes.

Malbim too makes the same point:

"Imo" — "along with him" implies equality, *itam*, that one of them is in control. God had bidden him merely to go with them, preserving his independent and separate point of view, accompanying them with no intention of harming Israel, whereas he went along with them. On this the Midrash commented "rejoicing in the discomfiture of Israel like them".

Targum Jonathan similarly hints at this distinction in translating the divine command at the beginning as: "Rise and take a walk with them", and Balaam's action as: "And he went along with them". Rashi too must have alluded to this distinction since he comments on the phrase: "And he went along with them" —

Being of the same mind.

Rashi would not have interposed such a comment without having a warrant in the text.

On the basis of this distinction in the wording of the text, God had not changed his mind. Balaam had not acted in accordance with the spirit of the divine command, but unlike Abraham the patriarch rushed not to do the will of his Maker but to violate it.

Isaac Arama in his *Akedat Yizhak* expresses the same idea but without regard to the distinction in the wording of the text:

We all know that it is impious to ask for evil or forbidden things to be permitted to us. Is it conceivable that when a man should propose to his friend that they should worship idols in secret, that he should answer, We'll go and ask the Sage if we may do it or not. Surely the prohibition is absolute and irrevocable! Should he ask, it is out of wickedness. How much more so if the seducer is a sage and prophet or near to God, that he should not say, Wait and I shall find out what my God has to say about it. But he should have said that such a thing was inconceivable and unheard of and even refused under threat of death . . .

311

Now Balaam knew that God had taken one nation from the midst of another by trials, signs and miracles and led them through a wilderness forty years etc. It should have been obvious to him that when he was tested by this mission, that he should not have asked or tried God but immediately have answered them, Far be it from me to destroy the herd of the Lord and the flock of His pasture; he should have striven with and upbraided the messengers of Balak. But he did not do so but was misled by his evil desires and agreed to ask the Father whether he should make war on His son and kill him in His very Presence. Surely this was a criminal and a mortal unforgivable sin!

Nevertheless, on the first occasion, the Lord in His goodness and lovingkindness answered him: "Thou shalt not go with them, thou shalt curse the people for blessed are they". When he was told, "thou shalt not go with them", it was implied that he should on no account go with them, as the wisest of men stated (Proverbs 1): "Should they say, Come with us, let us lie in ambush for them, let us waylay the innocent, without cause . . . walk not thou in the way with them, restrain thy foot their path" — even if it is not for the same purpose, go not with them, since their path is an evil one. "Thou shalt not curse the people" — warning him regarding the deed itself, and informing him that "every weapon formed against thee shall not prosper, and every tongue that shall rise against thee in judgement, thou shalt condemn" (Isaiah 54, 17).

But on the second occasion when he returned like a dog to its vomit and said, "Now, therefore, I pray you, tarry ye also this night, that I may know what the Lord will speak unto me more", the anger of the Lord burned and answered him that he should go in spite of everything and his shame and reproach would be witnessed before the princes, in whose eyes he had thought to be honoured . . .

We find in the *Akedat Yizḥak* a dramatic description of the inner process going on in Balaam's soul, in choosing between right and wrong, in making use of his freewill. When the emissaries came to him the first time, he stood free to accept or reject their approaches. As Maimonides has taught us:

Freewill is given to every man. If he wishes, he can choose the good path and be righteous or the evil path and be wicked . . . no one forces him or predestines him or predisposes him to any one of the two paths, but he chooses the path he so desires of his own absolute freewill and knowledge.

312

Neverthless, in spite of the absolute freewill given to man, as described so starkly by Maimonides, the Almighty does not leave man completely to his own resources, to make the awful decision between the two paths, but in His grace affords him assistance, a lending hand, guidance and enlightenment:

> What is the implication of David's statement: "Good and upright is the Lord, therefore He instructed the sinners in the way, He guideth the humble in justice" (Ps. 25, 8—9)? It refers to the sending of the prophets to them to make known the ways of the Lord and strengthen them in repentance. Moreover, He gave them ability to learn and understand. This gift is to be found in every man. The more he is drawn to the ways of wisdom and righteousness, the more he longs for them and pursues them. This is what our Sages referred to in the words: "He who comes to purify himself, is assisted from on High".
>
> (Maimonides, Laws of Teshuvah 6, 5)

The Lord was helpful enough in Balaam's case to give him the unequivocal answer, "Thou shalt not go with them, thou shalt not curse the people, for blessed are they". But he remained deaf to good counsel and would go, in spite of all. He asked a second time, despite the first refusal. This time the Lord did not prevent him doing what he wanted, as his free choice dictated. "Arise, go with them", came the Divine reply. What is described at length and figuratively in the *Akedat Yiẓḥak* is vividly dramatised for us in the Midrash:

> "If but to call thee, the men are come, rise up and go with them" — from here you may learn that man is led down the path he chooses to tread. For at the beginning he was told: "Thou shalt not go . . .". As soon as he brazened it out to go, he went, as it is written: "And the anger of the Lord was kindled". Said the Holy One blessed be He to him: Villain! I desire not the destruction of the wicked. But since you are bent on going to your own destruction, rise up and go.
>
> (Bamidbar Rabbah   20, 11)

The saying: "Man is led down the path he chooses to tread" is borne out by daily experience. We know too that the more a man

313

follows the good path which he has found after triumphing over many obstacles, the easier it becomes for him to resist temptation to stray from it. He will feel himself aided by an unseen force and that is the significance of "he who comes to purify himself is assisted from on High".

Conversely, the more one follows an evil path, the harder it becomes to forsake it; all too easy becomes the progress to one's ruin. "Once a man sins and repeats his transgression, it becomes permissible to him" (Talmud Yoma 86b). "He who comes to defile himself, the way is opened for him".

But even at this juncture, God did not forsake Balaam and leave him completely to the tender mercies of his evil inclination, in spite of his intent to defile himself. God added the proviso: "But only the word which I speak unto thee that shalt thou do".

Balaam, however, did not impart this proviso to the princes for fear they might decide to forego his services. He accompanied them and even got up early in the morning in his eagerness to enjoy the possible opportunity to curse Israel. (Contrast Abraham's rising early in the morning, inspired by a different intent.) Not only did he get up early but saddled his own ass. Our Sages observed that he did not rely on his own servants, as was his usual custom, since "hate blinds a man to social rules". (Contrast Abraham's saddling of his own ass in contravention of social norms because as our Sages taught us "love blinds a man to social rules".)[2] Since Balaam fulfilled God's bidding to go with them in such a manner, with such relish and joy, no wonder He was angry with him. And if we recall the implications of the subtle linguistic distinction in the use of the prepositions "with" and "along with" referred to earlier, the Divine wrath becomes even more understandable.

Similarly, we may understand why, after God had made the last effort to stay him from evil, in the shape of the angel stopping his path, and the stubbornness of his ass, why he stood deprived of further free choice. Ironically he could no longer turn back even when he hypocritically said to the angel on the third occasion: "If it be displeasing to 'hee, I shall go back". Now we may feel the·true force of the angel's retort: " Go *along* with (*im*) the men." Man is inexorably led down the path he chooses to tread and no one stands in his way.

NOTES

1   This phrase echoes Isaiah 14, 32.
2   See *Studies in Bereshit*, p. 198 also, *Studies in Shemot:* p. 248.

BALAAM'S PARTING SHOT

Hirsch draws attention to the identity of the various locations to which Balaam was brought by Balak, from which he was bidden to observe the Israelites for the purpose of cursing them. The three places were: Bamoth-baal (22, 41); the field of Zophim (23, 14); the top of Peor (ibid. 28); Hirsch detected ulterior motives and designs in Balak's bringing Balaam to precisely these places.

In bringing him to Bamoth-baal, the god of fertility and material plenitude, Balak wished to provoke Balaam to attack Israel economically. Should they not be attacked and weakened from the aspect of their material wealth and laid low in the name of the Baal, the gods of plenitude?

In bringing Balaam to the field of Zophim, Balak wished to strike at the second source from which every people derives its vitality — its spiritual power. Should not their spiritual foresight (Zophim — "watch", "overlook") their capacity for coping with the future be weakened and destroyed?

When however Balak perceived that nothing helped and that he could not prevail against this people either in the realm of the flesh or spirit, he made a third and decisive attempt in bringing Balaam to —

ראש הַפְּעוֹר הַנִּשְׁקָף עַל־פְּנֵי הַיְשִׁימֹן:

The top of Peor that looketh down upon the desert.

(23, 28)

Here is the substance of Hirsch's comment on this text:

316

A nation can be blest with every spiritual and material gift and still be condemned to perdition. It can be blest with material and spiritual wealth but still be corrupted within. Its wealth will only act as a stumbling block and the corruption make it unfit to benefit this wealth. This corruption comprises licence, a shameless indulgence in sensual pleasures. After Balak perceived that he had failed to harm them, both from Bamoth-baal and the field of Zophim he made a third attempt, taking Balaam to Peor, the god of sexual licence whose role was to awaken the beast in man. It was as if he impressed upon Balaam that the secret of the Jewish people lay in their chastity and purity — the foundation of every nation's health and progress, and that this was the point which had to be attacked . . .

Balaam however replied in his parable that Israel could not be harmed even from this vantage point — because the tents of Jacob were goodly. The same idea is found in the words of our Sages in the Midrash:

> Balaam too looked at them and his eye came out as he gazed upon them; for he could not touch them, as it is stated: "And Balaam lifted up his eyes and saw Israel" — implying their standards. He began to say: Who can harm such people? They know their ancestry and their families (their family life is pure), as it is stated: "Dwelling according to his tribes". From here we understand that the standards were a source of greatness and protection to Israel (from promiscuity, since the standards implied a recognition of their family identity).

(Bamidbar Rabbah 2, 3)

But after he had completed this parable — a song of praise to the purity of Israel in its "tents" — on its wanderings, and in its "dwelling places" — on settling down in its homeland, and after the spirit of the Lord had left him, he uttered the following strange statement to the despairing Balak:

לְכָה אִיעָצְךָ אֲשֶׁר יַעֲשֶׂה הָעָם הַזֶּה לְעַמְּךָ בְּאַחֲרִית הַיָּמִים:

Come and I will announce to thee what this people shall do to thy people in the end of days.

(24, 14)

317

Abravanel finds the second word of the passage — here translated "announce", but in Hebrew *i'azekha,* from the word *ezah* meaning "counsel" or "advice" — out of place. How can the word counsel or advice be applied to what would happen in the latter days? Furthermore the word advice cannot be applied to what a third party, which has no connection with us, ı ɔing to do. Admittedly, Balaam could "advise" Balak regarding what Israel would do in the latter days in the sense of revealing to him or announcing to him — one of the interpretations indeed suggested and underlying the English version, as we shall see later. But there are, first of all, commentators who take the word *ezah* in its usual sense of guidance and counsel. But they separate it completely from the next phrase "what this people shall do . . ."

> Regarding that matter, your dread of the Israelite multitude that stands opposite you and out of fear of whom you sent for me, I shall counsel you — not to provoke them. You have nothing to fear from them; they will not harm you nor your people all your days; for what this people will do to your people will be in the latter days and not now.
>
> (Bechor Shor)

Abravanel makes a similar point:

> The plain sense of the verse is that Balak should have no fears of Israel, because whatever Israel would do to his people would only take place in the end of days. In his days, however, peace and quiet would reign. There is no better advice than this, to stop worrying and leave matters to take their course.

Accordingly, Balaam's advice involved no positive action, setting Balak's mind at rest, counselling to do nothing. The verse would thus read, as Hirsch indeed translates it: "I will give thee some advice: what this people shall do to thy people will be in the end of days". Rashi and Rashbam adopt a different approach, regarding the counsel as something concrete, a course of action for the present:

"Come I will give thee counsel" — what you should do. What is the counsel? — their God detests immorality . . .¹ You may know that he gave them this advice to mislead them into immorality from the text (Num. 31, 16): "Behold these caused the children of Israel to sin through the counsel of Balaam"² "what this people shall do to thy people" — this is an elliptical passage meaning "I will counsel thee how to mislead them and tell you how they are destined to do evil to Moab at the end of days".

(Rashi)

In the same vein Rashbam comments:

"I will give thee counsel": counsel how to mislead them, since I know that the harm this people will cause thy people is destined to be in the end of days. But at the present time, by your life, there is nothing to fear from them! This was the counsel referred to in the passage "Behold these caused... Israel to sin through the counsel of Balaam". Here Moses did not explicitly narrate what the advice was, because Balaam whispered this to Balak, so that the advice did not become known until Moses divulged it when it became necessary.

Both the above commentators refer to the same piece of advice but they explain the connection between both clauses of the verse differently, Rashbam connecting "I will counsel thee" to the next clause by a causative link — "because or since I know the harm . . ."; Rashi, on the other hand inserting a new predicate: "I will counsel thee *what to do* and I will tell you . . ."

But as mentioned previously there are commentators, on which the English rendering is based (and Buber-Rosenzweig) who explain the term *ezah* here in a different sense from usual, in the sense of "announce" or "divulge". The term *ezah* is used for anything which is transmitted quietly and not meant for public consumption — advice in the sense of letting one into a secret.

Naḥmanides gives a similar but more detailed explanation:

In my view Balaam said: Let me tell you of the design that God has announced about that which this people will do to yours in the end of days. Cf.: Isaiah 14, 26: "This is the purpose (*ezah*) that is purposed upon the whole earth"; Jeremiah 49, 20: "Hear the *counsel* of the Lord that he hath taken against Edom".

319

This prophecy refers to the Messianic age . . . at the beginning he said that the Lord was his portion and inheritance and secondly added their conquest of the land and slaying of the kings, and thirdly referred to the advent of a king who would conquer Amalek . . .

Now on this the fourth prophecy, he referred to the Messianic era and therefore placed it very remote: "I see it but not now, I behold it but not at hand", phrases he did not employ in the first prophecies and he said that this was the design the Lord had planned for the end of days.

According to the above explanation, the phrase "I will announce to thee . . ." makes no reference to any of Balaam's impending designs to mislead the people, but is exclusively a prologue to his Messianic prophecy, referring to events that were to happen in the remote future. In other words, this verse (14) and the following ones show Balaam as the prophet of the Lord, the knower of the knowledge of the Most High. It was only after he had left Balak, when the Divine spirit had left him that he was once more overwhelmed by his baser thoughts and gave that notorious advice to Balak on how to mislead the Jewish people, and do to them what all his intended curses and witchcraft had failed to accomplish — to destroy them, had not Phinehas stood in the breach.

This change in Balaam's state of mind is reconstructed for us in Joseph Schechter's *Pirkei Hadrakha Ba-tenakh* (Chapters of Instruction in the Bible) in which he places the following words in the mouth of Balaam:

I left enchantments, I wanted the spirit of the Lord to inspire me and it did indeed. The Lord opened my eyes and I saw the grace and blessing that descend from on High on the heads of the upright. This time my blessing outdid all my previous ones — I gave them a perfect blessing, one of fullness and fertility, upstandingness, triumph and sovereignty, strength and vigour, that Israel should be the source of blessing . . .

When the Holy Spirit forsook me I arose and went my way; Balak too went his way, full of disappointed anger. On the way I pulled myself together and regained my former confidence. I recalled the third occasion on which Balak stood there by his offering at the top of Peor and a new idea came to my mind. Full of designs I raced to Balak, overtook him and caught him by his garments and said to him: I have some advice to give you ... the gates of enchantments are closed but not the gates of counsel. Our daughters will break the strength of Israel ... we have to inflame the fire of their sexual passion which will consume them body and soul. My counsel is treacherous but only by treachery can we drive them out of the land.

Questions for Further Study

Cf.:

Balaam to Balak's messengers (22, 18)	*Balaam to Balak* (24, 13)
Though Balak give me his house full of silver and gold I cannot transgress	Though Balak give me his house full silver and gold I cannot transgress
The word of the Lord my God	The word of the Lord
To do either a small or great matter.	To do either good or evil from my heart; that which the Lord will speak that will I speak.

1. Rashi on 24, 13:

   "Transgress the word of the Lord". Here the text does not say "my God", as previously, since he knew that he was abhorrent to the Lord and driven from His presence.

   Try to explain the reason for the other deviations.

2. "Flee thou" (24, 11) — an expression of swiftness as in Canticles 8, 14: "Flee my beloved ...". I said I would surely honour thee, that you would return to your land heavy with silver and gold and cattle, but now you can flee as quickly as possible, carrying nothing with you, because I will give you nothing.

   (Bechor Shor)

   What unusual expression in the text prompted the above comment?

NOTES

1 For the whole passage see further *Pinhas*, p. 328.
2 For a reason why the details of Balaam's advice were not alluded to till later see our detailed explanation further: *Matot*, p. 375.
3 Published by Newman, Jerusalem, Tel Aviv 1960.

BALAAM: THE HEATHEN MOSES

We have previously dealt with Balaam's approach to the gift of prophecy and noted the difference between him and the Hebrew prophets in this matter. The latter do not run after prophecy but, on the contrary, try to avoid it, sensing their own inadequacy. Balaam, however, seeks it, endeavours by magical means to force it into his service through seven altars, seven bullocks, by going to meet enchantments and, in the words of Naḥmanides, "wished to harness the Divine will".

This time we shall see how the Midrash depicts the role of Balaam and his conduct as compared with that of the Hebrew prophets.

> "There has arisen no prophet in Israel like unto Moses" (Deut. 34, 10) — but in the Gentile world there has arisen. And who? Balaam the son of Beor.
> (Sifrei)

The contrast is further elaborated in the following Midrashim:

> "And Balak saw" (22, 2). To this may be applied the text: "The Rock — His work is perfect; for all his paths are just" (Deut. 32, 4). The Holy One blessed be He gave the heathen no excuse for saying, You kept us at a distance and did not grant us in the world what You did to Israel. What did the Holy One blessed be He do? Just as He raised up kings, sages and prophets for Israel so he did for the heathen. Israel's kings, prophets and sages were tested along with those of the heathen.
> He raised up Solomon king over all the earth and so he did Nebuchadnezzar ... the former built the Temple and uttered many songs and supplications, the latter destroyed it, reviled and cursed and said (Isaiah 14, 14): "I will ascend above the heights of the clouds, I will be like the Most

High". He gave David wealth — he used it for a house in His name. He gave Haman wealth — he purchased with it an entire nation to the slaughter. The heathen received a corresponding share of all the greatness bestowed on Israel. He appointed Moses for Israel, who spoke with Him whenever he desired. He appointed Balaam for them; he spoke with Him whenever he desired. See the difference between the prophets of Israel and those of the heathen! The Hebrew prophets warn the nations against transgression, as it is stated: "I have made you a watchman for the nations" (combination of Ezek. 3, 17; Jer. 1, 5), whereas the prophets He raised up for the heathen, created a breach (i.e. undermined morality) depriving mankind of their Hereafter. What is more, all the prophets were inspired by the attribute of compassion towards both Israel and the nations, as Isaiah states: "Therefore my heart moans like a harp for Moab" (Isa. 16, 11) and Ezekiel (27, 2): "Take up a lamentation for Tyre". The prophets of the Gentiles, however, were motivated by cruelty; for this one designed to exterminate an entire nation for no reason at all.

For this reason the story of Balaam is told to make known why the Holy One blessed be He deprived the Gentiles of the Holy Spirit, because one had it and look what he did!

(Tanḥuma Balak 1)

In a similar strain we have in *Tanna Debe Eliyahu*:

As soon as Noah and his sons came into the world the Holy One blessed be He said to Shem, the son of Noah: My beloved Shem! Had the Torah been there during the first ten generations (of human history), do you think I would have destroyed My world? Now that all the heathens have been created I shall see whether they will accept My Torah. Go and prophesy to them! There was there a certain Gentile ("son of Noah") who prophesied to the heathen for four hundred years but the heathen paid no heed. Henceforth Eliphaz the Temanite, Bildad the Shuhite, Zophar the Naamathite, Elijah the son of Berachiah the Buzite, Job from the land of Uz, Baor the father of Balaam, and finally, Balaam himself prophesied to the heathen.

The Holy One blessed be He withheld nothing from Balaam. Why? Because it was revealed and known to Him blessed be He that all the heathen repudiators of the Law were destined to argue before Him on the day of Judgement: Lord of the universe! Had you given us a prophet like Moses we would have accepted your Torah; therefore the Holy One blessed be He gave them Balaam who was superior in wisdom to Moses . . .

See what is written with regard to Balaam (Micah 6, 5): "My people, remember now what Balak the king of Moab counselled and what Balaam the son of Baor answered him". Balaam only came to Balak to curse Israel. Go forth and learn from the first words Balaam spoke when Balak sent him emissaries. Balaam should have told Balak's emissaries that he would not curse Israel. But he did not do so, but, on the contrary, rejoiced exceedingly at the opportunity of cursing Israel even more than Balak had asked for . . .

The trend of both Midrashim is the same. Professor Urbach has aptly summed it up in his article on: "Gentile prophets and the story of Balaam in the Midrash".[1]

From these rabbinic dicta emerges the outlook that prophecy is not the exclusive gift of Israel, is no "racial characteristic" of this people. On the contrary, prophecy, i.e. direct communion with God, was bestowed, at the outset, on all human creatures.

The bestowal of the gift of prophecy on all human creatures was designed to impress upon the world that the choice of Israel was no arbitrary one, but the reward for Israel's readiness and willingness to accept the Torah. R. Yoḥanan's famous words to the effect that God offered the Torah first to all the nations, one by one, but all refused, only Israel accepting, is explained in the Gemara as the rejoinder to the arguments of the nations: Did you ever offer us the Torah that we refused it? In this way, later sources motivate the gift of prophecy to the Gentiles.

The Midrashim do not limit themselves to indicating that prophecy was indeed granted to all men and that there were Gentile prophets, but they deal with the question: Why did the Holy One blessed be He take the Holy Spirit away from them? Again, no arbitrary decision was involved, neither the choice of Israel nor the giving of the Torah to Israel were to blame, but the deeds of the Gentile prophets, their conduct, their misuse of this precious mantic gift were their undoing. This is how Urbach explains the Midrash:

Whilst the Hebrew prophets preoccupied themselves not only with the reform of their own people but also with that of other peoples Balaam went forth to corrupt Israel and to bring disaster on them . . .

Balaam represents the type of man who has been given the opportunity to

325

scale the loftiest spiritual heights but fails to stand the test and forfeits his status.

An important lesson can be learnt from this. Man's natural qualities do not determine his spiritual status, nor do the talents bestowed on him from Above. Even the supreme gift of prophecy cannot turn him into a saint against his will or without his own endeavours. Man's own will is the sole factor determining whether he will use his qualities, talents and even the gift of prophecy bestowed on him for good, or, God forbid, misuse them, for evil. It depends solely on his own freewill to aspire to the sainthood of a Moses or descend to the villainy of a Balaam.

Questions for Further Study

1. What is the trend of thought common to these two Midrashim?

2. Explain how David used his wealth "for a house in His name" and how Balaam created a breach, depriving *mankind* of their Hereafter (and not merely Israel).

3. Can you find in our chapter and the verses discussed in this chapter a trace of any resemblance between Moses and Balaam?

4. What trace did our Sages find in *Balak* that Balak "rejoiced exceedingly at the opportunity of cursing Israel?"

5. Whence the Midrash that: "Balaam came to Balak only to curse Israel" and that his first words to Balak's emissaries indicate this? Surely he specifically told the emissaries that he must first consult the Lord, and did not agree to follow them?

6. Cf. Balaam's gradually changing reactions to Balak's importunings: 22, 38: "Can I say anything? Whatever God shall put in my mouth *that shall I speak*". 23, 12: "Surely that which

God shall put in my mouth *that shall I observe to speak.* 23, 26: "Surely I have told you saying: All that the Lord shall speak *that shall I do*". 24, 13: "I cannot violate the word of the Lord *to do good or evil out of my own heart,* that which the Lord shall speak, that shall I speak".

Can you explain the reason for the changes and note any specific trend of development? In what direction?

NOTE

[1] Tarbiẓ, vol. 25, 3.

COPING WITH ZEAL

The beginning of our sidra concludes the story of Balaam's malicious efforts to discredit Israel in the eyes of the Almighty, by seducing them to commit immorality. The background to this story is filled in by the following excerpt from the Talmud (Sanhedrin 106a) which discusses the subject:

אמר להם בלעם: "אלוהיהם של אלה שונא זימה הוא. והם (ישראל) מתאוים לכלי פשתן. בוא ואשיאך עצה: עשה להם קלעים . . ." וכשישראל אוכלין ושותין ושמחין ויוצאים לטייל בשוק, אומרת לו . . . "הרי אתה כבן בית, שב, ברור לעצמך!" וצרצורי של יין עמוני מונח אצלה. אמר לו: "רצונך שתשתה כוס יין?" כיון ששתה, בער בו. אמר לה: "השמעי לי". הוציאה יראתה מתוך חיקה. אמרה לו: "עבוד לזה". אמר לה: "הלא יהודי אני!" אמרה לו: "מה איכפת לך . . . ולא עוד שאיני מניחה אותך, עד שתכפור בתורת משה רבך!" וזהו שנאמר (הושע ט): "המה באו בעל פעור וינזרו לבשת ויהיו שקוצים כאהבם".

Balaam said to them: Their God detests immorality. The Israelites hanker after linen garments. Let me give you some advice. Set up stalls and instal in them harlots to sell them linen wares ... When the Israelites were eating and drinking and rejoicing and strolling in the market place, she would say to him: Thou art like one of the family, sit down and choose for thyself! Gourds of Ammonite wine stood by her ... Said she to him: Wouldst thou drink a cup of wine? As soon as he had drunk it, the evil inclination burned within him and he said to her: Yield to me! She then took her idol out of her bosom and said to him: Worship this! He said to her: Am I not a Jew? Said she to him: What carest thou ... moreover I shall not yield to thee till thou hast repudiated the Law of Moses thy Teacher, as it is stated (Hosea 9, 10): "They went to Baal Peor, and separated themselves unto that shame; and their abominations were according as they loved".

At the end of the foregoing sidra, it is related how Pinḥas stepped into the breach to turn away the wrath of God. In his zeal for his God, he slew a man on the spur of the moment, without trial, or offering previous warning, without legal testimony being heard, and in defiance of all the procedures of judicial examination prescribed by the Torah, which in practice render a conviction well nigh impossible. His deed of summary justice, taking the law into his hands, constituted a dangerous precedent, from the social, moral and educational angle. Yet what has the Torah to comment on his action?

וַיְדַבֵּר ה׳ אֶל־מֹשֶׁה לֵּאמֹר:
פִּינְחָס בֶּן־אֶלְעָזָר בֶּן־אַהֲרֹן הַכֹּהֵן
הֵשִׁיב אֶת־חֲמָתִי מֵעַל בְּנֵי־יִשְׂרָאֵל
בְּקַנְאוֹ אֶת־קִנְאָתִי בְּתוֹכָם
וְלֹא כִלִּיתִי אֶת בְּנֵי־יִשְׂרָאֵל בְּקִנְאָתִי:

And the Lord spake unto Moses saying:
Pinḥas the son of Eleazar, the son of Aaron the priest,
hath turned My wrath away from the children of Israel, while
he was zealous for My sake among them,
that I consumed not the children of Israel in My jealousy.
(25, 10—11)

It sounds strange that such a reward is prescribed for such a deed.

The Sages in the Jerusalem Talmud state that Pinḥas' deed did not meet with approval of the religious leaders of his time, that is of Moses and the elders. One of them goes so far as to say that they wanted to excommunicate him, had not the Holy Spirit leapt forth and declared:

וְהָיְתָה לֹּו וּלְזַרְעוֹ אַחֲרָיו בְּרִית כְּהֻנַּת עוֹלָם
תַּחַת אֲשֶׁר קִנֵּא לֵאלֹהָיו עַל בְּנֵי־יִשְׂרָאֵל:

**And he shall have it, and his seed after him, even the covenant
of an everlasting priesthood;
because he was zealous for his God, and made an atonement
for the children of Israel.**

(25, 13)

Rabbi Baruch Epstein, the author of the Pentateuch commentary
Torah Temimah interprets the attitude of the Sages in the following
manner:

> Such a deed must be animated by a genuine, unadulterated spirit of zeal to
> advance the glory of God. In the case, who can tell whether the perpetrator
> is not really prompted by some selfish motive, maintaining that he is doing it
> for the sake of God, when he has actually committed murder? That was why
> the Sages wished to excommunicate Pinḥas, had not the Holy Spirit testified
> that his zeal for God was genuine.

Rabbi Kook makes a similar point in his commentary to the
Prayer Book on the *birkat haminim* (Blessing against the Heretics)
which occurs in the weekday *amida.* This prayer beginning "For the
slanderers let there be no hope..." breathes vengeance on those
traitorous to their people. Curiously enough, this unusually bitter
prayer was formulated in its present form by the Talmudic sage
known as Samuel Ha-katan distinguished for his love of his fellow
creatures and whose motto, according to *Pirke Avot,* was enshrined
in the verse (Proverbs 24, 17): "Rejoice not when thine enemy
falleth, and let not thine heart be glad when he stumbleth".
Rabbi Kook explains:

> Any sage distinguished for his piety and learning is capable of formulating
> prayers breathing sentiments of mercy and love. But such a prayer as this
> one, so full of hate and condemnation is bound to arouse the private feelings
> of animosity and spite, on the part of the author, against the enemies and
> persecutors of his people. Such a prayer must therefore originate with one
> noted for the holiness and purity of character and entire lack of the passion
> of hatred. Such a man was Samuel Ha-katan. One could be sure that he was

dominated by completely unselfish considerations and inspired by the purest of motives, and had removed from his heart all private feelings of hatred for the persecutors of his people.

Now, perhaps, it is easier to understand the connecting link between Pinḥas' deed, terrible in itself, and the reward prescribed by God:

לָכֵן אֱמֹר הִנְנִי נֹתֵן לוֹ אֶת־בְּרִיתִי שָׁלוֹם:

Behold I give unto him my covenant of peace.

(25, 12)

We do not need to accept Abravanel's suggestion that it implied Divine protection against the next-of-kin of the victim, Zimri, who was of a distinguished family, and who would, no doubt, wish to avenge his death. The covenant of peace need not be interpreted as a Divine guarantee of personal safety from molestation, but rather in the sense understood by Rabbi Zvi Yehuda Berlin, the renowned principal of Volozhin Yeshiva in his commentary *Ha'amek Davar*: The Divine promise of a covenant of peace constitutes rather a guarantee of protection against the inner enemy, lurking inside the zealous perpetrator of the sudden deed, against the inner demoralization that such an act as the killing of a human being, without due process of law is liable to cause.

The Neẓiv (Naphtali Zvi Yehuda Berlin) expressed this idea in the following manner:

In reward for turning away the wrath of the Holy One blessed be He, He blessed him with the attribute of peace, that he should not be quick-tempered or angry. Since, it was only natural that such a deed as Pinḥas' should leave in his heart an intense emotional unrest afterward, the Divine blessing was designed to cope with this situation and promised peace and tranquility of soul.

331

Questions for Further Study

1. "And the name of the Israelite that was slain was Zimri, a prince of the chief house among the Simeonites" (Numbers 25, 14)

להודיע שבחו של פנחס שאף על פי שזה היה נשיא, לא מנע פנחס את עצמו מלקנא לחלול ה׳, לכך הודיעך הכתוב מי הוא המוכה.

To make known the praiseworthiness of Pinḥas, that although a prince was involved, this did not prevent Pinḥas from being zealous for the profanation of the name of God. That is why the verse reveals to thee the name of the victim.

(Rashi)

"And the name of the Midianitish woman that was slain was Cozbi the daughter of Zur; he was head over a people, and of a chief house in Midian" (Numbers 25, 15).

להודיעך שנאתם של מדינים, שהפקירו בת מלך כדי להחטיא את ישראל.

To let thee know the extent of the hatred of the Midianites who went so far as to prostitute a king's daughter in order to bring Israel into sin.

(Rashi)

The Maharal of Prague (18th century), author of the work *Gur Aryeh,* asks why Rashi did not make the same comment on the second as on the first verse, to the effect that it was intended to reflect credit on Pinḥas, who did not stop at slaying a princess, in order to sustain the honour of God's name? Find in Rashi's own words an answer to this question.

2. On the same two verses, the author of the Pentateuch commentary, *Or Ha-ḥayyim,* asks if the Torah intended, in the last resort, to divulge the names of the victims and not leave them under a veil of anonymity as in the case of the man "who gathered sticks on the Sabbath day" (Numbers 15, 32), then why did it not immediately insert their names in Chapter 35, 6

at the beginning, instead of waiting till now and having to repeat the phrases: "And the name of the man", "and the name of the woman?"

Suggest why the names of the victims of Pinḥas' zealous deed were inserted in our sidra and not in the previous, at the beginning of the story.

DESIGNS ON ISRAEL'S SOUL

וַיְדַבֵּר ה' אֶל־מֹשֶׁה לֵּאמֹר:
צָרוֹר אֶת־הַמִּדְיָנִים וְהִכִּיתֶם אוֹתָם:
כִּי־צֹרְרִים הֵם לָכֶם בְּנִכְלֵיהֶם אֲשֶׁר־נִכְּלוּ לָכֶם עַל־דְּבַר פְּעוֹר
וְעַל־דְּבַר כָּזְבִּי בַת־נְשִׂיא מִדְיָן אֲחֹתָם
הַמֻּכָּה בְיוֹם־הַמַּגֵּפָה עַל־דְּבַר פְּעוֹר:

And the Lord spoke unto Moses, saying:

Harass the Midianites, and smite them;

for they harass you, by their wiles wherewith they have beguiled you in the matter of Peor,

and in the matter of Cozbi, the daughter of the prince of Midian, the sister, who was slain on the day of the plague in the matter of Peor.

(25, 16—18)

This was the second people the Israelites encountered on their journey from Egypt to the Promised Land, whom they were ordered by the Almighty to do evil to. The first people were the Amalekites, whom the Israelites were ordered to wipe out. The Midianites were to be "harassed". On the surface this command to harass a people offends our moral susceptibilities, especially when we are used to the "ways of peace" that are the keynote of the Torah. In our study of *Ki Teze*[1] we endeavour to understand the Divine command to wipe out the memory of Amalek. Amalek, we understood to be, not a racial concept but rather the embodiment of cruelty and wanton aggression. But what was the sin of the Midianites?

The passage with which we opened this chapter alludes to this, in its double emphasis on "the matter of Peor". Rashi enlightens us in his comment on this phrase:

> They (the Midianites) prostituted their daughters in order to mislead you into worshipping Peor.

Naḥmanides elaborates on this theme:

> It was the elders of Midian who initiated the idea, and it was from them that Moab received the design to prostitute their daughters in order to seduce them away from the true God. Furthermore, the Midianites even prostituted their own princess for the purpose: "In the matter of Cozbi, the daughter of the prince of Midian". This must have been done with the connivance of the Midianite rulers. Otherwise what would a Midianite princess be doing at Shittim where the Israelites had encamped? But she was a very beautiful woman and the Midianite elders wished to corrupt the Israelites through her. We may assume also that Balaam participated in this design, since on his way back from Moab he passed through Midian.

Naḥmanides here tries to solve the riddle why the Israelites were commanded to harass the Midianites and not the Moabites, since it is stated distinctly in chapter 25, 1: "... And the people began to commit harlotry with the daughters of Moab". The Midianites initiated the idea and the Moabites joined them, at their prompting. Hirsch gives a different answer, based on the fact that the text states "harass the Midianites ... for they harass you" — in the present tense. According to Hirsch, the text wishes to emphasize that, though the Moabites had ceased their wiles, the Midianites "harass" or literally "are harassing" you. The Midianites still persisted in their misconduct towards Israel.

It may be said that Amalek threatened the body of the people, whilst Midian threatened its soul. The strength and continued vitality of the Jewish people stem from the purity of its family life. Our Sages interpreted Balaam's design as aimed chiefly at undermining this. According to our Sages, Balaam opened by observing:

335

אֱלֹהֵיהֶם שֶׁל אֵלּוּ שׂוֹנְאֵי זִמָּה הוּא.

Their God (i.e. of Israel) hates immorality.

(Sanhedrin 106a)

The Torah itself stresses that Israel's existence depends on sexual purity:

וּשְׁמַרְתֶּם אַתֶּם אֶת־חֻקֹּתַי וְאֶת־מִשְׁפָּטַי וְלֹא תַעֲשׂוּ מִכֹּל הַתּוֹעֵבֹת הָאֵלֶּה
הָאֶזְרָח וְהַגֵּר הַגָּר בְּתוֹכְכֶם:
כִּי אֶת־כָּל־הַתּוֹעֵבֹת הָאֵל עָשׂוּ אַנְשֵׁי הָאָרֶץ אֲשֶׁר לִפְנֵיכֶם
וַתִּטְמָא הָאָרֶץ:
וְלֹא־תָקִיא הָאָרֶץ אֶתְכֶם בְּטַמַּאֲכֶם אֹתָהּ
כַּאֲשֶׁר קָאָה אֶת־הַגּוֹי אֲשֶׁר לִפְנֵיכֶם:

**Ye therefore shall keep My statutes and Mine ordinances, and
shall not do any of these abominations; neither the home-born,
nor the stranger that sojourneth among you —
for all these abominations have the men of the land done, that
were before you,
and the land is defiled —
that the land vomit not you out also, when ye defile it, as it
vomited out the nation that was before you.**

(Leviticus 18, 26—28)

Our Sages dwelt on the fact that Israel was famed for the purity of
its family life:

"And they assembled all the congregation together on the first day of the
second month, and they declared their pedigrees after their families, by their
fathers' houses..." (Numbers 1, 18) — When the Israelites received the
Torah the nations of the world were envious. They said, why have they been
privileged to come closer to Him than the nations. The Holy One blessed be
He silenced them and said unto them: Bring Me your family trees, as it is

stated: "Bring to the Lord the families of the peoples" (Psalms 96, 7), just the same as My children do bring, as it is said: "And they declared their pedigrees after their families, by their fathers' houses". Therefore He numbered them at the beginning of this book, after giving them the commandments, as it is stated: "These are the commandments, which the Lord commanded Moses for the children of Israel in mount Sinai" (Leviticus 27, 34). After this it is stated: "And the Lord spoke unto Moses in the wilderness of Sinai . . . take ye the sum of all the congregation of the children of Israel, by their families . . ." (Numbers 1, 1—2): "They merited the gift of the Torah, only on account of their pedigrees.

(Yalkut Shimoni)

במדבר רבה ב':

אף בלעם הביט בהם ויצאה עינו כנגדם, שלא היה יכול ליגע בהם שנאמר (במדבר כד):
"וישא בלעם את עיניו וירא את ישראל שוכן לשבטיו" — אלו הם הדגלים. התחיל
אומר: מי יכול ליגע לבני אדם אלו, מכירין את אבותיהם ואת
משפחותיהם, שנאמר "שוכן לשבטיו". מכאן למדנו שהיו הדגלים גדולה
לישראל.

"And Balaam lifted up his eyes, and he saw Israel dwelling tribe by tribe . . ." (Numbers 24, 2) — these are the ensigns of their tribes. Balaam began to say as follows: Who can do hurt to these people who recognize their own fathers and families, as it is said: "Dwelling tribe by tribe".

(Bamidbar Rabbah 2, 3)

It was the purity of Jewish family life then which thwarted Balaam's malicious designs. It was not a racial purity but a moral one, which only persisted so long as the Israelites preserved their moral integrity. But as soon as they fell victim to the wiles of the Midianites and strayed from the true path, they forfeited this purity in which lay their strength.

The plague which overtook Israel as a punishment for this fall from grace, contained within itself, the penalty and the atonement, for restoring the wrongdoers again to favour. Divine retribution possesses a twofold quality, healing where it wounds. An allusion to the remedy and healing that the punishment brought in its train, can be found in parenthesis, within the sentence telling of the plague.

וַיְהִי אַחֲרֵי הַמַּגֵּפָה
וַיֹּאמֶר ה׳ אֶל־מֹשֶׁה וְאֶל אֶלְעָזָר. . .
שְׂאוּ אֶת־רֹאשׁ כָּל עֲדַת בְּנֵי־יִשְׂרָאֵל. . .

**And it came to pass after the plague,
that the Lord spoke unto Moses and unto Eleazar...
Take the sum of all the congregation of the children of
Israel...**

(26, 1—2)

Our Sages interpreted the link between the plague and the
recording of the pedigree and families of the Israelites as implying a
tribute to Jewish standards of domestic morality which preserve the
people.

זה שאמר הכתוב (תהלים צד): "אם אמרתי מטה רגלי — חסדך ה׳ יסעדני". בשעה
שקבלו ישראל את התורה, נתקנאו אומות העולם. אמרו: מה ראו להתקרב מכל
האומות? סתם הקב"ה פיהן, אמר להן: הביאו לי יוחסין שלכם! "הבו לה׳ משפחות
עמים..." (תהלים צו), כשם שבני מביאין, שנאמר (במדבר א)" "ויתילדו על
משפחותם". לכך מנאם בראש הספר אחר המצוות: "אלה המצוות אשר צווה ה׳ את
משה אל בני ישראל בהר סיני" (ויקרא כז, לד). אחר כך (במדבר א, א)" וידבר ה׳ אל
משה במדבר סיני... שאו את ראש כל עדת בני ישראל" — שלא זכו ליטול את התורה
אלא בשביל יוחסין שלהם. "גן נעול אחותי כלה... אחת היא יונתי" (שיר השירים ד),
"שמעו האומות — אף הן התחילו מקלסין להם..." אלא כשבאו לשיטים "ויחל העם
לזנות (במדבר כה, א(שמחו האומות ואמרו: "אותה העטרה שהיתה בידן כבר בטלה,
אותו השבח שהיו משתבחין הרי בטל! שוים הם לנו!" כשבאו לידי נפילה זקפן המקום,
שנאמר: "אם אמרתי מטה רגלי, חסדך ה׳ יסעדני", — נגף המקום את כל שנתקלקל
והעמידן על טהרתן.

"If I say: My foot slippeth, Thy mercy, O Lord, holdeth me up" (Psalms 94,
18). When Israel received the Torah, the nations of the world were envious.
They said, why have they been privileged to come closer to God than all the
other nations? The Holy One blessed be He silenced them by saying: Bring
Me your family trees. Bring to the Lord the families of the peoples (cf.
Psalms 96) the same as My children bring, as it is said: "And they declared
their pedigrees after their families . . .". Therefore He numbered them at the
beginning of the book after he gave them the commandments: "These are the
commandments, which the Lord commanded Moses for the children of
Israel in Mount Sinai" (Leviticus 27, 34). They merited the gift of the Torah

only on account of their pedigrees. "A garden shut up is my sister, my bride... My dove... is but one" (Song of Songs 4, 12; 6, 9). When the nations heard (of the purity of Israel's family life) they too joined in the praises. But when the Israelites came to Shittim "And the people began to commit harlotry" (Numbers 25, 1) the nations rejoiced, saying: Gone is that crown which they possessed, gone is that attribute for which they were praised. They are equal to us. When they (the Israelites) came to their downfall, the Omnipotent lifted them up, as it is said "If I say: My foot slippeth, Thy mercy, O Lord, holdeth me up". The Omnipotent smote all who committed misconduct and then restored them to their former purity.

(Yalkut Shimoni)

The commentary *Or Ha-ḥayyim* elaborates on this Midrash, and explains that the plague came on the Israelites as a punishment for what the Israelites had done at Peor, bringing them into disrepute among the nations. The latter rejoiced at Israel's fall from grace. But the gloating of the nations did not cease with the suspension of the plague. The Israelites' moral prestige was only restored when they were numbered and their family purity was re-established, each one's pedigree declared according to his father's house. Then they were restored to Divine grace.

Will Israel continue to cherish "the crown" of sound family life "for which they were praised" down the ages?

NOTE

[1] In *Studies in Devarim*, Ki Teze 6

A SHEPHERD FOR THE CONGREGATION

התקן עצמך ללמוד תורה, שאינה ירושה לך.

Qualify thyself to study Torah, since it doth not come to thee by inheritance.
(Pirke Avot 2, 12)

ומפני מה אין מצויין תלמידי חכמים לצאת תלמידי חכמים מבינהם? אמר רב יוסף:
שלא יאמרו תורה ירושה היא להם.

Why do not the children of scholars usually turn out to be scholars? Said Rabbi Yosef: That it should not be said that the Torah came to them by inheritance.

(Talmud, Nedarim, 71a)

The same principle embodied in the above citation from the words of our Sages governed the question of Moses' successor which is treated in our sidra. Moses' children did not inherit their father's exalted position, nor were they, indeed, granted any appointment. Their names are not even referred to in the passage concerned where it is stated that a man be appointed over the congregation "who may go out before them and who may go in before them and may lead them out and bring them in" (Numbers 27, 17). Nowhere in Moses' prayer regarding his successor is there any echo of the faithful shepherd's grievance that he had brought his flock thus far, and was not even granted to lead them to the longed-for, final goal. Neither do we find any trace of a suggestion by Moses to nominate his sons to succeed him. All that finds expression is his concern for the welfare

340

of his flock Israel — "that the congregation of the Lord be not as sheep which have no shepherd" (ibid.).

However our Sages in the Midrash who always sought the universal application in the Biblical account and not merely its immediate, transitory implications detected a hint of Moses' own sense of grievance at being so summarily dismissed, before he had finished his mission. Moses, the greatest of prophets but nevertheless human, could not resign himself to the cruel fate that "decreed his bones should fall in the wilderness on the threshold of the promised land, after he had run like a horse before the people for forty years" (Midrash).

The duplication in the opening phrases of Moses' request served as the basis for our Sages' interpretations:

אֲשֶׁר יֵצֵא לִפְנֵיהֶם וַאֲשֶׁר יָבֹא לִפְנֵיהֶם
וַאֲשֶׁר יוֹצִיאֵם וַאֲשֶׁר יְבִיאֵם

Who may go out before them, and who may go in before them, who may lead them out and bring them in.

(27, 17)

The Midrash (Bamidbar Rabbah 21, 16) thereon states:

משל למלך שראה אשה אחת יתומה, בקש ליטול אותה לאשה. שלח לתובעה, אמרה:
"איני כדאי להנשא למלך!" שלח לתובעה שבע פעמים ולא היתה מבקשת. לבסוף
נשאה לו. לאחר זמן כעס עליה המלך ובקש לגרשה. אמרה: "אני לא בקשתי להנשא
לך, אתה בקשת אותי! הואיל וכך גזרת לגרשני וליטול אחרת, אל תעשה לזו כשם
שעשית לי". כך הקב"ה. אמר ר' שמואל בר נחמני: שבעה ימים היה מפתהו הקב"ה
שילך בשליחותו והיה אומר לו (שמות ד): "שלח נא ביד תשלח", "לא איש דברים
אנכי . . ." לאחר זמן פייסו הקב"ה והלך בשליחותו ועשה את כל אותם הנסים על ידו.
בסוף אמר לו (במדבר כ, יב): "לא תביאו את הקהל הזה לארץ". אמר לו משה: "רבונו
של עולם, אני לא בקשתי להלוך, א ת ה החילות (מתנות כהונה: החילות לשלוח אותי
לפרעה, למנות אותי מלך עך ישראל). הואיל וגזרת עלי, אותו שיכנס אל תעשה לו
כדרך שעשית לי, אלא: "אשר יצא לפניהם ואשר יבא לפניהם!"

It may be compared to a king who saw a certain orphan maiden and wished to take her to wife. When he sent to seek her hand in marriage she answered: I am not worthy to become the wife of a king! Whereupon he sought her hand seven times, but she still did not accede. In the end she married him. Subsequently the king became angry with her and wished to divorce her. Whereupon she said: I did not seek to marry you; you sought me! Since however you have thus decreed to divorce me and take another, do not to her as you have done to me.

It was the same with the Holy One Blessed be He. Said Rabbi Samuel bar Naḥmani: Seven times did the Lord seek to entice Moses to accept His mission but he (Moses) replied: "Send I prithee with whom thou wilt send I am not eloquent . . ." (Exodus 4). Subsequently, the Lord prevailed upon him and he went on His mission and performed all those miracles through him. In the end He said to him: "Thou shalt not bring this assembly to the Land" (Numbers 20, 12). Said Moses to him: Lord of the Universe! I did not seek to go in the first instance; Thou didst begin. Since, however, Thou hast thus decreed regarding me, him who will enter, do not to him as Thou didst to me, but "who may go out before them and go in before them!"[1]

Similarly, our Sages assumed that Moses did not lightly give up the idea of seeing his sons succeed him:

"יפקד ה'," מה ראה לבקש הדבר הזה אחר סדר נחלות? אלא כיון שירשו בנות צלפחד אביהן, אמר משה: "הרי השעה שאתבע בה צרכי; אם הבנות יורשות, כדין הוא שירשו בני את כבודי!" אמר לו הקב"ה (משלי כז): "נוצר תאנה יאכל פריה" — בניך ישבו להם ולא עסקו בתורה, יהושע הרבה שרתך והרבה חלק לך כבוד והוא היה משכים ומעריב בבית הוועד שלך, הוא היה מסדר את הספסלים והוא פורס המחצלאות; הואיל והוא שרתך בכל כחו, כדאי הוא שישמש את ישראל, שאינו מאבד שכרו. "קח לך את יהושע בן נון" לקיים מה שנאמר (משלי כז): "נוצר תאנה יאכל פריה".

"Let the Lord . . . set a man over the congregation" (27, 16). What prompted Moses to make this request immediately after the chapter dealing with the laws of inheritance? — Since the daughters of Zelophehad inherited their father, Moses said: Now is the time to make my claims. If daughters inherit, then it is only right that my sons inherit my glory! Said the Holy One blessed be He to him: "Whoso keepeth the fig tree shall eat the fruit thereof" (Proverbs 27, 18). Thy sons idled away their time and did not occupy themselves with study of the Torah; but, as for Joshua, much did he minister to thee and much honour did he apportion thee. He would betake himself early morning and late in the evening to thy meeting house, arranging the benches and spreading the mats. Since he served thee with all his might, it were meet for him to minister to Israel, that he lose not his reward. "Take to thee Joshua the son of Nun" — in fulfillment of the text (Proverbs ibid.): "Whoso keepeth the fig tree, shall eat the fruit thereof".

This drives home to us the lesson that "the Torah doth not come to thee by inheritance". Only those who labour in it inherit it. Now let us note how Moses ordained his successor in front of the congregation. For this purpose we shall carefully compare the ordination rite as commanded by God with the way it was implemented by Moses.

The Divine Command (27, 18—20)	*The Implementation* (27, 22—23)
1. Take thee Joshua...	And he took Joshua
2. And lay thine hand on him	And he laid his hands on him
3. And set him before Eleazar	And set him before Eleazar...
4. The priest and before all the congregation	And before all the congregation
5. And give him a charge	And gave him charge.
6. And thou shalt put some of thine honour upon him.	

Our Sages drew attention to the difference between the command "lay *thine hand*" in the singular, and Moses' implementation in the plural: "He laid *his hands*".

Let us quote Rashi on this point:

וסמך את ידיו: בעין יפה — יותר ויותר ממה שנצטווה, שהקב"ה אמר לו: "וסמכת את ידך", והוא עשה בשתי ידיו, ועשאו ככלי מלא וגדוש ומלאו חכמתו בעין יפה.

"And he laid his hands" — generously (literally — with a generous hand), in much greater measure than he had been commanded. For the Holy One blessed be He said to him: "Thou shalt lay thine hand" in the singular, and he had done it, with both his hands, making him as a vessel full to the brim and heaped up; so he filled him with a generous helping of his wisdom.

However, in one particular detail in the command to give of his honour or majesty to Joshua, there is no equivalent in the ordination ceremony, as carried out by Moses. This would seem to imply that, in this matter, Moses did not behave generously. But this is far from being true. The Italian Jewish commentator Isaac Reggio has aptly explained this omission:

> "And thou shalt put some of thine honour upon him". This refers to the charisma and authority with which the ruler should be endowed. Compare: "And bestowed on him royal majesty" (I Chronicles 29, 25 with reference to Solomon's assumption of sovereignty). Similarly Joshua was charged with charisma when Moses ordained him and appointed him. This charisma gave him the respect of the children of Israel. This is the force of the text: "That the congregation of the children of Israel may be obedient" (Numbers 27, 20). Now it layeth not with any man to bestow his spirit on others. The Lord, however, promised that if Moses laid his hands on Joshua and set him before the congregation and gave him a charge in their sight, then He would grant him some of Moses' charisma.

Moses overcame all pangs of envy, and it was in no jaundiced spirit, but generously and magnanimously that he ordained his successor. Truly "There arose not a prophet since in Israel like unto Moses" (Deut. 34, 10).

Questions for Further Study

1. "And Moses spoke unto the Lord, saying: Let the Lord the God of the spirits of all flesh . . ." (Numbers 27, 15—16) — To reflect credit on the righteous who, when they depart the world, leave their own affairs, and concern themselves with the public welfare.

    (Rashi)

    ## What prompted the above comment of Rashi?

2. "Who may go out before them . . ." (ibid. 17). Note like the kings of the nations who sit at home and send their armies into battle; but as I did, when I fought Sihon and Og, as it is stated (Numbers 21, 34): "Fear him not", and as Joshua did . . . and regarding David (1 Samuel 18, 16) "for he went out

and came in before them", the first to lead them out and the first to bring them in.

(Rashi)

(a)   What difficulty does the text present?

(b)   Where can you find in Rashi on another text in the Torah an allusion to this same idea of "not like the kings of the nations who sent their armies into battle?"

3.   The expression of "going out" almost invariably precedes that of "coming in" in a description of movement to and from a city, in the Bible. Cf. our text 27, 17; Deuteronomy 2, 2; Joshua 6, 1. Can you explain the reason for this?

4.   "Take thee Joshua ... a man in whom is spirit" (Numbers 27, 18). Every living person has spirit, but what is meant is, as in 1 Kings 2, 2 "be thou strong, and show thyself a man".

(Ibn Ezra)

"A man in whom is spirit" — receptive to the light of the King, as in Exodus 21, 6: "In the hearts of all that are wise-hearted I have put wisdom".

(Sforno)

(a)   What difficulty did both the above commentators detect in the text?

(b)   How does Ibn Ezra try to overcome the difficulty and what do we gather from 1 Kings 2, 2?

(c)   What other difficulty do you find in the text?

5.   "And lay thy hand upon him" as one who kindles one lamp from another. "And thou shalt put of thy honour upon him" — as one who empties from one vessel to another.

(Bamidbar Rabbah 21, 16)

(a)   Explain the difference between the two similes.

(b)   Explain why the simile of the lamp is used with regard to the laying of hands and that of the emptying from a vessel with reference to the putting of honour.

NOTE

[1]   i.e. finish the job and lead them into Eretz Israel (T).

THE KINDNESS OF THY YOUTH
(Haftarah, Jeremiah 1, 1—2, 3)

Though we read on the three Sabbaths between Shiv'a Asar
Be-tammuz and Tish'a Be-Av passages from the Prophets full of
reproof and indignant admonition, as befits the period of mourning
for the destruction of the Temple, the selectors of these Haftarot
could not bear ending on an unpleasant note, as do the words of the
prophecy imparted to Jeremiah:

מִצָּפוֹן תִּפָּתַח הָרָעָה עַל כָּל־יֹשְׁבֵי הָאָרֶץ: . . .
וְדִבַּרְתִּי מִשְׁפָּטַי אוֹתָם עַל כָּל־רָעָתָם
אֲשֶׁר עֲזָבוּנִי לֵאלֹהִים אֲחֵרִים
וַיִּשְׁתַּחֲווּ לְמַעֲשֵׂי יְדֵיהֶם:

From the north the evil shall open forth on all the inhabitants
of the earth...
and I will utter My judgements against them touching their
wickedness,
in that they have forsaken Me, and have offered up unto other
gods,
and worshipped the work of their own hands.

(Jer. 1, 14—16)

(The concluding verses of the chapter contain words of
encouragement to the prophet himself and are not directed at the
people as a whole.) For this reason the opening verses of the next
chapter are attached to the Haftarah so as not to end on a note of

347

anger and reproof but to conclude the prophetic reading on a note of hope and promise of the kindnesses of the Lord:

אַהֲבַת כְּלוּלֹתָיִךְ   זָכַרְתִּי לָךְ חֶסֶד נְעוּרַיִךְ

בְּאֶרֶץ לֹא זְרוּעָה: לֶכְתֵּךְ אַחֲרַי בַּמִּדְבָּר

רֵאשִׁית תְּבוּאָתֹה   קֹדֶשׁ יִשְׂרָאֵל לַה׳

רָעָה תָּבֹא אֲלֵיהֶם   כָּל אֹכְלָיו יֶאְשָׁמוּ

I remember for thee the affection of thy youth   **the love of thine espousals**

Thy going after Me in the wilderness   **in a land that was not sown.**

Israel is holy to the Lord   **the first of His produce**

All that devour him shall be held guilty.   **evil shall befall them.**

(Jer. 2, 2—3)

Our commentators have differed regarding the reading of the above two verses.

> Should you return to Me, it would be My desire to be merciful to you, since I remember the kindness of your youth and the love of thine espousals when I brought you to the bridal canopy. What is the kindness of youth? Your going after My messengers Moses and Aaron. You went forth from an inhabited land into a wilderness without provisions, because you believed in Me.
>
> (Rashi)

> Though I bring on you evil for your misdeeds, I shall not utterly destroy you, because I remember the kindness of your youth, as the Targum Jonathan has it "I remember the good deeds of olden times, the love of your forefathers who believed in My words".
>
> (Radak)

The difference between both these commentators is not great. According to Rashi if Israel would but open their heart to

348

repentance, even so much as the eye of a needle, the Holy One would open a gate as wide as a hall, since the merit of their fathers lay to their credit and the Lord remembered the loyalty of the generation of the wilderness. Should it be objected that we find no allusion to the loyalty of the generation of the wilderness in the Torah and that, on the contrary, we find them depicted as grumblers and rebels, we cite here the views of the *Mekhilta* on this subject:

> "And Moses led Israel onward from the Red Sea". R. Eliezer said: To redound to the credit of the Israelites. As soon as Moses said to them, "Arise and journey", they did not say, How can we go forth into the wilderness, without any provision for the journey? But they had faith and went after Moses. To this refers the prophetic text: "I remember the kindness of thy youth, the love of thine espousals, thy going after Me in the wilderness, in a land that was not sown".

According to Radak the indulgence of the Creator is even greater in not even making His grace dependent or conditional at all on their repentance. In virtue of the kindness of their youth He promises us that He will never make a complete end of Israel. The difference in approach between the two commentators is well expressed in their very opening words. Rashi begins with the conditional "Should you return to Me", Radak with "though . . .". Shadal (Luzzatto) gives, however, a completely different explanation:

> *Hesed* — "kindness" is a quality in the lover and *hen* "favour" (or "charm") in the beloved. (See Gen. 39, 21: "But the Lord was with Joseph, and showed kindness (*hesed*) unto him, and gave him favour (*hen*) in the sight of the keeper of the prison".
> Our text implies that I remembered the kindness and closeness which I showed towards you in the days of your youth and I loved you in the days of your youth and I loved you in the days of your espousals. Therefore if I punish you, My kindness shall not depart from you and Israel is holy unto the Lord. Nevertheless I am forced to reprove you to your face and say to you, "What iniquity have your forefathers found in Me".
> The closeness of man to God is not termed *hesed*, kindness, even though the one who loves God is termed *hasido* — his pious one or saint. The term

hesed will only be found to describe a relationship between man and man or shown by God to man. It was only later (in *Nehemiah* and *Chronicles*) that the goodness of man to God began to be termed "kindnesses" *hasadim*.

What is the difference between Luzzatto and the two previous commentators? Rashi and Radak maintain that the whole of verse 2 alludes to the attitude of the generation of the wilderness to God, whereas Luzzatto explains that it speaks both of the attitude of God to them and of theirs to God i.e. of their mutual relationship. According to Rashi and Radak, both parts of the verse are synonymous, "the kindness of thy youth and the love of thine espousals" referring to the same thing — their wandering in the wilderness. According to Luzzatto, no parallelism is involved and both parts of the verse complement each other.

Let us test the correctness of Luzzatto's explanation in the light of the text: Is his definition regarding the use of the word *hesed* borne out by the facts? This verse from Hosea (6, 6) would seem to contradict his principle: "For kindness (*hesed*) I desired and not sacrifice, and the knowledge of God more than burnt offerings". However, the context of this verse indicates there is no contradiction. What does the Lord demand? Surely the doing of kindness by one man to another. The second phrase "the knowledge of God" goes to prove that this is the meaning. In Jeremiah we have an exact definition of "the knowledge of God". In speaking of King Josiah Jeremiah said:

$$. . . \text{וְעָשָׂה מִשְׁפָּט וּצְדָקָה:}$$
$$\text{דָּן דִּין־עָנִי וְאֶבְיוֹן} . . .$$
$$\text{הֲלֹא הוּא הַדַּעַת אֹתִי}$$

. . . And do justice and righteousness,
he judged the cause of the poor and needy.
Is not this to know Me?

(Jer. 22, 15—16)

Even more explicit is the following text where the knowledge of God is represented as an absolute ideal in contrast to the relative ones of wisdom, might and riches:

כִּי אִם־בְּזֹאת יִתְהַלֵּל הַמִּתְהַלֵּל
הַשְׂכֵּל וְיָדֹעַ אוֹתִי
כִּי אֲנִי ה׳ עֹשֶׂה חֶסֶד מִשְׁפָּט וּצְדָקָה בָּאָרֶץ
כִּי־בְאֵלֶּה חָפַצְתִּי נְאֻם־ה׳ :

But let him that glorieth glory in this,
that he understandeth Me, and knoweth Me,
that I am the Lord who exercise mercy, justice and
righteousness in the earth;
for in these things I delight, saith the Lord.

(Jer. 9, 23)

This definition of the knowledge of the Lord evidently preceded Jeremiah and is also alluded to in Hosea.

There is therefore no contradiction of Luzzatto's principle. It may be however that the structure of the verse itself cannot be harmonised with his explanation. According to him, both parts of the verse are not parallel; the first part, "I remembered the kindness of thy youth, the love of thine espousals" refers to the attitude of the God to Israel, whereas the "going after Me in the wilderness" refers to Israel's loyalty to God. It may be argued that other prophetic texts regard this journeying through the wilderness as an example of God's kindness to Israel, as further in the same chapter we read:

הַמּוֹלִיךְ אֹתָנוּ בַּמִּדְבָּר
בְּאֶרֶץ עֲרָבָה וְשׁוּחָה
בְּאֶרֶץ צִיָּה וְצַלְמָוֶת
בְּאֶרֶץ לֹא־עָבַר בָּהּ אִישׁ
וְלֹא יָשַׁב אָדָם שָׁם :

351

That led us through a wilderness,
through a land of deserts and pits,
through a land of drought and of the shadow of death,
through a land no man passed through
and where no man dwelt.

(Jer. 2, 6)

The prophet here follows what is described in Deuteronomy where Israel's journeyings through the wilderness are taken to exemplify God's kindness rather than their loyalty to Him:

הַמּוֹלִיכְךָ בַּמִּדְבָּר הַגָּדֹל וְהַנּוֹרָא
נָחָשׁ שָׂרָף וְעַקְרָב וְצִמָּאוֹן אֲשֶׁר אֵין־מָיִם
הַמּוֹצִיא לְךָ מַיִם מִצּוּר הַחַלָּמִישׁ:
הַמַּאֲכִלְךָ מָן בַּמִּדְבָּר . . .

Who led thee through the great and terrible wilderness,
wherein were serpents, fiery serpents and scorpions and thirsty
ground where was no water,
who brought thee forth water out of the flinty rock,
who fed thee in the wilderness, with manna . . .

(Deut. 8, 15—16)

Both these texts however afford no proof for an interpretation of our text, since both of them speak of "leading" (*ha-molikh*) and not as here of "thy going after Me". We must conclude that the second part of our verse speaks of Israel's attitude to God and not the reverse. Let us now study the subsequent verse in the light of Luzzatto's approach:

קֹדֶשׁ יִשְׂרָאֵל לַה׳   רֵאשִׁית תְּבוּאָתֹה
כָּל־אֹכְלָיו יֶאְשָׁמוּ   רָעָה תָּבֹא אֲלֵיהֶם

Israel is holy to the Lord	**the first of His produce**
All that devour him shall be	
culpable	**evil shall befall them.**

(Jer. 2, 3)

Apparently this verse treats only of God's relationship towards Israel, His love for them, His care for them, indicating good grounds for Luzzatto's explanation. But only apparently. In actuality, the verse "Israel is holy to the Lord, the first of His produce" refers likewise to the attitude of Israel towards God. Israel would not have been holy to the Lord, had they not been the first of His produce. This quality of being first: *reshit* to the Lord was peculiar to Israel and their chief merit in His eyes. Let us study this metaphor closer. Israel was not always termed *reshit* at the time the people were first chosen and experienced the Divine revelation. In *Haazinu* we read that "He found him in a desert land and in a waste, howling wilderness. He compassed him about, He cared for Him, He kept him as the apple of His eye".

Our Sages in the *Sifrei* wish to interpret this passage to our credit:

> "He found him in a desert land" — i.e. Israel, as it is stated: "Like grapes in the wilderness I found Israel" (Hosea 9, 10).

Rashi too follows in the *Sifrei's* footsteps and interprets the whole passage as praise of Israel:

> He found them faithful in the desert land, in that they accepted the Torah, His kingdom and yoke, in contrast to Esau and Ishmael. Even in a waste howling wilderness they followed the true faith and did not say to Moses, How can we go forth into the wilderness?

Nahmanides however disagreed with this interpretation and asserted that, on the contrary, the text reproves Israel and recalls the kindnesses shown by God to them which they requited with evil. This first encounter of God and Israel did not redound at all to the latter's credit. Israel was passive. They were not chosen for their own goodness or merit. An even blacker picture of Israel's complete lack of merit is painted in Ezekiel 16, 4—8:

וּמוֹלְדוֹתַיִךְ בְּיוֹם הוּלֶּדֶת אוֹתָךְ
לֹא־כָרַת שָׁרֵּךְ וּבְמַיִם לֹא רֻחַצְתְּ לְמִשְׁעִי
וְהָמְלֵחַ לֹא הֻמְלַחַתְּ וְהָחְתֵּל לֹא חֻתָּלְתְּ׃
לֹא־חָסָה עָלַיִךְ עַיִן לַעֲשׂוֹת לָךְ אַחַת מֵאֵלֶּה לְחֻמְלָה עָלָיִךְ
וַתֻּשְׁלְכִי אֶל־פְּנֵי הַשָּׂדֶה בְּגֹעַל נַפְשֵׁךְ
בְּיוֹם הֻלֶּדֶת אֹתָךְ׃
וָאֶעֱבֹר עָלַיִךְ וָאֶרְאֵךְ מִתְבּוֹסֶסֶת בְּדָמָיִךְ
וָאֹמַר לָךְ בְּדָמַיִךְ חֲיִי וָאֹמַר לָךְ בְּדָמַיִךְ חֲיִי׃
רְבָבָה כְּצֶמַח הַשָּׂדֶה נְתַתִּיךְ וַתִּרְבִּי וַתִּגְדְּלִי וַתָּבֹאִי בַּעֲדִי עֲדָיִים
שָׁדַיִם נָכֹנוּ וּשְׂעָרֵךְ צִמֵּחַ וְאַתְּ עֵרֹם וְעֶרְיָה׃
וָאֶעֱבֹר עָלַיִךְ וָאֶרְאֵךְ וְהִנֵּה עִתֵּךְ עֵת דֹּדִים
וָאֶפְרֹשׂ כְּנָפִי עָלַיִךְ וָאֲכַסֶּה עֶרְוָתֵךְ וָאֶשָּׁבַע לָךְ
וָאָבוֹא בִבְרִית אֹתָךְ נְאֻם אֲדֹנָי ה׳ וַתִּהְיִי־לִי׃

And as for thy nativity, in the day thou wast born
thy navel was not cut, neither wast thou washed in water for cleansing;
thou wast not salted at all, nor swaddled at all.
No eye pitied thee to do any of these things to thee, to have compassion upon thee;
but thou wast cast out in the open field in the loathsomeness of thy person,
in the day that thou wast born.
And when I passed by thee, and saw thee wallowing in thy blood,
I said unto thee: in thy blood, live; yea I said unto thee: In thy blood live:
I caused thee to increase, even as the growth of the field. And

thou didst increase and grow up, and thou camest to excellent
beauty;
thy breasts were fashioned and thy hair was grown; yet thou
wast naked and bare.
Now when I passed by thee and looked upon thee and behold
thy time was the time of love,
I spread my skirt over thee and covered thy nakedness; yea, I
swore unto thee
and entered into a covenant with thee, saith the Lord God, and
thou becamest Mine.

Israel is depicted here not only as devoid of all merit, not only
naked and bare, but in her natural uncouthness, with the aim of
emphasising the love of He who chose her and the abundance of His
grace. In spite of Israel's lack of all beauty, defilement and
unattractiveness God chose them. On the other hand, the picture of
"the first" which Jeremiah depicts is altogether different. In this he
was preceded by Hosea:

כַּעֲנָבִים בַּמִּדְבָּר מָצָאתִי יִשְׂרָאֵל
כְּבִכּוּרָה בִתְאֵנָה בְּרֵאשִׁיתָהּ רָאִיתִי אֲבוֹתֵיכֶם:

Like grapes in the wilderness did I find Israel,
like the first-ripe in the fig tree at her first reason did I see your
fathers.

(Hosea 9, 10)

The Divine choice of Israel is pictured here not as directed to a
people devoid of all intrinsic merit, and even burdened with liabilities,
an object of God's grace, but rather as fully meriting their
distinguished treatment. Buber thus elaborates on the theme of this
verse: 'The Lord "found" Israel in the wilderness'.

355

This finding is compared to the find of grapes in the wilderness by the wanderer. In other words, the finder discovered a treasured object in a place where he least expected. He saw the encampments of those camping at the foot of mount Sinai and they appeared to him as first ripe figs at their season, producing fruit for the first time. The great fig of God, mankind, was yielding fruit for the first time and its fruit were the camps of Israel in the wilderness.

In our verse Jeremiah expands the comparison still further. Humanity is the field of God, his produce; Israel his firstfruit, dedicated, consecrated to the Lord. Again Jeremiah's words echo the Torah:

כֹּל חֵלֶב יִצְהָר וְכָל־חֵלֶב תִּירוֹשׁ וְדָגָן
רֵאשִׁיתָם אֲשֶׁר־יִתְּנוּ לַה׳

All the best of the oil, all the best of the wine and of the corn,
the first part **of them which they give to the Lord . . .**

(Num. 18, 12)

רֵאשִׁית דְּגָנְךָ תִּירֹשְׁךָ וְיִצְהָרֶךָ
וְרֵאשִׁית גֵּז צֹאנְךָ תִּתֶּן־לֹו׃

The firstfruits of the corn, of thy wine, and of thy oil
and *the first* **of the fleece of thy sheep shalt thou give him.**
(Deut. 18, 4)

Evidently the text speaks wholly in praiseworthy terms of Israel's merit, as the firstborn son of the Lord, the first of His produce. He was the first to acknowledge his Maker; he was the first to say "let us do and hear"; on him first shone the Divine light when "darkness covered the earth and thick darkness the nations". Radak's comment therefore seems fully justified:

Though I bring evil on you for your misdeeds, I shall not utterly destroy you, because I remember the kindness of your youth.

Questions for Further Study

1. Cf. with our text Jeremiah's statement: "And an everlasting love I have loved thee, therefore have I drawn thee with affection" (31, 2). Does this text support Luzzatto's explanation or not?

2. Cf. with our text Amos' statement: "Woe to them that are at ease in Zion, and to them that are secure in the mountains of Samaria, *the notable men of the first of the nations*" (6, 1). What is the difference in the force of the epithet "first" (*reshit*) here and in our verse from Jer. 2, 2?

3. You have forgotten the kindness I showed you in your youth, when I redeemed you from the burdens of Egypt and led you in the wilderness and supplied your wants there forty years. Behold I now remind you of the kindness I showed you in your youth when you went after Me in the wilderness in a land not sown and I called you holy, as it is written: "Ye shall be to Me a kingdom of priests and a holy people" (Ex. 19, 6). In other words, I gave you this title at that period in your history. Perhaps you ask, What benefit is there in it? What is the purpose of being called by this title of "holy?" It is a great thing for you. Had you not profaned My name with transgressions, you would be as a hallowed object. Just as whoever benefits from the sacred things is liable to bring a guilt offering, so with Israel — "All who devour it shall be held guilty".

(Joseph Kara*)

Is the above explanation of our text similar to Radak's or Luzzatto's or does it take quite a different line?

* A commentator of the school of Rashi (T).

AN ALMOND ROD I SEE
(Haftarah, Jeremiah 1, 1—2, 3)

We shall preface this chapter with some observations on the three Haftarot read on the three Sabbaths between the fasts of 17th Tammuz and 9th Av:

> It is stated in Pesikta: From Bereshit till 17th Tammuz the Haftara has some connecting link with the sidra. Henceforth it all depends on the time and event: three on the theme of retribution, seven, consolation and two of repentance. The mnemonic signs are *DaSHaḤ*.
>
> (Abudarham)

The Haftarot are cited in Tosafot (Megillah 31b):

> It is our usage to read the three passages of retribution before Tisha Be'Av: *Divrei Yirmeyahu* ("The Words of Jeremiah") (Jer. 1, 1—2, 3); *Shim'u Devar Ha-shem* ("Hear ye the word of the Lord") (Jer. 2, 4—28; 3, 4); *Ḥazon Yeshayahu* (Isaiah 1, 1—27).

Rabbi Zevin in his *Ha-mo'adim Ba-halakhah* writes:

> Special importance attaches to these Haftarot: Though our Sages instituted the reading of prophetic portions on festivals and sabbaths they did not exactly specify the particular portion to be read. With regard to the Haftarot from 17th Tammuz onwards they specifically ordained which portions had to be read. On account of this the latter Haftarot are more important and in the event of the reader forgetting to recite the specifically ordained portion on one sabbath, two portions must be read on the next.

The three Haftarot of Retribution were therefore ordained not as a connecting link with the Sidrot read on those sabbaths but to recall the dire events commemorated during that period — the three weeks of mourning for the Destruction of the Temple between 17th Tammuz and 9th Av.

Indeed the opening words of Jeremiah in the Haftarah of our sidra are bitter and grim, foretelling destruction and desolation. The following passage may be considered the central one and the focal point of all his prophecies:

רְאֵה הִפְקַדְתִּיךָ הַיּוֹם הַזֶּה עַל־הַגּוֹיִם וְעַל־הַמַּמְלָכוֹת
לִנְתוֹשׁ וְלִנְתוֹץ וּלְהַאֲבִיד
וְלַהֲרוֹס
לִבְנוֹת וְלִנְטוֹעַ :

**See, I have set thee today over all the nations and kingdoms,
to root out and to pull down, and to destroy
and overthrow;
to build and to plant.**

(1, 10)

Jeremiah's role is defined here in six verbs, four of destruction and two of construction. Significance may be attached to the fact that the first four are joined by the conjunctive *vav,* the last two are not — separating them. This multiplicity of verbs must not be regarded as an indiscriminate piling up of synonyms for rhetorical effect only, but we should try to detect the specific significance of each one of them.

Malbim who is the commentator *par excellence* for detecting the difference between apparently synonymous words in Scripture has the following to say:

The verb *natash* (to root out) specifically applies to plants, the uprooting of plants from their place, corresponding to *nataz* and *haras* which are specific to building, since he is speaking of just these two kinds of operations, as it is said: "to build and to plant". Similarly it is stated further (45, 4): "That which I have built will I break down (*hores*), that which I have planted I will pluck up (*notesh*)"; and "I will build them and not pull them down and plant them and not pluck them up" (24, 6).

Ule-ha'avid (to destroy) adds something to *li-ntosh,* since that which is uprooted still exists whereas that which is destroyed is completely annihilated. It is similarly stated further (12, 17): "If you will not hearken, then I will pluck up that nation plucking up and destroying" (i.e. the plucking up will not allow replanting but will be destined for complete destruction). Similarly *la-haros* adds something to *li-ntoz,* since they are both two different operations. The latter can apply to even one stone, whereas the former refers to building in general. Thus *harisah* is a much broader term.

Malbim explains further how a kingdom is compared to a house, to a building, because it is a structure made by man by putting one stone on another, as a kingdom is gradually built up. The "nation" on the other hand, is an organic natural growth and is pictured in Scriptures as a wood bringing forth trees (Isaiah 10, 18; 10, 32; Zech. 11, 1—3). Now we may understand the verse which sets the prophet over the nations and kingdoms — over the nations, to uproot and destroy, over the kingdoms to pull down and demolish. The order here, placing destruction before construction aptly corresponds to the operation of removing evil before doing good. Rebuilding and re-planting can have no permanency so long as the old have not been uprooted and pulled down. Jeremiah says the same thing negatively, elsewhere, employing an agricultural metaphor:

נִירוּ לָכֶם נִיר וְאַל־תִּזְרְעוּ אֶל־קֹצִים:

Break up for you a fallow ground, and sow not among thorns.
(4, 3)

Rashi explains the foregoing as follows:

Learn from the tillers of the soil who plough it up in the summer to kill the weeds by the roots so that thorns should not sprout up during the winter sowing — that they should not be like the one who sows without previously ploughing up the soil so that it becomes thorn-ridden.

Alshikh thus sums up the consolatory message of our verse:

> The purpose of your prophecies is not to uproot and pull down but to
> prompt them to repentance and mend their ways since they possess free will.
> It is the same idea that is expressed in the saying: the destruction of the
> elders is constructive. Furthermore even the very prophecy of uprooting and
> pulling down has the constructive purpose of building and planting, since the
> evil tidings — their retribution for failure to repent — is for the purpose of
> rebuilding and replanting, to prompt them mend their ways ...

The prophet now applies to his task immediately and shows us
two visions. Here is the first:

וַיְהִי דְבַר־ה׳ אֵלַי לֵאמֹר
מָה אַתָּה רֹאֶה יִרְמְיָהוּ
וָאֹמַר
מַקֵּל שָׁקֵד אֲנִי רֹאֶה:
וַיֹּאמֶר ה׳ אֵלַי
הֵיטַבְתָּ לִרְאוֹת
כִּי־שֹׁקֵד אֲנִי עַל־דְּבָרִי לַעֲשׂתוֹ:

And the word of the Lord came unto me saying:
Jeremiah, what seest thou?
and I said,
I see a rod of an almond tree *(shaked).*
Then the Lord said,
Thou hast well seen;
for I watch over *(shaked)* **my word to perform it.**

(1, 11—12)

Both the vision and the sound of the word are portentous. What is
so frightening about the rod of an almond tree? In what way does it
have any retributive significance? First *makel* — rod. Malbim
distinguishes three homonyms *makel, matteh, mishe'net. Matteh* —
staff — is a symbol of office and glory (Ezekiel: 19, 14) "*matteh* of

361

strength, sceptre to rule"); *mishe'net* refers to the stick used by the old and infirm for support (cf.: Exodus 21; Zech. 8, 4). *Anaf* is the Hebrew word used for a branch, arousing associations of growth and fruitfulness. For this reason the prophet chose the word *makel* which implies a rod associated with beating. Balaam used a *makel* to beat his ass. It symbolised therefore the rod of correction for the sinner.

The choice of the *shaked* was dictated by its botanical characteristics. As Radak observes, the retribution foretold would come quickly on Israel, just as the almond tree is the earliest tree to blossom in the spring. Our Sages however went into more detail in distilling for us the symbolic associations of the almond, in this context:

> Just as the almond tree takes twenty one days to produce its fruit after it blossoms, so every decree (all the catastrophes that befell Israel) took no longer than from 17th Tammuz till 9th Av (i.e. 21 days).
>
> (Kohelet Rabbah 12, 5)

But the symbolism specifically emphasised here is not just visual — the vision he saw, the form of the rod and the properties of the almond tree but lies in the verbal association with a root meaning to expedite: "I watch over (*shoked*) My word to perform it". Cf.: 44, 27: "I watch over (*shoked*) them for evil and not for good".

The picture of remorseless and expeditious retribution came to dispel the illusions of the complacent who imagined that disaster was afar off (we may recall that Jeremiah began first to prophecy in the reign of Josiah when all was tranquil), "that the scouring scourge shall pass through but not come to us" (Isa. 28, 15).

But there are other commentators who detect, even in this prophecy of doom, a message of comfort, fulfilling the duty of pronouncing a blessing on evil tidings just the same as on good ones, since man does not know what good may spring from evil or what he regards as evil at the time. Expounding the verse in Daniel (9, 14): "The Lord God hath expedited the evil and brought it upon us; for the Lord our God is charitable..." the Talmud observes (Gittin 88a):

> Is the Lord then charitable towards us in expediting evil? But the Lord dealt charitably with Israel by antedating the exile of Zedekiah whilst the exile of Jechoniah was still in existence.

Rashi explains the foregoing as follows:

> The exile of Jechoniah i.e. Jehoakin preceded that of Zedekiah by 11 years. This was the Almighty's charity. He expedited the destruction of His house in order to exile Zedekiah's generation to Babylon whilst the sages of Jehoakin's exile were still living, so that they could teach the new exiles Torah, since the majority of the Sages were exiled with Jechoniah...

Malbim explains, with the help of the Talmudic excerpt we have quoted, that Jeremiah's retribution too was also expedited for the benefit of Israel and not for its rue. He analyses the uses of the word *shaked* and shows that it always refers to constant watching over with diligence and industry, as in Psalms 126, where the watchman is credited with this action.

> Sometimes God brings evil on man by hiding His face, by a negative action, the evil emerging automatically, as in Deut. 32, 20: "I will hide My face from them, I will see what their latter end shall be". Sometimes He brings evil providentially, as in Daniel 9, 14: "And the Lord expedited the evil". Here the meaning is "I watch over my words" — how to implement them and perform the matter providentially. In this way we may interpret the Divine answer: "You have seen well", in the sense of: "You have seen that all this expedition is for the ultimate good of Israel.
>
> (Malbim)

Questions for Further Study

Compare the following visions:

What seest thou Jeremiah and I said, I see the rod of an

almond tree. And the Lord said to me, Thou hast well seen. What seest thou, and I said, I see a seething pot . . . and the Lord said to me, out of the north the evil shall break forth.

(Jer. 1, 11—13)

The Lord showed me and behold two baskets of figs. And the Lord said unto me, *What seest thou Jeremiah.* And I said, Figs . . . And the word of the Lord came unto me . . . Thus saith the Lord . . . like these good figs . . .

(Jer. 24, 1—4)

Thus He showed me; and behold the Lord stood beside a wall made by a plumbline. And the Lord said unto me, *What seest thou, Amos?* And I said, A plumbline. Then said the Lord, Behold I will set a plumbline in the midst of My people Israel.

(Amos 7, 7—8)

Thus the Lord God showed me; and behold a basket of summer fruit. And He said, *Amos, what seest thou.* And I said, A basket of summer fruit. Then the Lord said unto me; the end is come upon My people.

(Amos 8, 1—2)

Thus the Lord God showed me; and behold He formed locusts in the beginning of the shooting up of the latter growth . . . so I said, O Lord God forgive, I beseech Thee; how shall Jacob stand?

(Amos 7, 1—2)

Thus the Lord God showed me; and behold the Lord called to contend by fire . . . then said I, O Lord God, cease, I beseech Thee; how shall Jacob stand? for he is small.

(Amos 7, 4—5)

1. Can you explain the reason why the Lord asked the prophet "what seest thou" in the three visions of Jeremiah (two in our

chapter and one in chapter 24) and the two of Amos (7, 7; 8, 1)
and not in the first two visions in Amos 7?

2. Why did the Lord answer Jeremiah in the first vision, "You have
   seen well", a phrase not recurring in all the prophetic literature?

   Radak gives the following answer:

   > Evidently he saw the rod without leaves and blossoms. Yet with prophetic
   > insight he realised it was from an almond tree. Therefore God complimented
   > him on seeing well. Had he seen it with leaves and blossoms where would he
   > have displayed any particular gift of insight? It would have been easy for
   > him to recognize.

   Try to give another answer, paying attention to the whole
   context from the beginning of the chapter till this point.

3. In what way was the second vision in our chapter more
   fearsome than the first?

I AM A CHILD[1]

The title alludes to Jeremiah's reaction to the Divine mission imposed on him. Here is the passage in full:

וַיְהִי דְבַר-ה׳ אֵלַי לֵאמֹר:
בְּטֶרֶם אֶצָּרְךָ בַבֶּטֶן יְדַעְתִּיךָ
וּבְטֶרֶם תֵּצֵא מֵרֶחֶם הִקְדַּשְׁתִּיךָ
נָבִיא לַגּוֹיִם נְתַתִּיךָ:
וָאֹמַר אֲהָהּ אֲדֹנָי ה׳ הִנֵּה לֹא-יָדַעְתִּי דַּבֵּר
כִּי-נַעַר אָנֹכִי:

The word of the Lord came unto me saying:
Before I formed you in the belly I knew you,
and before you came forth from the womb I sanctified you;
I have appointed you a prophet to the nations.
Then said I: Ah, Lord God! behold I cannot speak; for I am a
child.

(Jer. 1, 4—6)

His reaction is therefore one of refusal, rejection and excuse. Jeremiah was not the first prophet to be charged with a prophetic mission. Moses, father of the prophets repeatedly refused[2] to accept the Divine mission advancing a variety of reasons. This, on the surface, seems strange. For the prophet knows, and this knowledge is foremost, that he does not transmit his own message to the people but that of his sender. This is often emphasised by all the prophets, and particularly so, by Jeremiah. This attitude so characteristic of

366

prophecy has been aptly formulated by Heschel in his work on prophecy[3]:

> The spiritual character of the prophets emanates from their conviction that it is God who puts His word in their mouth. Their right to prophesy, their demand that their words be obeyed is based on the very fact that it is the spirit of God speaking through them. Their message does not derive its value or weight from its content or any aesthetic, logical or other qualities it happens to possess, but from its *source*. The prophet's authority is derived from the Divine inspiration prompting his words. Everywhere and always do they emphasise this starting point of their message. They do not unburden to the people the vision of their own heart but only the message the Divine spirit has imparted to them.

The question therefore arises: why do the prophets refuse to accept this mission to be the emissaries of the true God?

Jeremiah motivates his refusal with the words we have quoted, but they call for explanation. What does he mean by "I am a child?" Let us hear some of our commentators on this:

> He was young in years literally . . . he objected to the Divine mission saying: How can You say that You have endowed me with knowledge and instruction when I do not know how to speak and properly arrange Your message . . .?
>
> (Abravanel)

Radak elaborates on the same point:

> "I cannot speak" — words of reproof since I am a child and how can I reprove a whole people? But there is nothing out of the ordinary in the fact that prophecy was bestowed on him at a tender age: for Samuel too was a child when he became a prophet and the prophetic spirit made them wise, though they were children.
>
> Possibly the word *na'ar* (translated: "child") means a ministrant. Though he is grown up he is still called *na'ar*, as we have in (Ex. 33, 11): "But his minister Joshua, a *na'ar* (here translated: 'young man') departed not from the tent". Similarly, Jeremiah ministered to another prophet or sage, and the text means that God could have imposed this mission on a more adult

person. But the commentators explain that he was a lad in years just the same as Samuel.

According to the foregoing two commentators the word *na'ar* refers only to his tender age and that is the motivation for his refusal. Rashi however does not accept this view but extends the connotation of the word *na'ar*:

> (Jeremiah says:) I am not worthy to reprove them. Moses reproved them close to his death. He had already achieved standing with them through the many miracles he had performed for them: he had brought them out of Egypt, divided the sea for them, brought them down the manna, had wafted to them the quail, given them the Torah and produced the well. I am at the very beginning of my mission, how can I go and reprove them![4]

Here the word *na'ar* "child" is taken in the sense of being as inexperienced as a child, as far as his career of leadership and prophecy were concerned. He had not yet proved his mettle, won their confidence. How could he appear before them as a preacher and admonisher?

Alshikh makes a similar point with a slight difference of emphasis:

> To be an emissary to Jerusalem, its kings, princes and all the people of Israel, a man with the gift of eloquence was needed, and I am but a raw youth whom they will not respect and whose words will have no effect. They will say: Who has appointed you as public prosecutor?

Alshikh finds a similarity between Jeremiah's excuse and Moses', but it is difficult to find a basis for it in the text. At any rate, all explanations have this in common: that Jeremiah's refusal was motivated by his concern for the success of his mission. In the interests of the matter itself he rejected the Divine charge. His youth, lack of eloquence, inexperience, lack of public standing, all these would hamper the Divine purpose which he was being asked to further. It was therefore better to send someone who was not a *na'ar*.

An entirely different approach is found in the Midrash:

. . . אמר לו הקב׳׳ה: ״בטרם אצרך בבטן ידעתיך״ — עד שלא יצרתיך במעי אמך
מניתיך להיות מתנבא על עמי. ענה ירמיהו ואמר לפני הקב׳׳ה: ״רבונו של עולם! איני
יכול להתנבאות עליהם, איזה נביא יצא להם ולא בקשו להרגו?! העמדת להם משה
ואהרן — לא בקשו לרגום אותם באבנים? העמדת להם אליהו בעל הקצוות — היו
מלעיגים ומשחקים עליו: ׳הרי מסלסל קווצותיו! שמו איש בעל שער!׳ (מלכים ב א,
ח); העמדת להם את אלישע — היו אומרים לו (מלכים ב ב, כג): ׳עלה קרח! עלה
קרח!׳ איני יכול לצאת ידי ישראל! לא ידעתי דבר, כי נער אנכי׳׳. אמרה לו רוח
הקדש: הלא לנער אני אוהב, שלא טעם מזח חטא. גאלתי את ישראל ממצרים
וקראתים נער, שנאמר (הושע יא, א): ״כי נער ישראל ואהבהו׳׳, ובאהבת נער אני נזכר
לכנסת ישראל, שנאמר (ירמיהו ב, ב): ״זכרתי לך חסד נעורוך׳׳.

The Holy One blessed be He said to him: "Before I formed you in the belly I knew you". Before I fashioned you in your mother's belly I appointed you to prophesy concerning My people. Jeremiah answered and thus addressed the Holy One blessed be He: Lord of the universe! I cannot prophesy concerning them. What prophet would go forth to them whom they would not seek to slay? You appointed Moses and Aaron for them. Did they not seek to stone them? You appointed Elijah the hairy one. They mocked and taunted him: Look how he fancies himself with his locks! His name is the hairy one! (2 Kings 1, 8); You appointed for them Elisha. They said to him (2 Kings 2, 23): "Go up you baldhead! Go up you baldhead!" I cannot satisfy Israel, "I cannot speak; for I am a child". The Holy Spirit said to him: But it is indeed a child that I love who has not experienced the taste of sin. I redeemed Israel from Egypt and called them: "child", as it is stated (Hosea 11, 1): "When Israel was a child I remember the assembly of Israel, as it is said (Jer. 2, 2): "I remember the kindness of your childhood" (or "youth").

(Yalkut Shimoni 262)

According to the Sages therefore Jeremiah's hesitations are not based on concern for his actual mission itself as for his own welfare. Should it be asked on what the Sages based their diagnosis that Jeremiah was concerned for his own safety, since our text contains no mention of Jeremiah being afraid, it may be answered that they read between the lines.

What is the Lord's answer to Jeremiah's hesitations?

וַיֹּאמֶר ה׳ אֵלַי אַל־תֹּאמַר נַעַר אָנֹכִי
כִּי עַל־כָּל־אֲשֶׁר אֶשְׁלָחֲךָ תֵּלֵךְ וְאֵת כָּל־אֲשֶׁר אֲצַוְּךָ תְּדַבֵּר:

אַל־תִּירָא מִפְּנֵיהֶם
כִּי־אִתְּךָ אֲנִי לְהַצִּלֶךָ . . .

But the Lord said unto me: Say not I am a child;
For to whomever I send you you shall go, and whatever I
command you you shall speak.
Be not dismayed before them
for I am with you to deliver you . . .

(Jer. 1, 7—8)

We see, then, that though Jeremiah did not explicitly express his fear, the All-knowing One is aware of man's innermost thoughts even if not expressed. Therefore God reassured him: "Be not afraid".[5] The Almighty did not say this but once, but, at the end of the first prophetic message repeated His reassurance:

אַל־תֵּחַת מִפְּנֵיהֶם . . . וַאֲנִי הִנֵּה נְתַתִּיךָ הַיּוֹם לְעִיר מִבְצָר וּלְעַמּוּד בַּרְזֶל
וּלְחֹמוֹת נְחֹשֶׁת . . .

Be not dismayed before them . . .
For behold I have made you this day a fortified city and an
iron pillar and brazen walls . . .

(1, 17—18)

We see then that the text itself bears witness to the fact that Jeremiah's refusal, according to the plain sense of the Scriptures, is as elicited in the Midrash.

Out of plain human weakness, fear of a public which persecuted and even slew its prophets he tried to shirk his mission. The Sages were not afraid of denigrating the prophet's moral stature by uncovering this truth. On the contrary: the Almighty does not transmit His message to His people through the medium of a puppet or machine. The chosen person even though destined for this mission from childhood is a human being with human feelings and frailties.

This human material the Creator fashions, kneads and shapes. It is
not for nothing that prophecy is described as "the hand of the Lord
upon the prophet". The prophet undergoes many vicissitudes before
he leaves behind this preliminary level of refusal, doubt and desire to
shirk the mission and achieves that higher level to which expression
is subsequently given:

נִמְצְאוּ דְבָרֶיךָ וָאֹכְלֵם
וַיְהִי דְבָרְךָ לִי לְשָׂשׂוֹן וּלְשִׂמְחַת לְבָבִי כִּי־נִקְרָא שִׁמְךָ עָלַי ה' אֱלֹהֵי
צְבָאוֹת:

Your words were found and I did eat them;
And Your words were unto me a joy and the rejoicing of my
heart, because Your name was called upon me, O Lord, God
of hosts.

(Jer. 15, 16)

But even when he had reached this pinnacle of prophetic
inspiration, communion with God and the tasting of the sweetness of
His words with all their bitterness and dread, even then, he was no
mere trumpet or channel for the Divine message. But his heart
remained human and full of feeling, as is evidenced by what
immediately follows:

לֹא־יָשַׁבְתִּי בְסוֹד־מְשַׂחֲקִים וָאֶעְלֹז
מִפְּנֵי יָדְךָ בָּדָד יָשַׁבְתִּי . . .
לָמָּה הָיָה כְאֵבִי נֶצַח וּמַכָּתִי אֲנוּשָׁה . . .

I sat not in the assembly of them that make merry nor rejoiced.
I sat alone because of Your hand;
Why is my pain perpetual and my wound incurable?

(15, 17—18)

371

Further, similar sentiments are voiced[6]:

פִּתִּיתַנִי ה' וָאֶפָּת
חֲזַקְתַּנִי וַתּוּכָל
הָיִיתִי לִשְׂחוֹק כָּל־הַיּוֹם כֻּלֹּה לֹעֵג לִי:
כִּי־מִדֵּי אֲדַבֵּר אֶזְעָק חָמָס וָשֹׁד אֶקְרָא
כִּי־הָיָה דְבָר־ה' לִי לְחֶרְפָּה וּלְקֶלֶס כָּל־הַיּוֹם:

O Lord you enticed me and I was enticed.
You have overcome me and have prevailed;
I am become a laughing-stock all the day; everyone mocks me.
For as often as I speak I cry out, I cry: Violence and spoil;
Because the word of the Lord is made a reproach unto me and
a derision all the day.

(Jer. 20, 7—8)

Accordingly, Jeremiah remained in spite of his elevation to the heights of prophetic inspiration keenly sensitive not only to the tribulations and sufferings of his people but also to the persecutions and clashes that he experienced at their hands.

That same dread expressed, according to the Midrash, in his words "I am a child" remained with him afterwards, though he scaled the heights of prophecy and there was fulfilled in him the Divine promise that "You shall be like My mouth".

The Deity chose no one else but man to be His partner in Creation — that frail, unreliable creature, torn by conflicting instincts whose life is marked by constant ascents and descents. The Almighty chose none other as His partner in the reformation of the world, as a prophet to transmit His message to mankind — a mortal who with all his spiritual achievements remains but a mortal. For only a man can be the emissary of God to man.

NOTES

[1] This is the first of the three Haftarot of Retribution read on the Sabbaths between the Fast of the 17th Tammuz and Tisha Be Av. See also the previous chapter.

[2] Regarding Moses' repeated refusals to accept his mission. See *Studies in Shemot*, pp. 64ff.

[3] Abraham Heschel: *Die Prophetie*, Krakau, 1936.

[4] Rashi's words find an echo in the Sifrei cited by him on Deut. 1,1,4: These are the words which Moses spoke to Israel . . . after he smote Sihon: "Moses said: If I reprove them before they have entered into at least a small part of the Land they will say: What right has He to preach to us? What good has he brought us? He has only come to find fault and seek a pretext because he has not the power to bring us into the Land! He therefore waited till he had overthrown Sihon and Og and given them possession of their territory. After that he reproved them".

[5] This development from a low grade of prophecy, from hesitation and dread to the highest and brightest grade of prophecy, Maimonides, basing himself on the Midrash, observes in Moses (*Guide* 1, 5). "The latter did not dare at the beginning of his prophetic career to rush into a matter so vast and important without first becoming versed in several branches of science and knowledge and thoroughly refining his moral character . . . he must not decide any question by the first idea that suggests itself to his mind or at once direct his thoughts and force them to obtain a knowledge of his Creator, but he must wait modestly and patiently and advance step by step . . . In this sense we must understand the words "And Moses hid his face for he was afraid to look upon God" (Ex. 3, 6). This act of Moses was highly commended by God who bestowed on him a well-deserved portion of His goodness as it is said: "And the similitude of the Lord shall he behold" (Num. 12, 8). This, say our Sages (Talmud Berakhot 7a), was the reward for having previously hidden his face lest he should gaze at the Eternal". Moses' fear, as Maimonides explains, was of the prophecy itself, of its blinding light which he was not yet capable of withstanding, whereas Jeremiah's fear, as our Sages explained, was of the consequences of his prophecy, of the hatred of his people, the taunts of his audience and the persecutions and clashes they were destined to bring.

[6] Note that all the Patriarchs were told by God not to fear. Cf. Gen. 15, 1; 26, 24; 46, 3, and with respect to Moses too in Num. 21, 34. In all these cases we are not told directly that they were afraid, but the Divine reassurance indicates their inner state of mind which He anticipated. The Rabbis commended these "fearers" and applied to them the text in Prov. 28, 14: "Happy the man who

fears always". Cf. too *Tanna Debe Eliyahu's* comment: "The admonition "fear not" is only addressed to him who is a truely godfearing person". Cf. also *Ḥukkat* 6, p. 267.

THE LESSON OF BALAAM'S END

הֵן הֵנָּה הָיוּ לִבְנֵי יִשְׂרָאֵל
בִּדְבַר בִּלְעָם
לִמְסָר־מַעַל בַּה׳ עַל־דְּבַר פְּעוֹר . . .

Behold, these caused the children of Israel,
through the counsel of Balaam,
to revolt so as to break faith with the Lord in the matter of
Peor . . .

(31, 16)

This is the first occasion on which the Torah names Balaam as the instigator of the plot to lead the Israelites into sin at Baal Peor. During the whole of the Scriptural account of the deed in the previous chapters, no mention is made of Balaam's connivance at the deed. On the contrary:

וַיָּחֶל הָעָם לִזְנוֹת אֶל־בְּנוֹת מוֹאָב:

And the *people* began to commit harlotry with the daughters of Moab.

(25, 1)

We noted how the Almighty vented His wrath on the Israelites for their backsliding and how He commanded them to harass the Midianites for their complicity in the deed of "the matter of Peor". But Balaam's share is not alluded to. Luzzatto comments as follows on this omission:

On his way back home Balaam passed through Midian and heard how the Israelites had committed harlotry with the daughters of Moab and had thereby been led into idolatry. He then realized that this was the only sure method of undermining Israel. He therefore advised the Midianites to send their choicest maidens to seduce the Israelites into idolatry. In this way they would forfeit the Almighty's protection.

The question why Balaam's share in the matter of Peor is not immediately recorded still remains to be answered. As we have noted on other occasions, the Torah often omits in one part of the narrative important details, only to allude to them, at a later stage. Our Sages referred to this phenomenon in the following phrase:

דברי תורה עניים במקומם ועשירים במקום אחר.

The Scriptures record matters briefly in their original context only to elaborate at greater length elsewhere. (Literally: "The words of the Torah are poor in their place and rich elsewhere").

Here we shall select two other examples of this from the many that abound in Scriptures. In the story of Jacob and Laban (Genesis 31, 36—42), the former only details the conditions under which he worked and refers to Laban's exploitation of his devotion at the very end. During the whole time that Jacob worked for Laban described in chapters 29 and 30, the narrative makes no mention of the conditions under which Jacob worked and how Laban changed his wages ten times. Only when Jacob had left Padan Aram and Laban catches up with him, are we treated to a graphic description of those conditions, in Jacob's outburst of righteous indignation (ibid. 31, 36—42). These details fill in what was lacking in our previous vague picture of Jacob's relations with Laban.

Another instance is afforded us in 1 Samuel 28, 3. Only in the part of the narrative where King Saul stands helpless and "the Lord answered him not, neither by dreams . . ." and he turns to the witch, are we told of his earlier struggle to destroy the sorcerers and soothsayers in Israel (ibid. 28, 9).

Naḥmanides refers to this literary device in Genesis 31, 7:

> "Your father hath mocked me, and changed my wages..." — this was literally true, though the narrative makes no mention of this in the Torah. ...Scripture is often brief in one context only to elaborate in another.

But why did the Torah omit details in one context only to put them in later? The explanation in the two examples we quote above is not hard to discover. The narrative is silent so long as Jacob himself was silent and controlled his indignation, all the time he worked for Laban. But after twenty years of exploitation, Jacob gave vent to all that he kept within him during that time. Had these details been coldly reported to us in their strict chronological order, would they have touched the deepest chords of our feelings in the same way? Similarly in the case of Saul, had the narrative first described to us the king's struggle to wipe out the soothsayers at a time when he had assumed kingship and was carrying out the will of God, it would have borne no special significance for us. He was, after all, merely carrying out the command of the Torah. It is only when King Saul himself has to go and consult one of them, that the point is driven home how low he had been brought and how deeply he had been humiliated.

Now let us try to understand why the Torah deferred mentioning Balaam's complicity in the matter of Peor till after his death at the hands of the Israelites, described in this sidra. Why was not Balaam's responsibility for the matter of Peor recorded in the context of that story?

Evidently the Torah wished to teach us a special lesson.

Though it was Balaam who instigated the daughters of Midian to strike a blow at the purity of Jewish family life, though he was the evil genius who thought out the plan, the moral responsibility ultimately rested on the Israelites themselves. They were guilty:

וַיָּחֶל הָעָם לִזְנוֹת

And the *people* began to commit harlotry.

(25, 1)

The narrative only recorded the sin of the Israelites and their retribution. Every individual is responsible for his own acts. Provocation does not free the victim of responsibility.

"דברי הרב ודברי התלמיד — דברי מי שומעים?"

The words of the Master (God) and the words of the disciple — whose word must we obey?

Man's first loyalty is to the moral law, to God. But that does not imply that the provoker to immorality, the misleader is free from responsibility. When therefore the retribution that overcame Balaam is alluded to — when he was slain in battle by the Israelites:

וְאֶת בִּלְעָם בֶּן־בְּעוֹר הָרְגוּ בֶּחָרֶב:

Balaam also the son of Beor they slew with the sword.

(31, 8)

— his complicity in the sin of the Israelites is also referred to:

הֵן הֵנָּה הָיוּ לִבְנֵי יִשְׂרָאֵל בִּדְבַר בִּלְעָם לִמְסָר מַעַל בַּה' עַל דְּבַר פְּעוֹר . . .

Behold, these caused the children of Israel,
through the counsel of Balaam,
to revolt so as to break faith with the Lord in the matter of Peor...

(31, 16)

MAMMON OR ERETZ ISRAEL

This sidra discusses, among other things, a highly topical issue touching on the problem of, or dilemma between the choice of a career — personal advancement — or the fulfilment of a mission. It is a choice which has faced and continues to face Jewish youth, especially those intent on discharging the cardinal precept of settlement in the land of Israel. We find the application of the term *haluzim* to the "armed men" of the two and a half tribes who agreed to help their brethren conquer the Holy Land. That term has now entered the everyday vocabulary of Jews, the world over, and has come to represent the pioneer who deliberately forsakes all considerations of career for the mission of building with his own hands the future of his people in Eretz Israel. It is now a platitude to say that the State of Israel was built up by generations of such *haluzim*.

In chapter 27 we find highly significant negotiations taking place between those members of the two and a half tribes privileged to constitute the first generation to enter the Promised Land and Moses the veteran leader of Israel, father of the prophets who led his people out of Egypt and for forty years in the wilderness. Here we are confronted by two diametrically opposed points of view. There were those whose interests revolved round material possessions, concern for their cattle, who lived on bread alone and saw not the hand of God.

In contrast to them stood the one who, never for a moment, forgot the Divine mission he had been charged with, and the way the Almighty had brought His people with signs and miracles thus far.

Transjordan had been conquered and the Israelites stood by the plains of Moab and had only to cross the Jordan to possess the land promised them by the Almighty. But again an obstacle presented itself. This time it was not the report of spies attempting to dissuade them from entering the land, of yearnings for the fleshpots of Egypt but a desire to settle down comfortably in the first stretch of fertile, cultivated country that they encountered, rather than move on into the Promised Land. This time they were deflected from their goal not by the Paradise they considered they had left behind them but by the one in which they found themselves.

וּמִקְנֶה רַב הָיָה לִבְנֵי רְאוּבֵן וְלִבְנֵי־גָד עָצוּם מְאֹד
וַיִּרְאוּ אֶת־אֶרֶץ יַעְזֵר וְאֶת־אֶרֶץ גִּלְעָד וְהִנֵּה הַמָּקוֹם מְקוֹם מִקְנֶה:

**Now the children of Reuben and the children of Gad had a
very great multitude of** *cattle:*
**And when they saw the land of Jazer and the land of Gilead,
that, behold the place was a place for** *cattle . . .*

(32, 1)

Note that this verse sums up as it were the spiritual outlook of the children of Reuben and Gad, as beginning and ending with *cattle* (*mikneh* in the Hebrew text). The Reubenites and Gadites forthwith address themselves to Moses. A careful study of their words reveals they made in reality two distinct approaches to Moses. First:

וַיָּבֹאוּ בְנֵי־גָד וּבְנֵי רְאוּבֵן וַיֹּאמְרוּ אֶל מֹשֶׁה וְאֶל־אֶלְעָזָר הַכֹּהֵן וְאֶל־נְשִׂיאֵי
הָעֵדָה לֵאמֹר: עֲטָרוֹת וְדִיבֹן . . . הָאָרֶץ אֲשֶׁר הִכָּה ה' לִפְנֵי עֲדַת יִשְׂרָאֵל
אֶרֶץ מִקְנֶה הִוא וְלַעֲבָדֶיךָ מִקְנֶה: וַיֹּאמְרוּ אִם־מָצָאנוּ חֵן בְּעֵינֶיךָ יֻתַּן אֶת־
הָאָרֶץ הַזֹּאת לַעֲבָדֶיךָ לַאֲחֻזָּה אַל־תַּעֲבִרֵנוּ אֶת־הַיַּרְדֵּן:

**The children of Gad . . . and Reuben came and spake unto
Moses and to Eleazar the priest and the princes . . . saying:
Ataroth and Dibon . . . even the country which the Lord smote**

**before the congregation of Israel is a land for cattle, and thy
servants have cattle.
And they spake: if we have found grace in thy sight, let this
land be given to thy servants for a possession and bring us not
over the Jordan.**

(32, 2—5)

What is the significance of the twofold nature of their address
implied in the repetition of the introductory ויאמרו — "they spake?"
At the outset, they merely placed the facts of the situation before
Moses. We have cattle and here is a land ideal for cattle. They were
sounding Moses. They paused and waited for Moses to make the
next approach, and perhaps himself suggest what they had not as yet
been bold enough to ask for. But no such advance was forthcoming
from Moses. So they plucked up courage and broached their
suggestion, as delicately as possible:

וַיֹּאמְרוּ אִם־מָצָאנוּ חֵן בְּעֵינֶיךָ
יֻתַּן אֶת־הָאָרֶץ הַזֹּאת לַעֲבָדֶיךָ לַאֲחֻזָּה
אַל־תַּעֲבִרֵנוּ אֶת הַיַּרְדֵּן:

**And said they: If we have found grace in thy sight,
let this land be given to thy servants for a possession,
and bring us not over the Jordan.**

(32, 5)

Moses thereupon poured forth a torrent of rebuke and reproof on
them making comparisons with the backslidings of their parents,
recalling past history from which they had evidently learnt nothing.
Full of foreboding for the future and concern for the Divine mission
they had been charged with, he demanded, above all, an equal
sharing of responsibility with their brethren:

הַאַחֵיכֶם יָבֹאוּ לַמִּלְחָמָה וְאַתֶּם תֵּשְׁבוּ פֹה:

Shall your brethren go to war, and shall ye sit here?

(32, 6)

After the two and a half tribes had discussed matters among themselves, they present new proposals to Moses: "And they came near unto him and said". They made their well known offer to go up as *haluzim,* armed at the head of the camp, with their brethren into the land, in exchange for inheriting Transjordan, to be allotted immediately to their women and children. Moses accepted their proposals and repeated them in his own words with significant emendations. The proposals as worded by the two and a half tribes and Moses are placed here side by side for comparison and contrast:

The Tribes	*Moses*
And they came near and said unto him, we will build sheepfolds here for our cattle and cities for our little ones (32, 16).	And Moses said unto them if ye will do this thing, if ye will go armed *before the Lord* to war (32, 20).
But we ourselves will go ready armed before the children of Israel, until we have brought them to their place and our little ones shall dwell in the fenced cities because of the inhabitants of the land (32, 17).	And will go all of you armed over Jordan *before the Lord,* until he hath driven out his enemies before him (32, 21). And the land be subdued *before the Lord*: then afterwards ye shall return and be guiltless *before the Lord* and before Israel and this land shall be your possession *before the Lord* (32, 22).
We will not return unto our houses until the children of	But if ye will not do so, behold, ye have sinned *against the Lord*

382

Israel have inherited every man his inheritance (32, 18).

and be sure your sin will find you out (32, 23).

For we will not inherit with them on yonder side Jordan, or forward; because our inheritance is fallen to us on this side Jordan eastward (32, 19).

Build your cities for your littles ones and folds for your sheep; and do that which hath proceeded out of your mouth (32, 24).

The abyss separating their two outlooks stands revealed here. The two and a half tribes saw it in the light of a quid pro quo between themselves and the rest of Israel; they would contribute their share in helping to conquer the land and, in return, would be allotted the region they desired. Not so Moses. He stated everything in terms of responsibility to and dependence on God who alone drives out the enemy and apportions the land.

One more variation between Moses' and the tribes' declarations is noted by Rashi (echoing Midrashic sources) which again is characteristic of the spiritual chasm separating the two sides. They placed their concern for their cattle — material possessions — before concern for their little ones. Moses corrects them. Here are the actual words of Rashi:

> They evinced more concern for their own money than their sons and daughters, as they placed their cattle before their little ones. Said Moses to them, Do not so! Put first things first and secondary things second! "Build you first cities for your littles ones and afterwards, folds for your sheep".

Moses does not argue with them over this but quietly corrects them in the course of giving his resumé of their declaration.

Did they take the hint? Let us study their reply.

וַיֹּאמֶר בְּנֵי־גָד וּבְנֵי רְאוּבֵן אֶל־מֹשֶׁה לֵאמֹר
עֲבָדֶיךָ יַעֲשׂוּ כַּאֲשֶׁר אֲדֹנִי מְצַוֶּה:
טַפֵּנוּ נָשֵׁינוּ מִקְנֵנוּ וְכָל־בְּהֶמְתֵּנוּ יִהְיוּ־שָׁם בְּעָרֵי הַגִּלְעָד: וַעֲבָדֶיךָ יַעַבְרוּ

383

כָּל־חָלוּץ צָבָא
לִפְנֵי ה' לַמִּלְחָמָה כַּאֲשֶׁר אֲדֹנִי דֹּבֵר:

And the children of Gad . . . and Reuben spake unto Moses saying,

thy servants will do as my lord commandeth.

Our *little ones, our wives,* our flocks, and *all our cattle* shall be there in the cities of Gilead.

But thy servants will pass over, every man armed for war, *before the Lord,* to battle as my lord saith.

(32, 25—27)

Note their concluding refrain "as *my* lord saith", not as *we* originally stated. They agreed against their will to Moses' proposals.

A similar picture portraying them as the embodiment of worldliness and material greed is evoked by the Midrash:

ה ל כ ה: שלש מתנות נבראו בעולם, זכה באחת מהן, נטל חמדת כל העולם; זכה בחכמה — זכה בכל; זכה בגבורה — זכה בכל; זכה בעושר — זכה בכל. אימתי? בזמן שהן מתנות שמים ובאות בכוח התורה, אבל גבורתו ועשרו של בשר ודם אינו כלום. שכן שלמה אומר (קהלת ט): "שבתי וראיתי תחת השמש כי לא לקלים המרוץ ולא לגבורים המלחמה וגם לא לחכמים — לחם; וגם לא לנבונים — עושר; וגם לא לידעים — חן, כי עת ופגע יקרה את כולם". וכן ירמיהו אומר (ירמיה ט): "כה אמר ה': אל יתהלל חכם בחכמתו ואל יתהלל הגבור בגבורתו ואל יתהלל עשיר בעשרו כי אם בזאת יתהלל המתהלל: השכל וידוע אותי, כי אני ה' עושה חסד ומשפט וצדקה בארץ, כי 'באלהחפצתי, נאום ה' '." ומתנות אלו בזמן שאינן באין מן הקב"ה, סופן להפסק ממנו.

". . . Now the children of Reuben and Gad had much cattle". Three gifts were created in the world (wisdom, strength and wealth). If a man is privileged to possess one of them, he can attain as his own the most precious things in the whole world. If he is privileged to possess strength, he has attained everything; if he is privileged to possess wealth, he has attained everything. When does this apply? When they are gifts of Heaven and come by dint of the Torah, but the strength and wealth of mortals are nought, as is borne out by what Solomon says: "I returned, and saw under the sun that the race is not to the swift, nor the battle to the strong neither yet bread to the wise, nor yet riches to men of understanding, nor yet favour to men of skill; but time and chance happeneth to them all" (Ecclesiastes 9, 11).

Jeremiah, in the same strain says: "Thus saith the Lord: Let not the wise man glory in his wisdom, neither let the mighty man glory in his might, let not the rich man glory in his riches, but let him that glorieth glory in this, that he understandeth and knoweth Me" (Jeremiah 9, 22—23). These gifts when they do not emanate from the Holy One blessed be He, will ultimately fail a man.

שנו רבותינו: שני חכמים עמדו בעולם, אחד מישראל ואחד מאומות העולם: אחיתופל מישראל ובלעם מאומות העולם ושניהם נאבדו מן העולם. וכן שני גבורים עמדו בעולם, אחד מישראל ואחד מאומות העולם: שמשון מישראל וגלית מאומות העולם; ושניהם נאבדו מן העולם. וכן שני עשירים עמדו בעולם, אחד מישראל ואחד מאומות העולם: קרח מישראל והמן מאומות העולם ושניהם נאבדו מן העולם. למה? שלא היתה מתנתן מן הקב"ה אלא חוטפין אותן להן. וכן אתה מוצא בבני גד ובבני ראובן, שהיו עשירים והיה להם מקנה גדול וחבבו את ממונם וישבו להם חוץ מארץ ישראל, לפיכך גלו תחילה מכל השבטים, שנאמר (דברי הימים ה, כו): "ויער אלוקי ישראל את רוח פול מלך אשור ויגלה לראובני ולגדי ולחצי שבט מנשה ויביאם לחלח וחבור . . ." ומי גרם לכך? על שהפרישו עצמם מן אחיהם בשביל קנינם. מניין? ממה שכתוב בתורה (במדבר לב, א): "ומקנה רב היה לבני ראובן ולבני גד עצום מאד".

Our Rabbis taught: Two wise men arose in this world, one in Israel and one among the gentiles — Ahitophel in Israel and Balaam among the nations of the world — and both of them were destroyed from the world. Similarly two strong men arose in the world — Samson in Israel and Goliath among the Gentiles — and both of them were destroyed from the world. Likewise two rich men arose in the world, one in Israel and one among the gentiles — Korah in Israel and Haman among the gentiles, and both of them were destroyed from the world. Why? Because their gifts emanated not from the Holy One blessed be He, but they snatched it for themselves. Likewise in the case of the children of Reuben and Gad, you find it that they were rich, possessing large numbers of cattle, *but they loved their money and settled outside the land of Israel.* Consequently they were the first of all the tribes to go into exile as is borne out by the text, "And He carried them away, even the Reubenites and the Gadites and the half tribe of Menasseh (Chronicles 5, 26). What brought it on them? The fact that they separated themselves from their brethren because of their possessions. Whence can we infer this? From what is written in the Torah (Numbers 32, 1), "Now the children of Reuben had much cattle".

"ומקנה רב היה לבני ראובן ולבני גד" — זה שאמר הכתוב (תהלים עה): "כי לא ממוצא וממערב ולא ממדבר הרים, כי אלוקים שופט, זה ישפיל וזה ירים". מהו "כי לא

ממוצא וממערב?'' לא ממה שאדם יוצא ועמל בסחורה והולך מ מ ז ר ח ל מ ע ר ב
נעשה עשיר; אפילו פורש בספינות והולך ממזרח למערב וחוזר על המדבריות ועל
ההרים, אינו נעשה עשיר. מהו ''ולא ממדבר הרים?'' אמר ר' אבא מרומניה: ''כל
'הרים' שבמקרא — הרים הם, חוץ מזה שהוא — 'רוממות', שאין אדם מ ת ר ו מ ם
מן הדברים האלה. מה הקב''ה עושה? נוטל נכסים מזה ונותן לזה! שנאמר (תהלים
עה): 'כי אלוקים שופט, זה ישפיל וזה ירים.'' לכן נקרא שמם ' נ כ ס י ם ' שנכסים
מזה ונגלים לזה. ולמה נקרא שמם ' ז ו ז י ם ? ' שזזים מזה ונותנים לזה. 'ממון?' מה
אתה מונה? — אינו כלום!

Consider the Scriptural text: "For neither from the east, nor from the West, nor yet from the wilderness cometh *lifting up (harim)*. For God is judge. He putteth down one, and lifteth up another" (Psalms 75)? What is the implication of the expression "For neither from the *east (moẓah)* nor from the west?" It is not from the fact that a man *goes out (yoẓeh)* and works hard to do business, going from east to west, that he becomes rich. Nay, even if he sails away in ships and travels from east to west going backwards and forwards in the deserts and on the *mountains (harim)* he does not become rich. What is the significance of the expression "Nor yet from the wilderness *harim*?" R. Abba of Serungaya (other texts — Romania) explained that in all instances in Scripture *harim* denotes mountains, except in this one which signifies exaltation; the expression implying man is not exalted by them. For what does the Holy One blessed be He do? He takes away wealth from one and gives it to another; as it says: "God is judge, He putteth down one and lifteth up another".

Questions for Further Study

1. Compare the reply of the two tribes in verses 25—27 with their subsequent reply to Moses' words in verses 31—32. Can you detect a similar tendency to retreat from their original position and follow the line adopted by Moses, as we found to be the case above in verses 25—27?

2. Explain and elaborate on the theme of the aggadah cited above regarding the gifts of wisdom, strength and wealth shared by Ahitophel, Samson, Korah which they snatched but did not emanate from God.

386

3.   Compare Nahmanides' evaluation of the behaviour of the two tribes with what we have said above.

> The children of Gad were more valiant than Reuben as it is said "He (Gad) dwelleth as a lion and teareth the arm with the crown of the head!" (Deuteronomy 33, 20). They were therefore not afraid to dwell alone in the land of the side of the Jordan. Moses thought perhaps that they did not want to enter Eretz Israel because they were afraid and had no trust in God, after the manner of the spies who said they could not conquer the land, since its inhabitants were too strong. The two tribes thereupon reassured Moses that they would go armed across the Jordan with their brethren and be the first to do battle with the enemies of the Lord.

(a)   In what way does Nahmanides' attitude differ from that adopted in our lesson?

(b)   Which do you consider to be more faithful to the plain sense of the narrative?

(c)   Do you find in the incident involving the two tribes described in Joshua support for the attitude adopted by the Midrash?

THE LESSON OF AN ITINERARY

This sidra begins with a long listing of the forty two stages in the Israelites' wanderings in the wilderness. With the exception of a number of asides recalling some incident that befell the Israelites in the course of these journeyings, we are confronted by forty verses recording nothing more than place names.

What significance does the Torah which, on the evidence of the Psalmist in Psalms nineteen "enlightens the eyes", "rejoices the heart" and "restoreth the soul", find in this dry list of names that are undoubtedly an important object of study for archaeologists and geographers interested in identifying them? Surely it is the Psalmist's definition of the qualities of the Torah and not considerations of archaeological, historical geographical and scientific importance that has been accepted by its students in every generation. They sought in the Torah what it itself promised them: "For a good doctrine have I given you". What is the good doctrine embedded in this listing? As if to warn us not to dismiss lightly this list of place names which, apparently, contains nothing of significance, the Torah itself prefaces the chapter with the portentious words:

וַיִּכְתֹּב מֹשֶׁה אֶת־מוֹצָאֵיהֶם לְמַסְעֵיהֶם עַל־פִּי ה'

Moses wrote their goings forth, stage by stage, by the commandment of the Lord.

(33, 2)

Admittedly, Ibn Ezra wished to connect the phrase "by the

commandment of the Lord" with the words "stage by stage", as if to say that the stages of their journey were in accordance with a travel schedule planned and directed by the Almighty Himself. But Nahmanides objects quite rightly. He maintains that the passage implies that the recording of the stages of their wanderings in the Torah was itself a Divine command. It's reason was not revealed to us, because they encamped "by the word of the Lord" and journeyed "by the word of the Lord".

The question of what was the point of this record has preoccupied our commentators. We shall cite here several of their explanations, beginning with the father of Hebrew Bible commentators, Rashi who gives us two answers:

> Why are these stations recorded here? In order to publicise the loving acts of the Omnipresent; that although He had decreed to move them about, and make them wander in the wilderness, you should not think they wandered and moved about from one stage to another, the whole forty years and that they had no rest, for you see that there are here only fort two stages . . .

In other words, the stages of their wanderings were mapped out for us in the Torah in order to publicise the mercies of the Almighty and demonstrate how He remembers His compassion even in the midst of anger. Rashi further shows, citing the authority of R. Moses the Preacher how the forty two stopping points were distributed over the forty years. Fourteen of them were their stopping points in the first year of their wanderings and eight were visited the last year. It follows then that during the whole of the intervening thirty eight years they made only twenty journeys. They were thus enabled to rest and settle down for extended periods of time.

Nevertheless Rashi was not satisfied with this explanation alone and he added another, in the name of Rabbi Tanḥuma from the Midrash Tanḥuma:

> "These are the stages of the children of Israel" — A parable. To what may it be compared? To a king whose son was ill and whom he took to a distant

place to cure. As soon as they returned home the father began to enumerate all the stages, saying to him, Here we slept, here we caught cold, here you had a headache. So the Holy One blessed be He said to him: Moses! Enumerate all the places where they provoked Me to anger. For this reason it is written: "These are the stages of the children of Israel".

Rashi's supercommentary *Be'er Yizhak* aptly compares Rashi's observations with other contexts in the Torah where similar listings are to be found, in the census taken of the people in Numbers. In those cases, too, the numerical information would seem to be of statistical, historical or geographical interest only. What spiritual lesson can we learn from them? Here are the words of the *Be'er Yizhak*:

How aptly did R. Tanhuma expound it, since most of what is recorded in the Torah is concerned with Israel, the commandments and admonitions directed at them, the story of what befell them, the retribution for their sins and reward for their obedience. He similarly expounded the reason for the counting of the children of Israel on each occasion to make known how beloved they were to the Omnipresent. God commanded a census be taken of them because they suffered decimation in the plague, the Almighty thus indirectly apprising us of how deeply the death of even one member of Israel distressed Him, as it were. This was the lesson to be learnt from the counting, to know how many had survived, like a father consoling himself after the loss of his children with those who still survived and yearning for them.

A similar reason underlay the recording of the stages of Israel's journeyings. Since the Holy One blessed be He brought them out of Egypt till they arrived at the gates of the land of promise, much had befallen them, both favourable and unfavourable. This short listing of the stages of their wanderings was designed as reading material for them after they settled down in their homeland. Each stage that they noted in their reading would enable them to recall what had befallen them, at that place. They would accordingly take to heart the kindness shown to them by the Omnipresent and the sufferings they endured for their disobedience so that, in future, they would act rightly and not sin.

This chapter draws our attention to the love of the Holy One blessed be He for His people. After their return to their homeland the faithful Father imparted to them a record in everlasting memory of what had befallen them on the way enabling them to appreciate the security they had achieved and their true happiness — the love and fear of the Lord.

The first chapter of our sidra thus contains the message of historical continuity, evokes the memory of the sufferings attending the achievement of our goal, making us look back to the history of our ancestors down the ages.

Maimonides gives a different explanation of the significance of this chapter in his *Guide for the Perplexed* in dealing with the general problem of "those accounts in the Torah which many think serve no purpose":

> With reference to such passage, I will first state a general principle and then proceed to discuss them separately . . . Every narrative in the Torah serves a certain purpose in connection with religious teaching. It either helps to establish a principle of faith, or to regulate our actions, and to prevent wrong and injustice among men . . .
>
> When we therefore come across narratives in the Torah which have no connection with any of the commandments, we are inclined to think that they are entirely superfluous, or too lengthy, or repetitious; but this is only because we do not see the particular details which make those narratives noteworthy. Of this kind is the enumeration of the stations of the Israelites in the wilderness. At first sight, it appears to be entirely useless. To remove such a misconception the Torah states: "And Moses wrote their goings forth, stage by stage, by the commandment of the Lord". It was indeed most necessary that these should be recorded. For miracles are only convincing to those who witnessed them; coming generations, who know them only at second hand may consider them as figments of the imagination . . . Now the greatest of all miracles in the Torah is the stay of the Israelites in the wilderness for forty years with a daily supply of manna. This wilderness as described in the Torah consisted of places "wherein were fiery serpents and scorpions and drought, where there was no water"; places very remote from cultivated land and naturally not adapted for the habitation of man. "It is no place of seed, or of figs, or of vines, or of pomegranates, neither is there any water to drink" (Num. 20, 5); "A land no man passed through and where no man dwelt" (Jer. 2, 6). In reference to the stay of the Israelites in the wilderness the Torah relates: "Ye have not eaten bread, neither have ye drunk wine or strong drink" (Deut. 29, 5). All these phenomena were miraculous and public. But God knew that in future people might doubt the

authenticity of these miracles, as they doubt the accuracy of other narratives; they might think that the Israelites stayed in the wilderness in a place not far from inhabited land, where it was possible for man to live in the ordinary way; that it was like those deserts in which Arabs live at present; or that they dwelt in such places in which they could plow, sow and reap or live on some vegetable that was growing there; or that manna always came down in those places as an ordinary natural product; or that there were wells of water in those places. In order to remove all these doubts, and to establish firmly the accuracy of the account of these miracles, the Torah enumerates all the stations, so that coming generations may see them, and learn the greatness of the miracle which enabled human beings to live in these places forty years.

Similarly, the words: "At the commandment of the Lord they journeyed and at the commandment of the Lord they pitched" would suffice as a simple statement of the facts; and the reader might at first sight consider as unnecessary additions all the details which follow, viz., "and when the cloud tarried long . . . and so it was when the cloud was a few days . . . or whether it were two days . . .". But I will show you the reason why all these details were added. For they serve to confirm the account and to contradict the opinion of the nations, both of ancient and modern times, that the Israelites lost their way and did not know where to go; that "they were entangled in the land" (Ex. 14, 3); wherefore the Arabs unto this day call that desert *Al-tih,* "the desert of going astray", imagining that the Israelites blundered around and did not know the way. The Torah therefore clearly states and emphatically declares that it was by God's command that the journeyings were irregular, that the Israelites returned to the same places several times, and that the duration of the stay was different in each station; whilst the stay in one place lasted for eighteen years, in another place, it lasted one day and in another one night. There was no blundering. The journey was regulated by "the rising of the pillar of cloud" (Num. 9, 17). Therefore all these details are given. The Torah clearly states that the route was near, known and in good condition; I mean the way from Horeb, to which they came intentionally, according to the command of God, "Ye shall serve God upon this mountain" (Ex. 3, 12), to Kadesh Barnea, the beginning of inhabited land, as the Torah states, "Behold we are now in Kedesh, a city in the uttermot part of the border" (Num. 20, 16). That way was a journey of eleven days; cf.: "Eleven days journey from Horeb, by the way of mount Seir, unto Kadesh Barnea" (Deut. 1, 2). They could not possibly have got lost; their zigzagging and stopping were deliberate for which the Torah states the real cause.

(Guide 3, 50)

But Maimonides was not satisfied with this explanation and the two reasons he had given outlining the necessity of all this detail and the religious message the passages contained. He laid down a general rule for all such passages that appear superfluous dry, technical and trivial. He concludes:

> In like manner there is good reason for every passage the object of which we cannot see. We must always apply the words of our Sages: "It is not a vain thing for you" (Deut. 32, 47), and if it seem vain, it is your fault.
>
> (T. Yerushalmi Peah 1, 1)

In other words, the lack of thought content, the dearth of a religious message must be traced to the incapacity of the student in failing to detect the eternal inner significance underlying the apparent dry, technical, historical details. "If it seem a vain thing — it is your fault".

Sforno however propounds another solution, drawing a somewhat different lesson from the place names:

> "These are the stages . . .". The Lord blessed be He desired that the stages of the Israelites' journeyings be written down to make known their merit in their going after Him in a wilderness, in a land that was not sown so that they eventually deserved to enter the land. "And Moses wrote" — he wrote down their destination and place of departure. For sometimes the place for which they were headed was evil and the place of departure good. "And these are their stages, according to their goings forth".
>
> Sometimes the reverse happened. He wrote down too the details of their journeyings because it involved leaving for a new destination without any previous notice, which was very trying. Despite all this, they kept to the schedule. On each occasion, it is recorded that "they journeyed" from a particular place and "encamped" at a particular place indicating that both the journeying and the encamping were trying experiences.

In other words, according to Sforno the Torah shows us both sides of the coin. We have been shown an Israel composed of rebels and grumblers, having degenerated from the lofty spiritual plane of their religious experience at mount Sinai, having become slaves to their selfish passions, ungrateful and quarrelsome, hankering after the fleshpots, the onions and garlic of Egypt. Now the Torah changes its note and shows us the other side of the picture, Israel loyal to their trust, following their God through the wilderness in a land that was not sown (Jer. 2). They followed Him in spite of all the odds, through the wilderness of Sinai, the wilderness of Etham, the wilderness of Paran and the wilderness of Zin as well as through the wilderness of exile amongst the nations down the ages. That was also a place of fiery serpents and scorpions and drought where there was no water, where our continued existence would have been impossible, were it not for the grace of God which ceased not, and in virtue of which we have come thus far.

עַל פִּי ה' יַחֲנוּ וְעַל פִּי ה' יִסָּעוּ

By the word of the Lord they encamped and by the word of the Lord they journeyed.

(9, 20)

Question for Further Study

Cf. the following two verses: "And they journeyed from Rameses in the first month, on the fifteenth day of the first month" (Num. 33, 3): "And the children of Israel journeyed from Rameses and they pitched in Succoth" (ibid. 5). What is the reason for the repetition? In this connection cf.: Num. 14, 14: "And they will say to the inhabitants of the land"; and ibid. 15: "Then the nations which have heard . . . *will say*". Cf. also Gen. 28, 5: "And Isaac sent forth Jacob and he went to Padan Aram", and ibid. 10: "And Jacob went forth from Beersheba and went to Haran". Vide Rashi ad loc.

THE COMMANDMENT TO SETTLE (IN) ERETZ ISRAEL

וַיְדַבֵּר ה' אֶל־מֹשֶׁה בְּעַרְבֹת מוֹאָב עַל־יַרְדֵּן יְרֵחוֹ לֵאמֹר:
דַּבֵּר אֶל־בְּנֵי יִשְׂרָאֵל וְאָמַרְתָּ אֲלֵהֶם
כִּי אַתֶּם עֹבְרִים אֶת־הַיַּרְדֵּן אֶל־אֶרֶץ כְּנָעַן:
וְהוֹרַשְׁתֶּם אֶת־כָּל־יֹשְׁבֵי הָאָרֶץ מִפְּנֵיכֶם
וְאִבַּדְתֶּם אֵת כָּל־מַשְׂכִּיֹתָם
וְאֵת כָּל־צַלְמֵי מַסֵּכֹתָם
תְּאַבֵּדוּ וְאֵת כָּל־בָּמוֹתָם תַּשְׁמִידוּ:
וְהוֹרַשְׁתֶּם אֶת הָאָרֶץ
וִישַׁבְתֶּם בָּהּ
כִּי לָכֶם נָתַתִּי אֶת־הָאָרֶץ לָרֶשֶׁת אֹתָהּ:

And the Lord spoke unto Moses in the plains of Moab by the
Jordan at Jericho, saying:

Speak unto the children of Israel, and say unto them:
When ye pass over the Jordan into the land of Canaan,

Then ye shall drive out all the inhabitants of the land from
before you,
and destroy all their figured stones,
and destroy all their molten images,
and demolish all their high places.

And ye shall drive out the inhabitants of the land,
and dwell therein;
for unto you have I given the land to possess it.

(33, 50—53)

The passage beginning with the phrase: "When ye pass over the Jordan . . ." belongs to a class of Biblical statements which occurs quite frequently elsewhere, particularly, in the book of Deuteronomy. They are all distinguished by making the observance of the precept enunciated therein dependent on the children of Israel entering the Holy Land. Thus we have: "When thou art come unto the land which the Lord thy God giveth thee . . ." (Deuteronomy 17, 14; 26, 1); "And it shall come to pass, when the Lord thy God shall bring thee into the land whither thou goest to possess it" (ibid. 11, 29). In Leviticus too (19, 23) we have: "And when ye shall come into the land".

In cases such as these it is not always clear where the conditional clause "when ye come . . ." ends, and where the main clause, setting forth the commandment which applies on entering the land, begins. The reason for this is a grammatical ambiguity peculiar to the Hebrew language in the use of the *vav* joining the clauses together. It may mark merely a continuation of the conditional clause: "If or when this happens *and* also this, then . . ." or the beginning of the main or operational clause implying: "If or when this happens, *then* observe such and such a command". In our context it will become clear, after closer study, that the conditional clause finishes with verse 51 (with the words: "to the land of Canaan") and the command which the Israelites are called upon to observe begins with the phrase: "then ye shall drive out all the inhabitants of the land from before you".

Twice in the verses with which we introduced the chapter the expression: *ve-horashtem* "And thou shalt possess them" occurs. From a superficial glance, it would seem that verse 53 is merely a repetition of verse 52. But as several commentators have pointed out this is not so. In 52 it is stated: "Thou shalt dispossess the inhabitants of the land". Whereas in 53, it is stated: "Ye shall possess[1] the land and dwell therein". Rashi takes the second *ve-horashtem* to imply a precondition for their subsequent settlement rather than an outright command:

והורשתם את הארץ: והורשתם אותה מיושביה — אז ״וישבת בה״, להתקיים בה, ואם
לא — לא תוכלו להתקיים בה.

"Ye shall possess the land" — take possession of it from its inhabitants, then "ye may dwell therein" — safely exist there. Otherwise ye will not be able to exist there.

The two verses do not then duplicate each other, repeating the order to inherit or occupy the land by dispossessing the inhabitants. The second verse adds the warning that *if* the Israelites do not dispossess the inhabitants first, they will never succeed in maintaining themselves in the country safely. Naḥmanides interprets the verse differently:

> In my opinion, this constitutes a positive command of the Torah wherein He commanded them to settle in the land, and inherit it; for He gave it them; and they should not reject the heritage of the Lord! Should it enter their mind, for instance, to go and conquer the land of Shinar (Babylon) or Assyria or any other country and settle therein, then they would have transgressed a commandment of the Lord . . .

Ve-horashtem does not imply, therefore, "dispossession" of the indigent inhabitants, as Rashi explains, but rather the "inheritance" of one's patrimony. The emphasis is not on securing themselves in the country but rather on the taking up of the Divinely granted heritage; "For He hath given it to them, that they should not reject the heritage of the Lord". Just the same as a Jew is not morally free to do what he likes with his own life but has a duty to preserve it, so he cannot live where he likes. But the place where he should spend his Divinely granted gift of life is prescribed for him. Should a Jew harbour any imperialistic designs and choose to conquer, shall we say, "Shinar" or "Assyria" and not the Land promised and destined for his people he is violating the Divine will.

Naḥmanides outlines the duty of settling Eretz Israel at greater length in his strictures on Maimonides' *Sefer Ha-miẓvot* (Book of Divine Precepts) which are devoted to explaining the points on which he differs from the latter in his method of numbering the 613 precepts of Judaism. In this case, Naḥmanides takes Maimonides to task for his not including the duty to settle Erez Israel as a separate *miẓvah*. Maimonides dwells at length in many parts of his works on the paramount and indispensable importance of Eretz Yisrael, in the perspective of Judaism, but does not specify its settlement as one of the 613 precepts referred to in the Torah.

But here are the words of Naḥmanides:

> We have been commanded in the Torah to take possession of the land which the Lord, Blessed be He granted to our forefathers, Abraham, Isaac and Jacob and not to leave it in the hands of others or allow it to remain desolate, as it is stated, "Thou shalt possess the land and dwell therein, for to you have I given the land and ye shall inherit the land which I swore to your fathers". The exact boundaries of the territory covered by this religious obligation are delineated for us in the Torah (Deuteronomy 1, 7). A proof that this is a special *miẓvah* can be adduced from the Almighty's order to the spies, "Go up and *possess it, as the Lord hath spoken* to you, fear not and be not dismayed" (ibid. 1, 21) ... And when they refused to go up, it is written, "And you rebelled against the word of the Lord . . ." This indicates that we are dealing with a specific precept and not merely a promise.
>
> I consider that the hyperbolic statements of our Sages regarding the greatness of the *miẓvah* of residing in the Holy Land proceeded from their concern to carry out this explicit command of the Torah. They stated, for instance, that he who leaves Eretz Yisrael for the diaspora shall be in thine eyes as him that committed idolatry as it is written: "For they have driven me out this day from abiding in the inheritance of the Lord, saying: Go, serve other gods" (1 Samuel 26, 19).
>
> The *miẓvah* applies for all time, even during the exile, as is evident from many places in the Talmud. Compare the Sifrei: "It happened that Rabbi Judah ben Batira and R. Matya ben Ḥarash and R. Ḥanina the nephew of R. Joshua and R. Yoḥanan were journeying to the diaspora. On reaching Palatium (a place outside Eretz Israel) they recalled Eretz Israel and their eyes filled with tears and they rent their garments and applied to themselves the following verse: "Thou shalt possess them and dwell in their land", whereupon they retraced their steps and went back home, saying: Residence in Eretz Israel is equal in weight to all the *miẓvot* in the Torah".

We may appreciate the force of the last mentioned rabbinic statement as well as the other sentiments, if we bear in mind that there can be no complete observance, in all spheres of life, of the precepts of the Torah, except in Eretz Israel. That is why King David is held to have implied that his expulsion from the Holy Land by Saul was tantamount to telling him to go and worship idols:

תנו רבנן: לעולם ידור אדם בארץ ישראל, אפילו בעיר שרובה עובדי כוכבים ואל ידור
בחוץ לארץ אפילו בעיר שרובה ישראל, שכל הדר בארץ ישראל דומה כמי שיש לו
אלוה, וכל הדר בחוץ לארץ דומה כמי שאין אלוה, שנאמר (ויקרא כה, לח): ''לתת לכם
את ארץ כנען להיות לכם לאלוהים''. וכל שאינו דר בארץ ישראל אין לו אלוה?! אלא
לומר לך: כל הדר בחוץ לארץ כ א י ל ו עובד עבודת כוכבים. וכן בדוד הוא אומר
(שמ''א כו, יט): ''כי גרשוני היום מהסתפח בנחלת ה' לאמר: לך עבוד אלוהים
אחרים''. וכי מי אמר לו לדוד: לך עבוד אלוהים אחרים? אלא לומר לך: כל הדר בחוץ
לארץ כ א י ל ו עובד עבודת כוכבים.

At all times should a man reside in Eretz Israel, even in a city inhabited mostly by heathens. Let him not reside outside the Land, even in a city mostly inhabited by Jews. Since whoever resides in Eretz Israel is like to him who has a god, whilst whoever resides outside it is like him who has no god, as it is stated (Leviticus 25, 38): "To give you the land of Canaan, to be your God."Do you mean to say that whoever does not reside in the land of Israel has no god?! But what is meant is — Whoever resides outside the land is *as if* he worships idols. David said so too: "For they have driven me out this day from abiding in the inheritance of the Lord (i.e. in Erez Israel, from where he fled from the anger of Saul), saying, Go, serve other gods" (1 Samuel 26, 19). But whoever told David to go serve other gods? But this teaches you that whoever resides outside the Land of Israel is as if he served idols.

(Ketubot 110b)

In other words, the Torah cannot be observed in its entirety except in a society wholly governed by its precepts and not in an alien framework ruled by other ideals. Admittedly there are personal religious obligations that can be observed anywhere, even by a Jewish Robinson Crusoe on his desert isle, but the Torah, as a whole, implies a complete social order, a judiciary, national, economic and political life. That can only be achieved in the Holy Land and not outside it.

The precept enjoining us to occupy Eretz Israel and make it our permanent home: "Ye shall possess the land and dwell therein", is motivated by one good reason —

כִּי לָכֶם נָתַתִּי אֶת־הָאָרֶץ לָרֶשֶׁת אֹתָהּ:

For unto you have I given the land to possess it.

(33, 53)

It is the above assumption which Rashi utilises in his celebrated first comment to the Pentateuch, in explaining why it begins with the story of Genesis:

שאם יאמרו אומות העולם: לסטים אתם שכבשתם ארצות שבעה גויים, הם אומרים להם: כל הארץ של הקב״ה היא, הוא בראה ונתנה לאשר ישר בעיניו, ברצונו נתנה להם (לשבעת הגויים) וברצונו נטלה מהם ונתנה לנו.

Should the nations of the world say: Ye are robbers in occupying the land belonging to the seven nations, Israel replies: The whole world belongs to the Holy One blessed be He; He created it and giveth it to whomsoever He desireth. In accordance with His will He gave it to them (the seven nations), originally, and in accordance with His will He took it from them and gave it to us.

This was the sole reason for our title to the Land. The Almighty ordered us to take possession of it. In the whole book of Genesis no mention is made of the good properties of the land, that it flowed with milk or honey. On the contrary, we are told, on many occasions, that there was a famine in the land. The Patriarchs' loyalty to it was tested. Abraham returned to it after leaving it in time of famine and Isaac was not permitted to forsake it, even in time of famine. The reason that is given is simply:

כִּי־לְךָ וּלְזַרְעֲךָ אֶתֵּן אֶת־כָּל־הָאֲרָצֹת הָאֵל

For unto thee, and unto thy seed, I will give all these lands.

(Genesis 26, 3)

It is the Almighty who determines the boundaries of nations. He alloted Israel its place in the world just the same as He did for other peoples:

הֲלוֹא אֶת־יִשְׂרָאֵל הֶעֱלֵיתִי מֵאֶרֶץ מִצְרַיִם
וּפְלִשְׁתִּיִּים מִכַּפְתּוֹר
וַאֲרָם מִקִּיר

Have not I brought up Israel out of the land of Egypt,
And the Philistines from Caphtor,
And Aram from Kir?

(Amos 9, 7)

What then is the difference between Israel's relationship to its homeland and that of other nations to theirs? The difference is just this. Israel is aware that this land was granted it by the Almighty. This is not just a matter of history but involves for Israel a moral obligation, the responsibility to observe a particular way of life in that land. According to Naḥmanides, the Israelites were specifically commanded to take possession of Ereẓ Israel and live there to fulfil their religious mission.

This perhaps is the implication of that strange statement in the Midrash regarding the Almighty's words to Jacob, ordering the Patriarch to return to his homeland, after twenty years of exile and servitude in Laban's house:

"שוב אל ארץ אבותיך ולמולדתך ואהיה עמך" — אביך מצפה לך, אמך מצפה לך —
אני בעצמי מצפה לך.

"Return unto the land of thy fathers, and to thy kindred; and I will be with thee" (Genesis 31, 3) — Your father is waiting for you, your mother is waiting for you — *I Myself am waiting for you.*

(Bereshit Rabbah 77)

401

Naḥmanides also emphasises that just as it is obligatory to wrest the land from the peoples who defiled it with their evil deeds and not to emigrate therefrom, so it is equally important not to leave the land desolate.

> We should not leave it in the hands of others or allow it to remain desolate.

This task of conquering and taming the desert on God's earth had already been implied in the first command given to man "Fill the earth and conquer it" (Genesis 1, 22) on which Naḥmanides comments:

> He granted man power and government in the land to do as he wished ... to build, uproot, plant and mine metal from its hills.

The picture is however not complete without referring to its other side. Just as the former inhabitants of the land had been expelled for their misdeeds so would "God's own country"[2] vomit the Israelites, should they contaminate it with their practices. The Divine gift of the Land was not unconditional but, as stated at the end of our sidra (35, 33—34):

וְלֹא תַחֲנִיפוּ אֶת הָאָרֶץ אֲשֶׁר אַתֶּם בָּהּ . . .

וְלֹא תְטַמֵּא אֶת הָאָרֶץ אֲשֶׁר אַתֶּם יֹשְׁבִים בָּהּ

אֲשֶׁר אֲנִי שֹׁכֵן בְּתוֹכָהּ

כִּי אֲנִי ה' שֹׁכֵן בְּתוֹךְ בְּנֵי יִשְׂרָאֵל

So shall ye not pollute the land wherein ye are, defile not therefore the land which ye shall inhabit, wherein I dwell; for *I, the Lord dwell among the children of Israel.*

Questions for Further Study

1. What is the syntactical structure of verse 53 according to the explanation of Rashi and Naḥmanides cited above?

2. What prompted Rashi to add at the end his comment: "Otherwise, you will not be able to exist there", though there is no hint in the text for his statement?

3. Then shall those that remain be as thorns in your eyes, and as pricks in your sides.

(Numbers 33, 55)

On this phrase "then shall those that remain", Rashi adds the words, "they shall be to your hurt".[3] What prompted Rashi to add this comment? What do they add to the meaning of the text?

NOTES

[1] The Authorised Version has "drive out the inhabitants" in both cases.

[2] For a study of Naḥmanides' (Ramban) approach to Eretz Israel, see "The Centrality of Eretz Israel in Naḥmanides" by Aryeh Newman, *Tradition* 10, 1, 1968 (T).

[3] יהיו לכם לרעה.

THE CONSEQUENCES OF FOLLOWING VANITY
(Haftarah, Jeremiah 2, 4—28)

Our Haftarah[1] opens with a rhetorical question in which reproof, regret and pain are interfused:

כֹּה אָמַר ה׳
מַה־מָּצְאוּ אֲבוֹתֵיכֶם
בִּי עָוֶל כִּי רָחֲקוּ מֵעָלָי
וַיֵּלְכוּ אַחֲרֵי הַהֶבֶל וַיֶּהְבָּלוּ׃

Thus saith the Lord:
What iniquity did your fathers find in Me, that they became estranged from Me,
and have walked after things of nought and are become nought?

(Jeremiah 2, 5)

What is the implication of the Hebrew *'avel* (here rendered "unrighteousness")? It evidently bears the same meaning as it does in Deuteronomy 32,4 in the Song of Moses "A God of faithfulness and without *'avel* ("iniquity")" where it is obviously the opposite of faithfulness. Our text would thus read: Have I then violated My trust with your ancestors that they have gone far from Me? Note that the text does not speak of being far away but of having *gone* far away, of someone who was once near, close to God having become divorced from Him. The regret is infinitely greater than when the person was never close. The Talmud explains it through the medium of a parable:

404

R. Shimon b. Yoḥai stated: We do not say, Examine the camel, examine the swine! (for a sacrifice to see whether it is free from blemish, since it is disqualified from the beginning. Strictly speaking it cannot be declared unfit since it never was fit.) But we say, Examine the lamb! (for a sacrifice) perhaps it has become blemished and unfit. (A man who was originally fit can be declared unfit). To whom does such a principle refer? To a scholar who divorced himself from the Torah. R. Judah b. Lakish stated to any scholar who has divorced himself from the Torah apply the texts (Proverbs 27, 8): "Like a bird that wandereth from her nest so is a man that wandereth from his place", and (Jer. 2, 5): "What unrighteousness have your fathers found in Me that they are gone far from Me?"

Malbim's explanation lends greater force to the Divine regret:

One may forsake the object of affection either because (1) he has found some defect, moral or otherwise in it — regarding this text states: "What unrighteousness have your fathers found in Me" or (2) because the new object of affections is superior in some way; regarding this the text observes, that even this is not the case: "They have walked after things of nought and it availed them nought".

Malbim thus takes the last clause of the text to imply that they went after inferior not superior things and no profit or benefit accrued to them from this shift in their affections and behaviour. Other commentators including the Targum Jonathan and Abravanel take this text to mean simply that they followed vanity and they became as nought — becoming as empty and vain as the objects of their worship and affections. Which is then the correct meaning?

We find the same phrase in 2 Kings 17, 10—16 where the history, sin and retribution of the ten tribes are summarised:

וַיַּצִּבוּ לָהֶם מַצֵּבוֹת וַאֲשֵׁרִים עַל כָּל־גִּבְעָה גְבֹהָה . . . וַיְעַד ה'
בְּיִשְׂרָאֵל . . . בְּיַד כָּל נְבִיאֵי . . . לֵאמֹר שֻׁבוּ מִדַּרְכֵיכֶם הָרָעִים . . . וְלֹא
שָׁמְעוּ וַיַּקְשׁוּ אֶת־עָרְפָּם כְּעֹרֶף אֲבוֹתָם . . . וַיִּמְאֲסוּ אֶת־חֻקָּיו וְאֶת־
בְּרִיתוֹ . . . וְאֶת עֵדוֹתָיו . . . וַיֵּלְכוּ אַחֲרֵי הַהֶבֶל וַיֶּהְבָּלוּ
וְאַחֲרֵי הַגּוֹיִם אֲשֶׁר סְבִיבֹתָם
אֲשֶׁר צִוָּה ה' אֹתָם לְבִלְתִּי עֲשׂוֹת כָּהֶם: וַיַּעַזְבוּ אֶת־כָּל־מִצְוֹת ה' . . .

405

**And they set them up pillars and Asherim upon every high
hill ...
Yet the Lord had forewarned Israel by the hand of every
prophet ... saying, Return from your evil ways ...
But they would not hear but stiffened their neck, like to the
neck of their fathers.**

**They rejected His statutes and His covenant ... and His
testimony,**
they went after things of nought and became nought
**and after the nations that were round about them,
Concerning whom the Lord had charged them that they
should not emulate them;
And they forsook all the commandments of the Lord ...**

From the context which is a listing of all the sins the Israelites
committed it is clear that this phrase is not referring to any external
consequence of their going after nought, or to what they achieved or
failed to achieve by their actions, but is describing their very actions.
Of course it is possible that this same phrase may have a different
implication in another context. Let us revert to our passage: "What
unrighteousness have your fathers found in Me that they are gone far
from Me and have walked after things of nought and are become
nought?" The subsequent three verses are merely a detailed
elaboration of the different sections of this verse. Corresponding to
"what unrighteousness have your fathers found in Me" we have "and
they did not say, Where is the Lord ...". Corresponding to "that
they are gone far from Me" we have: "But when ye entered ye defiled
My land and made My heritage an abomination and the rulers
transgressed against Me". Corresponding to "and they went after
things of nought and are become nought" we have: "The prophets
also prophesied by *Baal and walked after things that do not profit*".

From the foregoing correspondence the text evidently speaks of
the unprofitableness of their new course of action as Malbim

observed. Accordingly, our text is in direct contrast to the preceding passage which formed the first paragraph of the chapter which is not included in this week's Haftara.[2]

There Israel "went after" their God — "how thou wentest after Me in the wilderness"; but now they had gone far away from him; not only that, but had even "walked after things of nought". There the result of their loyalty was Divine guardianship: "All that devour him shall be held guilty". Here the result of their disloyalty: a lack of all benefit and no further protection "and walked after things that do not profit". Later the text relates that they would become a prey at which the young lions would roar and their land would be made desolate.

What were then the kindnesses of God which they had ignored and to which they had preferred vanities? The text specifies "that brought us up from the land of Egypt: that led us through the wilderness", as if to say the deliverance from Egypt by itself would have been sufficient but, in actuality, it constituted but the first of a long list of His kindnesses. Subsequently the grim realities of that trek in the wilderness are pictured for us:

בְּאֶרֶץ עֲרָבָה וְשׁוּחָה
בְּאֶרֶץ צִיָּה וְצַלְמָוֶת
בְּאֶרֶץ לֹא־עָבַר בָּהּ אִישׁ וְלֹא־יָשַׁב אָדָם שָׁם:

Through a land of deserts and pits,
Through a land of drought and of the shadow of death,
Through a land that no man passed through and where no man dwelt.

(2, 6)

'*Arava* — "desert" implies arid land distinguished for lack of vegetation paralleling the phrase "land that was not sown" at the beginning of the chapter, and the opposite of *eretz ha-karmel* "a land of fruitful fields" in the next verse. "Pits" hamper the going, since

407

there is no proper highway but pits and ditches. "Drought" aggravates the physical suffering since the worst hardship is thirst. The same idea was expressed by the Israelites in their grumblings (Num. 20, 5):

לְהָבִיא אֹתָנוּ אֶל־הַמָּקוֹם הָרָע הַזֶּה
לֹא מְקוֹם זֶרַע וּתְאֵנָה וְגֶפֶן וְרִמּוֹן וּמַיִם אַיִן לִשְׁתּוֹת:

To bring us to this evil place, not a place of seed or fig, vine or pomegranate and where there is no water to drink.

"Shadow of death" — refers to their mental hardship. Surely there is no place like the desert for its light, the glare and blackness? But the implication emerges in the next clause — loneliness. "In a land that no man passed through" — where there is no hope of meeting anyone and no sign even of wayfarer. "And where no man dwelt" — where there in no hope of coming upon a place of habitation — complete isolation from human beings.

In all these situations it was the Lord who led you and guarded you. But besides guarding you He bestowed on you His bounty:

וָאָבִיא אֶתְכֶם אֶל־אֶרֶץ הַכַּרְמֶל לֶאֱכֹל פִּרְיָהּ וְטוּבָהּ

And I brought you to a land of fruitful fields to eat the fruit thereof and the good thereof.

(2, 7)

We must keep our eyes open to every detail of the prophet's words. We may note how the word *erez* — "land" keeps recurring. All the kindnesses of the Almighty are inextricably interwoven with the Land: "Who brought us up from the *land* of Egypt, who led us through a desert *land,* a *land* of drought, in a *land* where no man passed through, and I shall bring you to a fruitful *land*".

The sins of Israel too are expressed correspondingly with reference to the land: "You came and defiled My *land*".

Note too the change in the person. The prophet opened with a rhetorical question regarding previous generations: "What unrighteousness did *your fathers* find in Me" i.e. they, your fathers did not say, did not remember who brought *them* out of Egypt. On the other hand, when the prophet began to speak of the qualities of the Land he changed his form of address. He did not continue: "Who brought *us*" (in continuation of "who led us" etc.) and, in shifting to the first person did not express himself "I brought them to a fruitful land" but addressed himself directly to his own generation, to his listeners:

וָאָבִיא אֶתְכֶם אֶל־אֶרֶץ הַכַּרְמֶל לֶאֱכֹל פִּרְיָהּ וְטוּבָהּ

And I brought *you* to a land of fruitful fields to eat the fruit thereof and the good thereof.

(2, 7)

With respect to the entry in the Land, you, the people who dwell therein every day and hour of your lives, you should be sensible of the kindnesses of the Lord who brought you to this land. If out of an abundance of goodness in a good land you forgot the evils, the suffering of Egypt, the kindness of God in the wilderness, how could you forget the kindness of the Almighty to you every day in the land whose fruit you eat and whose bounty you enjoy daily? In spite of all this you did not say: "Where is the Lord . . .".

What is the meaning of this question "Where is the Lord", for the not asking of which the prophet condemned them? — It is presumably an expression of desire to be near to God, to look for His providence and see in everything the work of His hands. This was the question they did not ask. Abravanel finds the wording difficult. How can such an anthropomorphic phrase as "where is" be used of God? Surely He cannot be located in one particular place. Such a question

409

is suitable with respect to a finite physical entity, but not to the infinite and Omnipresent. The prophet should rather have condemned them for not saying: "Let us go and run to know the Lord!" Abravanel explains that the text implies that they should have searched for God who had hidden His face from them. They should have probed for the reason for this withdrawal of Divine favour, recognized His providence everywhere and longed for His presence. But they did not ask this question. It was this oblivion, this forgetting of God reflected in the absence of this question, "Where is the Lord" for which the prophet indicted Israel and their leaders as well:

הַכֹּהֲנִים לֹא אָמְרוּ אַיֵּה ה׳
וְתֹפְשֵׂי הַתּוֹרָה לֹא יְדָעוּנִי
וְהָרֹעִים פָּשְׁעוּ בִי
וְהַנְּבִיאִים נִבְּאוּ בַבַּעַל
וְאַחֲרֵי לֹא יוֹעִילוּ הָלָכוּ:

The priests said not, Where is the Lord?
And they that handle the Law knew Me not,
And the rulers transgressed against Me;
The prophets also prophesied by Baal
And walked after things that do not profit.

(2, 8)

They asked not regarding the presence of God and "knew" Him not.

Since we have tried to understand the above verses, perhaps we can now decide which explanation of the opening passage of our *Studies* is to be preferred. Does not this whole picture of a people and its priests, both great and small forgetting the Divine bounty indicate that they themselves have become as nought? The correspondence between their action and its consequence is deliberate: they walked after nought and became as nought.

On the other hand, this does not rule out the other interpretation. The prophet presumably charged his words with two meanings just as he did in the immediately previous passage, where he speaks of Israel's loyal following after God in the wilderness. There it states that Israel is "holy to the Lord", in two senses — holy in its conduct and being, and therefore like a hallowed portion may not be molested or misused ("all that devour him shall be held guilty"). Similarly when they proved disloyal and went after vanity and nought, it is stated *va-ye'hebalu*, with two meanings: their being, their conduct and character was vain and empty "they *are* nought" and therefore their achievements, their status among the nations is as nought, "they have *achieved* nought". Their external discredit has followed their inner discredit.

Questions for Further Study

1. Compare the various translations given for the passage with which we have headed this chapter:
    Luther: Und hingen an den unnuetzen Goetzen, da *sie doch nichts erlangten.*
    Landesdorfer (Catholic translation, Bonn, 1927): Sie waren dem Nichtigen nachgewandelt so dass sie *selbst dem Nichtigen verfielen.*
    Revised Version: And have walked after *vanity* and *and become vain.*
    Version d'Ostervald: ... marcher après la vanité et *devenir vains.*
    Buber: Und gingen dem Tande nach, *wurden zu Tand.*
    Which of our commentators do they each follow and which seems the most faithful to the spirit of the text?

2. "They did not say, Where is the Lord . . .". Cf.: the question in Jer. 2, 6—8 in which they were condemned for not asking,

with the following texts where the prophet condemns them for asking: "Behold they say to me, Where is the word of the Lord, let it come to pass" (Jer. 17, 15); "Why should the nations say, Where is their God?" (Joel 2, 17); "My adversaries have made me a reproach in saying to me daily, Where is their God?" (Psalms 42, 4); "Why should the nations say, Where is their God" (ibid. 79, 10); "Why should the nations say, Where now is their God" (ibid. 115, 2). Explain the difference between the two types of questions — the one which should have been asked and the one which shouldn't.

3.   "You came and defiled My land and My inheritance you made an abomination" (Jer. 2, 7). Cf.: Leviticus 18, 24—30; Numbers 35, 32—34.

(a)   What connection is there between Israel's conduct and the situation of Erez Israel?

(b)   Do you know any texts in the Torah (Genesis) from where it appears that, according to the Torah, there exists a connection not only between Israel and its land but also between man as a whole and the land — the world as a whole?

NOTES

[1]   The second of the three passages of reproof or retribution (*shelosha depuranuta*) read in the three week mourning period. See infra *Pinḥas* 5 for further details.

[2]   See *Pinḥas* 4, infra pp. 348ff.

THOUGH YOU WASH YOURSELF WITH NITRE
(Haftarah, Jeremiah 2, 4—28)

The reader of this prophecy (which begins at verse 4) will sense from verse 20 a change in the general atmosphere. The first part opens with a question:

מַה־מָּצְאוּ אֲבוֹתֵיכֶם בִּי עָוֶל כִּי רָחֲקוּ מֵעָלָי

What iniquity did your fathers find in Me that they became estranged from Me?

(2, 5)

The sin of ingratitude and the regret underlying the words of reproof are emphasised. An attempt is also made to extenuate their behaviour by placing the blame on the leaders, the shepherds who misled them, the priests, those who held fast to the Law, the prophets who did not guide but caused them to err. The fathers are mentioned: "What iniquity did your *fathers* find in Me?", the previous generations likewise being guilty. Speaking to the present generation with whom he pleads the cause of the Lord, he addresses them nevertheless as "My people" — "But My people has changed its glory for that which does not profit"; "For My people have committed two evils" — the very same title bestowed on them at the beginning by the Lord when He spoke with Moses at the burning bush when He first apprised him of the message of redemption (Ex. 3, 7):

רָאֹה רָאִיתִי אֶת עֳנִי עַמִּי

413

I have surely seen the suffering of My people.

The use of this same title in this context underlines the anguish of the Father who sees His son who is destined to be His people becoming estranged from Him: "They have gone after things of nought and have become nought". These verses are more concerned with a last attempt to convince the people of their folly and bring them to their senses than to reprove them.

But starting with verse 20 the general tone changes to one of bitter indignation and angry upbraiding. They are no longer called My people. The Lord addresses them directly and applies to them various epithets:

כִּי מֵעוֹלָם שָׁבַרְתִּי עֻלֵּךְ
נִתַּקְתִּי מוֹסְרוֹתַיִךְ
וַתֹּאמְרִי לֹא אֶעֱבוֹר

For of old time I have broken your yoke
And burst your bands
And you promised not to transgress any more.

The figure is one of a beast of burden, perhaps of a stubborn ox but after the figure of the vine that disappoints the grower we are treated to another figure:

כִּי אִם־תְּכַבְּסִי בַּנֶּתֶר וְתַרְבִּי־לָךְ בֹּרִית
נִכְתָּם עֲוֹנֵךְ לְפָנַי נְאֻם אֲדֹנָי ה':

For though you wash yourself with nitre and use much soap
Yet your iniquity is marked before Me, says the Lord God.
(2, 22)

Here we have the figure of the washerwoman who strives in vain to take the stains out of the bloodstained garment. Then we have the

figure of the swift young camel traversing its ways, the wild ass used
to the wilderness followed by yet another figure: the adulteress who
goes after her lovers, the strangers, and then the thief caught
redhanded.

Evidently the indignant prophet cannot check his flow of words by
finding another figure or elaborating it and exhausting all its aspects
(as Isaiah in the figure of the vineyard in Isa. 5). Evidently the fury of
his indignation forces him to pass from figure to figure in quick
succession once another picture fills his mind in which he sees his
people and its treachery, crowding out the previous one.

Like all metaphors, they are not purely ornamental, an elaboration
of the actual idea but an expression of the idea itself. Were we to
strip the metaphorical garb from the idea it embodies we would be
confronted with a scarecrow no more resembling his prophecy than
a man's shadow does the man himself.

Let us study two of these metaphors more closely and thereby
endeavour to lay bare their significance and extract the prophet's full
meaning: We quote again the metaphor of the washerwoman:

כִּי אִם־תְּכַבְּסִי בַּנֶּתֶר וְתַרְבִּי־לָךְ בֹּרִית
נִכְתָּם עֲוֹנֵךְ לְפָנַי

**For though you wash yourself with nitre and use much soap;
Yet your iniquity is marked before Me.**

(2, 22)

This verse is puzzling, a fact already noted by our Sages. The text
would seem to run counter to the idea of repentance, saying as it
were: All is lost, no human effort will avail, no manifestation of
goodwill will help. Even more puzzling is Jeremiah's resort to that
same metaphor in order to arouse them to repentance when he said:

כַּבְּסִי מֵרָעָה לִבֵּךְ . . .
לְמַעַן תִּוָּשֵׁעִי

415

**Wash your heart from wickedness
That you may be saved.**

(4, 14)

Radak tried to solve this contradiction:

> "Though you wash yourself with nitre": just as a garment is laundered with
> soap and nitre to take out the stains, so if you wash yourself and clean
> yourself, i.e. repent, in spite of that, I shall punish you for your iniquity, so
> enormous is it.
>
> Now it is stated: "Wash your heart from wickedness that you may be
> saved?" The answer to this question is that, at any rate, if the Israelites of
> that generation repented, they would be saved from the enemy and He would
> not exile them but they would receive the punishment of their heavy iniquity
> in their own land. For there is an iniquity which cannot be atoned for by
> repentance alone but by sufferings which completely purge the iniquity after
> repentance. Our Sages raised an objection from these verses and answered:
> Here (4, 14) we are dealing with a decree not accompanied by a Divine
> adjuration (e.g. "As I live") and there in our text we are dealing with a decree
> accompanied by a Divine adjuration; for a decree accompanied by an
> adjuration cannot be annulled.

Abravanel strongly attacks these words of the Sages:

> If we accept the argument of the Sages that the decree could not be retracted
> because it was accompanied by an adjuration, then this will raise an
> objection to the mission of the prophets and their daily reproofs. All their
> words will be vain and worthless. Moreover the virture of repentance suffers
> greatly and we have been given to understand that nothing can withstand
> repentance. The words of Ezekiel insist on this supreme virtue of repentance.

Abravanel accepts in principle Radak's explanation — that there
are iniquities whose punishment can be reduced by repentance. But
sufferings are still necessary for the sinner, for the repentant, more
then anyone else, to *purge* him. He does not agree, however, with
Radak at all with regard to our text, answering our question in
another way, taking account of the general context:

In my view no such question arises in this verse since it does not say: "Though you wash your heart from wickedness" which implies sincere repentance as in the other verse: "Wash your heart from wickedness". Our verse does not use this expression because the prophet did not mean: Though you repent it will be of no avail! But what he meant was that his contemporaries were wicked in secret and showed themselves pious in public. Regarding this he said: Though publicly you act like pious folk, the Almighty knows your inward evil. This is the force of: "Though you wash yourself with nitre and use much soap" referring to the materials used for laundering. Apart from all the deeds that you openly commit with guile and deceit, your iniquity is marked before Me, that is to say, the hidden iniquity is registered before Me. This is followed naturally by: "How can you say: I am not defiled, I have not gone after the Baalim?" The reproof was against their hypocritical conduct — outwardly pure but inwardly rotten.

Abravanel seems to us to have succeeded in plumbing the depths of the prophet's meaning, first, because, as mentioned, he took account of the general context as emerging from the subsequent verses (many other verses in our chapter bear him out, as we shall see further) but also because, more than Radak, he paid attention to the details of the imagery. The laundering alluded to in our text has not the same implication as in chapter 4 where the washing clean of the heart is meant but merely depicts the laundering of a garment. This is the key to understanding the verse and the solving of the difficulty with which both our Sages and Radak grappled.

We shall meet the idea emerging from Abravanel's precise analysis of the imagery of the text again in the figure in verse 26; but first let us glance at the intervening verses.

In the face of Israel's denial that "I was not defiled, nor did I go after the Baalim" (note that in vv. 4—19 the accusation is a political one. It refers to going after strange peoples depicted in the metaphor of the thirsty person wandering after empty cisterns instead of repairing to the source of living water. Here, on the other hand, the treachery lies in the running after idols pictured as harlotry). The prophet shows them once again through imagery their treachery:

רְאִי דַרְכֵּךְ בַּגַּיְא דְּעִי מֶה עָשִׂית . . .

See your way in the valley, know what you have done...
(2, 23)

In the face of proofs from reality they can no longer deny and indeed this time they admit:

אָהַבְתִּי זָרִים וְאַחֲרֵיהֶם אֵלֵךְ:

I have loved strangers and after them I shall go.
(2, 25)

But this is no admission of one turning over a new leaf but an admission that is not even accompanied by remorse. It is most certainly not characterised by a forsaking of the sin. The prophet comments:

כְּבֹשֶׁת גַּנָּב כִּי יִמָּצֵא
כֵּן הֹבִישׁוּ בֵּית יִשְׂרָאֵל
הֵמָּה מַלְכֵיהֶם שָׂרֵיהֶם וְכֹהֲנֵיהֶם וּנְבִיאֵיהֶם:

As the thief is ashamed when he is found,
So is the house of Israel ashamed,
They, their kings, their princes, and their priests and their prophets.
(2, 26)

Once again the comparison raises difficulties. Is a thief ashamed? The Targum Jonathan thus tries to overcome the difficulty:

> Like the shame of a man who is regarded as trustworthy and turns out to be a thief.

418

But it is hard to find a trace of this idea in the wording of the text. What is more, such a comparison is scarcely effective since the prophet's argument is that Israel are not ashamed but impudently admit: "I have loved strangers and after them I shall go".

This was why Radak did not follow the Targum but tried to explain it simply in the sense that Israel *should* have been ashamed. But this explanation is forced. For if this verse is not a description of their actual behaviour but a demand to adopt a more worthy course of conduct, a call to be ashamed of their deeds, then what is the force and point of the image of the thief? Malbim's explanation therefore strikes us as more plausible:

> The thief caught in the act is not ashamed of the action of stealing but only of his failure. His shame is only in being found out but not in the deed itself . . . Behold as the thief is ashamed, whose shame is not prompted by the theft but only by the being "found", being caught, so is the house of Israel ashamed; not shame for their evil conduct but for the misfortunes that have befallen them as a result.

Note Malbim's approach to the text. He not only notices the word "found" which adds something to the picture, since it does not state: "As the thief is ashamed so are they ashamed" nor: "As the thief who is caught in his theft" but: "When he is found" *ki yimaze*. He does not explain the *ki* in the time sense of "when", but in the causative sense of "because": "as the thief is ashamed on account of being found". In this way the text fits in with the rest of the chapter.

Israel's sin is not only ingratitude but the absence of any desire to repent. If they appeal to the Lord "in the time of their evil" or misfortune and cry: "Arise and save us" this is only a pretence, words, external actions, a counterfeit remorse but not true repentance.

419

INDEX OF BIBLICAL AND RABBINICAL SOURCES

References marked * occur in footnotes. References marked ° occur in questions for further study.

Genesis
2:8-10 — 294
3:7 — 246
3:13 — 107
3:24 — 35
6:5 — 270
8:8 — 264°
12:3 — 295
14:13 — 269
15:3 — 252
18:20 — 270
21:1 — 18, 63
22:2 — 277
22:12 — 275
23:16 — 107
24:60 — 92
26:3 — 400, 401
28:5 — 394°
28:10 — 394°
31:3 — 401
31:14 — 261
32:4 — 261
33:16 — 76
39:21 — 349
40:19 — 69

Exodus
2:14 — 267
2:17 — 229
3:6 — 267, 373*

3:7 — 413, 414
3:7-8 — 207
3:12 — 392
3:16-17 — 207-208
3:17 — 135
4:13 — 341, 342
5:1 — 261
5:7 — 75
5:14 — 74, 75
5:18 — 97
7:4 — 7
12:2 — 131
13:5 — 208
13:17 — 261-262
14:3 — 392
14:11 — 260
14:31 — 230, 231
15:7 — 90, 91
15:14-15 — 255
15:22 — 349
16:3 — 99, 118, 119, 231
16:4 — 244
16:8 — 241
16:12 — 240
16:13 — 113
17:1 — 114, 258
17:2 — 244
17:4 — 244
17:5 — 241, 244
17:7 — 114

Thanks are due to Dr. Marvin Ring who compiled the indices of Biblical sources, commentators, authors and subjects.

421

17:11 — 217
18:23 — 245
19:6 — 183, 357°
19:12 — 1
19:21 — 1
19:22 — 1
21:15 — 276
22:20 — 42
22:21 — 190
24:7 — 356
24:16 — 6
25:8 — 6
30:12 — 17, 21
32:10 — 185°, 197
32:11 — 227
32:11-13 — 158-159
32:12 — 159, 160
32:32 — 122
33:1-3 — 208, 209
33:11 — 367
35:27 — 77
36:3 — 131
36:7 — 77
40:19 — 6
40:35 — 6

Leviticus
1:1 — 6
1:2 — 275
4:13 — 151
5:21 — 40
5:12-24 — 50°
5:21, 23 — 45
14:12 — 38
18:26-28 — 336
19:2 — 183
19:15 — 70
19:19 — 188
19:26 — 131
19:28 — 58°
20:6 — 69-70

21:10 — 53
25:26 — 43°
25:38 — 399
26:3-6 — 67
26:6 — 295
26:9 — 72
26:44 — 16
27:2 — 273, 276
27:29 — 278
27:34 — 337, 338

Numbers
1:1 — 11
1:1-3 — 10
1:2 — 17, 337
1:3 — 13
1:18 — 336, 338
1:49-50 — 12
1:51 — 1
2:2 — 4
2:3 — 7
4:15 — 25
4:15-16 — 29°
4:16 — 2
4:18 — 25
4:18-20 — 24
4:19 — 26
4:20 — 1, 26
5:6 — 39, 40, 42, 43°
5:6-7 — 44
5:7 — 42°, 46, 48, 50°
5:7-8 — 47
5:8 — 40, 41, 43°
5:12 — 39
5:18 — 39
6:1-11 — 51-52
6:5 — 39, 55, 58°
6:6-7 — 53
6:8 — 53, 56
6:11 — 30°, 54, 58°
6:14 — 54

6:22-27 — 60
6:23 — 61
6:24-26 — 67, 68
6:25 — 69
6:26 — 66, 69, 70-71
6:27 — 61, 65
7:2 — 74
9:17 — 392
9:18 — 90, 94, 212
9:20 — 394
10:11-12 — 94
10:29 — 11, 13
10:35-36 — 88
10:36 — 91
11:1 — 105
11:2 — 227
11:4 — 106, 107
11:4-5 — 106
11:4-6 — 96-97, 119
11:10 — 103°, 106
11:11 — 121
11:12 — 119
11:13 — 108
11:14 — 119
11:14-15 — 121-122
11:16-17 — 123-124
11:18 — 108
11:18-20 — 109
11:20 — 240
11:21-22 — 110
11:24-29 — 124-125
11:26 — 125
11:27 — 127, 130
11:29 — 127, 133
11:33 — 119
12:1 — 129, 132
12:2 — 129, 133°
12:3 — 212-213
12:7 — 110, 111
12:8 — 267, 373*
13:2 — 135

13:3 — 136
13:18-20 — 136-137
13:27-28 — 137
13:27 — 148, 209
13:28 — 138
13:30 — 137
13:31 — 137-138, 139
13:32 — 138, 141
13:32-33 — 147
13:33 — 142°, 259
14:1 — 142°, 143
14:1-4 — 144-145
14:2 — 165
14:2-4 — 148
14:4 — 149, 154, 168
14:11 — 227
14:12 — 158
14:13-19 — 158-159
14:14 — 212, 394°
14:15 — 394°
14:15-16 — 157
14:16 — 160
14:28 — 165
14:29 — 143, 165
14:31 — 141
14:33-34 — 165, 166
14:34 — 169°
14:37 — 166
14:40 — 166, 170°
14:41-43 — 166-167
14:45 — 167
15:22 — 152
15:22-24 — 151
15:22-31 — 149, 150
15:30 — 154
15:32 — 332°
15:38-39 — 171
15:39 — 171, 173, 177
15:39-40 — 175°
16:1 — 203
16:1-2 — 192°

16:1-3 — 186
16:3 — 182-183, 192°, 194, 203,
   205, 213
16:4 — 155°, 227
16:4-10 — 205
16:5 — 183-184, 227
16:6-7 — 226
16:7 — 30°
16:8 — 204, 206
16:9 — 183, 206
16:10 — 206
16:12-14 — 204
16:13 — 184, 205, 206, 207, 209,
   260
16:16 — 202*
16:19 — 195, 197, 201°
16:20 — 195, 196, 197
16:22 — 185°, 196, 198
16:24 — 196, 210°
16:26 — 199, 200
16:28 — 225, 226, 244
16:29 — 226, 286
16:29-32 — 228, 243
16:32 — 213
16:34 — 213, 230
16:35 — 213
17:1-3 — 219
17:3 — 220
17:3-5 — 223
17:6 — 200, 201, 213, 230
17:10 — 197
17:11-13 — 216, 217
18:5 — 1
18:12 — 356
18:14 — 188, 189
19:2 — 233
20:1 — 249
20:5 — 391, 408
20:6 — 155°-156°
20:8 — 245
20:10 — 239

20:12 — 238, 241, 243, 248, 341,
   342
20:12-13 — 236
20:13 — 240
20:14 — 248, 253°
20:14-17 — 249-250
20:16 — 392
20:17 — 253°
20:18 — 253°
20:19 — 250
20:20 — 251
20:23-24 — 236
21:1 — 255, 257
21:5 — 260,262
21:6 — 261, 262
21:7 — 263
21:8 — 218, 263, 265°
21:9 — 264, 265°
21:22 — 253°
21:24 — 272
21:26 — 266
21:33-34 — 266
21:34 — 344°
22:2 — 323
22:6 — 301
22:12 — 310, 312, 313
22:17 — 309
22:18 — 321°
22:19 — 312
22:20 — 310, 313, 314
22:21 — 310
22:21-22 — 310
22:22 — 306, 310, 313
22:34 — 314-315
22:35 — 315
22:38 — 326°
23:1-3 — 283
23:5 — 284, 304
23:11 — 291
23:12 — 326°-327°
23:14-16 — 284

23:23 — 300, 303
23:26 — 327°
23:28 — 316
24:1-2 — 286, 290
24:2 — 317, 337
24:3 — 286
24:5 — 288°, 292
24:6 — 288, 294
24:13 — 321°, 327°
24:14 — 300, 317, 320
24:15 — 286
24:17 — 320
25:1 — 335, 339, 375, 378
25:10-11 — 329
25:12 — 331
25:13 — 329, 330
25:14 — 332°
25:15 — 332°
25:16-18 — 334
26:1-2 — 338
27:12-14 — 237
27:14 — 114, 238, 239
27:16 — 342
27:17 — 340, 341
27:18-20 — 343
27:20 — 344
27:22-23 — 343
31:8 — 378
31:16 — 319, 375, 378
32:1 — 380, 384, 385
32:2-5 — 380-381
32:5 — 381
32:6 — 381, 382
32:16 — 382
32:17 — 382
32:18 — 382-383
32:19 — 383
32:20 — 382
32:21 — 382
32:22 — 382
32:23 — 382-383

32:24 — 383
32:25-27 — 383-384
32:31 — 227
33:2 — 388, 391
33:3 — 394°
33:5 — 394°
33:50-53 — 395
33:51 — 396
33:52 — 396
33:53 — 396, 400
33:55 — 403°
35:33-34 — 402

Deuteronomy
1:1-4 — 373*
1:2 — 392
1:21 — 167, 398
1:26 — 398
1:27 — 148
1:37 — 240
2:9 — 305
2:26-29 — 253°
4:20 — 131
6:5 — 178
7:6 — 183
8:5 — 252
8:7 — 252
8:7-11 — 37*
8:10 — 71
8:15 — 94-95, 262, 391
8:15-16 — 352
10:14 — 309
10:16 — 63-64
10:17 — 70-71
10:19 — 42
11:29 — 396
12:29 — 398
14:1 — 7
15:12 — 262
15:19 — 188, 189
17:14 — 396

425

18:4 — 188, 189, 356
19:23 — 396
20:3 — 269
21:22 — 15
22:7 — 262
22:10 — 188
22:12 — 172
23:6 — 304-305
24:17 — 190
24:19-20 — 190
26:1 — 396
29:5 — 391
29:13-14 — 154
30:3 — 92
30:6 — 36, 64
32:4 — 323,404
32:10 — 6-7, 353
32:20 — 363
32:47 — 393
32:48-51 — 237-238
32:51 — 238
33:8 — 114
33:20 — 387°
34:10 — 323, 344

Joshua
2:9 — 305
2:9-11 — 256
5:1 — 257, 258
7:9 — 160
7:11 — 185°
10:12 — 244
10:14 — 245
13:22 — 282
22:20 — 185°, 197
24:9-10 — 305

Judges
1:24 — 144
11:13 — 272
11:15 — 280°

11:17 — 280°
11:30-31 — 273
11:31 — 274, 276
11:34-35 — 274
11:37 — 276, 278
11:39 — 276, 277
13:3-5 — 81
13:5 — 83
13:7 — 81
13:10 — 86°
14:2 — 85
14:5-6 — 84
16:28 — 85

Samuel I
1:11 — 277
1:18 — 70
2:30 — 39
4:21 — 83
12:13-14 — 123
15:24-25 — 170°
18:16 — 344°-345°
24:1-2 — 115
24:4 — 115
24:6 — 115
24:11-12 — 116
24:17-20 — 116-117
26:2-3 — 115
26:8 — 115
26:9-11 — 115-116
26:16, 23-25 — 116
26:19 — 398,399
26:21 — 116
26:25 — 117
28:3 — 376
30:17 — 76, 77

Samuel II
24:2-10 — 19-20
24:3 — 22
24:17 — 197

Kings I
2:2 — 345°
14:13 — 270
17:1 — 243
18:22-40 — 214-215
18:37 — 216

Kings II
1:8 — 369
2:23 — 369
3:27 — 276, 277
17:10-16 — 405, 406

Isaiah
1:18 — 234
3:12 — 25
7:4 — 167
13:17 — 41
14:14 — 323-324
14:26 — 319
16:11 — 324
28:15 — 362
40:26 — 178
44:26 — 228, 243
54:17 — 312
58:11 — 293
60:2 — 356
63:17-19 — 231-232

Jeremiah
1:4 — 282
1:4-6 — 366
1:5 — 324
1:7-8 — 369-370
1:10 — 168, 359
1:11-12 — 361
1:11-13 — 364°
1:12 — 362
1:14-16 — 347
1:17-18 — 370
2:2 — 349, 351, 369, 407

2:2-3 — 348
2:3 — 457°, 407, 411
2:5 — 404, 405, 406, 409, 413, 414
2:6 — 351, 352, 391, 406, 407, 408,
409, 411°
2:6-7 — 408
2:7 — 406, 407, 408, 409, 412°
2:8 — 406, 407, 410
2:11 — 413
2:13 — 413
2:20 — 414
2:22 — 414, 415
2:23 — 417, 418
2:25 — 418, 419
2:26 — 418
2:27 — 419
4:3 — 360
4:14 — 415, 416, 417
5:22 — 174
9:22-23 — 384, 385
9:23 — 351
12:17 — 360
15:16 — 371
15:17-18 — 371
17:8 — 293
17:15 — 412°
19:5 — 275
20:7-8 — 372
22:15-16 — 350
24:1-4 — 364°
24:6 — 360
31:2 — 357°
31:11 — 293, 294
44:27 — 362
45:4 — 359-360
49:20 — 319

Ezekiel
1:3 — 282
3:17 — 324
8:3 — 172

427

16:4-8 — 354-355
18:31 — 36, 64
19:14 — 361-362
20:1 — 153
20:32-33 — 153
27:2 — 324
36:17-36 — 161-162
36:26 — 36, 64

Hosea
1:1 — 282
2:4 — 33
2:7 — 33, 34
2:10 — 34
2:18-19 — 32, 36-37
2:19 — 35
6:3 — 34
6:6 — 350
9:10 — 7, 328, 353, 355
11:1 — 369

Joel
1:1 — 283
2:17 — 412°
3:1 — 128

Amos
2:11 — 56, 57°
6:1 — 357°
7:1-2 — 364°
7:4-5 — 364°
7:7-8 — 364°
8:1-2 — 364°
9:7 — 401

Micah
6:5 — 324-325

Zephania
13:9 — 37

Zechariah
2:12 — 90, 91

2:15 — 92-93
8:13 — 295-296

Malachi
1:2 — 253°

Psalms
1:1 — 187, 188
1:3 — 293
8:4 — 179
8:4-5 — 178
15:3 — 248
15:4 — 132
19:8 — 55, 388
19:9 — 191, 388
25:8-9 — 313
29:11 — 23
31:17 — 70
42:3 — 178
42:4 — 412°
51:5 — 47
55:3 — 278
68:18 — 6
71:1 — 21
73:28 — 73
74:23 — 90, 91
75:78 — 385, 386
78:18-19 — 104°, 108
78:24 — 95
78:25 — 95
78:49 — 264°
79:10 — 412°
83:2 — 91
91:1 — 243
94:12 — 252
94:18 — 338, 339
96:7 — 337, 338
106:7-25 — 95-96
106:23 — 157
106:32 — 241, 248, 249

115:2 — 412°
115:16 — 27
124:1-2 — 16
131:1 — 21
135:19 — 41
135:20 — 41-42
146:8 — 41

Proverbs
1:11 — 312
4:2 — 388
6:23 — 252
8:17 — 41
9:1 — 89
11:30 — 273
12:10 — 100
24:17 — 330
27:6 — 287
27:8 — 405
27:18 — 342, 343
28:14 — 373*-374*

Song of Songs
3:9 — 172
4:12 — 339
6:9 — 339
8:14 — 321°

Lamentations
2:2 — 24-25

Ecclesiastes
7:16 — 56
7:23 — 233
9:11 — 384
9:18 — 271

Daniel
9:14 — 362-363

Nehemiah
8:13 — 153

Chronicles I
5:26 — 385
21:3 — 21, 22-23
23:13 — 29°
29:10 — 63
29:25 — 344

MISHNAH

Rosh Hashana
3, 3 — 217-218
3, 5 — 263-264

Avot
1, 6 — 270
2, 4 — 90
2, 12 — 340
4, 24 — 330
5, 6 — 297
5, 17 — 181
5, 24 — 11

BABYLONIAN TALMUD

Berakhot
6b — 216
7a — 373*

Shabbat
89a — 64
115b — 88
116a — 89

Yoma
23 — 28
86b — 314

Rosh Hashana
3a — 256
17b — 70-71

Ta'anit
11a — 54-55
20a — 287-288
29a — 142°

Megillah
31b — 358

Ketubot
110b — 399

Nedarim
71a — 340

Gittin
88a — 363

Sotah
9b — 85

Bava Kamma
103a — 41

Sanhedrin
17a — 125-126
105b — 127, 284
106a — 328, 336

Zevaḥim
116a — 257-258

Menaḥot
43b — 171, 173, 175

Ḥullin
49a — 61
122a — 234

PALESTINIAN TALMUD — 329

Peah
1, 1 — 393

MEKHILTA
Beshalaḥ — 349
Yitro — 257

AVOT DERABI NATHAN — 130

SIFRA
Vayikra — 43°
Beḥukotai — 66-67

SIFREI

Numbers
Naso — 50°, 62
Beha'alotkha — 89, 90-91, 97, 102
Shelaḥ — 146, 176°
Ḥukkat — 259
Pinḥas — 341
Masei — 398

Deuteronomy
Devarim — 373*
Ha'azinu — 353
Vezot Haberakha — 323

SIFREI ZOTA — 62

MIDRASH RABBA

Bereshit (Genesis)
38, 13 — 199
60 — 274
77 — 401

Bamidbar (Numbers) — 25-26
2, 3 — 317, 337
2, 5 — 6-7
4, 20 — 29°-30°

8, 2 — 41-42
8, 3 — 39
10, 16 — 86°
11, 6 — 66
11, 14 — 69-70, 71
12, 19 — 77
12, 20 — 74
15, 16 — 74
19, 7 — 248-249
19, 8 — 235
20, 11 — 313
20, 12 — 300-301, 303
20, 13 — 301
20, 15 — 286
20, 16 — 285
21, 16 — 341, 342, 345°

Devarim (Deuteronomy)
3, 6 — 309

Kohelet (Ecclesiastes)
12,5 — 362

MIDRASH TANḤUMA

Naso — 61-62
Koraḥ — 184, 192°, 204
Ḥukkat — 252
Balak — 323-324
Masei — 389-390
Niẓavim — 153-154

TANḤUMA YASHAN

Behukotai — 273-276, 279

ZOHAR — 175

YALKUT SHIMONI — 336-337, 338-339

7,59 — 233
262 — 369

MIDRASH TEHILLIM — 117

TANNA DEBE ELIYAHU
324-325,374*

TARGUMIM

Onkelos
  Numbers
    12:1 — 130
    14:32 — 169°

Jonathan
  Numbers
    22:20 — 311
    22:21 — 311

  Jeremiah
    2:2 — 348
    2:5 — 405
    2:26 — 418

INDEX OF COMMENTARIES AND AUTHORS

Abravanel, Don Isaac
  Exodus 30:12 — 18, 19; 32:12 — 161
  Numbers
    Introduction — 3-4; 1:1-2 — 17; 4:19 — 27; 6:24 — 68-69; 6:27 — 63;
    11:5 — 99; 11:26 — 126; 12:2 — 133°-134°; 17:2 — 223°;
    22 — 305; 22:12 — 303; 22:20 — 308; 24:14 — 318
  Deuteronomy 10:16 — 35
  Judges 11:15 — 280°; 11:35 — 278; 13:5 — 82-83; 13:7 — 81, 82
  Samuel II 24:10 — 21
  Jeremiah 1:6 — 367; 2:5 — 405; 2:6 — 410; 2:22 — 416-417
Abudarham, David ben Joseph — 358
Agnon, S. Y. — "Samukh Venir'eh" — 163
Akedat Yizhak — see Arama
Albo, Joseph — "Sefer Ha-ikkarim" — 228, 243-244
Alshikh, Moshe
  Numbers 11:8 — 112°; 16:26 — 200
  Judges 13:7 — 82
  Jeremiah 1:6 — 368; 4:3 — 361
Arama, Isaac — "Akedat Yizhak — 78, 154
  Exodus 32:12 — 161
  Numbers
    1:2 — 15; 6:23 — 61; 11:1 — 106-107; 11:11 — 122; 11:29 — 127;
    13:28 — 139; 14:4 — 145, 155; 14:23 — 146; 14:31 — 141;
    14:34 — 169°; 14:45 — 167; 16:13 — 206; 16:22 — 185°, 197;
    16:23 — 198; 16:24 — 198; 17:3 — 220, 222; 20 — 239, 244;
    22:20 — 311-312
Astruc, Anselm Solomon — "Midrashei Ha-torah"
  Numbers 6:11 — 57; 11:5 — 99-100; 22:12 — 306
Bahya Ibn Pekkuda — "Hovot Ha-levavot" — 15-16, 132, 178, 179
Be'er Yizhak — see Horowitz
Bekhor Shor, Joseph
  Numbers 11:22 — 133; 19:2 — 233-234; 20:8 — 114; 24:11 — 321°;
    24:14 — 318
Berlin, Naphtali Zvi Yehuda (Neziv) — "Ha'amek Davar"
  Numbers 6:24 — 65, 66; 17:3 — 30°, 221-222; 22:5 — 307°;
    25:12 — 331

Biur — see Wessely
Buber, Martin — 33, 355-356
  "Moses" — 127
  "The Teaching of the Prophets" — 168
Buber, M — *Rosenzweig, F.* — "Die Schrift und ihre Verdeutschung" —
  211*, 319
Caro, Isaac — "Toledot Yizhak" — 103°·104°
Cassuto, Umberto — "Sefer Hakinus" — 38-39
Chamiel, H. — "Studies in the Book of Judges" — 87*
Chavel — 281*
Da'at Zekenim — Numbers 10:36 — 91-92
Darkhei Ha'aggadah — see Heinemann
Epstein, Baruch — "Torah Temimah" — 330
Falk, Haim Joseph — 198
Gersonides — see Levi b. Gershon
Gur Aryeh — see Yehuda Leib b. Bezalel
Ha'amek Davar — see Berlin
Ha-Ketav Veha-kabbalah — see Mecklenburg
Hefez, Moshe — Numbers 4:20 — 28

Heinemann, Isaac — "Darkhei Ha'aggadah" — 75-76
Heschel, A.J. — "Die Prophetie" — 367, 373*
Hirsch, Shimshon Raphael —
  Exodus 40:33 — 5-6
  Numbers 4:20 — 26-27; 6:23 — 63; 6:26 — 72-73; 7:2 — 78,
    10:35 — 90; 10:36 — 92; 11:29 — 128; 21:6 — 262, 265*,
    21:9 — 264; 24:1 — 287; 23:28 — 317; 24:14 — 318; 25:18 — 335
Hizkuni, Ben Manoah — Numbers 16:19 — 202*

Horowitz, Isaac — "Be'er Yizhak"
  Numbers 33:1 — 390-391
Ibn Attar, Haim — "Or Ha-hayyim" —
  Numbers 16:24 — 198-199; 17:3 — 224°; 20:12 — 245;
    25:14-15 — 332°; 26:1 — 339
Ibn Ezra, Abraham —
  Numbers 5:7 — 50°; 6:7 — 57°; 6:11 — 58°; 10:36 — 92;
    11:5 — 97-98; 15:39 — 175; 16:12 — 210°; 16:13 — 209;
    16:14 — 211°; 17:6 — 216; 20:6 — 242-243; 21:1 — 258;
    27:18 — 345°; 33:2 — 388-389
Ibn Kaspi, Joseph — 130-132, 133°, 298
  "Mezaref La-kesef" — 257
  "Tirat Kesef" — 304-305

Isserles, Moses (Rama) — 58°

Jacob, Benno — 2

Judah Halevi — "Kuzari" — 2-3

Kalish — "Prophecies of Balak" — 288°

Kara, Joseph — Jeremiah 2:2 — 357°

Kariv, Abraham — "From the strong goeth forth sweet" — 80, 83, 85-86, 87*

Karo, Yoseph ben Ephraim — "Kesef Mishneh"   271*

Kaspi — Ibn Kaspi

Kaufmann, Yehezkel — "History of Israelite Religion" — 299-300

Kimḥi, David (Radak) —

Judges 11:31 — 276; 11:39 — 276

Jeremiah 1:6 — 367-368; 1:12 — 365°; 2:2 — 348, 356; 2:22 — 416

Hosea 2:18 — 33; 2:19 — 35

Kli Yakar — see Solomon, Ephraim ben Aaron

Kook, Avraham Yiẓḥak Ha-cohen — 330-331

Leḥem Mishneh — 271*

Leibowitz, Nehama —

"Studies in Bereshit" — 120*, 211*, 315

"Studies in Shemot" — 79*, 211*, 315*, 373*

"Studies in Vayikra" — 43*, 170*

"Studies in Devarim" — 37*, 211*, 232*; 280*; 339*

Levi ben Gershom (Gersonides, Ralbag)

Judges 11:31 — 277

Samuel II 24:10 — 21

Lieberman, S. — "Hellenism in Jewish Palestine" — 93*

Lifshitz, Israel — "Tiferet Israel" — 268-269, 297

Luzzatto, Shemuel David (Shadal)

Numbers 2:2 — 4-5, 11:5 — 100; 14:5 — 155°; 16:24 — 196; 20:24 — 246; 22:28 — 298-299; 25:1 — 376

Deuteronomy 2:9 — 305

Jeremiah 2:2 — 349-350; 2:3 — 352, 353

Maharal — see Yehuda Leib b. Bezalel

Maimonides — see Moshe b. Maimon

Mecklenburg, Jacob Zvi — " Ha-ketav Veha-kabbalah" —

Numbers 4:20 — 30°-31°; 20:8 — 246-247; 22:20 — 310-311

Meir, Yehudah Leibush ben Yehiel Michal (Malbim) — 170°

Numbers 15:39 — 176°, 179; 16 — 181-182, 184°; 16:24 — 199; 22:20 — 311

Judges 13:7 — 82; 14:6 — 84

Jeremiah 1:10 — 359-360; 1:11 — 363; 2:5 — 405; 2:26 — 419

Mizrahi, Eliyahu

Numbers 5:7 — 48-49

Moshe ben Maimon (Maimonides, Rambam) — 169, 297-298, 312

"Guide for the Perplexed" — 109, 225, 229, 285, 298, 373*, 391-392

"Mishneh Torah" (Code of Judaism) — 48, 178

De'ot — 55-56

Gezelah Va-avedah — 47

Avodah Zarah — 180

Teshuva — 46, 270-271, 313

Sefer Hamizvot — 397

"Shemonah Perakim" — 55, 239-240, 247

Moshe ben Nahman (Nahmanides, Ramban) — 14, 299, 398, 402

Genesis 1:22 — 402; 31:7 — 377

Numbers — Introduction — 1, 5; 1:3 — 18; 1:45 — 12-13; 6:14 — 56;
11:4 — 107; 11:5 — 98; 11:21 — 111; 13:2 — 144; 14:20 — 163;
15:22-31 — 150-155; 15:39 — 173; 16 — 187; 16:5 — 227, 228-229;
16:21 — 196, 197; 17:3 — 220, 221; 20:8 — 241; 20:12 — 240, 242,
245-246; 21:1 — 258; 22:20 — 308-309; 23:1 — 323; 23:5 — 285;
24:14 — 319-320; 25:18 — 335; 32:2 — 387°; 33:2 — 389;
33:53 — 397

Deuteronomy 20:8 — 14

Judges 11:31 — 278-279

Samuel II 24:10 — 21

Nahmanides — see Moshe b. Nahman

Newman, Aryeh — "The Centrality of Eretz Israel in Nahmanides" —
403*

see also under Translator's notes in subject index

Pollak, H.Y. — 65

Radak — see Kimhi

Ralbag — see Levi b. Gershom

Rambam — see Moshe b. Maimon

Ramban — see Moshe b. Nahman

Rashba — see Shelomo b. Aderet

Rashbam — see Samuel b. Meir

Rashi — see Solomon Yizhaki

Reggio, Isaac — Numbers 27:20 — 344

Saadia Gaon — Hosea 2:19 — 37

Samuel b. Meir (Rashbam)

Numbers 1:2 — 4, 11; 1:50 — 4; 4:2 — 4; 4:20 — 24-25; 6:27 — 61;

435

15:38 — 173; 16:13 — 209; 24:2 — 286-287; 24:14 — 319
Schechter, Joseph — "Pirkei Hadrakha ba-tanach" — 320-321, 322*
Sefer Ha-ḥinukh — 19, 46
Sefer Zikkaron — Numbers 20:15 — 251
Segal, D. — 279°, 280*
Sforno, Ovadiah —
  Numbers   4:20 — 28; 6:25 — 69; 10:36 — 92; 13:32 — 141;
    15:39 — 175, 180; 18 — 234; 20:18 — 253°; 22:22 — 310;
    27:18 — 345° — 33:1 — 393
Shadal — see Luzzatto
Shoḥer Tov — Psalms 1:1 — 188-189
Singer's Prayer Book — 109, 112*
Solomon b. Aderet (Rashba) — "En Ya'acov" — 70
Solomon, Ephraim ben Aaron — "Kli Yakar" —
  Numbers   15:38 — 174; 16:22, 24 — 201°
Solomon Yizḥaki (Rashi)
  Genesis 1:1 — 400; 24:55 — 250; 33:16 — 76; 43:20 — 210°
  Exodus 17:8 — 261; 30:12 — 17; 32:7 — 210°
  Leviticus 5:23 — 45
  Numbers 1:2 — 18; 4:20 — 25; 5:6 — 40; 5:7 — 48; 5:8 — 41;
    6:11 — 58°; 6:24 — 65, 66; 6:26 — 69; 11:8 — 112°; 11:10 — 103;
    11:21 — 110, 111; 11:22 — 100; 12:1 — 130; 13:2 — 135;
    13:31 — 140; 14:1 — 155°; 14:4 — 149; 14:32 — 169°; 15:38 — 172;
    15:39 — 176°, 177; 16:1 — 191, 192°-193,° 198; 16:4 — 227-228;
    16:12 — 210°; 16:14 — 211°; 16:15 — 185°; 16:19 — 145;
    17:3 — 224°; 17:11 — 217; 17:3 — 220; 17:5 — 223; 20:12 — 247;
    20:14 — 251; 20:15 — 251; 21:5 — 260-261; 21:34 — 269;
    22:2 — 307°; 22:21 — 311; 22:23 — 300; 23:9 — 291; 24:5 — 292;
    24:13 — 321°; 24:14 — 319; 25:14 — 332°; 25:15 — 332°;
    25:18 — 335; 27:15-16 — 344°; 27:17 — 344-345; 27:23 — 343;
    32:16 — 383; 33:1 — 389; 33:53 — 396-397; 33:55 — 403°
  Deuteronomy 1:42 — 210°; 32:10 — 353
  Jeremiah 1:6 — 368; 2:2 — 348; 4:3 — 360
  Hosea 2:18 — 32
  Psalms 78:24 — 95
  Ecclesiastes 9:18 — 271*
  Gittin 88a — 363
Soloveitchik, Joseph Dov — "The Halakhic Personality" — 52
Tiferet Yisrael — see Lifshitz
Translations —

Buber — 411°
Landesdorfer — 411°
Luther — 411°
Revised Version — 411°
Version d'Ostervald — 411°
Tzedah La-derekh (Issachar\ Ber Eilenburg) — 192°
Urbach, E. — "Gentile prophets and the history of Balaam in the Midrash" — 325-326, 327*
Wessely, Naphtali Hertz — "Biur" —
Numbers   15:38 — 172; 17:5 — 223
Yehuda Leib ben Beẓalel (Maharal) — "Gur Aryeh" —
Numbers 5:7 — 49; 25:14-15 — 332°
Zevin — "Ha-mo'adim Ba-halakha" — 358

SUBJECT INDEX

Aaron 3, 12f, 25f, 28, 114, 129ff, 140, 147, 182, 187ff, 191, 196ff, 216, 220f, 228, 237, 240ff, 246, 256, 348, 369; sons of 63, 222
Abishai 118
Abraham 117, 132, 199, 225, 252, 269, 275, 277, 295, 297, 311, 314, 398, 400
Achan 197f
Achijah the Shilonite 287
Adam and Eve 107, 246
Ahitophel 385
Almond tree 361f
Amalek 77, 217, 257, 261, 320, 334f
Amalekites 334
Ammon 272, 274
Ammontes 278
Amorites 3, 13, 256, 258, 266
Arad 255ff
Ark 25f, 28, 83, 88ff, 167, 212
Asham 41, 47, 49
Assyria 397
Atharim 255, 257f
Atonement 42, 47f, 49, 151, 221f
'avel 404

Baal 33f, 37, 316, 406; prophets of 214
Baal Peor 328, 375
ba'ali 32, 35
bala' 25
Balaam 3, 282ff, 290ff, 297ff, 303ff, 308ff, 316ff, 323ff, 328, 335, 337, 375ff, 385
Balak 3, 283, 291f, 301, 304f, 309f, 316ff, 323, 325
Bamoth-baal 316f
birkat haminim 330
Booths 153
Burning Bush 413
Burnt offering 152, 274, 276ff, 350

438

Caleb 137ff
Cannanite(s) 167, 255, 257f
Census 10ff; designed to call attention to miracle of our existence 15
Chosen People 259, 355
Confession 40, 46
Covenant 160, 331
Cozbi 335

dabber be... 129
Dathan and Abiram 181f, 186, 194, 197, 199f, 203ff, 225, 260
David 19, 21f, 47, 55, 76, 114ff, 119, 178f, 197, 229, 324, 399
Delilah 81, 84
Divine Name 161, 163, 178, 309
Divine Presence 2f, 5, 39, 174, 197, 287, 312
Divine Providence 80, 94, 135f, 140, 212, 216f, 242f, 247, 262, 264
Divine Retribution 337
Divine Revelation 148, 195f, 353
Divine Will 6, 163, 174, 284, 287, 290, 397

Edom 248, 251
Edomites 305
Egypt 7, 13, 74, 77, 106, 118, 143, 146, 154f, 160, 168, 184, 208f, 230, 240, 245, 252, 260, 267f, 304, 334, 368, 379, 407ff, fleshpots of 95ff, 119, 209, 231, 380, 394
Eldad and Medad 126f, 130
Eleazer 2, 219
Elijah 214f, 243, 324, 367
Elisha 369
Eretz Israel 11, 141, 163, 252, 379, 397ff
Esau 76, 252, 304, 353
Evil inclination 132, 314
ezah 318f
Ezra 153

Firepan(s) 219ff, 228
Freewill 312f

Gad 3; children of 380, 384f; sons of 227
Gadites 380, 385
Garden of Eden 294

gezel 41
Golden Calf 2, 39, 107, 122, 157ff, 187, 197, 208, 227
Goliath 385
Guilt offering 38f, 46, 48

haluẓim 379, 382
Haman 324, 385
Haran 199
Hereafter 252, 324
Heresy 180
hesed 349f
High Priest 53f, 78, 216
Hillel and Shammai 181f
hillul ha-shem 159, 161, 239, 306
hinam 97ff, 101
hitvadeh 46f
Holy Land 14, 22, 146, 379, 396, 398, 400
Holy Spirit 229, 285f, 320, 324f, 329, 369
Horeb 392

Ichabod 83
Idolatry 109, 149, 152ff, 180, 299, 376, 398
imo 311
Isaac 209, 225, 297, 398, 400
ishi 32, 35
Ishmael 353
Israel 2, 7, 32f, 35, 39, 41, 61ff, 72, 86, 91f, 118, 143, 147, 163, 183, 187, 197, 222, 251, 255ff, 287, 290ff, 304ff, 309, 311, 314, 316ff, 324f, 335, 337f, 341f, 344, 349, 351ff, 363, 369, 376, 383, 385, 390, 393f, 400f, 407, 410f 419; camp of 2ff, 13, 38, 167, 212, 258, 268, 356; princes of 74ff, 182, 187
Israelite(s) 7, 27, 39, 42, 80, 82f, 94, 98, 100f, 111, 118f, 135, 144, 153f, 196, 198f, 208f, 217f, 240, 258f, 263, 266, 300, 303ff, 316, 328, 334ff, 339, 375ff, 380, 388, 391ff, 397, 402, 408, 416
itam 310f

Jacob 41, 76, 182, 209, 225, 261, 303f, 376f, 398, 401
Jechoniah 363
Jephthah 272ff
Jeroboam 153, 270

Jethro 257f
Jezebel 215
Joab 21f
Joseph 182; tribe of 187
Joshua 126, 131, 140, 144, 160, 187, 244f, 305, 342ff
Josiah 350, 362
Judah 7, 182

Kadesh 114, 248f
Kadesh Barnea 392
Karet 27
Kibrot Hataavah 187
Kohath, sons of 3, 25f, 28
Korah 3, 66, 181ff, 222f, 225, 227, 241, 244, 385
kushit 130f

Laban 376f, 401
Levi 182; sons of 184, 204, 206; tribe of 216
Levites 2, 4ff, 12, 25ff, 41, 187, 222
Lot 269

Menasseh 3, 385
Manna 105, 113, 118f, 148, 241, 262, 368, 391
Manoah 81f
Massah 113f
Matnot Kehunah (priestly portions) 38
Matriarchs 291
Media 41, 49
Meribah 111, 113f, 239f, 248f, 261
Meribath-Kadesh 238
Midian 3, 208, 229, 335, 376f
Midianites 334f, 337, 375f
mimenu 139f
Miracle(s) 14f, 95, 144, 154, 160, 213, 215f, 229ff, 243f, 255, 263, 297ff, 368, 379
Miriam 129f, 132
Moab 3, 255, 305, 319, 335; daughters of 376; King of 266, 272, 275, 277, 301, 325; plains of 380; princes of 308ff
Moabites 305, 335
Moses 3, 6f, 11, 13f, 22, 25f, 64f, 77, 88ff, 99, 102, 106ff, 113, 119, 121ff,

129ff, 136, 138, 140, 143f, 147f, 157ff, 163, 167, 181ff, 194, 196ff, 204ff, 212, 216ff, 226ff, 236ff, 258, 260, 263, 267ff, 299, 319, 323f, 326, 328f, 337f, 340ff, 348f, 353, 366, 368f, 379ff, 390f, 404, 413; "Father of the Prophets" 225
Mount Carmel 214
Mount Sinai 1ff, 102, 186, 191, 268, 337f 356, 393; parallel with Tabernacle 5f

na'ar 367f
Naboth 66
Nazarite 3, 38f, 51ff, 82ff
Nazarite vow 52, 56f, 80, 82ff, 221
Nebuchadnezzar 323
Negev 258
nitnah rosh 149
Noah 324

Og 3, 269
ohel 233

panim 70ff
Passover 208
Patriarchs 160, 225, 291, 400
Peor 316f, 320, 335, 339, 375ff
Pharoah 74f, 98f, 261
Phillistines 80, 82f, 85
Phinehas 274, 320
Pinḥas 329ff
Priest 41, 61ff, 153
Pristly Blessing 38, 60ff
Promised Land 4f, 95, 135, 138, 141, 145, 147f, 154, 160, 207, 209, 266, 292, 334, 379f
Prophesy 168, 229, 285ff, 292, 320, 325f, 367, 371, 415
Proselyte 39f, 41f

Rahab 305
Red Heifer 3, 233ff
Red Sea 105, 230, 255, 258, 260, 349
Repentance 37, 47, 167, 169, 416, 419
Rephidim 244, 261

Reuben 3, 182; children of 380, 384f; sons of 227
Reubenites 187, 222, 380, 385
Reward 34
Robbery 40, 45, 49, 180
Rod 361f
Rove 179f

Sacrifices 150f, 154, 216
Samson 80ff, 385
Samuel 86, 122, 277f, 367
Sanctuary 2, 220
Saul 114ff, 234, 376f, 399
Shinar (Babylon) 397
Shittim 339
shuv 91f
Sihon 3, 266, 272
Sin offering 54ff, 151f
Solomon 56, 229, 323, 344, 384
sota 38f
Spies 13f, 135ff, 143f, 147f, 155, 160, 165ff, 187, 208, 227, 241, 258f, 380, 398

Taberah 105, 187
Tabernacle 1ff, 11, 18, 24, 77, 220; parallel with Mt. Sinai 5f
tallit 139, 175
Tent of Meeting 1f, 54, 126, 195, 243
Temple 168, 323, 347; destruction of 359
terumah 153
Torah 2, 6, 12, 14, 17, 22, 27, 40, 42, 46, 53, 55f, 57, 62f, 77f, 85, 88, 91, 102, 118, 121, 129ff, 135, 144, 152f, 154, 171, 173f, 177, 180, 183, 186f, 189ff, 213, 219f, 229f, 233ff, 242ff, 249, 252, 257, 267ff, 273, 278, 298f, 301, 303, 324f, 329, 336ff, 340, 342, 349, 356, 368, 375ff, 384, 388ff, 394, 397ff, 405
Translators notes 93*, 199*, 271*, 346*, 357*, 403*
Trespass 40f, 197, 244, 246, 251

Urim and Thummim 3

vav 45, 276, 396

Wilderness of Etham 394
Wilderness of Paran 187, 394
Wilderness of Sinai 215, 337, 394
Wilderness of Zin 113f, 238, 294

Yissa 69ff

Zedekiah 363
Zelophehad, daughters of 342
Zimri 331
Zipporah 130f
ẓiẓit 3, 171ff
Zophim 316f

ערך לדפוס / אבנר טומשוף

עיונים בספר במדבר

בעקבות

פרשנינו הראשונים והאחרונים

מאת

נחמה ליבוביץ

מהדורה אנגלית תורגמה ועובדה ע״י

אריה ניומן

המחלקה לחינוך ולתרבות תורניים בגולה

של ההסתדרות הציונית העולמית

ירושלים